UNIVERSITY OF
WOLVERHAMPTON
KNOWLEDGE • INNOVATION • ENTERPRISE

Harrison Learning Centre
City Campus
University of Wolverhampton
St. Peter's Square
Wolverhampton
WV1 1RH
Telephone: 0845 408 1631
Online Renewals: www.wlv.ac.uk/lib/myaccount

2 6 MAR 2014		
1 6 FEB 2017		
- 2 MAR 2017		

Telephone Renewals: 01902 321333 or 0845 408 1631
Online Renewals: www.wlv.ac.uk/lib/myaccount
Please return this item on or before the last date shown above.
Fines will be charged if items are returned late.

Dedication—40 Years Later

In 1966 I was one of 75 students in a classic course at the University of Chicago, "The Modern City." A wonderful pair of professors taught us— Harold Mayer[1] and Gerhard Meyer.[2] They presented the fundamentals of urban geography and urban economics, respectively, and their teachings have guided my thinking ever since. Each of them had minor handicaps— Mayer with his misformed arms and Meyer with his bad eyesight and stammer, which gave students time to write everything down. In class, Mayer swung the old slide projector up to the table, then showed us wonderful photographs from cities of past and present. His pictures were not for amusement; every picture illustrated a general point that stuck in the mind afterward.

Not only were Mayer's publications widely known, but he was also very active in urban and regional planning. Later he moved to the University of Wisconsin–Milwaukee, contributing to the local and regional planning process. His wonderful photographic collection is now archived in their library.

Gerhard Meyer had escaped the Nazis and was a personal friend of the famed theologian Paul Tillich. He published almost nothing, instead having his influence indirectly through his students. Meyer was appreciated by his colleagues, but they unfortunately required two decades to promote him to full professor.

Both Mayer and Meyer were masters at organizing information. Their good humor always reinforced learning, rather than distracting from it. One has been dead for 30 years, and the other for 10, but I have not forgotten them or what they taught me.

Notes

1. American geographer and urban planner (1916–1994). Served in the U.S. Office of Strategic Services during World War II, the Philadelphia City Planning Commission, and the Chicago Plan Commission, where he helped to develop the St. Lawrence Seaway. Professor at University of Chicago (1950–1967), Kent State University (1968–1974), and the University of Wisconsin–Milwaukee (1975 until his death).

2. American economist of German origin (1903–1973). Emigrated in 1933 to France, in 1935 to Great Britain, and in 1937 to the United States. Taught at the University of Chicago from 1937 onwards, and was appointed full professor after 1965. Meyer also taught the economics module in the core curriculum.

Crime
and
NATURE

Marcus Felson

Rutgers University, School of Criminal Justice

SAGE Publications
Thousand Oaks ▪ London ▪ New Delhi

For information:

Sage Publications, Inc.
2455 Teller Road
Thousand Oaks, California 91320
E-mail: order@sagepub.com

Sage Publications Ltd.
1 Oliver's Yard
55 City Road
London EC1Y 1SP
United Kingdom

Sage Publications India Pvt. Ltd.
B-42, Panchsheel Enclave
Post Box 4109
New Delhi 110 017 India

Printed in the United States of America.

Library of Congress Cataloging-in-Publication Data

Felson, Marcus, 1947-
Crime and nature / Marcus Felson.
    p. cm.
Includes bibliographical references and index.
ISBN 0-7619-2909-6 (cloth) — ISBN 0-7619-2910-X (pbk.)
    1. Criminal psychology. 2. Criminal behavior. I. Title.
HV6080.F295 2006
364.3—dc22

                                          2005031627

This book is printed on acid-free paper.

06   07   08   09   10   11   9   8   7   6   5   4   3   2   1

Acquisitions Editor:	Jerry Westby
Editorial Assistant:	Kim Suarez
Project Editor:	Tracy Alpern
Copy Editor:	Cate Huisman
Typesetter:	C&M Digitals (P) Ltd.
Indexer:	Will Ragsdale

Contents

List of Exhibits

Preface

In 1916, Ernest W. Burgess published a classic but forgotten paper that marked the beginning of the ecology of crime.[1] Almost 10 years later, his book, *The Growth of the City,* defined the delinquency area of an American, city.[2] That was an important example of crime research by the Chicago School—so-called because it studied Chicago as a social laboratory and was centered at the University of Chicago.[3] Clifford R. Shaw and Henry D. McKay applied similar ideas in 1942 with an extended study of Chicago's delinquency areas, later applied to other American cities.[4]

These scholars drew ideas from the life sciences, especially the larger field of ecology. Such ideas helped them understand cities and crime within them. Unfortunately, little conceptual progress has followed after their efforts.[5] More recent knowledge about ecology has not been adequately applied to crime. The task of this book is to borrow once more from the life sciences to help tell the story of crime in neighborhood, city, metropolis, and beyond.

Two special groups of life-scientists can help us in practical ways. *Naturalists* know how to gather and synthesize information about plants and animals and their natural history, as well as their daily nurture. They show us how to put together information about crime as well. *Ecologists* can relate diverse forms of life interacting and adapting, both locally and within a larger world. Even without genetic change, organisms adapt to their environment—in ways highly relevant to crime. This book is a chronicle of how such adaptations occur, and how it is relevant to crime prevention as well.

I have designed this volume for students who have already been exposed to standard theories of crime. I shall not repeat these theories. Instead, this book pushes ahead. My purpose is to synthesize diverse crime information within a single coherent framework. The *tangible* features of the social and physical world help achieve such a synthesis. That's why I have looked beyond criminology for assistance. Naturalists and ecologists gaze widely in space and time, and are masters of synthesis. They have learned how to make practical decisions and push forward. They will help us organize what's known and can be known about crime.

Notes

1. E. W. Burgess, "Juvenile Delinquency in a Small City," *Journal of the American Institute of Criminal Law and Criminology* 6 (1916): 724–728.

2. E. W. Burgess, *The Growth of the City* (Chicago: University of Chicago Press, 1925).

3. The term "Chicago School of sociology" is often used. But that was not really a coherent or unified school of thought, but a "school of activity." On the myth of a "Chicago School," see H. Becker, "The Chicago School, So-Called," *Qualitative Sociology* 22, no. 1 (1999): 3–12. Available from Howard Becker's webpage, http://home.earthlink.net/~hsbecker/). I return to this issue in Chapter 5.

4. C. R. Shaw and H. D. McKay, *Juvenile Delinquency and Urban Areas* (Chicago: University of Chicago Press, 1942). Other important references to their work are offered in the endnotes of the last chapter of this book.

5. But see subsequent work by A. Hawley, *Human Ecology: A Theory of Community Structure* (New York: Roland, 1950). I regret not spending more time here on Professor Hawley's contribution, which played an important role in my intellectual development.

Acknowledgments

I thank three colleagues at Rutgers University for their assistance: Ronald V. Clarke provided ideas and read a messy draft, helping me over several decades to refine my understanding of crime. Michael Maxfield offered useful suggestions, including the book's title, and I much appreciate a man who reads so many books, and thinks about them. Mercer Sullivan has argued with me politely and incisively. Richard Felson offered major criticism, and I listened too him—even though he is a younger brother. My nephew, Alex Felson, also helped me understand Charles Darwin (whose ideas have to be selected for and adapted to the study of crime). Gloria Laycock (of the Jill Dando Institute of Crime Science at University College, London) contributed many thoughts about crime science over the course of many years. Johannes Knutsson of the National Police Academy, Norway, gave several useful suggestions in the course of many visits. Arlen Egley of the National Youth Gang Center allowed me to pester him with e-mail questions. Scott Decker, of the University of Missouri–St. Louis, made some worthwhile comments about gangs. Malcolm Klein, who pretends to be retired, was critical as always, and I took many of his thoughts into account. Richard Block of Loyola University offered useful comments about juvenile gangs, as did Wesley Skogan of Northwestern University. Nick Ross (of the BBC in London) suggested the term "crime science." Paul and Patricia Brantingham assisted me personally and intellectually over too many years and in too many ways to reconstruct.

The following reviewers are gratefully acknowledged:

Matt DeLisi
Iowa State University

Travis C. Pratt
Washington State University

Marc Swatt
Northeastern University

Jerome McKean
Ball State University

Ken Venters
University of Tennessee at
  Chattanooga

Shawna Cleary
University of Central Oklahoma

Anthony Luongo
Temple University

Richard Block
Loyola University

Mark Colvin
Kent State University

Keith Clement
University of West Florida

Marny Rivera
Southern Oregon University

These webpages proved very useful for writing this book:

Center for Problem-oriented Policing www.popcenter.org
Jill Dando Institute for Crime Science www.jdi.ucl.ac.uk/
Crime Reduction, UK www.crimereduction.gov.uk/toolkits/

Many students have offered ideas and examples in the context of class.
Members of the annual meeting for ECCA—the International Seminar on
Environmental Criminology and Crime Analysis—have offered useful comments. My wife, Mary A. Eckert, has been a source of inspiration, influence,
and patient encouragement and has actively offered solutions.

How to Use This Book

Teaching Purpose	Chapters Especially Relevant
To understand crime within a larger system	1, 2, 4, 8, 9, 11, 22
To understand crime's tangibility	3, 5
To recognize crime's diversity	1, 10, 13
To define and classify crime	2, 21
To see what locations foster crime	5, 6, 7
To see how crime draws from other activities	11–14
To learn how offenders find crime targets	15–17
To understand how people defend themselves	18, 19
To isolate the purpose of juvenile gangs	20

PART I

Introduction

The true mystery of the world is the visible, not the invisible.

—Oscar Wilde[1]

Life is an offensive, directed against the repetitious mechanism of the Universe.

—Alfred North Whitehead[2]

I am interested in those things that repeat and repeat and repeat in the lives of the millions.

—Thornton Wilder[3]

Reality must take precedence over public relations, for nature cannot be fooled.

—Richard P. Feynman[4]

1

Crime and Life

Crime is a lively process. Offenders, victims, guardians against crime are active before, during, and after crimes occur. This chapter explains how crime fits the larger definition of life and draws upon naturalists to help us understand its liveliness. For example, Charles Darwin (1809–1882) watched hundreds of plants over 24-hour periods; he then wrote an entire book about their motions.[5]

This book is about crime in motion, its living processes.[6] Life has seven special requirements: *organization, adaptation, metabolism, movement, growth, reproduction,* and *irritability*.[7] This book examines how crime meets

Exhibit 1.1   Crime and the Seven Requirements of Life

Life's Seven Requirements	Crime Examples
Organization	Lone offender fences stolen goods. Two youths rob a store. An illicit drug organization
Adaptation	Drug sellers find a new spot. Victims are more careful now.
Metabolism	Burglary follows daily work cycles. Vandalism follows school cycles.
Movement	Offenders travel to crime site. Victims travel to crime site. Co-offenders go to hangout.
Growth	A high-crime decade develops. Crime rates fall.
Reproduction	New youths enter crime-prone ages. Offenders find new accomplices.
Irritability	Offenders react to adversity. Opportunity tempts new offenders.

these requirements, in the context of its larger environment (see Exhibit 1.1). This chapter introduces the seven concepts, with some initial examples of them.

That environment changes in ways that impinge greatly on crime. In the 19th century, manufacturers discovered combination locks that make safes more difficult to break into. Then a man named George Bliss, who liked to break into banks, got tired of struggling with these locks. He studied how the new locks worked and constructed a wire device called "the Little Joker." It required him to break into each bank twice. During his first break-in, he would insert the Joker into the lock and leave it. The bankers did not know that his simple device was recording the numbers scratched most often. In his second burglary, he could see the combination etched into the wire, and open the safe quickly.[8] In time, safe companies learned what to do to stop this, and safecracking virtually died out. You can easily see that crime and its prevention are dynamic aspects of a living world.

This is an interesting example, but our task is to put many examples together in order to understand how crime works in a larger world. That is a challenge to me as a theorist and to you as a student of crime. In wrestling with the facts of crime in the real world, I try to take Einstein's suggestion for good science: "Things should be made as simple as possible, but not any simpler."[9]

To apply that advice, we study how crime varies, but we also seek regularities to make sense of it all.

Organization and Living Crime

Like the rest of life, crime can be organized in many forms—primitive and elaborate, informal and formal, short term and long, small scale and large, single layer and multilevel. Fortunately, some crime experts are very attuned to organizational variety. Professor Peter Reuter of the University of Maryland has shown that illegal gambling and drugs display diverse forms of organization.[10] For example, "numbers rackets" are rather dispersed illegal gambling operations, with central control largely impractical. On the other hand, dispersed illegal gambling operations often depend on centralized "banks" to fund their payouts to customers.

Professor David Friedrich of the University of Scranton has shown us a great organizational variety, too, in white-collar crimes.[11] Some such crimes involve only one or two persons, while others develop elaborate conspiracies, even involving entire corporations. What *seem* to be the most "organized" criminal activities are usually not that fancy at all. Many drug sales networks are really *sequences* of simple illegal events, involving different persons rather than a simultaneous organization. As we shall see, crime is organized in the naturalist's sense of that word, not necessarily the televised version. In later chapters, this book explains many of crime's organizational forms in the context of larger ecology.

Adaptation and Living Crime

Human genes have produced a rather flexible species, able to live in heat and cold, dark and light, mountain and valley. People from Africa can live in Alaska and vice versa, without appreciable genetic shift. To make these adaptations, humans are able to use a vast array of tools and techniques, including coats, heaters, air conditioners, lighting, and shades. The flexible human species can adapt between legality and illegality, and among the various forms of illegal action. Parts of this book deal with adaptation in its many forms. I consider how people exploit new crime opportunities with changing technology—such as the emergence of Internet fraud. I also examine how people adapt to reduced crime opportunities—sometimes by following the law more often.

Not only offenders but also potential victims adapt to a changing environment. People manufacture automobiles with better locks and other theft-thwarting features. Urban parks are rebuilt for security, and public transit systems are designed to keep people from jumping turnstiles, painting graffiti, or mugging customers. Many forms of situational crime prevention have removed crime opportunities, without adding arrests or criminal justice costs.

Although new crime forms emerge, older forms sometimes adjust to new circumstances. For example, shoplifters can learn to avoid the sweep of surveillance cameras or find new targets as old ones become less suitable for theft. Credit-card fraudsters try to adjust when new procedures interfere with their efforts. Older crime forms might disappear. Safecracking faded as safes became formidable and easier crime targets emerged.[12] Drug markets can shift from heroin to cocaine, then back again in response to availability and fashion, as well as the morbidity and mortality of users. Once-popular drugs fade and new designer drugs emerge.[13] Those preventing crime also learn to do a better job, as we shall see. Chapter 10 is entirely devoted to adaptation. Crime's variety convinces me more than anything else that we must study it as a living process.[14]

Crime Rhythms and Movement

Imagine a police cadet, age 22, studying at the police academy. He starts with an image of crime derived from television. Then the academy teaches him by the book, without going into crime's detailed realities. After graduating from the academy, the new officer goes to work, only to be surprised about crime's regular and irregular features.

Crime has a metabolism, a rhythm of life responding to other rhythms. The daily life of a city provides the targets for crime and removes them. The sleeping, waking, working, and eating patterns of offenders affect the metabolism of crime.[15] You can see the metabolism of the city by going several stories up in a building, pulling up a chair, and watching people and vehicles over the course of an entire day, then into darkness.

The daily movement of activities away from residential areas makes burglary easier. And so the metabolism of the metropolis is essential for understanding how crime thrives. We must study these rhythms of life if we wish to understand crime, for the energy of crime draws from the energy of life. Residential burglars depend on weekday flows of people away from home. Certain robbers rely on the motion of people near money machines. Offenders have their own metabolism, perhaps sleeping late to recover from a late night's partying. Residential burglars depend on the rhythmic shift of residents away from home in the morning, and they better watch out for their return later. Each community breathes both illegal and legal activity, with offenders, targets, and guardians all moving with respect to one another. Accordingly, street prostitutes select "strolls" that make it easier to pick up customers on their way home from work. Robbers heed the motions of their victims as well as the motions of others who might interfere with their crimes. For example, they notice people who stagger home, drunk and alone. A car thief responds to a vehicle moving into his range and to the owner's walking out of sight. Burglars save more difficult tasks for times when they have pickup trucks available to remove heavier items.

Movements include the offender's trip to crime, the victim's trip to be attacked personally, or the guardian's motion away from the site of the target. Accomplices move toward a common location from which they commence their joint offending. We must also consider the trip after crime, with burglars and thieves evading potential captors and going to unload the loot.

The motions of the living metropolis, city, town, village, and countryside greatly affect vulnerability to and security from every type of criminal activity. Crime is in motion—daily, hourly, and momentarily, on large scale and small. Exhibit 1.2 shows that the daytime share of crime varies greatly from one offense to another. While 62 percent of purse snatching and pocket picking occurs between 6:00 a.m. and 5:59 p.m., only 20 percent of motor vehicle theft takes place during those daytime hours. While unarmed assaults and robberies tend to occur during daytime, the armed versions of the same crimes tend to take place at night. (If you look ahead to Exhibit 1.4, you will see that crime events can shift greatly by a single hour of day and night.) Clearly crime has a metabolism that we must try to understand.

Growth and Crime

Mark Twain explained growth as basic:

What is the most rigorous law of our being? Growth. No smallest atom of our moral, mental, or physical structure can stand still a year. It grows—it must grow; nothing can prevent it.[16]

Exhibit 1.2   Victimizations Before 6:00 p.m., United States, 2002, Selected Offenses

Crime Type	Percent Reported Incidents 6 a.m.–6 p.m.	(Base N in 1000s)
Purse snatching, pocket picking	62.4	154
Assault by unarmed offenders	58.3	3,061
Robbery by unarmed offenders	51.3	189
Assault by armed offenders	43.1	815
Robbery by armed offenders	39.1	215
Rape, sexual assaults	35.0	248
Motor vehicle theft	20.3	989

SOURCE: National Crime Victim Survey, 2002, Tables 58 and 59. Available from Bureau of Justice Statistics, www.ojp.usdoj.gov/bjs/abstract/cvusst.htm.

NOTE: This table omits those crime types whose times are unknown or unavailable more than 10 percent of the time. Non–personal property crimes (e.g., burglary) are subject to more error; these victims often discover that an offense occurred some time afterward.

Young bodies grow into crime-prone ages, affecting not just individuals but the crime rates of large societies. Criminal participation of many types begins and peaks during teenage years, often extending at high rates into the 20s. However, many crimelike behaviors begin at earlier ages. Children steal candy from stores at ages too young to be treated criminally. They poke and shove one another at young ages; but teachers and parents can normally manage transgressions that small kids with puny muscles perpetrate within confined areas. Upon reaching puberty, their potential damage to person and property multiplies with size, muscularity, and increasing range of daily movement. Transgressors can no longer be dealt with entirely within family and school. Girls develop the capacity to get pregnant and boys to impregnate. Youths can now fight more seriously and break rules at a much more serious level. But the teenage years pass. Crime then decreases as people age, spending more evening hours at home, avoiding risks of offending and victimization alike. Of course, this is just the simple model of crime and age. Offenses on the job can increase with employment and changing levels of authority—counter to the usual expectation that aging reduces crime participation. Once more we see that crime is alive; hence its change is not a mechanical process.

Crime can also grow as offenders become more efficient for any one type of crime, learn to find more lucrative targets, or broaden to other types of crime. Offenders multiply their damage through repeat offending against the same or similar targets. One criminal activity can also feed additional crime activities in the vicinity, such as the drug seller who provides an incentive for nearby burglary and theft.

A whole chapter of my prior book examines how one crime leads to another.[17] Offenders bring in other offenders. Illegal markets encourage more and more crime. Victims commit crimes to offset their losses. Offenses lead to illegal retaliations. Illegal use of public settings feeds additional criminal activity. Public parks can be dominated by the tougher youths, driving out others. Courtyards of public housing projects become the scene for drug sales and turf battles. Malls might be privately owned, but their public access affects crime. Malls enable shoplifting and employee theft, easily becoming hangouts that help offenders find accomplices. Thus crime is part of a larger system.

Reproduction and Crime

Like all living processes, crime has an ability to produce more of itself. Crime reproduces sexually with a delay. Neonates are too young for crime; crime-prone ages take a decade or more to arrive. Moreover, the offending patterns of parents are not simply passed on to their children. Yet sexual reproduction must not be dismissed as we study changing crime rates.[18] New babies augment the population, entering the crime rate's *denominator*, pushing crime rates down. As youths reach adolescence, they help increase the *numerator* of a crime rate.

Human reproduction occurs at uneven rates, producing birth cohorts of different sizes. For example, relatively more Americans were born in the baby boom years, 1947–1960, than in 1978–1987. Add 16 years, and you have a partial predictor of American burglary rates. Burglary was higher in 1975, when 19 percent of Americans were ages 15–24. But the burglary rate was lower in the year 2002, when only 14 percent belonged to that same age group.[19] The baby boom birth cohort—into which I was born—wreaked more havoc. Later birth cohorts had to work much harder to do the same amount of damage.[20]

To fully understand the impact of youths on crime, we must divide their possible roles as offenders, targets, and guardians against crime. Youths are likely offenders, but also tend to become targets of personal crime. Adolescence and young adulthood are prime ages for falling victim to assault, having an apartment broken into or a car stolen or vandalized, etc. From the onset of puberty through young adult years, people spend more time away from home, putting persons and property at greater risk. Arguably, the impact of youth on crime is age-squared, so a 5 percent increase in the number of youths might lead to a 25 percent increase in burglary. Moreover, youths probably interfere with crime less than parents.[21] A youth population thus adds more offenders and targets, while subtracting people likely to prevent crime.

Population processes might have their greatest impact in getting people *out* of crime. Offenders are always getting older, and aging out of prime crime ages. In addition, many of the most active offenders get sick or injured, and some even die from their fast and dangerous lives. Crime rates cannot persist without new generations to augment and replace the old.

Without replenishment, the number of offenders will decline with time. Replenishment is not automatic.[22] Not all youths reaching crime-prone ages will follow their predecessors into crime and delinquency at similar levels. Since most young offenders do not act alone, they need to find accomplices – normally youths of similar ages. Delinquent-prone youths best find one another if the community provides them adequate settings for doing so. In such settings, one can (1) find new recruits to crime, and (2) improve one's efficiency at crime by helping one another *immediately* to carry out criminal acts. Quickly recruiting accomplices is crime's fastest form of reproduction.[23]

In these terms, crime has a breeding season. At specific times of year, current offenders become more active and find new recruits. The onset of the school term assembles youths at suitable ages for crime and generates certain offenses within school settings or in the vicinity (especially during the transition period at the end of the school day). Although crime quiets down after Christmas, it picks up again as spring breaks out—especially in climates that are more seasonal. Better weather and longer days not only provide more crime targets, but also enhance the social circumstances for finding accomplices. It is quite a challenge to learn the many avenues through which crime grows and reproduces.

I have gone through six of the seven requirements of life, applying them to crime. The least of the requirements, irritability, is especially interesting and important for understanding crime.

Crime Responds to Stimuli

If you take a stick and poke it in the face of an insect, it will respond to the irritations—proving to you that it is alive. Crime, too, demonstrates living responses. *Irritability* refers to how living beings, including offenders and their victims, quickly respond to external *stimuli*. A poorly supervised bank

stimulates a robber; a valuable garment entices a shoplifter; a vulnerable pedestrian activates a street tough.[24] Fortunately, crime prevention experts have learned to provide stimuli that *discourage* criminal acts. One of my main reasons for writing this book is to explain how that happens.

Responses to these stimuli are in stark contrast to *mechanical* cause and effect. Living things might respond in *varied* ways to the exact same challenge. I once looked out the window to discover a cat attacking a squirrel. The cat ran with greater speed but the squirrel was a master: feinting right, stopping suddenly, jumping left, arriving at a tree, then climbing beyond reach. The squirrel's repertoire for evading danger kept him alive. Another squirrel might have used that same repertoire in a different order, as might that very squirrel on the next occasion of danger. Even plants, with no brain to think about it, have evolved methods for adjusting and varying their responses. The larger tree grabs most of the sunlight, but the smaller plants find an opening. The first branch moves into the best position, but the next growth works its way around to its own sliver of light. To adapt to conditions, offenders and victims of crime must vary their responses, too. That is what we mean by improvisation. That is not to say that offenders are highly creative—merely that they sometimes try doing different things in different ways or places. Like the rest of life, crime mixes causation and evasion, structure and confusion, direction and zigzag.

Crime's Diverse Responses

Accordingly, crime responses are diverse, often creative, and seldom absolutely determined. Given more crime opportunities, some offenders would simply finish earlier, satisfied with their current level of illegal gain. Other offenders would respond by committing more crimes and having more parties. Exhibit 1.3 lists eight alternative responses to an aversive stimulus: tighter security at a department store. An offender might respond by giving up crime entirely, or for the time being, or finding another shady activity, or finding a new type of crime, or changing modus operandi, or finding new targets, or going back at a better time, or continuing the same offense at a lower rate.[25] The exhibit offers examples of both irritability and adaptation, demonstrating that we can and must study crime in terms of life's general creativity and diversity of choice.

Life can also tempt a nonoffender to give up innocence, even at a relatively advanced age. As H. L. Mencken sees it, "Temptation is an irresistible force at work on a movable body."[26]

Or someone who has turned away from crime for some time might turn back to it, responding to a new stimulus. Our inability to predict all

Exhibit 1.3   Different Offender Responses to the Same Adverse Stimulus

ADVERSE STIMULUS: A department store introduces new crime-control techniques to thwart shoplifters	
Diverse Responses	*Examples for a Single Offender*
1. Give up crime entirely.	Decide to live off a part-time job.
2. Give up crime for now.	Rely on other sources for a while.
3. Find a shady activity.	Become bouncer in a tough establishment.
4. Switch to new type of crime.	Stop shoplifting; start robbing convenience stores.
5. Change modus operandi for same offense.	Learn another way to stash the loot and walk out undetected.
6. Give up old targets in search of new one.	Stop stealing from Store A; shift to Store B.
7. Switch times.	Go back to the store when they are too busy to interfere with your crime.
8. Continue the same offense at a lower rate.	Select fewer and better times to steal.

criminal behavior in mechanical fashion reflects the basic difference between life sciences and abiotic sciences, such as physics or chemistry.[27] Alternative responses to crime stimuli are, after all, a part of life.

Crime's Sudden Bursts of Life

Seeds that have lain dormant for years can explode with luxuriance when conditions are perfect. So it is with crime. During the 1950s, crime rates were low in the United States. Certain developments were in process, but had not yet converged. Plastics, aluminum, and transistors were beginning to appear in valuable goods that were light in weight and easy to steal. But the crime wave did not yet emerge. Much of the population was dispersing into single-family suburban homes that were easy to burgle, but still crime rates remained relatively low. Several important conditions for a crime wave had not yet converged.

Some new changes made a crime wave possible, especially during the 1960s. Shopping centers (not yet enclosed malls) were spreading in suburbs, providing new opportunities for shoplifting, employee theft, and auto theft. The vast expansion of the female labor force left suburban houses empty during the day, making burglary easy. Working women were increasingly exposed to theft away from home, even to personal attack. With men and women away, teenagers were better able to evade supervision. Many more single-adult households formed, generating millions of new crime targets and reducing guardianship.

These trends coalesced in the late 1960s, when individuals in the post–World War II baby boom entered the teenage years. Vast numbers became teenagers, discovering a great array of new crime opportunities—also providing targets themselves. No one of these conditions alone could have produced the quadrupling of crime rates that followed. Like plants that lie dormant, then suddenly bloom abundantly, crime rates accelerated to an extent not seen before.

Crime can burst forth, not only for the community and larger society, but also in particular situations. I was once waiting in line in a perfectly respectable and popular restaurant when the two men ahead of me exploded into a fistfight. They were strangers to one another, waiting to be seated. One thought the other had taken his place. They had a conflict of interest, but perhaps additional irritations or aversive stimuli exacerbated their disagreement and led to a quick escalation.[28] Violence sometimes explodes, surprising those present, maybe even the instigator. Although the current book neglects the social psychology of crime situations, that's a very important topic for understanding crime's escalations and surprises.[29]

Crime Lives but Has Boundaries

Life delivers surprises, but that does not mean it is without structure. Some local settings impair crime almost always. Other settings invite crime often. Other settings can go either way. Environments limit choices, punishing and rewarding decisions very unequally. An offender can suffer immediate disaster from burgling in the wrong place, abusing drugs at higher dosages, or living among dangerous people. An offender can also gain immediate benefit, but experience disaster later. Thus substance abuse brings quick pleasures with a price to pay in the future.

Crime conditions change, sometimes gradually, sometimes suddenly—like a candle flickers. Small-town police can modify local burglary by moving a single offender into detention, then out again. A new mall in a quiet town might enhance shoplifting and related drug abuse for the entire region. In the last decade, Wal-Mart and other huge retailers have transformed the business procedures of rural areas and towns in the United States and other nations. Before its arrival, local shops were small, and not as suitable for theft. After large stores arrived, it was easier to shoplift, with more merchandise watched by fewer sales personnel. Employee thefts are easier when stores have huge floors, docks, and storage areas. Thefts from parking areas include cars, car parts, and car contents. The very crime opportunities that were brought to the suburbs in the 1960s appeared in towns some years later. And so we see that crime is a mix of structure and surprise.

Offenders confuse us because they are alive. They make adjustments. To understand crime's regularities and surprises, think of the natural world as *narrowing the range* of likely or possible responses to any given stimulus. For example, improving the management of a parking lot serves to reduce theft from it, but might still allow room for some thefts at the edge of the lot.[30] The use of conductors in Britain's public transport interferes with thefts and vandalism, but also generates more attacks on conductors. The interplay of *constraints, choices,* and *outcomes* makes crime ecology a fascinating field.

Crime in Terms of "Stimulus and Response"

The liveliness of crime impels us to examine the very vocabulary we use to describe it. Some common social science terms are too confusing, including "independent versus dependent variable" and "free will versus determinism."[31] Real offenders are neither entirely independent of nor dependent on their surrounding environment. However, the terms, "stimulus" and "response" remind us that stimuli demand attention; the environment imposes limitations, but living things do not respond mechanically. Stimulus and response are *not perfectly paired.* That allows some surprise in the world of crime. At the same time, choices are not infinite, so we can make predictions. Fortunately, situational crime prevention has greatly improved its ability to predict which settings and products invite crime and how to prevent it.

Clearly, offenders engage in a good deal of calculation—seeking to maximize their own benefit. At the same time, offenders can *mis*calculate, which is not the same as *non*calculation. People misjudge their risks, when to commit a crime, or what they have to gain. They ignore eventual harm to their health or safety. Crime doesn't pay, and it does—depending on the periods examined and the span of rewards or punishments one considers.

In many ways, this book examines how crime stimuli are delivered to potential offenders. Really, the whole book considers the cues that life gives us, leading us toward or away from illegal action.

Consider for now a healthy young man and a healthy young woman who immigrate separately to a city where they do not know the local language and cannot speak to one another. But they can still communicate about some things. They can enjoy music without a common language, and can dance together in a primitive way. They can share rudimentary sports—such as kicking a soccer ball—without a common language. They can have sex with one another, or think about it, without verbalizing. One can commit a crime against the other without much talk.[32] They can even commit a crime together with minimal verbal communication. Even people who hate one another can communicate, as can one person trying to escape another. My point is that diverse cues are emitted in the course of life, and that some of these cues impel people toward crime.

Crime Dynamics Aren't Easily Studied

Crime dynamics mix different processes together, making them hard to untangle. Crime, as a living activity, is self-altering. It unfolds and transforms its own habitats and niches, and these changes feed back on it. Not only does crime drive people away from certain places, but their abandonment makes things worse, still. Life mixes causes and effects, making crime difficult to study. For example, neighborhood deterioration feeds crime, but crime also drives people out of a neighborhood, enhancing deterioration. We can say that crime is self-altering, since it changes its own environment. To get a better handle on crime's self-altering processes, we have to work out the pieces of many puzzles.

To study crime we also need to study how good and bad phenomena mix. For example, a pleasant evening out with friends is a good experience, but that also provides offenders an opening to act against one's empty home or parked car, or against one of the celebrants going home late. Offenders sometimes find innocent victims, but they also attack the person or property of other offenders. As we shall see, the line between good and evil is not as clear as some people tell you.

As noted earlier, crime changes rapidly, even shifting over the months of adolescence, the school calendar, the days of the week, the hours of the day, and the minutes of an hour.

In the year 2000, some 406 robberies were reported to the police department in Albany, New York. Exhibit 1.4 shows tremendous variation by hour. For the entire year, only one robbery occurred during the period 7:00 to 7:59 a.m. In contrast, 35 robberies occurred from 8:00 to 8:59 p.m. The exhibit shows how the number of robberies rises slightly in the morning, takes a dip, then accelerates in early afternoon. It takes another dip during

Exhibit 1.4   Robberies Reported to Police, Albany, New York, 2000, by Hour of Day

Hour Beginning	Number of Incidents
5:00 a.m.	8
6:00	8
7:00	1
8:00	7
9:00	9
10:00	11
11:00	5
12:00	15
1:00 p.m.	16
2:00	16
3:00	22
4:00	18
5:00	9
6:00	18
7:00	20
8:00	35
9:00	31
10:00	14
11:00	28
12:00	22
1:00 a.m.	29
2:00	18
3:00	28
4:00	18

SOURCE: Table 1 of M. Felson and E. Poulsen, "Simple Indicators of Crime by Time of Day," *International Journal of Forecasting* 19 (2003): 595–601. Original data provided by Albany police department.

NOTE: Time spans are 5:00–5:59 a.m., 6:00–6:59 a.m., etc.

rush hour, then accelerates again with darkness. Crime reports for big-city police departments often show much larger differences than this, with crime reports over 100 times greater in prime hours than from 5:00 to 6:00 a.m. on a weekday.[33]

Police activity also varies greatly by hour. In 2003, Utah State University police made some 114 arrests. Only one of these was between 6:00 a.m. and

7:59 a.m. Arrests did not pick up until noon. But the real peak was 24 arrests from midnight to 2:00 a.m.[34] We can conclude that crime and police activity vary dramatically in the course of an average day.

Crime variations are also highly evident for individuals. In the course of a single school year, a 13-year-old undergoes substantial new experiences. The new assembling of youths in September as school begins can only disrupt the pecking order. Last year's strongest boy has to prove it again or lose his berth.[35] The dramatic changes within the first month of school are neglected by most datasets and theories of crime. In some cases, the boy whose puberty had lagged begins to develop new muscles as autumn progresses; perhaps by November he will gain revenge for the bullying he suffered in September. These disruptions are also found when a new chicken is introduced to the barnyard, and has to fight the others to reestablish the pecking order.[36]

Exhibit 1.5 illustrates the dramatic changes in age of burglary arrest in California, even without considering the shifts in adolescent experience over a year.[37] The peak age of burglary arrest is 17, which becomes the index year of 100. In comparison, ages 10–12 have only 15 arrests per 100 at the comparison age. The arrests accelerate through age 15, then decelerate after age 17. By age 24 there are only about one-fourth as many arrests as there were for age 17. After age 24 (not shown), arrests for burglary decline dramatically. On the other hand, arrests for drunk driving and public drunkenness decline much less with age.

Day by day and month by month, crime and delinquency fluctuate even more.[38] Youths tend to flounder and vacillate as they make their way through the prime crime ages. They quickly and dramatically change behaviors, including substance abuse and predatory crime participation.

The unevenness and surprise of crime might appear at any level. National robbery rates have been known to rise almost 10 percent in one year; if you compound that percent you will see why it is possible for national crime rates to quadruple in a single decade. Crime rates within particular localities fluctuate even more. In recent years, some cities have seen their crime rates decline 30 percent or more over a two-year period, but smaller locales might see even greater fluctuations than that.

Crime's Quickness Confuses Research and Theory

Crime's rapid changes can wreak havoc with those studying it. On the one hand, many crime theories focus on rather sluggish features of society. Social norms, poverty, and inequality shift at a glacial pace compared to the pace at which crime shifts. Broad business cycles can move rapidly, but they

Exhibit 1.5   Arrests for Burglary, California, 1998, by Age

(Age 17 indexed at 100)	
Age	*Arrests*
10–12	15
13–14	59
15	92
16	98
17	100
18	91
19	71
20	53
21	44
22	34
23	31
24	27
(Arrests for burglary decline dramatically beyond age 24—not shown.)	

SOURCE: Calculated from Table 8 in Office of Attorney General, *Report on Arrests for Burglary in California, 1998* (Sacramento, CA: Criminal Justice Statistics Center, August 1999) (Report Series, Volume 1, no. 2).

NOTES:

1. Total burglary arrests at age 17 = 4,347.

2. To even up category widths, the age 10–12 arrests are divided by 3, and the age 13–14 arrests are divided by 2.

do not predict crime trends and cycles consistently. As you proceed through this book, you will find that crime ecology is sensitive to rapid changes in crime and community.

Crime as a living process eludes those empiricists who ignore changes in the course of a day, week, or month. Crime participants are real people with blood running through their veins. "Data smoothing" is the unfortunate tendency to average out crime statistics over periods that have little to do with real life. Teenagers do not organize themselves to fit long-term life trajectories, so I cannot understand the researchers who claim that they do. The pace of real life is much too fast for standard crime theory or summarized data. To explain crime and its changes over time, we must consider crime as a quick event responding to other quick events.[39] Crime is a volatile part of the fast changes in everyday life.

Nature Shrinks and Changes Form

Sometimes natural events disappear or shrink in surprising ways. Mark Twain explained, in *Life on the Mississippi*, how the great river broke through and cut off some of its own loops, making itself shorter by many miles. The lower section of the Mississippi River (from Cairo to New Orleans) was 1,215 miles long around 1700, but only 973 miles long in 1883.[40] Just as a river can shrink, so can crime. A cooler winter can keep more people safe at home. Prolonged drought can force people to migrate. Good weather can produce a bumper crop of opiates, whose increased purity sends drug abusers to a premature death. To keep track of crime's changing environment, we must keep our eyes open and be ready to adjust to new realities.

Crime Prevention Must Be Lively, Too

As we seek to prevent crime, we must understand it as a living activity. Sometimes offenders adjust to new circumstances. Other times entirely new offenders discover a crime opportunity, having nothing to do with the first group. Professor Ronald V. Clarke studied how people used slugs to cheat their way into the London Underground.[41] Replacing the token machines led *to a two-thirds reduction in the crime,* then some people cheated the new token machines, too. This appeared to be a "displacement," and many people claimed no progress had really been made. Clarke took a closer look and found that different offenders were involved in cheating the new machines. He also found they stole less from the new machines than had been stolen from the old ones. Crime and its prevention, alike, reflect the diversity of a living system.

The Living *Study* of Crime

A few years ago, I received a letter from a professor nearing retirement who was asked to teach criminology again after a 40-year lapse. He found that the same issues were still being discussed as before, with little or no progress toward solutions!

In contrast, natural science professors can't get six months behind, or they might never catch up. The rapid growth of knowledge in the natural sciences occurs first because scientists emphasize detailed description of every structure and process they study. Consider Henry Gray (1825–1861), who wrote one of the greatest books in medical history.[42] *Gray's Anatomy* is still in daily use by physicians. It includes 1,247 illustrations and provides a travelogue of the human body, inside and out.[43] Gray wrote in great detail with absolute clarity. For example,

> The abdomen is the largest cavity in the body. It is of an oval shape, the extremities of the oval being directed upward and downward. The upper extremity is formed by the diaphragm, which extends as a dome over the abdomen, so that the cavity extends high into the bony thorax, reaching on the right side, in the mammary line, to the upper border of the fifth rib. On the left side it falls below this level by about 2.5 cm. The lower extremity is formed by the structures, which clothe the inner surface of the bony pelvis. . . . These muscles are sometimes termed the diaphragm of the pelvis. The cavity is wider above than below, and measures more in the vertical than in the transverse diameter.

Only a methodical and dedicated person could have written 13,000 entries like that. If you think it's easy, you ought to try it. But if you learn to describe crime and its circumstances in detail, you can make a very valuable contribution.

Science is more than description, however. Natural scientists have learned to make more rapid progress as a group because they have worked out their *collective* processes. In particular, they have learned *not* to argue about the most basic issues and methods. Their *basics* are part of a working consensus, and they reserve inquiry and argument to the *details*.

The key to their consensus is a *scientific paradigm*. This is what holds a scientific discipline together. It is founded on a rigid set of rules about fundamental issues and methods. A scientific paradigm has a monopoly. There cannot be multiple paradigms, since that defeats the whole purpose—finding consensus on the basics. A paradigm is a very practical set of rules and assumptions for doing research, for making decisions, and for pushing ahead.[44] That helps teach students one set of principles, without confusing them on every issue.

All decisions are imperfect, but nothing is worse than never making decisions at all. The natural sciences have devised means for making decisions and pushing forward. Of course, that might not satisfy a physicist. Nobel Laureate Richard P. Feynman insisted, "The exception proves that the rule is wrong. That is the principle of science. If there is an exception to any rule, and if it can be proved by observation, that rule is wrong."[45]

Naturalists are a bit more forgiving than physicists. If a man is born without complete vertebrae, they do not then categorize him with an octopus. But naturalists still have rules and try very hard to keep them.

A scientific paradigm is a brilliant invention, since it closes the books on some topics in order to open inquiry on others. Naturalists and ecologists have managed to gather and organize vast amounts of information about life. They cooperate amongst themselves as much as they can, confining their quarrels to the smaller issues. In this book, I will repeatedly borrow from their cooperative bag of tricks.

Is There a "Criminal Man"?

For two centuries, students of crime have tried to isolate "criminal man," based on genes, psyches, personalities, or social group membership.[46] These efforts have been a scientific disappointment. Their greatest setback occurred while World War II was underway. Austin L. Porterfield, Professor at Texas Christian University, invented the self-report survey of crime and delinquency.[47] His 1943 article compared youths sent to the juvenile court with college students. It turns out college students had participated in a great deal of ordinary crime and delinquency, mostly without getting caught, and were willing to admit it.[48] Porterfield had demonstrated that crime is not just the province of the disadvantaged. (Nor did those more advantaged confine themselves to white-collar crime.)

In 1966, using better study methods, Martin Gold of the University of Michigan found even stronger evidence of the same point.[49] Youths of all backgrounds—not just members of special delinquent groups—reported committing delinquent acts at similar rates. Subsequent research has repeatedly confirmed that social, economic, and psychological variables are at best moderate predictors of criminal behavior. Worse still, the ability to predict who will commit crimes *has not improved* in several decades of research effort.

Criminologists in time gave up predicting ordinary crime, shifting their focus to a different type of prediction. They sought either to predict *violence* or to predict *very active offending.*[50] Their efforts led to no more than modest improvements in prediction, and surely did not solve the problem. Scholars also sought to predict the *shape of criminal careers* as an alternative rescue effort.[51] For example, criminal careers of youths can be "predicted" somewhat by looking *backward* in time; but if you try to look *forward,* you will not do very well predicting what crimes young people *will* do in the future. Indeed, the crime participation patterns of youths are not very orderly, unless you take pains to smooth out each youth's variations from month to month.

Some researchers have finally faced the fact that these ideas have failed. In 2003, Professors Robert Sampson (of Harvard University) and John Laub (of the University of Maryland) decided to jump ship. These leading experts publicly abandoned the search for a separate and distinct "criminal man."[52] From an otherwise polite and unaggressive article, these two sharp sentences are worth noting:

> Substantively meaningful [offender] groups or types *do not, in fact, exist.*

> We believe that statistical approaches for data reduction have *seduced* some criminologists by giving the *appearance* of distinct and predictable groupings ("super predator," "life-course-persistent offender") that are amenable to direct policy intervention. (Emphasis added.)

We are left with the problem that stable offenders and nonoffender groups have not been verified. That's why this volume

- focuses not on offenders, but rather on criminal acts, directly; and
- treats individuals and their criminal acts as rapidly changing phenomena, even from hour to hour, day to day, and week to week.

Waiting a year or several years to reinterview teenagers is a big mistake. For youths are very much alive, undergoing rapid changes and facing surprising experiences. Yet surprises can have a structure. This book offers some ideas for studying crime as a living activity, whose underlying structure is found within a larger system of activities. A natural perspective helps to find that structure. This book seeks to develop that perspective, learning from ecologists and naturalists how it might be accomplished.

Overview

Like larger life, crime has seven special requirements: organization, adaptation, metabolism, movement, growth, reproduction, and irritability. Crime is not committed by dead men. Its vibrancy comes out every moment, impelling crime prevention to be nimble, and challenging scholars. We must make sure our theoretical ideas about crime can keep up with it. Naturalists help us avoid sluggish categories or concepts. They help us study the multiformity, unevenness, and liveliness of crime. Often offenders learn something new, and so should we.

Central Points, Chapter 1

1. Life has seven components: organization, adaptation, metabolism, movement, growth, reproduction, and irritability. All seven apply to crime.

2. Crimes adaptations and growth can be extreme, reflecting changes in the larger society, the local community, or the age of the population.

3. Crime responds quickly to stimuli. This is reflected in how offenders act and how communities shift, even by the hour.

4. Convergences of offenders, targets, and guardians tell us when crime can occur, or not.

5. Organization of criminal activity takes on many forms, often simple but occasionally complex.

Exercises

1. Consider your personal movements in the course of your weekday, and how your crime vulnerabilities shift as you move.

2. Describe the metabolism of your campus. How do you think it affects crime?

3. Describe a campus bar and how its activities shift by hour of day and by day of week. Apply these changes to crime risks.

4. Observe the steps and parking lot of a local secondary school for a half-hour before and a half-hour after school lets out. Can you see some students leaving early? Do you see some students lingering on?

Notes

1. Anglo-Irish playwright, author (1854–1900). Quoted in *The Columbia World of Quotations* (New York: Columbia University Press, 1996).
2. British philosopher and mathematician (1861–1947). See part 1, Chapter 5 of Alfred North Whitehead, *Adventures of Ideas* (New York: Macmillan, 1933).
3. American writer (1897–1975). Quoted in *Simpson's Contemporary Quotations* (New York: Houghton-Mifflin, 1988).
4. Nobel Prize winner in physics (1918–1988). Quoted in *Simpson's Contemporary Quotations* (New York: Houghton-Mifflin, 1988).
5. For example,

> The cotyledons are in constant movement up and down during the whole day . . . [first rising] from 10.30 A.M. to about 3 P.M.; they then sank till 10 P.M., rising, however, greatly in the latter part of the night. [Note: Cotyledons are the "seed leaves" produced by a seed plant embryo, absorbing nutrients packaged in the seed, until the seedling is able to produce its first true leaves.] (p. 23)

From C. Darwin, *The Power of Movement in Plants* (London: John Murray, 1880). Available from the British Library, http://pages.britishlibrary.net/charles.darwin3 (accessed September 3, 2005).

6. Crime is biotic in three senses. First, the population of criminal acts lives and grows beyond the life of any single incident. Second, a criminal act has a life before it finally ends.

Third, a criminal act that appears deceased can flare up, leading to revenge, arrest, and reaction. Crime is not nearly as dead as the statistics that sometimes describe it.

7. This is a conventional list of life requirements, commonly found in biology texts, but there are variants. An interesting alternative list is presented by Professor Daniel E. Koshland, Jr., at the University of California, Berkeley, in an essay, "The Seven Pillars of Life," *Science* 295, no. 5563 (March 2002): 2215–2216. He lists program, improvisation, compartmentalization, energy, regeneration, adaptability, and seclusion. Some of these terms echo the more common list. The most interesting exceptions are compartmentalization and seclusion, which could be applied to behavior settings, discussed in Chapter 6 of this book.

8. P. Ekblom, "Less Crime, by Design," lecture at Royal Society of Arts, October 2000. Available from the European Designing Out Crime Association, http://www.e-doca.net/Resources/Lectures/Less%20Crime%20by%20Design.htm#thinking_thief (accessed September 3, 2005).

9. Widely attributed to Einstein. It was probably said in German and spread by word of mouth. For an extensive list of Einstein quotations and attributions, see the article on him at angelfire.com—http://www.angelfire.com/realm/firelight63/Words_Einstein_Albert.htm (accessed September 3, 2005).

10. P. Reuter, *Disorganized Crime: The Economics of the Visible Hand* (Boston: MIT Press, 1983). Also see P. Reuter and J. Haga, *The Organization of High-Level Drug Markets* (Los Angeles: RAND, 1989).

11. D. O. Friedrichs, *Trusted Criminals: White Collar Crime in Contemporary Society.* (Belmont, CA: Wadsworth, 2004).

12. Richard P. Feynman was also a talented safecracker, but his Nobel Prize was for something else.

13. R. Curtis and T. Wendel, "Toward the Development of a Typology of Illegal Drug Markets," in M. Natarajan and M. Hough, eds., *Illegal Drug Markets: From Research to Prevention Policy* (Monsey, NY: Criminal Justice Press, 2000) (Volume 11 in *Crime Prevention Studies* series).

14. The word "crime" is used in at least three different ways. Sometimes it refers to one incident; sometimes to many incidents as a class; and sometimes to the interdependencies among incidents. This book uses the word all three ways, depending on context. When I say crime is a living activity, I refer mainly to the last of the three usages. Perhaps as crime ecology matures we will find new rules to communicate with minimal confusion.

15. For students of nature, "metabolism" refers to the internal processes of a living body, while the external motions of those bodies are called "movements." But students of urban ecology reverse these scales. The latter use "metabolism" for the larger community, while movements apply to individuals or smaller groups within it. I adapt the latter usage because it applies better to the problem at hand. The metabolism of the metropolis, for example, takes into account the daily flow of its population to and from work.

16. Mark Twain was the pseudonym of U.S. author Samuel Langhorne Clemens (1835–1910). Quoted in *The Columbia World of Quotations* (New York: Columbia University Press, 1996). Of course, Mark Twain took the sun and other nutrients for granted, but it is possible to kill growth by blocking nutrition.

17. Chapter 8 in M. Felson, *Crime and Everyday Life,* 3rd ed. (Thousand Oaks, CA: Sage, 2002).

18. Sexual reproduction long preceded the human presence on earth. It supersedes human role theory and human cultural variations. The word "gender" cannot replace the word "sex." The second word applies to living things whose sex organs make contact, fertilizing eggs that grow into offspring. In many languages, inanimate objects have gender, e.g., *le table* and *la porte* in French. But a table and door cannot mate.

19. U.S. Census Bureau, "Table H-3. Population by Age: 1900–2002," in *Uncle Sam's Reference Shelf,* http://www.census.gov/statab/www/minihs.html (accessed September 3, 2005).

20. However, one can easily overstate the impact of age structure on crime. The property available to steal and the persons away from home tell us more.

21. Parents can sanction youths in ways they cannot sanction one another. This topic merits further exploration but is neglected in this book.

22. See M. Felson, 2003, "The Process of Co-offending," in M. J. Smith and D. B. Cornish, eds., *Theory for Practice in Situational Crime Prevention* (Monsey, NY: Criminal Justice Press, 2003) (Volume 16 in *Crime Prevention Studies* series).

23. This process is a form of asexual, nongenetic reproduction. I use the term "asexual reproduction" in a broad sense, given that crime produces more of itself.

24. "Irritability" has nothing to do with "feeling bad," or with "strain theory." Nor does it claim a *general* crime response. Rather, it considers *very specific* stimuli and responses.

25. For more on the crime displacement issue, see

  a. R. Hesseling, "Displacement: A Review of the Empirical Literature," in R. V. Clarke, *Crime Prevention Studies* (Monsey, NY: Criminal Justice Press, 1994) (Volume 3 in *Crime Prevention Studies* series).

  b. R. Barr and K. Pease, "Crime Placement, Displacement, and Deflection," in M. Tonry and N. Morris, eds., *Crime and Justice: A Review of Research* (Chicago: University of Chicago Press, 1990) (Volume 12 in series).

  c. R. Barr and K. Pease, "A Place for Every Crime and Every Crime in Its Place: An Alternative Perspective on Crime Displacement," in D. J. Evans, N. R. Fyfe, and D. T. Herbert, eds., *Crime, Policing and Place: Essays in Environmental Criminology* (London: Routledge, 1992).

  d. R. Clarke and D. Weisburd, "Diffusion of Crime Control Benefits: Observations on the Reverse of Displacement," in R. V. Clarke, ed., *Crime Prevention Studies* (Monsey, NY: Criminal Justice Press, 1994) (Volume 2 in *Crime Prevention Studies* series).

  e. D. Cornish and R. V. Clarke, "Situational Prevention, Displacement of Crime and Rational Choice Theory," in K. Heal and G. Laycock, eds., *Situational Crime Prevention: From Theory Into Practice* (London: Her Majesty's Stationery Office, 1986).

  F. S. Town, "Crime Displacement: The Perception, Problems, Evidence, and Supporting Theory," in *Practical Skills Online Papers,* the Jill Dando Institute for Crime Science, http://www.crimereduction.co.uk/skills10.htm (accessed September 3, 2005).

26. Extraordinary U.S. journalist and essayist (1880–1956). Quoted in *A Mencken Chrestomathy* (New York: Knopf, 1949).

27. However, some aspects of the physical sciences also provide surprise. Consider the motion of subatomic particles, taken one at a time.

28. For a review of instrumental aspects of violence and other forms of aggression, see J. Tedeschi and R. Felson, *Violence, Aggression and Coercive Action* (Washington, DC: APA Books, 1994). Tedeschi and Felson allow that aversive stimuli can enhance aggressive responses.

29. See Tedeschi and Felson, op. cit.

30. On parking lot crime, see R. V. Clarke, "Thefts of and From Cars in Parking Facilities" (2002), Center for Problem-oriented Policing, http://www.popcenter.org. See also C. Corbett, *Car Crime* (Cullompton, Devon, UK: Willan, 2003).

31. Some scientists believe that living beings and living systems are inherently probabilistic. Others follow Einstein, who exclaimed, "God does not play dice with the universe." That implies that all of nature is deterministic, and science uses probability only as a stopgap—until it learns to explain more precisely. But Einstein was a physicist, not a life scientist. Planets follow their marching orders rather better than do squirrels, offenders, police, or crime victims. Even if an ultimate determinism exists, its complexity will force us to study probabilities. Accepting the flexibility of life will help us learn about crime as a living process. On the other hand, we must not let flexibility and probability take over, or science will lose all laws.

32.   In Montreal, a bilingual city, robbers have no trouble with the language barrier. The word "stick-em-up" is universal. See T. Gabor and others, *Armed Robbery: Cops, Robbers and Victims* (Springfield, IL: Charles C Thomas, 1987).

33.   These variations would be even greater if we took shorter periods than an hour, or if we kept one day separate from another instead of averaging them together.

34.   Utah State University Campus Police, *2003 Statistical Report,* http://www.usu.edu/usupd/statistics/index-2003.cfm (accessed September 7, 2005).

35.   I infer this from statistics on assaults in September, but I admit that my evidence is indirect.

36.   The pecking order question is taken up again in Chapter 22.

37.   These are not the same youths followed over their different ages. Instead, this is based on age patterns observed during one time period. But real cohort studies find essentially the same thing. An exception is sometimes found for a subset of offenders who are very active over long periods of time and who have a substance abuse pattern. They drop off from crime participation later in their lives and their deceleration is slow.

38.   This only stands to reason. But real research unfortunately examines longer periods.

39.   It is all right to summarize data if you (1) try to stick close to daily life, and (2) admit to yourself and others that life spills out of the categories used to study it.

40.   In kilometers, it declined from 1,955 to 1,566.The entire Mississippi River is from 2,300 to 2,350 miles long, depending on the government agency measuring it. That is over 3,700 kilometers, almost equivalent to a transcontinental trip (e.g., across the United States, Europe, or Australia).

41.   R. V. Clarke, "Fare Evasion and Automatic Ticket Collection on the London Underground," in *Crime Prevention Studies,* ed. R. V. Clarke (Monsey, NY: Criminal Justice Press, 1993) (Volume 2 in *Crime Prevention Studies* series). Available from the Center for Problem-oriented Policing, http://www.popcenter.org/Library/CrimePrevention/Volume %2001/07clarke .pdf. See also R. V. Clarke, R. Cody, and M. Natarajan, "Subway Slugs: Tracking Displacement on the London Underground," *British Journal of Criminology* 34 (1994): 122–138.

42.   Not to be confused with Stephen Gray, father of modern electricity.

43.   Henry Gray (1825–1861) was a physician. This is one of the great classics of scientific literature. For the 20th edition, see H. Gray, *Anatomy of the Human Body,* 20th ed. (Philadelphia: Lea & Febiger, 1918). Available online from several sources, including Yahoo! Education, http://education.yahoo.com/reference (accessed September 3, 2005).

44.   This contrasts with a school of thought—a common system of beliefs among like-minded people. Common interest in social programs or social justice does not constitute a scientific paradigm. Nor is it sufficient simply to share membership in the same department or association. Interestingly, the Chicago School of sociology was not a paradigm or even a school of thought, but rather a "school of activity"—a group of scholars sometimes joining together for common purposes, despite their intellectual incompatibility on many issues. See H. Becker, "The Chicago School, So-called," *Qualitative Sociology* 22 (1999): 3–12. Available from Howard Becker's webpage, http://home.earthlink.net/~hsbecker (accessed September 3, 2005). Also see S. Gilmore, "Schools of Activity and Innovation," *Sociological Quarterly* 29 (1988): 203–219. Professor Samuel Gilmore distinguishes a school of thought from a "school of activity."

45.   R. P. Feynman, *The Meaning of It All* (Reading, PA: Addison-Wesley, 1998).

46.   "Criminal man" derives from Cesare Lombroso (1836–1909), known as the father of modern criminology. His works include *L'uomo Delinquente* (Criminal Man) first published in 1876. See the 1972 version in English: Gina Lombroso-Ferrero, *Criminal Man, According to the Classification of Cesare Lombroso* (Montclair, NJ: Patterson Smith, 1972) (Patterson Smith Reprint Series in Criminology, Law Enforcement, and Social Problems, publication 134).

47.   A. L. Porterfield, "Delinquency and Outcome in Court and College," *American Journal of Sociology* 49 (1943): 199–208. See also A. L. Porterfield, *Youth in Trouble* (Fort Worth, TX: Leo Potishman Foundation, 1946).

48. Porterfield compared college student offenses to a separate sample of court cases, showing that students tended to get away with their illegal acts.

49. M. Gold, "Undetected Delinquent Behavior," *Journal of Research in Crime and Delinquency* 3 (1966): 27–46. See also M. Gold, *Delinquent Behavior in an American City* (Belmont, CA: Brooks/Cole, 1970). Annual "Monitoring the City" studies confirm the same finding every year, under names of various authors, but easily found via the Internet.

50. The leader in this shift was Professor Marvin Wolfgang at the University of Pennsylvania, whose main work emerged from 1972 to 1985. See

    a. M. E. Wolfgang and F. Ferracuti, *The Subculture of Violence: Towards an Integrated Theory in Criminology* (Beverly Hills, CA: Sage, 1982).

    b. M. E. Wolfgang, R. M. Figlio, and J. T. Sellin, *Delinquency in a Birth Cohort* (Chicago: University of Chicago Press, 1972).

    c. M. E. Wolfgang, *The National Survey of Crime Severity* (Washington, DC: U.S. Department of Justice, Bureau of Justice Statistics, 1985).

51. Accordingly, Professor Terrie E. Moffitt, of the University of Wisconsin, presented a "developmental taxonomy" of crime and delinquency in 1993. See T. E. Moffitt, "Adolescence-limited and Life-course-persistent Antisocial Behavior: A Developmental Taxonomy," *Psychological Review* 100 (1993): 674–701.

52. See R. J. Sampson and J. H. Laub, "Life-course Desisters? Trajectories of Crime Among Delinquent Boys Followed to Age 70," *Criminology* 41 (2003): 555–592. Their ideas are amplified in a new volume: R. J. Sampson and J. H. Laub, eds., "Developmental Criminology and Its Discontents: Trajectories of Crime From Childhood to Old Age," special issue, *The Annals of The American Academy of Political and Social Science* 602 (November 2005).

You never get clarity . . . as long as a word is used by twenty-five people in twenty-five different ways.

—Ezra Pound[1]

Words are the daughters of earth . . . things are the sons of heaven.

—Samuel Johnson[2]

I never threw an illegal pitch. The trouble is, once in a while I toss one that ain't never been seen by this generation.

—Satchel Paige[3]

I shall not today attempt further to define [pornography] . . . but I know it when I see it.

—Justice Potter Stewart[4]

2

Crime Defined

Suppose that two vice-squad officers—one from California and the other from Australia—meet while on vacation. Both are concerned that women are illegally imported into their countries to be prostitutes. They discuss enforcing their relevant laws. Then the American officer learns that selling sex is usually quite legal in Australia. Can they still trade notes about prostitution?

My goal in this chapter is to help them find common ground. To study crime properly, we need to know its universal features. We need to find a general definition that applies in all countries and all places. Natural scientists, too, have often needed to separate universals from particulars. Their practical experience can help us define crime. We have to state, clearly and consistently, what all crimes have in common. This chapter offers a clear definition of crime, helping us think about when and how it occurs and what to do about it.

If you give me a list of all human behaviors, I should be able to tell you which ones are crimes and which ones are not. I should do this in very few words, being very practical.

Such a definition should not try to serve all purposes. It should not try to specify who's really guilty. Nor should it promise to count up every crime that real people do in real life. By setting aside these issues, this chapter takes on a focused task. But to define crime, we still have much to worry about.

It's hard to study crime for a general reason. Justice is a living process. Laws grow, meander, respond to stimuli, and stray from what is written. Not only do laws change names and coverage, but they vary from place to place. How, then, can we use earthly laws to define crime in a consistent fashion? Naturalists can help us think in terms of overall natural history, going beyond any one patch of land or moment in time. They have experience with definitions as devices assisting human comprehension.[5] Before we can borrow from naturalists, we first need to study in greater detail our problem—why it's hard to define crime.

Localities Are Not Consistent

Inconveniently, legal systems often treat the very same behavior differently. That does not help our search for a single definition of crime. Even felonies are subject to variations in legal action. Burglary usually draws more police attention in low-crime American towns or counties, while big-city authorities might not even send out a police car. But the greatest variations in legal policy and action are found with "vices."

Prostitution Policy Is Especially Uneven

Consider Canada's policy on prostitution. That policy began by banning soliciting sex for money. Then Canada removed that ban but continued to treat *other communication* for prostitution as illegal. Then it brought back its earlier policy.[6] Until 1999, Sweden prohibited pimping but permitted trading sex for money. In the Netherlands, prostitution itself has been legal since the time of Napoleon, but *organized* prostitution is illegal. Many jurisdictions have laws against sex selling, but enforce these laws unevenly, seldom, or not at all.[7]

Some places require prostitutes or houses of prostitution to have licenses, perhaps arresting those unlicensed. In other localities, police try only to arrest prostitutes if they are underage or overt. Still other jurisdictions permit houses of prostitution but prohibit street soliciting.[8] Nevada is the only American state that licenses brothels; and they are licensed only in some Nevada counties. The city of Las Vegas bans prostitution within its borders, but allows advertisements for licensed brothels not far away. Many local areas in other states tolerate massage parlors or seedy bars that front for prostitution.

Even within a jurisdiction, prostitutes can be banned from one street while another is left without much enforcement. Some police departments focus on *prostitutes themselves,* while others arrest their *customers,* or act against *owners* of illicit bars or buildings housing them.[9] Not just sex for pay, but *many* behaviors are treated differently under law—by nation, historical epoch, jurisdiction, or neighborhood.

Alcohol and Drug Control Policies Vary

Even greater variations are found in treatment of alcohol and drug offenses. In the American colonies, hemp—the crop from which marihuana is produced—was not only legally grown but inspected for export.[10] American soldiers in the 19th century carried marihuana with them as a normal matter. Indeed, marihuana did not become a public issue until the 20th century.[11]

Its significance varies greatly among jurisdictions. Consuming a small amount of marihuana is a felony in one place and a misdemeanor in a second place, while a third jurisdiction looks the other way entirely and a fourth deems it legal. "Small amount" means one thing here and another there. Some jurisdictions enforce their marihuana laws strictly and others mildly or rarely. A marihuana statute can be enforced in one decade, ignored in another decade, and repealed in a third.[12]

Sometimes administrative or civil ordinances or administrative rulings restrict a behavior that criminal law permits. It may be legal to serve a drink to a pimp, but letting him do business in your tavern could risk your liquor license. Accordingly, half-hour rooms for prostitutes could get a motel in trouble with the civil or administrative law.

Government Fights Crime With Diverse Tools

Defining crime is further clouded by the multiple ways public agencies can act against an activity they do not like. In many American cities, police departments have written letters to absentee owners of marginal businesses, asking them to make changes. "Civil abatement" has often been effective both at reducing undesired behavior and avoiding arrests, since respectable people—fearing bad publicity—tend to give up their unrespectable income.[13] They also have something to lose through noncriminal law.

A local government authority could disrupt drug abuse within a bar in at least these ways:

- Ask police to talk to owners or managers.
- Complain to the liquor board.
- Use administrative law against them.
- File a *civil* lawsuit claiming damages.
- Use *criminal* enforcement.

Also, authorities might interfere with an establishment in *practical* ways—parking a police car in front, strict enforcement of building codes, or spawning bad publicity.[14] Or they might do *nothing* at all.

Within the United States, we find tremendous variations in written law, case law, and enforcement among the 50 states and over time. We even find inconsistencies within a single criminal code in a single year. Criminal codes reflect public wrath, media pressure, regional priorities, and electioneering. Like too many cooks in the kitchen, lawmakers often write untidy legislation. Unfortunately, you can't get reelected for making the criminal code internally consistent.[15] Moreover, in the United States (a common-law nation), ongoing court cases shift and confuse crime definitions as we speak.[16] Even nations with one police force have local variations in what they really do. So how can we define crime?

Oddball "Crimes" Versus Rare Crimes

President Charles de Gaulle said of his beloved France, "How can anyone govern a nation that has 246 different kinds of cheese?"[17]

How can we make sense of crime when it has thousands of odd varieties? In American states, the following behaviors have been banned in a few places: Mourners at a wake may not eat more than three sandwiches. Snoring is prohibited unless all bedroom windows are closed and securely locked. Goatees are illegal unless you first pay a special license fee for the privilege of wearing one in public. It is illegal to go to bed without first having a full bath. Bullets may not be used as currency. Two people may not kiss in front of a church. It is illegal to eat peanuts in church. Women may not wear heels over three inches in length while on the common. It is illegal to dispose of used razor blades. It is unlawful to walk backwards after sunset. Only white Christmas lights are allowed for display. You aren't allowed to cross a street while walking on your hands. To stroll down the street playing a violin is against the law. Women must obtain written permission from their husbands to wear false teeth. You cannot sell the clothes you are wearing to pay off a gambling debt.[18]

Of course, many such laws are only found in one or two jurisdictions, and might not even be taken seriously there. A broad and useful definition of crime must exclude insignificant oddities. The problem is that these strange laws seldom exist and are seldom enforced. That helps us draw the line:

Rare crime: This behavior is criminalized in enough societies, but it either rarely happens or is rarely discovered and punished. It should be *included* as a crime, anyway.

versus

Oddball "crime": This behavior is criminalized in odd places and cases. To be practical, we must *exclude it* from our comprehensive crime definition.

This distinction is similar to one found among naturalists. A sheep born with three legs is not declared to be a new species. On the other hand, a rare species of bird can be defined if its members have some normalcy and generality, despite paucity.

Do Not Quit the Task

In despair, many scholars have abandoned the search for a comprehensive crime definition. They define crime for one locality at one time. We could define crime as "anything that violates local laws at any time," but that evades the question, offering no single and consistent list of crimes. To study crime scientifically, we must continue searching for a general definition of crime.[19] To quote Gertrude Stein, "Everything must come into your scheme, otherwise you cannot achieve real simplicity."[20]

Our task is to find a crime definition that neither depends on local variations nor ignores them.

Subsuming Crime Under a Larger Category

The problem is to reconcile local with universal. Some scholars try to avoid this problem by defining a category wider than crime. For example, many sociologists expand their inquiry to "social deviance." Studying "deviance from social norms" avoids local variations in legal systems. Unfortunately, a universal definition of deviance is also elusive. One society tolerates hashish but hates alcohol, while another society does the reverse. Homosexuality is okay in San Francisco, not that bad in Japan, but very bad in rural North Carolina. So we are back where we started—unable to find a consistent definition.

Some observers subsume crimes within a more objective and general category of harmful behavior. For example, Professors Michael Gottfredson and Travis Hirschi[21] avoid any particular legal system by studying "criminality"—a broad tendency to commit selfish acts that are harmful in some way. Legality is beside the point. Thus doing poorly in school, being a bad parent, performing badly on the job, and criminal behaviors often result from low self-control. According to this theory, some people commit illicit acts even beyond what they might prefer.[22]

Similarly, many psychologists write about "aggressive behavior" or "antisocial behavior." But is shoplifting aggressive if you do it calmly? Does it make sense to call a social group smoking marihuana "antisocial"? Wider categories often create more problems than they solve. To study crime we cannot run away; we must define its boundaries.

A Better Choice

In the past, scholars were forced to choose between (a) defining crime *differently* in each jurisdiction, or (b) defining something much *broader* than crime itself, then including crime within it.[23] I have not given up on a third option, a comprehensive definition. Fortunately, broader science teaches us how to find it.

A good naturalist has a local eye, but a comprehensive mind. Taking natural variation into account, a naturalist studies specifics without giving up generalities. Exhibit 2.1 shows how naturalists solve five problems of definition, and how their solutions can help us study crime. Row 1 considers variations among continents. The common American groundhog is absent from Australia, while the Australian koala is foreign to America. Naturalists simply define a larger category, such as "mammal," then subdivide that

Exhibit 2.1   Natural Variations in Flora and Fauna Compared With Those in Crime

	Flora & Fauna	*Crime*
1. *Variations among nations*	Australia has koalas, America has woodchucks	Prostitution legal in Australia, illegal in the United States
2. *Extinctions*	Dinosaurs	Hanging horse thieves
3. *New finds*	New butterfly species	Internet frauds
4. *Migrations*	Wolves migrate to a new habitat	Crack cocaine migrated from California
5. *Variations among individuals*	Plant colorings	Offenses by people in different social categories
6. *Ugly examples*	Hideous toads	Laws impinging on human rights

category to handle variations found around the world. Similarly, sex for pay is legal in Australia but illegal in most of the United States. A comprehensive definition of crime can take natural variations into account, too. It allows us to expand, divide, and link categories, as necessary.

Exhibit 2.1 illustrates how naturalists use comprehensive thinking to solve such problems. Their definitions include both living and extinct animals, such as dinosaurs. We too can include such extinct practices as hanging horse thieves. Just as naturalists incorporate new species, we can include emergent forms of Internet fraud. Animal migrations do not thwart the naturalist's definitions, nor should we be bothered that crime shifts from one place to another. If naturalists can handle plant colorings that vary within a category, we can handle crime variants, too. If naturalists can code ugly species, we can include crimes defined by tyrants to reduce individual liberty, even if we disapprove of such laws.

To define crime, we must perform two distinct tasks:

1. Formulate a definition

2. Study variations within each defined category

Thus *crime* can include behaviors that I personally think *should not* be banned, and *noncrime* can include behaviors I think *should* be banned.

A scientist avoids mixing up what *is* and what *ought to be*. If you forget that, you will confuse yourself and everybody else. A comprehensive crime definition transcends natural variations, finds a common denominator among them, and allows observers to classify variants later—while avoiding oddball crimes.

Now that I have set out my goal, the rest of the chapter tries to reach it.

A Comprehensive Definition of Crime

This section proposes a brief but pointed definition of crime, taking into account formal law, citizen violations, and official response to such violations. A crime is

> any *identifiable behavior* that
> an *appreciable number* of governments
> has *specifically prohibited* and
> *formally punished.*[24]

This 15-word comprehensive definition of crime requires that a law must be stated and enforced some time in human history. Some part of a law must be written for it to help define crime. Thus prehistoric people had no crime in the formal sense. Yet a crime can exist if the law is *not entirely* written down, so long as the banned behavior is specific and official.

I used the term "appreciable number" for a reason. That removes illegal acts that are quirks of a particular place, but have no general significance as crime. We can say for practical reasons that, to be a crime, a behavior must have been banned by at least 10 societies in history, and its violation must have been punished on at least 50 occasions in each of these societies. That eliminates the oddities.

It is easy to make a mess of crime definitions by mixing up two distinct questions:

1. What crimes do people commit—before anything is done about it?

2. How does the justice system *act* after it decides a crime has occurred?

The second question brings with it many more complexities: Whether a crime happened *this time;* whether *this person* did it; whether the accused are *treated* equally by the justice system; and how people in different places and times act or do nothing.

This chapter seeks to answer *only* the first question—what crime is *before* something is done about it. That just requires knowing that *some* offenders have been sanctioned some time in history for something they really did.

Crime considers behaviors prohibited by *governments*.[25] It excludes most bad behaviors of everyday life—which are handled outside government and have little to do with criminal law. Of course, governments can prohibit a behavior, yet act against it only occasionally. A crime by definition does not require the justice system to act every time. It requires that a specific behavior,[26] with an identifiable target of action,[27] be formally prohibited (by an appreciable number of governments), that this prohibition be subsequently violated, then that the violator be formally sanctioned (in an appreciable number of cases).

Thus crime's comprehensive definition includes past and present crimes, and leaves room for future crimes. At least for now, the list includes crimes that occur rarely (yet are not oddities), are found here but not there, then but not now, or now but not then. Like species, the list of crime types never shrinks, even with extinctions. The list grows longer as

- new criminal laws are enacted and acted upon;
- old legal codes are discovered along with evidence they were used;
- vague prohibitions are made specific, and enforced; or
- existing prohibitions are violated and sanctioned for the first time under criminal law.

You now have a rule for deciding what's a crime.

Be Practical!

You can usually designate a crime by asking a few questions. Did at least a few societies designate a specific behavior to be criminal? Did somebody engage in that behavior after it was banned? Did that society punish some offenders formally for their violations? If all three responses are positive, the behavior is a crime. If one of the answers is negative, the behavior is not a crime. This definition of a crime can incorporate the many variants of prostitution law or drug violations, even if not all variants are in force at all times and places. One then can study the many natural variations in crime just as naturalists study the distributions of rabbits, amphibians, or orchids.

This comprehensive definition overlaps with local and expansive definitions of crime.[28] Vague and ill-defined offenses, such as unspecified "disorderly conduct" or nonspecific "loitering," cannot fit the comprehensive definition, even if they are listed as illegal in a particular jurisdiction. Only if police procedures, custom, or case law make such a prohibition reasonably clear and specific could it be added to the comprehensive list.

A definition of crime must *never* include all or most human behavior. The definition committee might need a new rule in the future about what strange laws to omit. But violations should not be removed simply because they are strange. If a silly law is widely used, we have to include it within our comprehensive definition of crime.

Our assignment is now simpler. We might not agree on what *should* be criminalized. But we can probably agree that a behavior has often been *treated* criminally. Going back to the officers from California and Australia, they can discuss prostitution as a crime—in terms of the comprehensive definition—then consider how their local variations in law affect the behavior and its consequences. In other words, *Australian criminologists can study prostitution as a crime by the larger historical definition, even if it is not a crime by their own standards.* I think that's a simple and practical solution to the definition problem.

Overview

We now have a comprehensive crime definition. Later we will be able to classify our general list of crimes. Clearly, prostitution and drug violations are criminal acts in pragmatic and comprehensive terms, even though they do not always violate local laws. As Samuel Johnson noted, "A blade of grass is always a blade of grass, whether in one country or another."[29]

Our broad crime definition is not limited by local variations in law, by oddities of local law, or by what the justice system does, who is the culprit, or whether somebody was unjustly treated. Those are important issues, but should not confuse the task at hand—finding a comprehensive definition for crime that helps sort out which behaviors fit and which don't. This chapter offers a crime definition that can be put to work. After all, definitions are human devices to help us make sense of nature, else why do we have them?

Central Points, Chapter 2

1. Crime can be defined, despite local inconsistencies and oddities.

2. A stable and comprehensive definition is necessary if we want to study crime scientifically.

3. A crime is any identifiable behavior that an appreciable number of governments has specifically prohibited and formally punished.

4. Local definitions of crime are highly inconsistent over varying places and times. Regulation of drugs, alcohol, and prostitution is especially prone to variation in time and space.

5. Naturalists find definitions that allow variation, expansion, and extinction. Their thinking helps us define crime.

Exercises

1. Go online and find any criminal code. Then find any crime that seems vague and another that seems clear.

2. Can you think of a behavior that is probably a crime almost everywhere?

3. Write an agenda for a police meeting on prostitution control, where there will be officers from many parts of the world.

4. Interview two students who were victims of burglary and reported it, one in a big city and the other in a smaller place. Compare the police response.

Notes

1. U.S. poet, critic (1885–1972). Interview in G. Plimpton, ed., *Writers at Work* (New York: Viking Press, 1963) (The *Paris Review* Interviews, 2nd series).

2. A famous 18th-century figure (1709–1784) in Britain and beyond. He compiled the first real dictionary of the English language, and was a great writer and humorist. See Samuel Johnson, "Preface," *A Dictionary of the English Language: In Which the Words Are Deduced From Their Originals, and Illustrated in Their Different Significations by Examples From the Best Writers: To Which Are Prefixed, a History of the Language, and an English Grammar* (London: Printed by W. Strahan, for J. and P. Knapton, T. and T. Longman, C. Hitch and L. Hawes, A. Millar, and R. and J. Dodsley, 1755–1756). For a list of editions, see Vassar College Library special editions, http://specialcollections.vassar.edu/exhibits/johnson/editions.html (accessed October 19, 2005).

3. Great baseball pitcher in the Negro leagues (né: Leroy Robert Paige, 1906–1982), who only entered the major leagues late in life, after they were racially integrated. Quoted in P. Dickson, *Baseball's Greatest Quotations* (New York: Walker Books, 1991). Available from http://www.baseball-reference.com, then search for Paige (accessed September 3, 2005). For a biography of Paige, see "Satchel Paige," in Wikipedia, http://en.wikipedia.org/wiki/Satchel_Paige (accessed September 3, 2005).

4. Supreme Court Justice of the United States, in *Jocobellis v. Ohio*, where he voted with the majority to overturn a pornography conviction.

5. I argue throughout this book that naturalists and ecologists can help us make sense of crime. But they are not perfect. See M. L. Corn, "The Listing of a Species: Legal Definition and Biological Realities" (Washington, DC: Congressional Research Service Reports, 1992). Available from the National Council for Science and the Environment, http://www.ncseonline.org/NLE/CRSreports/biodiversity/biodv-10.cfm (accessed September 3, 2005).

6. This oversimplifies the variation but makes the point. Of course, Canada has provincial variations, even in federal features. The Royal Canadian Mounted Police are federal, but they do not act uniformly, wear red, or ride horses very often.

7. For a broad view of prostitution in society, see these books:
    a. F. Henriques, *Prostitution in Europe and the New World* (London: MacGibbon & Kee, 1963).
    b. L. L. Otis, *Prostitution in Medieval Society: The History of an Urban Institution in Languedoc* (Chicago: University of Chicago Press, 1985).
    c. N. Roberts, *Whores in History: Prostitution in Western Society* (London: HarperCollins, 1992).
    d. J. Walkowitz, *Prostitution and Victorian Society: Women, Class, and the State* (Cambridge, UK: Cambridge University Press, 1980).
    e. H. Reynolds, *The Economics of Prostitution* (Springfield, IL: Charles C Thomas, 1986).

8. For a brief but useful description of street prostitution in the Sydney, Australia, business district, see J. McCloskey and M. Lazarus, "Community Policing and the Policing Factor of On-Street Prostitution in the Kings Cross Police Patrol," in *Australian Institute of Criminology Conference Proceedings 14, Sex Industry and Public Policy* (1992). Available from the Australian Institute of Criminology, http://www.aic.gov.au/publications/proceedings/14/mcloskey.pdf (accessed September 3, 2005).

9. For a discussion of how prostitution enforcement varies within Canada, see E. N. Larsen, "The Effect of Different Police Enforcement Policies on the Control of Prostitution," *Canadian Public Policy* 22 (1996): 40–55.

10. K. B. Olds, "Public Export Inspections in the United States and Their Privatization," *The Cato Journal* 19 (1999). Available from the Cato Institute, http://www.cato.org (accessed September 3, 2005).

11. M. L. Mathre and A. Byrne, "Part 3: The U.S. Cannabis Prohibition and Beyond," *Drug and Alcohol Professional* 2 (2002): 4–9. For PBS coverage of this issue, see the PBS website, http://www.pbs.org/wgbh/pages/frontline/shows/dope/etc/cron.html.

12. For many details on drug law variations, see The Schaffer Library of Drug Policy's extensive online collection, http://www.druglibrary.org/toc.htm.

13. For the use of civil abatement against crime and related problems, see L. G. Mazerolle and J. Roehl, eds., *Civil Remedies and Crime Prevention* (Monsey, NY: Criminal Justice Press, 1998) (Volume 9 in *Crime Prevention Studies* series). Note especially one of the articles in that volume by J. E. Eck and J. Wartell, "Improving the Management of Rental Properties With Drug Problems: A Randomized Experiment." At least in the United States, civil and administrative laws are easier to impose than criminal laws. Levels of proof are lower and hearings are quicker. See also J. R. Brunet, "Discouragement of Crime Through Civil Remedies: An Application of a Reformulated Routine Activities Theory," *Western Criminology Review* 4 (2004), http://wcr.sonoma.edu/v4n1/brunet.html.

14. There is no better source of information on practical police methods and avoiding arrest than the website of the Center for Problem-Oriented Policing, http://www.popcenter.org. Browse through the online pamphlets on specific crime problems, as well as the library sources, pdf files, and weblinks.

15. See P. H. Robinson, M. T. Cahill, and U. Mohammad, "The Five Worst (and Five Best) American Criminal Codes," *Northwestern University Law Review* 95 (2000): 1–89. Of course, criminal codes are more consistent under Napoleonic law.

16. Common law nations derive from the British tradition, allowing law to build and change based on how courts interpret specific cases, not just the actions of legislatures.

17. French general, president (1890–1970). Quoted in *The Columbia World of Quotations* (New York: Columbia University Press, 1996).

18. For a collection of odd laws, see "Strange Laws," http://sbt.bhmedia.com/laws.html (accessed September 3, 2005).

19. This issue has been discussed before. See S. Henry and M. M. Lanier, "The Prism of Crime: Arguments for an Integrated Definition of Crime," *Justice Quarterly* 15 (1998): 609–629.

20. U.S. author and patron of the arts (1874–1946), who relocated to France. As quoted in R. B. Haas, *What Are Masterpieces* (New York: Pitman, 1970).

21. See M. Gottfredson and T. Hirschi, *A General Theory of Crime* (Palo Alto, CA: Stanford University Press, 1990). This approach has many desirable features, and helps us escape the mischaracterization of offenders. But it does not solve our definition problem.

22. You can add many other behaviors, including rudeness, bad driving, drinking, smoking, overeating, drug abuse, unhealthy diet, the lack of physical exercise, and suicidal behavior.

23. The juvenile courts in the United States were formed during the Progressive Era, receiving authority to supervise youths for delinquent behavior not clearly defined as a violation of criminal law. This fits a broader concept of disapproved behavior or deviance.

24. With all this analysis, I have learned to appreciate the *Webster's* dictionary definition of crime: "an act or the commission of an act that is forbidden or the omission of a duty that is commanded by a public law and that makes the offender liable to punishment by that law."

25. I did not define government, but I mean it to be formal and to exclude brief periods and isolated places where anything can happen.

26. This comprehensive definition of crime neglects crimes of omission. These offenses are more difficult to pinpoint in time and space, so they are antithetical to the thinking of this book. Think of them as local crimes.

27. I have extended my notion of target beyond my original works on routine activity theory that applied "target" only to predatory offenses.

28. The comprehensive, local, and expansive definitions overlap in real life. For instance, a vague local crime would not meet the test of the comprehensive definition. A deviant act never prohibited anywhere by law would not fit the comprehensive definition. But the comprehensive definition still absorbs many actions that fit the other definitions. See Appendix B, Exhibit A for a depiction of this relationship.

29. See endnote 2 on Samuel Johnson.

Transform a problem into one that you can solve.

—Richard P. Feynman[1]

It is still not enough for language to have clarity and content . . . it must also have a goal and an imperative. Otherwise from language we descend to chatter, from chatter to babble and from babble to confusion.

—René Daumal[2]

Rigidity in articulation is the price we . . . pay for easy mastery of a highly necessary symbolism.

—Edward Sapir[3]

The disordered fragments of raw experience can be fitted and arranged.

—W. V. O. Quine[4]

3

Crime's Stages

Always try to look beyond a single crime incident. Sort out the sequences of events *within* which a crime occurs, especially those nearest in time and space. Pay close attention to the offender's concerns, actions, and experiences soon before and soon after a given incident. How did he get there? What sequence of events led to the crime? Did another crime occur quickly, as a follow-up to the first one? By asking these questions, a detective might solve a particular crime, and a professor might explain a million crimes to a classroom full of students.

Crime's Three Stages

Look closely at the period just before a criminal act. In many cases offenders must be provoked to commit an act of gratuitous violence. Professor Richard Felson of Penn State University has studied in detail and in theory the situational elements of violent events.[5] He notes a sequence of insults, counterinsults, and escalations, occasionally leading to violence. Many assaults and even homicides begin as simple quarrels. Professor Richard Wortley at Griffiths University in Australia has filled out our understanding of provocation, even for violence within prisons.[6]

The period just before a property crime is also important. Often the first task is to evade supervision. An offender must find his target and move toward it. It's not that any single crime is so complicated. But to succeed, the crime has to fit into a larger sequence of events.

The same point applies to those buying or selling illegal goods or services. The buyer and seller must find one another, approach, and make some sort of bid. So whatever they type of crime, pay close attention to the period leading up to it. Drawing from Professors Vincent Sacco and Leslie W. Kennedy, we can divide the crime event into three stages:

1. The prelude

2. The incident

3. The aftermath[7]

The prelude includes whatever processes lead directly up to and into the crime, with some continuity—finding accomplices, going to the crime scene, getting drunk and angry, insulting somebody before a fight, scouting out what you are going to steal, waiting until nobody is looking, and more. The crime incident refers to the immediate event—breaking in, punching a nose, stealing a stereo, breaking a window, using somebody else's credit card.

The aftermath includes the offender's escape, fencing stolen goods, and trying to hide from police or pursuers. It can lead into many additional events, such as citizen reactions to crime, medical treatment to victims, and the actions of the criminal justice system.[8] In many cases, the aftermath to one crime becomes the precursor to the next. After an assault, one participant leaves to find friends or weapons for retaliation—the follow-up crime. I come back to this issue later in this chapter.

How an Event Unfolds

We should always be careful not to read too much into an incident. In the words of Rudyard Kipling,

> Ah! What avails the classic bent
>
> And what the cultured word,
>
> Against the undoctored incident
>
> That actually occurred?[9]

Of course, we still need to put an incident into context, and to dissect its events to some extent. A crime incident has an *immediate reality,* nested within a *larger reality.* The latter includes more than what happens during the immediate incident. Consider two examples:

> A burglar breaks into a house and grabs some jewels. The police are summoned, and code it as a petty larceny. Then the victim discovers the jewels were more valuable than previously thought, so the police change it to grand larceny. The incident itself did not change—but its aftermath changes how we *view* it.

> A bar patron hits the guy next to him with a shattered bar glass. The victim is taken to the hospital, expected to recover. The police code it as an aggravated assault. Then the victim takes a turn for the worse and dies in the hospital a month later. *In light of what happened afterwards,* the police change the charge to murder.

Police rewrote each crime incident based on what happened later. That's all right for the criminal justice system, which has to decide what crime to charge the criminal with and to mete out punishment.

But this book has a more limited task—to explain *how the crime event happened.* Murder is less an incident than an outcome.[10] Exhibit 3.1 depicts how the aftermath "leaks" back into the incident, affecting how people view it. In studying crime, you should try very hard not to let follow-up events prejudice your evaluation of earlier events.[11] That means screening out the aftermath when studying the earlier stages. It's fine to study crime's larger

Exhibit 3.1   As the Crime Unfolds, Its Story Changes

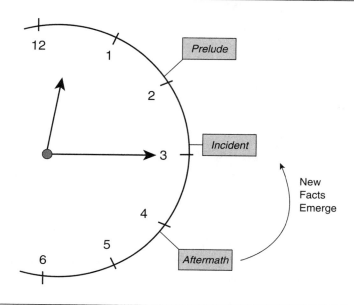

reality, just so you don't mix it in with the incident itself. Of course, we still want to know the offender's motive.

What the Offender Wants

The Roman philosopher, Cicero, tells us that "no one undertakes crimes without hope of gain."[12] This statement is basically true but needs to be qualified:

- Crime planning often takes no more than a fraction of a second. Someone perceiving an insult might respond with very quick revenge. A thief might see something and grab it right away.
- Gains are not necessarily financial. Thus gains include saving face and punishing others for misdeeds, if the offender thinks that should be done.[13]
- Gains are weighed against costs, risks, and difficulties. For any given crime, these might be rather simple. But for a bunch of crimes, these can diversify greatly.

The point is that offenders are oriented toward gain. This point is controversial, since a good deal of violence *appears* to be senseless—it produces no *material* gain. Many observers call this "expressive violence," arguing that it occurs almost for no reason at all. But Tedeschi and Felson provide an excellent argument that "expressive violence" does not exist. They show that such offenses occur for nonmaterial reasons, such as saving face. In their terms, Tedeschi and Felson say that he uses violence to meet at least one of these three general goals:

1. To get others to comply with his wishes

2. To restore justice (as he sees it)

3. To assert and protect his self-image

Tedeschi and Felson emphasize the offender's gains, but we can add to that the costs an offender must consider. Professor Ronald Clarke notes that offenders generally seek to gain benefits, avoid risks, and evade difficulties.[14] These allow us to prevent crime by denying offenders what they want and giving them what they don't want.

Offender Reckoning by Stage of Crime

To understand an offender's reckoning, we should distinguish a crime's immediate target from its real motive. The target might be a television, but the motive is the money it will bring. The offender might succeed in getting the television, only to discover he can't get any money for it. So what began as a success turned out a failure.

That's why we should study offender satisfactions in stages. In the prelude to the crime, the offender cannot yet get what he wants; but he might be turned away, arrested, or countered. Most of the offender's good and bad experiences occur during the incident and its aftermath, as Exhibit 3.2 indicates. During the incident itself, he wants to reach his crime target, and to avoid wasting effort or being harmed. In the aftermath, he wants to fulfill the motive, while steering clear of further troubles.

A car thief can run into trouble breaking into the car, or get caught in the act. Or perhaps he gets into the car and even gets hold of its sound system, but is arrested in the aftermath, or the fence won't give him a dime.[15] Even a crime such as vandalism, despite its immediate feedback, risks a failed escape. To understand what the offender wants, we should study each criminal event as it unfolds.

Sometimes we can read the future in the present, but not always. Oscar Wilde explains, "There is no such thing as an omen. Destiny does not send us heralds. She is too wise or too cruel for that."[16]

Exhibit 3.2   What the Offender Wants and Hopes to Avoid

	Offender Wants	*Offender Does Not Want*
During Crime Incident	To complete the crime successfully	To waste effort; to step into harm's way
After Crime Incident	To fulfill what motivated the crime	To find follow-up trouble or humiliation

It is easy to misunderstand offender intentions by forgetting the stages of a crime. Suppose a street robber demands a wallet from the victim, who fights him. He shoots the victim, who later dies. The wallet only contains a single dollar. The headline later reads, "Man murdered for one dollar!" That headline includes an outcome the offender did not anticipate. He began by hoping to get a good deal more than a dollar, and expecting the victim to comply. It didn't turn out that way.

I have presented the three stages of a criminal act. Now I show how to sort out each incident or group of incidents into a single sentence, and to diagram that sentence.

Sorting Out Crimes

The various people who study crime should be able to talk to one another. That includes a detective looking for a single culprit, a crime statistician making a big table, or a professor teaching a class or writing a book. I suggest describing each crime or type of crime with a single sentence, in a standard form:[17]

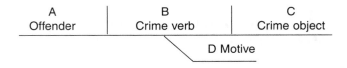

This diagram tells us that the offender or offenders did something illegal, acting upon some object (a person or thing), for some motive. Taking it step by step,

a. The *subject* of the sentence could be the offender, suspect, or many of them.

b. The *crime verb* tells what the offender(s) did, such as break, ingest, paint, pinch, punch, shoplift, smash, steal, trade, or vandalize. Some of these actions (e.g., shoplifting) are always illegal. Others are not always illegal. What makes "paint" illegal is painting the wrong thing.

c. Next you need a *crime object*—what the offender(s) acts upon. These might be the CDs pinched, noses punched, glass smashed, or walls defaced with graffiti.[18] The crime's direct object might also include a person with whom the offender exchanges contraband, such as a drug buyer or seller.

d. At the end of the sentence, the crime's *motive* is described with a prepositional or infinitive phrase.

This standard format helps us sort out crimes in several ways.[19]

Closer Examination of Legal Categories

A single category under criminal law often masks important behavioral variations. We can sort out those variations by separating specific actions, objects, and motives. The diagram above helps do just that. For example, one person assaults another for diverse motives, including:

To punish

To restore self-esteem

For thrills

To show off to friends

To disable and rob

Boys stealing a car sound system might differ in motive. One might want to transfer it to his own car. Another wants to sell it to get the money. Another wants to put on a show for his friends. Another just wants the thrill of the theft. These variations in motive affect prevention tactics. Removing opportunities to fence stolen auto parts interferes with the boys who steal the sound system with money in mind. But that has no direct impact on boys stealing for their own use, or to show off.

Even in the Same Crime Incident, Motives Can Differ

Three boys go into a store and shoplift some clothing. Their crime is ostensibly the same, but their motives can differ. One wants to wear some of the clothes. The other wants to sell some, and the third wants to show off to the other two. If they are apprehended later, none of this will matter for punishment. But as analysts, we want to know. To reduce shoplifting, the store might have different strategies for different motives.[20] Ink tags that ruin the garment make it hard to wear or sell, but have no impact on the thrill. Still, the theft will probably not occur if only one of the boys can get what he wants. In short, people with entirely different motives can carry out what appears as the same crime.

Same Motive, Different Crimes

People with the same motive can carry out different crimes. Suppose that three boys want money to buy beer for a party tonight. One of them shoplifts, another takes a car stereo, a third commits a burglary. These are three different crimes with *the same motive*. The legal descriptions of these crimes will miss their commonality. Moreover, security improvements at the store will thwart one offender, but have no impact on the other two.

Imagine four barkeepers who make money from illegal drug transactions, each in a different way. The first *sells drinks* to the crime participants to make his profit. He allows them to do illegal business, but does not *directly* participate in it. The second *takes a kickback* from each illegal drug sale. The third barkeeper *rents the use* of the bar to drug sellers for a fixed price. The fourth himself *sells drugs*. In all four cases, the motive is money, but the verbs and objects differ among them.[21] In studying crime, you might get lost in the details. But you can always go back to the above diagram to sort out the fundamentals.

Crimes in Sequence

This chapter has already presented crime's stages, and showed how to sum up one crime or crime type in a sentence. Now I consider how several offenses occur in sequence. Exhibit 3.3 shows how two crimes can overlap. Crimes often fit into a larger sequence, with the aftermath of one crime becoming the prelude to the next. Each step has an immediate motive, but the offender also has an eventual motive. For example, a drug offender wants to get high later that day. To get what he wants, he might go through four steps:

	[Subject]	[Verb]	[Crime's Object]	[Motive]
1.	He	steals	a television set	(to sell it),
2.		sells	the television set	(to buy the drugs),
3.		buys	the drugs	(to ingest them),
4.		ingests	a dosage	to get high.

Exhibit 3.3   The First Crime Leads Directly to the Second

1st Crime Sequence	2nd Crime Sequence	Time	Overall Sequence	
1. Prelude			A burglar approaches,	
2. Incident			then burgles a home,	Crime 1
3. Aftermath	3. Prelude		then leaves with the loot,	Overlap
	4. Incident		then sells the loot to a fence,	Crime 2
	5. Aftermath		then departs with the money.	

He might keep the *eventual* motive—to get high—in the back of his mind all along. Sorting out the specific steps helps a detective find the culprit, and assists in crime prevention. All you have to do is throw obstacles in the offender's path. If he cannot sell the booty, he cannot get the drugs, and might drop all four criminal acts.

Illegal and Legal Behaviors Are Intertwined

When an offender carries out a sequence of behaviors, some of them may be entirely legal.

- An offender enters a department store legally, picks out six items, puts three under his coat, pays for the other three, and exits.
- A drug manufacturer buys some over-the-counter drugs from the store, purifies them, then mixes them with something else, ends up with an illegal substance, then sells it. Some of these steps are probably legal, but the overall enterprise is not.

Fortunately, we can describe various legal and illegal behaviors in terms of who does what and why. The grammar of crime is also the grammar of life. A *legal* action can also be divided by who does it, what they do, to whom or what, and with what motive. Thus changes in laws or their variations from place to place do not stop us from studying the steps offenders go through. Canada's changes in its prostitution laws—discussed in the previous chapter—do not prevent us from sorting out these sequences. The challenge is to break down any complex crime process into its simple parts and sequences.

Sequences for House Prostitution

Sometimes offenders organize a sequence of crimes with one another. Perhaps they act as independent but cooperative offenders. Perhaps they act under a boss, with central control. Perhaps they act in different places, showing up only now and then to pass along contraband or money.

But sometimes offenders cooperate at a single location. Consider a house of prostitution—one way to sell sex, with quite a long history.[22] Consider its many names, current and obsolete: bad house, bagno, bag shanty, bawdy-house, beauty parlor, bird cage, bordello, boum-boum parlor, broad house, brothel, buttocking shop, cake-shop, cathouse, cavaulting school, chicken ranch, clap trap, coupling house, disorderly house, flesh factory, flophouse, funhouse, girly parlor, grinding house, hooker shop, hot house, house of assignation, house of ill repute, house of joy, house of sale, house of shame, house of sin, jab joint, knocking shop, maison de joie, man trap, meat factory, molly house, no-tell hotel, nunnery, parlor house, red-light house, seraglio, service station, sin bin, skin room, slut hut, snake ranch, sporting house, trick pad, whorehouse, and numerous other terms.

Which tasks are illegal will vary by nation, but these tasks must probably be performed to run a house of prostitution, wherever it is:

1. setting up the *house,*

2. recruiting the *prostitute,*

3. transporting *her* to the house,

4. managing the *ongoing operation,*

5. soliciting her *customers,*

6. negotiating the *price,*

7. providing the *sex,* and

8. collecting the *money.*[23]

Sometimes the same person will perform several of these tasks, and other times such tasks are divided among different people in cooperation. By sorting out tasks, we can better understand criminal activities, and compare them from place to place and time to time.

Sequences for Street Prostitution

Street prostitutes have a simpler task, but they still must carry out a sequence of behaviors to do business.[24] Perhaps a street prostitute first finds a street corner to work from, then she flags down a motorist or entices a pedestrian.[25] In New Jersey, each of these steps is criminalized. First, it is illegal to loiter for prostitution purposes in places of public access, including

> any public street, sidewalk, bridge, alley, plaza, park, boardwalk, driveway, parking lot or transportation facility, public library or the doorways and entrance ways to any building which fronts on any of the aforesaid places, or a motor vehicle. . . .[26]

More generally, it is illegal to wander, linger, or prowl in a public place with the purpose of engaging in or promoting prostitution. Second, New Jersey law prohibits the following *repeated* behaviors if they assist prostitution:

> Beckoning to or stopping pedestrians or motorists in a public place; attempting to stop motor vehicles or pedestrians, or to engage passers-by in conversation.[27]

Such repetitive behavior is important for street prostitutes to reach their customers. It can also irritate neighbors, who are likely to complain to the police.

Other prostitution laws might forbid enticing someone to become a prostitute, arranging appointments for a prostitute, living off the proceeds of prostitution, or owning a structure used for prostitution activities. As you look at these lists, you can readily see that crime is a complex of behaviors, having diverse objects and variants. Yet we can understand the different crime types if we tease apart these behaviors, studying them one at a time and finding their verbs, objects, and motives.

Crime and the Larger Flow of Life

Imagine a group of lingering boys, drinking beer underage. One of them pulls out some marihuana. The drugs sit on the table while their socializing continues. It is not clear who has possession of the marihuana at that stage, or even who knows it is sitting there. It is not clear who will smoke it, share it, saunter in, or slip out. Are boys in the next room participants, partial participants, or nonparticipants? Is it a crime to watch others smoke marihuana, or to inhale its secondhand smoke? What is the line between noticing and watching, or watching and joining? When does legal activity end and illegal activity begin? Fortunately, observers have learned orderly ways to study the flow of life, and we can apply that order to study crime.

Red Smith, the famous sportswriter, once said, "I like to get where the cabbage is cooking and catch the scents."[28] We can learn about the flow of life that way. But we also have to figure out how to take good notes and put them in order systematically. Ethologists[29] study movements and actions of living things in their natural environment. For example, a rattlesnake attacks in nine stages: placement, alertness, head turning, approach, preparation, strike, reapproach, head searching, and swallowing.[30] Kinesiologists and other experts also divide up the quick action of daily human life, suggesting how to maximize performance in baseball, golf, skiing, figure skating, and boxing. Choreographers also use detailed codes for dancers.[31] These many human endeavors come down to the same issue of motion in space and time. To quote Jack Handey, "To me, boxing is like a ballet, except there's no music, no choreography and the dancers hit each other."[32]

These specifics can also be assembled for academic purposes. Ecological psychology studies how human "behavior settings" organize the daily flow of life, a topic to which I shall return later. Geographers have used global positioning to study daily activities of citizens. Professor Clark McPhail (of the University of Illinois at Urbana-Champaign) has coded riots and other collective actions in terms of detailed and specific movements.[33] Even inanimate objects are studied minutely in space and time, including fireworks displays, artistic fountains, scenery for Broadway musicals, factory machinery and robots, fleets of trucks, containers, ships, taxis, and cars. To be sure, the artist and athlete are creative and surprising, but with excellent control they depart from the script by decision, not by accident. Crime is not always beautiful or interesting to watch, but it still has its sequences. A shoplifter enters, approaches, finds what he wants, takes it from the shelf, stashes it on or near his body in another part of the store, then exits. Illegal actions have specific steps and stages, helping us trace how they fit within a larger world.[34]

Repeat Victimization: An Interrupted Sequence

Not all crime sequences occur without a break. Some offenders return to the same victim—but their sequence is interrupted by time. That makes it more difficult for crime analysts to figure out the sequence, or for police to act accordingly. Fortunately, Professors Ken Pease and Graham Farrell in the United Kingdom discovered why this topic is important, how to study it, and how to do something about it.[35] (I come back to this in later chapters.)

Not all repeat victimizations involve the same offender, but some do. For example, a residential burglar might return to the same home to complete the task the next day, or a month later. Not only do repeats take up a large share of crime, but they are the most preventable. It is much easier to get someone's attention *after* the first victimization than before, so victims will listen better to crime prevention experts.

The topic of repeat victimization has recently been extended in an interesting way. Some British and Australian scholars have recognized the importance of *near*-repeat victimizations. This refers to victimizations against very nearby properties or places, but not exactly the same ones as before. Suppose that I break into your home this week, and your next-door neighbor's home next week—that's a *near* repeat.

Researchers Kate Bowers, Shane Johnson, Michael Townsley, Ross Homel, and Janet Chaseling have helped invent this topic.[36] Some settings and habitats—discussed in future chapters—invite crime repetitions for both a victim and a victim's neighbors. Moreover, a successful crime against one victim helps feed attempts and successes against others. Thus a local area that invites crime also helps multiply crime, since crime risk is communicable. Areas with a good deal of housing homogeneity suffer more repeat burglary, since a burglar knows better where to enter and how to find his way around, even in the dark. Repeat victimization and near repeats are interrupted sequences that help make sense of crime—going beyond the isolated incident.

Overview

Crimes can be complex, but we can break them down into simpler features. Each offense can be broken down into three stages. Very different crimes can be described with the same sentence structure and diagram techniques. We can link them into sequences, taking into account the prelude and aftermath of the crime incident itself. These techniques transcend historical periods and nations. Whether one at a time or in the millions, criminal acts have common as well as distinct features. Police detectives, professors, and students— from different nations and cities—should be able to communicate about crime. As a result, each may come to realize that crime depends on more than what's in front of a single person's nose.

Central Points, Chapter 3

1. A crime event has a prelude, an incident, and an aftermath.

2. We should study a crime as it unfolds, without letting its aftermath color our view of what happened in the incident itself.

3. Every legal and illegal act can be described in the same format, with a verb, object, and motive.

4. Often, illegal events fit into a sequence, with the aftermath of one providing the prelude for the next.

5. Offenders generally seek to gain benefits, avoid risks, and evade difficulties. Even violent crimes tend to be goal oriented.

Exercises

1. Discuss five different ways to steal a computer.

2. Write a fictional account of shoplifting, specifying its three stages.

3. Some teenagers are hanging out together. Imagine six steps leading them incrementally toward an illegal act.

4. Write a half dozen indicators that lead you to suspect the presence of prostitution.

Notes

1. These words are attributed to Feynman, but did he really say them?

2. French poet, writer, and critic (1908–1944). Quoted in *The Columbia World of Quotations* (New York: Columbia University Press, 1996).

3. E. Sapir, *Language: An Introduction to the Study of Speech* (New York: Harcourt-Brace, 1921).

4. U.S. philosopher (1908–2000). Quotation appears in W. V. O. Quine, *From a Logical Point of View* (Cambridge, MA: Harvard University Press, 1961).

5. He also happens to be my brother. His work on violence is the best you will find anywhere. This paragraph focuses on nonacquisitive violence, which still has a purpose for the offender. See J. Tedeschi and R. B. Felson, *Violence, Aggression and Coercive Action* (Washington, DC: APA Books, 1994).

6. His excellent work can be found in several places, including these:
   a. R. Wortley, *Situational Prison Control: Crime Prevention in Correctional Institutions* (Cambridge, UK: Cambridge University Press, 2002).
   b. R. Wortley, "A Classification of Techniques for Controlling Situational Precipitators of Crime," *Security Journal* 14 (2001): 63–82.
   c. R. Wortley, "A Two-stage Model of Situational Crime Prevention," *Studies on Crime and Crime Prevention* 7 (1998): 173–188.

7. I prefer to call this the "crime event" rather than the "criminal event," since the word "criminal" implies a person rather than an incident. However, the phrase "the criminal event" is still useful. See L. W. Kennedy and V. Sacco, *The Criminal Event: An Introduction to Criminology in Canada* (Toronto, ON: Nelson Thomson, 2002). Also see the work on the routine activity approach reviewed in any of the editions of M. Felson, *Crime and Everyday Life* (Thousand Oaks, CA: Sage, 2002).

8. A crime has an immediate aftermath, but it might also have an elongated period during which more happens, too. Not every burglar dispenses with the goods right away, and not every injured victim heals or worsens quickly. I could divide all three stages into substages, but let's save that for another day.

9. British writer of prose and poetry (1865–1936). See "The Benefactors" in *The Years Between* (London: Methuen, 1919).

10. Modified slightly from a comment made by Professor Michael Maxwell, personal communication. Also see analysis by R. B. Felson and H. J. Steadman, "Situational Factors in Disputes Leading to Criminal Violence," *Criminology* 21 (1983): 59–74.

11. Of course, the justice system might learn later what happened earlier.

12. Marcus Tullius Cicero (106–43 BC), Roman orator, philosopher, statesman. From *Pro Roscio Amerino*, 84. Quoted in *The Columbia World of Quotations* (New York: Columbia University Press, 1996). Cicero drew this idea from a famous judge of his time, L. Cassius.

13. See Tedeschi and Felson, op. cit.

14. I have already included many references to Professor Clarke's work. Note how he has elaborated crime prevention options over the years he has studied the topic. His techniques increased from 12 to 25. I have neglected here specific mention of offender excuses (neutralization). These techniques are presented in many places, including the website of the Center for Problem-oriented Policing, http://www.popcenter.org (accessed September 3, 2005), and the British Home Office Crime Reduction site, http://www.crimereduction.gov.uk/learningzone/scptechniques.htm (accessed September 3, 2005).

15. In effect, the first crime succeeded, but the follow-up crime failed.

16. Quoted in "Oscar Wilde, 1854–1900" (n.d.), The Free Library, http://wilde.thefree library.com (accessed September 9, 2005).

17. I hated diagramming sentences in high school. I never dreamed, then, that it would help me understand crime, now. For more on diagramming sentences, see C. L. Vitoo, *Grammar by Diagram: Understanding English Grammar Through Traditional Sentence Diagramming* (Peterborough, ON: Broadview Press, 2003).

18. In much of my work, I refer to crime "targets." These are the people or things that offenders attack or seize in carrying out criminal acts. Here I subsume crime targets into a larger category, "crime's direct object." I do this because the word "target" does not quite fit a drug house or house of prostitution set up illegally. Fortunately, English-language grammarians help us out here. I sometimes use the words "target" and "direct object" interchangeably. You will be able to tell what I mean from the context.

19. Exhibit B in Appendix B gives 11 examples of crimes parsed according to the format explained in this chapter.

20. See R. V. Clarke, "Shoplifting," in U.S. Department of Justice, *Problem-oriented Guides for Police* (2003). Available from the Center for Problem-oriented Policing, http://www.popcenter.org (accessed September 3, 2005).

21. Experts in drug offending could extend this list. See M. Natarajan and M. Hough, eds., *Illegal Drug Markets: From Research to Prevention Policy* (Monsey, NY: Criminal Justice Press, 2000) (Volume 10 in *Crime Prevention Studies* series).

22. For a longer view of prostitution, see references in Note 7, Chapter 2.

23. E.g., see B. S. Heyl, *The Madam as Entrepreneur: Career Management in House Prostitution* (New Brunswick, NJ: Transaction, 1979).

24. For an ethnographic account of street prostitution, see T. Sanders, "The Risks of Street Prostitution: Punters, Police and Protesters," *Urban Studies* 41 (2004): 9.

25. Although legalization varies, the street prostitution process has many international features. See J. McCloskey and M. Lazarus, "Community Policing and the Policing Factor of On-Street Prostitution in the Kings Cross Police Patrol," in *Australian Institute of Criminology Conference Proceedings No. 14, Sex Industry and Public Policy* (1992). Available from the Australian Institute of Criminology, http://www.aic.gov.au/publications/proceedings/14/mcloskey.pdf (accessed September 3, 2005).

26. N.J.S.2C:34-1.1 Loitering for the Purpose of Engaging in Prostitution. Certain subsections are run together and original punctuation changed slightly. This quotation does not consider the conditions for charging or convicting a particular offender, which go beyond these words alone.

27. See previous endnote for source.

28. Popular American sports columnist (1905–1982) who won a Pulitzer Prize in 1976. He said this while departing to cover California baseball games played by the Giants and Dodgers. Quoted in *Simpson's Contemporary Quotations* (New York: Houghton Mifflin, 1988).

29. Kinesiology focuses on the mechanics and anatomy of human movement. Ethology studies animals in their natural environment. Human ethology focuses on humans in their natural environment, overlapping a good deal with ecological psychology.

30. K. V. Kardong and V. L. Bels, "Rattlesnake Strike Behavior: Kinematics," *Journal of Experimental Biology* 201 (1998): 837–850.

31. Digital dance systems synchronize movements by attaching a dozen or more bending sensors to each ballet dancer. Even traditional square dancing has been programmed with precision, its calls manipulated, its formations scored in bitmap pictures, its sequences stored on laptop computers.

32. J. Handey, *Deep Thoughts: An Inspiration for the Uninspired* (New York: Penguin, 1991).

33. C. McPhail and R. T. Wohlstein, "Individual and Collective Behaviors Within Gatherings, Demonstrations, and Riots," *Annual Review of Sociology* 9 (1983): 579–600.

34. We might call this *crime kinesiology*. But we also want to relate this information to larger ecology.

35. To get started in the repeat victimization literature, see these papers:
   a. G. Farrell and K. Pease, eds., *Repeat Victimization* (Monsey, NY: Criminal Justice Press, 2001).
   b. S. Lloyd, G. Farrell, and K. Pease, *Preventing Repeated Domestic Violence: A Demonstration Project on Merseyside* (London: British Home Office, 1994) (Police Research Group, Crime Prevention Unit Paper 49).
   c. G. Farrell, and K. Pease, *Once Bitten, Twice Bitten: Repeat Victimization and Its Implications for Crime Prevention* (London: British Home Office, 1993) (Police Research Group, Crime Prevention Unit Paper 46).
   d. G. Laycock and G. Farrell, "Repeat Victimization: Lessons for Implementing Problem-Oriented Policing," *Crime Prevention Studies* 15 (2003): 150–175.

36. See these articles:
   a. M. Townsley, R. Homel, and J. Chaseling, "Infectious Burglaries: A Test of the Near Repeat Hypothesis," *British Journal of Criminology* 43 (2003): 615–633.
   b. K. J. Bowers and S. D. Johnson,"Who Commits Near Repeats? A Test of the Boost Explanation," *Western Criminology Review* 5 (2004): 12–24, http://wcr.sonoma.edu/v5n3/bowers.htm (accessed September 3, 2005).
   c. K. J. Bowers and S. D. Johnson, "Domestic Burglary Repeats and Space-Time Clusters: The Dimensions of Risk," *European Journal of Criminology* 2 (2005): 67–92.
   d. S. D. Johnson and K. J. Bowers, "The Stability of Space-Time Clusters of Burglary," *British Journal of Criminology* 44 (2004): 55–65.
   e. S. D. Johnson and K. J. Bowers, "The Burglary Rate as a Clue to the Future: The Beginnings of Prospective Hot-Spotting," *European Journal of Criminology* 1 (2004): 237–255.

PART II

Crime Within a System

Plants and animals remote in the scale of nature, are bound together by a web of complex relations.

—Charles Darwin[1]

The successful student must train [the] mind to adapt to the changing environment. . . .

—University webpage[2]

Holland has made pimps into landlords.

—Jim Lohse[3]

Some primal termite knocked on wood
And tasted it, and found it good!
And that is why your Cousin May
Fell through the parlor floor today.

—Ogden Nash[4]

4

Crime's Ecosystem

Thieves cannot survive stealing each other's booty. That's why crime must feed on a larger system. That system is interconnected, and our job is to figure out how. Each of us has given crime a helping hand, even when acting entirely within the law. Sometimes we can do nothing about this; but by learning how crime lives and feeds, we will have more tools to use against it.

The essential point of ecology is to figure out how a particular activity draws its life from something bigger. In Thornton Wilder's classic play, *Our Town,* an envelope was addressed to

> Jane Crofut; The Crofut Farm; Grover's Corners; Sutton County; New Hampshire; United States of America; Continent of North America; Western Hemisphere; the Earth; the Solar System; the Universe; the Mind of God.

The play moves slowly, and is often produced by inexperienced volunteers. Yet it has a certain charm and endurance. Wilder had a wonderful sense of time and place. He never lost sight of past or future and their links to the present. As he explained himself in 1938,

> An archeologist's eyes combine the view of the telescope and the view of the microscope. He reconstructs the very distant with the help of the very small. It was something of this method that I brought to a New Hampshire village.[5]

We, too, must fit our crime participants within a setting, contained in a locality, embedded in a region, a nation, then the earth and beyond. To understand this, we must turn to a central concept in ecology.[6]

Crime in Its Ecosystem

Eugene Odum (1913–2002) pioneered the concept of *ecosystem.*[7] An ecosystem is a dynamic, living system of different activities, each drawing upon one another and on nonhuman resources. To understand the concept, note the importance of articles—"the" or "an." *The ecosystem* includes many living and nonliving things, their interactions, the flows of energy from the sun via many routes, and the cycling of essential nutrients to *all* living organisms and activities, including crime.[8] *An ecosystem* is a regional or local system of living things and what they live from. But we cannot rely on the ecologists to do our work. We must apply their ideas to crime using our own brains.

A given crime's ecosystem takes into account its interactions with other crimes and the surrounding noncrime environment. It is a dynamic, living system that allows crime to survive and sometimes flourish.[9] Thus auto theft's ecosystem might consider the interplay among auto owner, thief, parts dealer, and repairmen; the relationship between alcohol, drugs, and crime; and how legitimate work leaves cars unsupervised. Crime ecology studies crime's ecosystems, large and small.[10]

Exhibit 4.1   The Span of Crime's Ecosystem

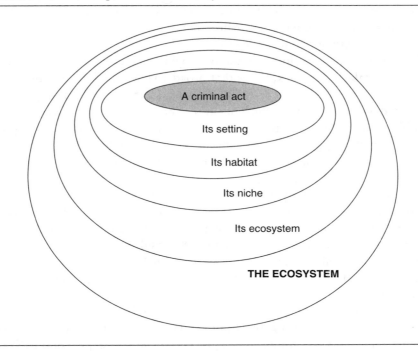

But we cannot stop with a crime's own ecosystem. We must link many crime ecosystems to one another and to the larger ecosystem. The *web of crime* is a complex living system that links legal and illegal activities within the larger ecosystem. The several circles in Exhibit 4.1 depict the web of crime, at least for one criminal act or type. That web is of course more complex because so many crimes are related to one another and to legal activities and nonhuman events. Fortunately, we can find some devices to keep from getting lost as we study crime in a larger world. This book teaches these devices one by one.

Whenever you are down in the specifics of crime, you should look up; whenever you are up in crime's larger environment, you should look down. The ecological perspective helps you link each crime to a larger world, then come back again.

The ecological perspective is both intellectual and empirical. It helps us think and tell a story afterwards. Experienced ecologists know how to study the systems of organisms—their niches, habitats, and myriad interdependencies.[11] Their experience helps us study crime. Now is a special moment in the history of crime theory, for we are beginning to understand better how crime details can fit into a coherent, tangible, framework. That allows us to put ecology to work. You will soon realize that crime ecology is a field pregnant with opportunity for students of crime.

Crime ecology must look far and near, while filling the steps in between. Now let's take a step back, to see that broader view. Exhibit 4.1 depicts the nested parts of the ecosystem leading to crime. A crime (such as shoplifting) is nested within its setting, which fits into its habitat; the habitat is contained within its niche, which is part of a larger crime ecosystem. That fits within something still bigger, the ecosystem for all of life.[12] Crime ecology poses a challenge to you: Can you expand your mind, thinking about crime in a larger system, without getting lost?

Exhibit 4.1 can help you keep track of where you are as you read this book. Chapters 1 to 3 give you an idea of the criminal act itself. These acts fit into crime settings, the topic of Chapter 6. These settings fit within crime habitats, discussed in Chapter 7. Chapter 8 considers something more elaborate, a crime's niche. Of course, the niches include the habitats, and the habitats include the settings, so the book keeps expanding, building, and reaching farther. Of course, crime's ecosystem includes many relationships and processes discussed in Chapters 9 through 20. After that, I seek to synthesize some of this information with the final chapters. If you get lost in any of this, remember that complexity is just a lot of simple steps. Look back at Exhibit 4.1, and you can probably find out where you are.

You could also use the crime diagrams from the previous chapter to describe a crime in its ecosystem. But you will need more than one sentence and more than a simple diagram. Consider these six steps:

1. Joe breaks into a car to steal its stereo.

2. The car is parked in a downtown street *setting*.

3. That setting is located within a *habitat* where cars are easily plundered.

4. That habitat is part of a *niche* with chances to sell stolen stereos.

5. That niche is part of a larger auto crime *ecosystem,* with drugs to buy.

6. That ecosystem is part of a world with agriculture and transport of such drugs.

As you proceed in this book, I hope to provide you the tools you need to sort out these features of crime's larger world. This book emphasizes one point above others: All offenders need to draw upon a larger system and its tangible resources. Theft depends on goods to steal, a way to steal and transfer them. Drugs depend on production and a network for distribution. Prostitution depends on customers and suitable settings to find them, then to carry out the act. Violent crimes imply sufficient power to overcome victims and some confidence that others will not interfere. In short, to study crime we must look beyond it. Ecology helps us do so.

The Tasks of Crime Ecology

Ecology derives from the Greek word for a house, *oikos*.[13] As you read farther in this book you will see how offenders live off the larger world, near and far, including the illegal activities of others. In very broad terms, crime ecology is the scientific study of the processes, interdependencies, transformations, distributions, and abundances of criminal activities. As these chapters unfold, those five long words will make more sense.

Crime ecology has three tasks: to learn how criminal activities (1) draw upon the larger ecosystem, (2) depend on one another, and (3) influence the larger ecosystem. An example of the first is to link crime to an abandoned lot down the street, or the poppy fields of Afghanistan. An example of the second is how prostitution, drug dealing, and auto theft interact.[14] An example of the third is how high crime rates drive people away from the inner city, contributing to its decline.[15] I give the third task less attention in this book—not denying its importance, but because we're busy enough with the first two tasks.[16]

The Fallacy of Misplaced Complexity

Some criminal events seem to be complex, but perhaps they can be broken down into simpler elements. The production, distribution, and sale of illicit drugs might involve a complex web of activities. But any single one of those activities might not be complex at all. Be on the lookout for a complex chain of simple events. Sometimes one person sells drugs to another, who sells to a few others, etc. Thus several simple transactions fit into a larger, more complex whole.

Do not assume that everybody involved in a chain of events meets in the same room and plans its complexity. From afar, perhaps you see complexity; but from close up, simplicity is the rule. *The fallacy of misplaced complexity* is the tendency to imagine central coordination and fancy organization that does not really exist. Unless proven otherwise, assume that each offender acts simply and locally, even when participating in something that reaches well beyond himself.

Crime's Food Web

Consider how offenders feed off a larger world.[17] That process has simpler parts that join into something more complex:

Predator-prey relationships: Street robbers pick wallets off those staggering home from the local bar.

Crime's food chains: Nastier robbers shake down weaker robbers, who harvest wallets from drunks.

The crime web: Thieves, fences, flea markets, customers, drug dealers, and prostitutes can be linked in a complex crime web.[18]

Consider the food web for marihuana. It starts with the plant *Cannabis sativa.* Marihuana is known by at least 200 names: ace, A-bomb, Acapulco, Afghani, African, Alaskan, Alice B. Toklas, ashes, Aunt Mary, baby, bag, baggie, bales, bamba, bangue, bar, BC-bud, bhang, blunt, bo, bobo, bonghit, boo, boo-boo bama, bricks, bud, Buddha, bush, burn-one, buzz, C. S., can, Canadian-black, canamo, canamo-indio, cest, chanvre, cheeba-cheeba, chronic, cocktail, Colombian gold, cryppie, cryptonite, dagga, dank, diambista, dirtweed, ditch, ditchweed, dobie, domestic-don-juan, doob, doobie, dope, doradilla, draf, fatty, fingerlid, fir, flowers, flowertops, fuma-d'Angola, gage, gangster, ganja, gash, gasper, giggleweed, goblet-of-jam, gold, golden, goldstar, gong, goody-goody, goof-butt, gram, grass, grasshopper, green, greenbud, green-sticky, gretta, griefs, griffa, guaza, gungun, haircut, hanma, hanf, harsh, hash, hay, hemp, herb, high, hint keneviri, hocuspocus, homegrown, hooch, hooter, hops, huang-ma, humboltd, huoma, Indian-hemp, indica, indo, instagu, J, jaysmoke, jive, joint, Juanita, kalakit, kee, kenevir, kif, killer, kilos, kineboisin, leaf, leño, loco-weed, ma-fen, ma-jen-chiu, mari , mariguana, mary-jane, Maui-wowie, method, Mexican, mj, mo, moocah, moota, nail, nigra, number, one-hit, ounce, owl, Panama red, panatela, parsley, pot, potlikker, pounds, PR, pretendica, puff, qunnab, ragweed, rainy-day woman, rasta, redbud, reefer, roach, root, seeds, sens, sensemilla, sess, shake, shit, sinsemilla, skunk, skunkweed, smoke, spliff, stash, stems, stone, ta-ma, tea, tekrouri, Texas-Tea, Thai-bud, Thai-stick, ThaistickSwisher, thumb, trees, twigs, twist, untoque, wahupta, weed, whacktabacky, whackyweed, wheat, wood, yeh, yerba, yerhia, yesca, and 420.[19]

Marihuana is from the class Magnoliopsida, order Rosales, family Cannabaceae, and has three species: *Cannabis sativa, Cannabis indica,* and *Cannabis ruderalis.* The marihuana plant grows 3 to 10 feet tall and has hairy leaves divided into about a half-dozen leaflets, often sticky with resin. Separate plants produce male and female flowers. Much marihuana is grown near where it is used, and handled only by a few people for personal use. Yet marihuana can also be linked to a larger world. It might be grown in a favorable climate, go from farmer to distributor to transporter, and be divided into smaller units as it moves along a crime chain toward the end consumer. Other drug chains can also have several links of producers, dealers, and customers. An outdoor drug market might require additional roles, including touts, lookouts, holders, runners, guards, and go-betweens.[20]

But the crime web goes farther. It includes any chemicals needed to grow and cure the product, receptacles, and other equipment and supplies. It includes the presences of those who feed the offenders and absences of those who might interfere. Indoor growth of marihuana requires construction of special buildings, sometimes underground or concealed in houses. Advanced marihuana cultivation uses specialized hydroponic equipment and lighting, with substantial consumption of electricity or other energy. That's why a crime web is often too messy to put on a single piece of paper.

Marihuana sales and usage can be linked to other illicit drugs. Interestingly, marihuana links ordinary citizens and legal businesses to a chain of diverse thieves, prostitutes, and robbery victims.[21] The crime web is so complex that we need to study it piece by piece in order to comprehend it at all.

I cannot do all of that in one chapter. But I can illustrate with one example how prostitution reaches near and far, and provide some discussion of what to do about it.

The Web of Crime Challenges Policymakers

The web of crime complicates traditional public policy, making it unclear where to focus punishment. One hesitates to punish misdemeanors severely, but a misdemeanor can set the stage for a felony. For example, an ordinary selling of sex occasionally leads to a murder. In other cases, a serious offense leads no further. Wife-murderers are unlikely to murder again, but society can hardly let them go unpunished. Several later chapters consider how various crimes relate to one another and to perfectly legal activities. Shall we close a restaurant for feeding drug dealers a hamburger, Coke, and French fries?

Yet the web of crime increases policy options, often making it easier to stop crime without locking up more people. Consider the problem of curb-crawling, where men circle the neighborhood in cars, trying to pick up prostitutes. A city can assign female police officers to decoy and arrest them—a highly inefficient and expensive practice. It's even more cumbersome to arrest and process prostitutes. Or the city can give people a traffic ticket for circling three times, leaving the offenders out of the criminal justice system. A third option is to change the Friday night traffic lights to keep traffic moving, impairing prostitution without requiring arrests. A fourth option is to block off certain streets on weekend evenings. Understanding crime's ecology helps us deal with problems more effectively and to redirect policy toward more efficient methods. For example, police can study how prostitution works in its environment, then seek to reduce its harm.

Even societies that do not *want* to regulate prostitution cannot ignore its relationship to other crime problems. The Netherlands might be the world's most innovative country in dealing with vice control, including prostitution. Dutch authorities experimented with a drive-in prostitution park, away from nearby residences, providing health inspection and police protection for the girls working there. It is called a *Tippelzone,* from the word for "walking in short steps"—a preautomotive word that implies street prostitution.[22] The Dutch set up Tippelzones in eight cities. Dutch authorities then began to toughen their enforcement against curb-crawling and streetwalking in other parts of these cities. In effect, they instituted a policy of *planned displacement*—pushing their prostitution toward the Tippelzones and away from the usual zones.[23]

The innovation in the largest city, Amsterdam, began in 1996 and was closed down on December 31, 2002. Although Rotterdam and The Hague will soon close their Tippelzones, several other Dutch cities will probably keep theirs in operation.[24] (In short, Tippelzones ran into trouble in the largest cities in the Netherlands, while proving rather more successful in the smaller cities. Often crime prevention efforts have the least success in very large crime ecosystems.)

Paul van Soomeren was project evaluator for the Amsterdam Tippelzone, and wrote a fascinating report about it.[25] I have adapted Exhibit 4.2 from his report. In the Tippelzone, authorities designed

- a pickup area, where prostitutes offer their services and negotiate with clients;
- a living room, which only prostitutes and health and welfare officials could enter; and
- the *afwerkplaats,* where sexual services were provided in cars.

The service area was divided up by aluminum partitions for privacy. After choosing a girl, the customer drove into one of the partitions for sex in the front seat. The partitions were designed so the girls could exit a car quickly, but the door on the man's side would bump the trash can, so she could get away from him. A smaller area served customers arriving by motorcycle or bicycle. The Amsterdam Tippelzone was designed to accommodate 80 prostitutes at any one time, and car movements ranged from 500 to 15,000 per night.

Van Soomeren concluded that the Amsterdam Tippelzone was, at least initially, safer than the usual street prostitution.[26] He found the experiment a short-term policy success, minimizing many problems, including complaints from neighbors in the areas formerly used by prostitutes.

Now you get to the point of the story. Tippelzones *at first* reduced those crimes linked to prostitution. But as time passed, the word got around to other nations; new prostitutes began to arrive, and illegal trafficking of women increased. More of the women were illegals, contrary to the goals of the project. These girls came not only from Eastern Europe but as far away as Central and South America. As a consequence the Amsterdam zone became overcrowded with sex workers. The increased litter and noise were just one result. The oversupply of girls drove down the price. That in turn led to fights among the girls. Pimps began to take advantage of the girls' illegal status. The Amsterdam Tippelzone was shut down.

An initial policy success in one nation turned sour, precisely because that nation's prostitution was part of a larger ecosystem. Regulating sex is a very difficult task in an urban and motorized world, with easy movement among nations. To quote van Soomeren,

> The success of the Tippelzone appears to have been its downfall, as the number of prostitutes using the zone increased exponentially and the zone could no longer be controlled.[27]

Many nations have tried to regulate vice. For over a century, New Orleans, Louisiana, was a center for quasilegal prostitution. Its zoned vice sector—Storeyville—is now called the French Quarter, and its prostitution was quite open. That gave rise to sex tourism (and related crime problems) long before Thailand gained that reputation.[28] Sex zones were found in many parts of America, including Newport, Kentucky, across the river from Cincinnati, where I grew up. If you start asking questions you will find that no region of the United States is without its sex zones, past and present.

Crime ecology helps us clarify the problems and potential solutions, but it does not offer a new utopia. World interdependence makes some problems difficult to *solve,* but still possible to *improve.* Further discussion of practical crime prevention is offered in the chapters ahead. We have to think very carefully, but it is possible to design parks and streets so most people can use them most of the time. Of course, sex parks, sex streets, and sex cities are not so easy to manage.

Exhibit 4.2   Amsterdam's Tippelzone and the Larger World

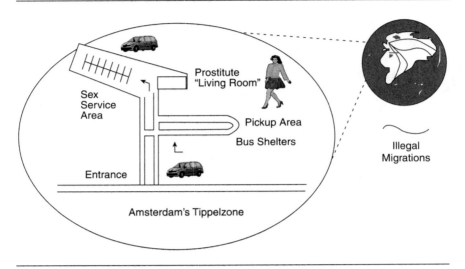

SOURCE: Adapted from P. van Soomeren, "Design Against Kerb-crawling: Tippelzones," paper presented at the International CPTED Conference, Brisbane, Australia, September 13–17, 2004.

Crime Ecology's Subfields

Ecology studies interdependencies. But in studying crime ecosystems, we do not insist that *everything* is closely related to everything else. Such infinite interdependence could only produce confusion.[29] To keep crime ecology in order, we divide it into three subfields, drawn from the larger ecological discipline:[30]

Regional crime ecology studies how features originating beyond a single city or locality affect crime. This branch of crime ecology more or less began in 1795, when Patrick Colquhoun traced London's tremendous crime wave to the mass of goods flowing through the city's docks and warehouses.[31]

Community crime ecology studies how the *larger* parts of a city or locality affect local crime. This branch of crime ecology can be traced to the 1930s, when Clifford Shaw and Henry McKay compared crime and delinquency in 75 community areas of Chicago.

Behavioral ecology pays the most attention to *specific* local environmental stimuli and activities, helping us study crime in its everyday environs. Crime nests itself directly and daily amid other activities quite near in time and space.

Even if the other branches of ecology are tremendously important for crime, behavioral ecology is most directly and immediate relevant to everyday crime. The behavioral ecology of crime has grown in the past few decades because of the following:

- More data are now available on a *very* local basis. Increasingly, it is possible to study crime by block, half-block, street corner, street face, empty lot, park, alley, address, and stairwell.
- More theoretical ideas now help us organize these data. These ideas go under headings such as situational crime prevention, routine activity theory, environmental criminology, rational choice theory, the geography of crime, and (more recently) crime science. People using these terms converse rather well with one another.

On the negative side, the triumph of the automobile has confused community analysis. In a modern society, people can easily drive across "community boundaries" for work, shopping, religion, friendship, and family contacts. Local behavior settings are more directly nested within a larger region than ever before. The ecology of Shaw and McKay no longer suffices because daily life spans a wider area than it did in 1940.

Crime Ecology Is Down-to-Earth

We must think of crime ecology in terms of what's very local and very distant, too. To avoid getting lost, we shall have to pay close attention to the tangible aspects of crime and the world upon which it draws.[32]

Not Just People

Crime ecologists keep their feet on the earth by combining crime's social aspects with its technical and physical requirements.[33] Crime's ecosystem includes buildings, tools, and techniques that offenders employ, and the artifacts they steal. Crime relies on items easy to carry away, illegal drugs that fit within a small pocket, cars parked for easy attack, places to get drunk, and locales for finding accomplices and picking fights. Crime is affected by good weather and bad. Of course, down-to-earth knowledge is not always simple. A crowbar helps a person change a tire or pry open a window. A rock is useful for landscapers and vandals. A cell phone assists friendships and drug dealing. Advertisements help jobseekers find work and prostitutes find customers. Good weather can reduce assaults at home, while enhancing those occurring away from home. Crime ecology has quite a bit to sort out.

Landforms Affect Crime

The crime ecologist notices the mountain that keeps those living on one side from attacking those on the other. Natural and artificial landforms affecting crime opportunity include the archipelago, barrier, basin, bay, beach, canal, canyon, cape, cliff, coastline, cove, creek, dam, ditch, delta, fault, fjord, harbor, highland, hill, inlet, island, isthmus, lagoon, lake, lowland, marsh, mesa, mountain, mouth of a river, mudflat, peninsula, plateau, port, reservoir, river, swamp, and valley. In many cases, landforms block access by outsiders or limit their convenience for entry or exit. In other cases access is easy. Flat and unimpeded entry and exit assists the offender. But it also gives the potential victim a chance to see who is coming. Castles and forts have long been located on hills surrounded by lowlands, combining a view of the distance with command of the heights.

Crime topography studies the localized and fine features of landscape and cityscape as these influence crime and its prevention. Topography affects crime rates in many ways.[34] A few Los Angeles suburbs are located at the edge of the mountains where they are accessible from one side only; they tend to have very low crime rates. In contrast, the flattest part of Los Angeles, with wide boulevards and easy entry and exit, generates the highest crime rates. This principle applies at a larger scale. The two most mountainous nations of Europe, Switzerland and Norway, benefited from narrow roads, huge mountains, and bad driving that long impeded offenders.[35] Haynes, Alaska, accessible only by ferryboat or a 10-hour drive, has had only one auto theft in memory. The thief ran out of gas in the mountains. But do not conclude that beauty causes low crime rates. Central Park in New York City is very pretty, but sometimes very dangerous. Clearly beauty and crime are highly compatible.

People Remake Environments

A famous quotation from Sir Winston Churchill is, "We shape our buildings; and thereafter they shape us."[36] Crime specialists have long recognized that construction affects crime opportunity in serious ways.[37] Humans affect crime by shaping landscapes, as well as the areas between buildings and the borders between buildings and gardens or streets. For example,

A *balustrade* creates a semiprivate space; its invasion might be noticed.

A *garden with transparent fences* allows offenders to be seen after entry and before departing; in contrast, solid walls hide the presence of offenders, except for the short time entering and leaving the perimeter.

A *belvedere, gazebo, open gallery, glade,* or other structure that commands a good view of the surrounding countryside often provides security if someone is there to look.

Thorn bushes or *cacti* block entry to windows, discouraging burglars while avoiding arrests.[38]

A p*arapet* or protective wall or railing decoratively sets off a walkway or embankment. It discourages trespassing, secures pedestrians on the walkway, and silences aesthetes.

To quote Tim Crowe, "Good design is safe design." Experts in crime prevention through environmental design have offered us many ideas for constructing environments that serve human needs while reducing crime risks.[39]

Artifacts, Tools, and Weapons

Some criminal acts depend on appropriate tools, such as those that assist a burglary, or equipment, such as a car for escape with the loot. Many offenses occur mainly after alcohol has reduced offender inhibitions.

The general term *facilitators* refers to diverse tools or features of daily life that assist illicit efforts. The screwdriver can facilitate auto theft, and alcohol can facilitate fights. A facilitator holds a specific position in the chain of events leading toward a criminal outcome. Removing it can break that chain, thus preventing many crimes.[40]

The concept of facilitator is best understood within a larger anthropological history. Human artifacts—including tools, weapons, and many products—provide things to steal and to steal them with, as well as means to attack others. They help people extend their criminal capabilities, as well as their defenses. Although the current book neglects facilitators and the history of artifacts, that does not say they are anything less than very important.

Social and Physical Factors, Combined

Social and physical factors often affect crime jointly. Many a crime prevention effort has fallen into disuse from poor management. Bushes are not clipped, so burglars use them as a foil. Employees leave obstructing boxes, behind which shoplifters stash their loot. Outside trash helps insiders hide what they steal from the docks. Trashcans turned over help somebody climb inside. Junk lying around is used to smash a window. Middle-aged decision makers often forget that youths have a wider repertoire than they.

The interplay of the social and physical worlds manifests itself in law, including traffic regulations. People probably stop at red lights more to protect themselves from the cross traffic than for fear of the police. But laws are not always self-enforcing; if legislators really want to reduce speeding, they would require stiffer gas pedals.

Even a law that was once self-enforcing can shift in significance with new practical conditions. The greatest growth in pornography in my lifetime as an American occurred during socially conservative presidencies. When Ronald Reagan held office, home videotape machines multiplied and the pornography business flourished. During the presidency of George W. Bush, the expanding Internet was a boon to visual sex.

The power of norms, including laws, must be studied within a larger tangible framework. Purely intangible constraints are not sufficient if committing a crime is easy.[41] Consider how people criticize the misbehavior of others and try to stop it. This process depends on the critic's ability to

1. see the violator's transgression *as it is about to start,* then

2. signal disapproval to the likely offender (e.g., with a dirty look or negative remark).[42]

This explains why some subway systems not only provide a camera for each station supervisor, but also a microphone to tell the guys to cut it out.

Specifics About the Crime Ecosystem

Crime control methods are very weak when not backed up by physical processes. For example, moral disapproval cannot alone stop crime if the physical world impairs such control. At the same time, criminal motivations are ineffective for producing crime without a physical means to put them into action. It is a mistake to think that "where there's a will, there's a way." Most offenders are not highly motivated to commit any particular crime, regardless of costs. To understand crime, we should pay close attention to physical opportunity to carry it out. That's why crime ecology pays so much attention to tangible aspects of crime and its prevention.

Illegal Drug Use and Its Many Interdependencies

Professor Howard Parker offers some remarkable insights into how young Britons obtain their illicit drugs.[43] He offers a 10-point scale, which I have adapted in Exhibit 4.3 and related to larger ecology in subsequent chapters. Some youths accommodate others who use drugs but do not use drugs themselves. Others use drugs only if offered, and never pay for them.

Exhibit 4.3   How Young Britons Obtain Their Drugs

	What Young Person Does	Rules of Engagement With Drug Market	Larger Implications
1.	Keep away from drugs	Have nothing to do with drugs. Keep away from those who do use them, if possible.	Neutralism, Chapter 11
2.	Accommodate others	Remain abstainer, but accommodate others involved with drugs.	Incidental support, Chapter 14
3.	Only if offered	Take minor drugs, only if offered and shared in safe social setting. Never seek drugs yourself.	Mutualism, Chapter 12
4.	Use but never pay	Never pay for drugs yourself. Always rely on partners or friends of drug dealer, pooled payments.	Food chains, Chapter 4; Parasitism, Chapter 13
5.	Only via friends	Buy drugs only from friend or acquaintance. Never buy hard drugs.	Mutualisms, food chains, food webs, and complex mutualisms, various chapters
6.	Only known dealer	Buy only from drug dealer you know. Act as intermediary for friends and acquaintances. Your own drug bill is covered.	
7.	Expand sometimes	Buy drugs only from real dealers in exceptional circumstances, and only ones you know.	
8.	Use established dealers	Buy drugs for personal use and friends, using realistic negotiations with established drug dealers.	Drug markets, various chapters
9.	Buy for others, too	Buy drugs to divide up and sell to cover your significant drug bill or to make a profit.	Various chapters
10.	Whomever, wherever	Buy drugs from any dealer or whomever you can, because you need them.	Foraging, Chapters 15, 16, and 17

Increasing engagement with drugs as your eye moves down the table.

SOURCE: Adapted from H. Parker, "How Young Britons Obtain Their Drugs: Drug Transactions at the Point of Consumption," Chapter 3 in M. Natarajan and M. Hough, eds., *Illegal Drug Markets: From Research to Prevention Policy* (Monsey, NY: Criminal Justice Press, 2000) (Volume 11 in *Crime Prevention Studies* series). Reprinted with permission from Criminal Justice Press.

Others only buy from a friend, and only use soft drugs. Others buy from a known dealer. Some youths are willing to buy any drug from anyone.

Of special interest is how drug purchases move between and across settings. Offenders vary among themselves, yet assist one another to violate laws. As you proceed in this book, you will develop more precise tools for spotting and classifying these links in everyday life.

Overview

Alfred North Whitehead remarked, "We think in generalities, but we live in details."[44] The job of ecology is to bridge the gap between generalities and details. It accomplishes that by generalizing about tangible things, seeking just the right words to do so.

Crime ecology pays close attention to the tangible aspects of crime, including landforms and the built environment. These social and physical features affect the capacity of offenders to move along physical paths, to overcome barriers, to employ tools, and ultimately to converge with their targets. Even organizational and electronic crimes require entry to buildings and use of equipment in the absence of interference. Certain products are much more likely to be stolen for very tangible reasons. Certain criminal acts generate many other related crimes and local problems. It is increasingly possible to link local crime to immediate circumstances, then to link these circumstances to a chain of events more distant in time and space. Crime ecology applies the general ecology paradigm, along with the experience and concepts ecologists have gathered up and boiled down. Over the next several chapters, you will see that crime ecology—despite its unique issues—is a branch of larger science.

Central Points, Chapter 4

1. Crime is nested within a complex, living system that allows it to survive—and sometimes flourish.

2. A criminal act is nested within its setting, habitat, niche, its own ecosystem, and the larger ecosystem—in that order.

3. Crime's ecosystem includes buildings, landscaping, natural landforms, and tools and techniques that offenders employ, as well as the artifacts they steal.

4. Crime sometimes fits a complex chain of simple events, lacking central organization.

5. Crime can at the same time be very local and connected to a wide-ranging system of events.

Exercises

1. Trace a local shoplifting to the other side of the earth.

2. List five ways that a burglar can sell stolen goods.

3. Compare a house of prostitution to street prostitution. Which one most often generates other crimes?

4. Look at Exhibit 4.3. Without telling anybody, figure out where *you* fit in.

Notes

1. Chapter 3, *The Origin of Species* (London: John Murray, 1859). Available from the Online Literature Library, http://www.literature.org/authors/darwin-charles/the-origin-of-species (accessed September 7, 2005) (Full title: *On the Origin of Species by Means of Natural Selection, or the Preservation of Favoured Races in the Struggle for Life*).

2. California State University, Long Beach, "CSULB Academic Assessment Plan." Available from http://www.nmmi.cc.nm.us/ir/assessstrategicplan.htm (accessed September 3, 2005).

3. "Prostitutes in Amsterdam and Holland," http://www.amsterdam-holland-travel.com (accessed November 3, 2005).

4. American poetic humorist, playwright, and lyricist (1902–1971). Quoted in *The Columbia World of Quotations* (New York: Columbia University Press, 1996).

5. "A Preface for *Our Town*," *New York Times,* February 13, 1938. See also pages 100–103 in Donald Gallup, ed., *American Characteristics and Other Essays* (New York: Harper & Row, 1979).

6. Most of these concepts can be found in standard ecological texts. An excellent option is M. Begon, J. L. Harper, and C. R. Townsend, *Ecology: Individuals, Populations, and Communities* (Boston: Blackwell Scientific, 1990). This is available in various editions. See Begon's other texts, too.

7. Before Odum, many ecologists studied local fields, forests, and marshes in isolation rather than parts of a larger system. Odum broadened the horizons of ecology by linking watersheds, weather patterns, plants, animals, and climate. He considered trees and forest, as well as their interplay with much larger systems of nature.

8. The broadest term, *the ecosystem,* is a dynamic, global, and interacting complex that takes into account all living organisms and all their activities plus all the components of their nonliving environment, and all the dynamics among these. The ecosystem incorporates plants, humans, animals, sunlight, nutrients, and more. Human criminal activities are but a small part of the ecosystem.

9. Mark Twain once expressed his displeasure with technical people who use "gigantic language [for a] microscopic topic." Quoted in *The Columbia World of Quotations* (New York: Columbia University Press, 1996). Of course, crime is a topic of substantial breadth, so terminology can help us. I hope Mr. Twain, were he alive today, would not be too harsh on me.

10. Although narrower definitions of ecology exist, Odum's broad definition best helps us study crime as it interacts with a wider environment.

11. For entry into the ecological literature, see C. Lévêque, *Ecology From Ecosystem to Biosphere* (Enfield, NH: Science Publishers, 2003). Also see J. T. Staley and A. L. Reysenbach, eds., *Biodiversity of Microbial Life: Foundation of Earth's Biosphere* (New York: Wiley, 2002).

12. I could elaborate further. Any given crime fits into the ecosystem for all of crime. Any given crime's habitat fits within the habitat for other crimes, etc. But the diagram is complicated enough, and I think you get the idea already.

13.   Crime is just one of many adaptive and contentious features of life. All living things must defend against dangers and threats to survival. What makes crime special is the presence of human law, and its sporadic intervention. But laws and other countermeasures cannot fully stop crime; instead, they enter the mix, contending within a larger, living system.

14.   See B. Cohen, *Deviant Street Networks: Prostitution in New York City* (Lexington, MA: Lexington Books, 1980).

15.   It is intriguing to consider how an entertainment district in Los Angeles can be destroyed by too much crime, then move elsewhere; but such a district in Paris lasts for decades, with gendarmes waiting in a truck to arrest people every Friday night.

16.   Other challenges include relating crime's origins to a broader natural history, adapting ecological ideas to crime ecology, and nesting the field of crime ecology within general ecology.

17.   See, e.g., E. C. Viano, J. Magallanes, and L. Bridel, *Transnational Organized Crime— Myth, Power and Profit* (Durham, NC: Carolina Academic Press, 2003).

18.   Similarly, deer, cattle, grass, bacteria, carnivorous hunters, and flu viruses are all linked in a complex food web. You will note that many of these ideas are drawn from larger ecology. But they are not analogies. The process is essentially the same.

19.   Collected from two websites. The first, Constitutional Patriots Opposing Prohibition, advocates legalizing marihuana, http://www.cpop.org (accessed September 3, 2005). The second is a high school website dealing with drug education at Cooper High in Abilene, Texas, http://coopercougars.com/curriculum/drugs/Slangtermlist.htm (accessed September 3, 2005). I cannot vouch for most of this information, and present it mainly because it illustrates proliferation.

20.   See B. Johnson, E. Dunlap, and S. Tourigny, "Crack Distribution and Abuse in New York," in M. Natarajan and M. Hough, eds., *Illegal Drug Markets: From Research to Prevention Policy* (Monsey, NY: Criminal Justice Press, 2000) (Volume 11 in *Crime Prevention Studies* series). Take note of other articles in that series, as well as the editors' introduction.

21.   See Exhibit 8.2 and parallel comments in Chapter 8 about prostitution markets.

22.   This distinguishes it from club prostitution, window prostitution, and home prostitution. Legality of prostitution depends on circumstances.

23.   This phrase is borrowed from Paul van Soomeren. See the next note.

24.   Personal communication from Paul van Soomeren, DSP Group, Amsterdam, September 3, 2005.

25.   P. van Soomeren, "Design Against Kerb-crawling: Tippelzones," paper presented at the International CPTED Conference, Brisbane, Australia, September 13–17, 2004. Available from the European Designing Out Crime Association, http://www.e-doca.net/Resources/Lectures/Design_against_kerb-crawling_tippelzones_(vice_zones).pdf (accessed September 4, 2005). A related report in Dutch is S. Flight, Y. van Heerwaarden, and E. Lugtmeijer, "Evaluatie Tippelzone Theemsweg Amsterdam 2003: Effect Extra Beheersmaatregelen," DSP Group, http://www.dsp-groep.nl/cms/frameset.htm (accessed September 3, 2005).

26.   This is probably controversial, especially if you consider the different stages of the process. I suspect that some people noticed bad features of the new Tippelzone without comparing it to the traditional form of street prostitution.

27.   See note, above.

28.   T. G. Bauer and B. McKercher, eds., *Sex and Tourism: Journeys of Romance, Love, and Lust* (New York & London: Haworth, 2003). Also see S. Thorbek and B. Pattanaik, eds., *Transnational Prostitution: Changing Patterns in a Global Context* (London: Zed Books, 2002).

29.   Of course, the impact of the larger world on crime is often indirect. For example, photosynthesis thickens the plants that conceal burglars at work. Other times, a more direct process occurs, such as the departure of residents to their workplaces giving the home burglar easy entry. In theory, crime ecology studies many crime ecosystems, their relationship to other

ecosystems, and their relationship to the overall ecosystem. In practice, this is too confusing to do all at once. That's why ecology pulls only a few strings out at a time.

30. Ecologists often divide their field into four: ecosystem ecology, population ecology, community ecology, and behavioral ecology. I am neglecting population ecology for now. Ecosystem ecology would include regional crime ecology.

31. See

   a. P. Colquhoun, *On the Police of the Metropolis* (London: C. Dilly, 1795).
   b. P. Colquhoun, *A Treatise on the Commerce and Police of the River Thames* (London: Joseph Mawman, 1800).
   (Both reprinted Montclair, NJ: Patterson Smith, 1969)

32. In the Conclusion (IV), I summarize the different levels of analysis linked in this book. If you get lost along the way, look there to clarify where I am going.

33. Thus we draw a line between "crime ecology" and "social ecology." When social or cultural factors related to crime also have a physical or technical manifestation, they can be considered by crime ecology. Anything that lacks such tangibility is normally turned over to other fields.

34. See M. Felson, "The Topography of Crime," *Crime Prevention and Community Safety: An International Journal* 4 (2002): 47–52.

35. See M. B. Clinard, *Cities With Little Crime: The Case of Switzerland* (Cambridge, UK: Cambridge University Press, 1978); M. Killias, *Les Suisses en Face au Crime* (Gruesch, Switzerland: Rueegger, 1989); and M. Eisner and M. Killias, "[Crime in] Switzerland," *European Journal of Criminology* 1 (2004): 257–293. However, their crime rates have increased lately, suggesting that topography is not the whole story when modern transport helps overcome it. Moreover, most of the population in these nations is now urban. For European crime data sources, see the European Union's area of freedom, security, and justice, http://europa.eu.int/comm/justice_home/eucpn/states_crime.html.

36. Quoted in *Simpson's Contemporary Quotations* (New York: Houghton Mifflin, 1988).

37. See Chapter 9 in M. Felson, *Crime and Everyday Life,* 3rd ed. (Thousand Oaks, CA: Sage, 2002). Also see an excellent article by T. D. Crowe and D. Zahm, "Crime Prevention Through Environmental Design," *Land Management* 7 (1994): 22–27. Available from the Center for Problem-oriented Policing, http://www.popcenter.org/Responses/Supplemental_Material/streetclosures/Crowe&Zahm_1994.pdf (accessed September 8, 2005).

38. Here are five more landscaping features and one architectural one: An eyecatcher is a structure built on a distant rise to carry one's eye outward; it can create greater supervision and hence security. A knot is a small Tudor garden of dwarf plants in interesting patterns. It can create beauty and interest without blocking visibility. A parterre is a carpet pattern of flowers, blocking off certain routes without interfering with supervision. A portico adds beauty and semiprivate space, without necessarily reducing security greatly. A topiary is a form of sculptured shrubbery that provides beauty without unnecessary obstruction. A Venetian window has a wide and tall arched opening, giving a useful view of the surrounding area combined with substantial beauty. But if the building is empty, intrusion is easy. For more on these concepts, see John Tatter, "Glossary of Terms: Landscape Gardening and Architecture" (n.d.). Available from Birmingham-Southern College, http://panther.bsc.edu/~jtatter/glossary.html (accessed September 8, 2005).

39. See the work of T. D. Crowe, *Crime Prevention Through Environmental Design* (Boston: Butterworth-Heinemann, 1991). See the many works of Paul and Patricia Brantingham, repeatedly cited in many chapters. Also, see endnote 37, above. For a review of classic works, see M. B. Robinson, "The Theoretical Development of 'CPTED': 25 Years of Responses to C. Ray Jeffery," in W. Laufer and F. Adler, eds., *Advances in Criminological Theory* (New Brunswick, NJ: Transaction, 1996).

40. See R. V. Clarke, "Situational Crime Prevention," in Michael Tonry and David P. Farrington, eds., *Building a Safer Society: Strategic Approaches to Crime Prevention* (Chicago:

University of Chicago Press, 1995) (Volume 19 in *Crime and Justice: An Annual Review of Research*, a series). Also see R. V. Clarke, "Introduction," in R. V. Clarke, *Situational Crime Prevention: Successful Case Studies*, 2nd ed. (Albany, NY: Harrow and Heston, 1997).

41. There is an underlying conversation between the current book and Travis Hirschi's classic 1969 work, *Causes of Delinquency* (Berkeley: University of California Press). This is discussed in M. Felson, "Linking Criminal Choices, Routine Activities, Informal Control, and Criminal Outcomes," in D. Cornish and R. V. Clarke, eds., *The Reasoning Criminal: Rational Choice Perspectives on Offending* (New York: Springer-Verlag, 1986).

42. In some cases, mere presence of another person suffices to discourage a potential transgressor.

43. H. Parker, "How Young Britons Obtain Their Drugs: Drug Transactions at the Point of Consumption," in M. Natarajan and M. Hough, eds., *Illegal Drug Markets: From Research to Prevention Policy* (Monsey, NY: Criminal Justice Press, 2000) (Volume 11 in *Crime Prevention Studies* series). See also H. Parker and others, *Illegal Leisure: The Normalisation of Adolescent Recreational Drug Use* (London: Aldrich, 1998).

44. Quoted in *The Viking Book of Aphorisms* (New York: Viking Press, 1966).

Always obey your parents, when they are present.

—Mark Twain[1]

The only difference between the saint and the sinner is that every saint has a past, and every sinner has a future.

—Oscar Wilde [2]

There are several good protections against temptations, but the surest is cowardice.

—Mark Twain[3]

. . . blanketed with anonymity and foul air.

—Alistair Cooke[4]

Hit 'em where they ain't.

—Wee Willie Keeler[5]

5

Crime and Supervision

Crime seeks times and spaces that are largely unsupervised. This chapter explains the process. To start out, I recommend moving next to a fire station, since firefighters are there most of the time, even leaving their large doors open in good weather—when crime rates happen to be higher. But I don't recommend living near a police station. Police are usually out on patrol or buried inside, ignoring the nearby street.[6] I have always tried to live next to retired people, whose presences during the day serve to discourage nearby burglary and theft. To study supervision further, let's begin with its fundamental elements.

The Crime Triangle

Six main elements anchor the tangible world of crime, summed up in John Eck's Crime Triangle (Exhibit 5.1).[7] The inside triangle contains the three elements leading to a crime incident, an offender, target, and place (or setting). The outside triangle has three elements paired with those of the inner triangle:[8]

1. A *handler* keeps an eye on the potential *offender*. This includes parents, teachers, or anybody else who supervises people in some personal sense.

2. A *guardian* keeps an eye on the potential *target* of crime. This includes anybody passing by, or anybody assigned to look after people or property. This usually refers to ordinary citizens, not police or private guards.

3. A *place manager* looks after a *place*, securing it from crime. This includes secretaries, apartment managers, and neighbors. Some place managers (such as a bar manager or schoolteacher) look after settings that do not persist for the whole day.

It is easy to confuse a guardian with a place manager. Sometimes the same person watches the place and the goods inside it. But when you carry your book bag around campus, you are really looking after the bag, not any particular place. In contrast, the doorman looks after the building, including the people and things going in and out, at least while they are in her domain. Perhaps a store manager performs both functions, looking after the place and the goods it contains.

The best example of a handler is a parent, but other family members, neighbors, and teachers can also be handlers. We should not assume that only those older discourage someone's misbehaviors, but often that's so. As Oscar Wilde explains, "The only thing one can do with good advice is to pass it on. It is never of any use to oneself."[9]

While handlers look after potential offenders, guardians focus on crime targets. Usually we think of guardians as looking after specific persons and property that could be targeted. A student looks after her own book bag. Two students walk home together at night, looking after one another in the process.

Exhibit 5.1   The Crime Triangle

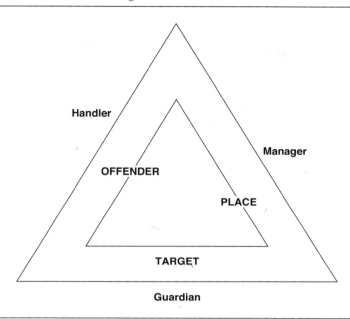

SOURCE: Modified from work by J. Eck, available in article by J. Eck and R. V. Clarke, "Classifying Common Police Problems," in M. J. Smith and D. B. Cornish, eds., *Theory for Practice in Situational Crime Prevention* (Monsey, NY: Criminal Justice Press, 2003) (Volume 16 in *Crime Prevention Studies* series). Reprinted with permission from Criminal Justice Press. Available from the Center for Problem-oriented Policing, www.popcenter.org.

That helps us understand why crime prevention depends on all three types of control agent—handlers, guardians, and place managers. Their importance varies by offense, setting, and offender age. At age 10, handlers are central, and criminal action depends on a dearth of parental supervision. At age 16, such supervision is much more difficult to carry out, so guardians of property and managers of places become more relevant for crime prevention.

Guardians have little to do with preventing cooperative crimes, such as drug trades. Both buyer and seller want the illegal sale to occur (although they might seek guardianship against related assaults). Someone old enough to buy or sell drugs has already evaded parental supervision. That leaves place managers as the key agents of control against illegal drug transactions.

In general, a crime is unlikely if a handler is supervising the likely offender, a guardian is watching the target, and a manager keeps track of the place. But persons in these roles need to understand what they have to do. Arguably, if

Exhibit 5.2   How Auto Theft Risk Varies by Location

Auto thefts per 100,000 cars, per 24 hours parked in a given location, England and Wales, 1997.

Where car is parked	Car crime risk
Public parking lot	454
Street outside home	117
Garage at home	2
Driveway, carport	40

SOURCE: Adapted from R. V. Clarke and P. Mayhew, "Preventing Crime in Parking Lots: What We Know and What We Need to Know," in M. Felson and R. Peiser, eds., *Reducing Crime Through Real Estate Development and Management* (Washington, DC: Urban Land Institute, 1998).

all citizens thought like a criminal, the crime rate would drop precipitously.[10] But when they do not know what to look for, or when their physical supervision is impaired or distracted, crime opportunities grow. For example, place managers can supervise some settings, but not always with perfection.[11]

Covering Space and Time

Many types of crime risk vary in accord with supervision of time and space. For example, car theft risk varies greatly by where you park your car. Using British Crime Survey Data (for England and Wales), Ronald Clarke and Patricia Mayhew examined car theft per 100,000 cars, per 24 hours parked in a given location.[12] Their results are presented in Exhibit 5.2.

These extreme variations tell us how important supervision can be. It's worth learning how space and time are supervised or neglected. As indicated in Exhibit 5.3, crime levels depend on whether those responsible for supervision seldom or never leave; leave and return unpredictably; leave and return on schedule; seldom show up, or never show up at all—in that order. The best supervision occurs when place managers never leave. But if they do leave, outside offenders have difficulty if their departure and return are unpredictable. On the other hand, scheduled arrivals and departures, if easily discerned, help outside offenders find the time for crime. Outside offenders have even greater freedom if supervisors show up seldom or abandon settings entirely.

Exhibit 5.3   Is Your Security Really Covered?

	Security Coverage of Place	
	A and B	*C and D*
Security Coverage of Time	*Can Watch Most or All of Property*	*Can Watch Some or Little of Property*
1. Never leave	Retired person in apartment	Manager of large apartment building
2. Leave and return unpredictably	College student apartment	Police and private security
3. Leave and return on schedule	College employees in a particular office	College employees and the larger building
4. Seldom show up	Vacation cottages	Large vacation estates
5. Never show up at all	Abandoned house	Abandoned lot or factory

Outsiders can still commit crimes if supervisors cannot see or hear what goes on for the full area. For example, one building on a factory complex might be occupied on the weekend, but that does not prevent burglars from sneaking into another building out of sight. Crime levels also depend on whether those responsible for the place occupy or secure

1. the entire property,

2. most of the property,

3. some of the property, or

4. little of the property.

The most supervision (top of second scale) is provided when those responsible for a setting can see all of it. In general settings are most secure if supervision covers more time and space.

These two scales can be combined (Exhibit 5.3, treating coverage of place as a dichotomy). At one extreme, a retired couple might leave seldom or never, watching their entire apartment. At the other extreme, an abandoned factory is never supervised, and too large to watch anyway.[13] For many college students, the main risk is being out more in the evenings and on weekends. But they have one advantage: Many college students come and go unpredictably, discouraging burglars.[14] With dormitories occupied off and on in the course of a day, students might face greater risks of theft from other students with building access, as opposed to total outsiders.

College and university employees come and go on a schedule, making it easier to break into offices or take things during the lunch hour. Within an office they have little area to cover, but the larger building is less easily supervised.

Exhibit 5.3 helps explain, too, why public police and private security cannot easily thwart crime using traditional patrol methods. They have tremendous ground to cover, and can spend very little time watching any one location. Given the high cost of labor in modern societies, it is not usually feasible to patrol very much of time and space. That's why modern societies need to use situational crime prevention, problem-oriented policing, and other more clever methods than trying to surprise offenders or to supervise every corner and cranny of daily life.

Of course, no setting is immune to crime. Even in a well-supervised place, somebody might be able to take a good look and find the right moment.[15] Quick theft of one small item takes little time, and can occur even in a supervised place if the offender picks the right moment. A thorough burglary requires a higher level of abandonment, but most burglaries take five minutes or less. To set up ongoing outdoor drug sales requires still more abandonment in time and space. To carry out a quick but noisy crime, an offender needs little time but enough space to buffer the sight and sounds. When supervision is low enough, a greater variety and number of offenses can be easily carried out.

I am not the only one who has considered the supervision of both spaces and times. Professor Jerry Ratcliffe of Temple University defines the "hotspot matrix," also based on crime risk. It considers broad categories of crime risk

A. over space:
1. *dispersed,* such as a poorly designed housing complex, with burglaries distributed across it;
2. *clustered,* such as a sports stadium, with many auto thefts in various parking areas, especially one or two; and
3. *hotpoint,* such as a particular parking lot with many auto thefts, while others are secure.

B. over time:
1. *diffused,* such as thefts in a vacation area, where people are out day and night;

2. *focused,* such as robberies distributed over the afternoon and evening, but especially during the evening rush hour; and
3. *acute,* such as assaults confined to a small period, when the bars let out.[16]

In the chapter so far, I presented the crime triangle as the foundation for studying supervision. I distinguished supervision of offenders, targets, and places. I showed how supervision varies by places, then by times, then by the combination of both. I offered my own approach to that, but gave you an alternative approach, offered by another professor. If you get lost among these ideas, simply go back to the crime triangle; you will find your way from there. Now I consider how chunks of metropolitan space are in some ways abandoned, available for crime.

Nobody Watching the Neighborhood

To understand crime, always ask whether somebody is watching. That question applies not only to single properties and parts of properties, but also to the vicinity.

In the 1930s Shaw and McKay noted that areas with substantial crime and delinquency also contained many abandoned properties. Shells of factories, closed businesses, abandoned residences, empty lots—all of these exemplify a deteriorated urban area.[17] Exhibit 5.4 lists 11 ways this can happen. Crimes occur on the spot, including brief acts of prostitution and ongoing drug houses.[18] Crimes occur near there, since abandoned places help offenders stash drugs or provide refuge, and since nobody is likely to supervise the vicinity. Abandoned properties also help youths converge, absent parental controls, forming and maintaining gangs and finding accomplices for crime and delinquency. A vicious cycle can develop, as remaining legitimate activities are driven out. In general, a failure of legitimate activities to control a local environment leaves a vacuum that crime then fills. Some metropolitan spaces and places are largely devoid of guardians, handlers, and place managers, and are thus quite suitable for setting up crime.

Outdoor Spaces and Crime Uses

Many urban scholars study land use in broad terms, such as "zoned for business," "multifamily housing," and "single-family dwellings." But to understand crime, we must look much more closely at particular slivers of space. The field of crime mapping is beginning to link crime locations to the

Exhibit 5.4   Abandoned Sites Feed Crime 11 Ways

(**Examples in italics**)

A. Crimes occur at abandoned sites, including lots or buildings.

1. Brief offenses are committed there	*Prostitutes take customers to abandoned sites*
2. Ongoing offenses committed there	*Abandoned sites used as drug houses*
3. Site itself a crime target	*Copper pipes stripped from abandoned sites*
4. Personal crimes occur there	*Squatters are easy targets for attack*

B. Crimes occur near abandoned site.

1. Place to stash contraband	*Local burglars hide the loot there*
2. Refuge for offenders	*People sell drugs outside, then take refuge*
3. Less supervision in vicinity	*Attacks occur on nearby streets*

C. An abandoned site nurtures crime beyond.

1. Escape from parental controls	*Excellent hangout for young offenders*
2. Criminal continuity	*Offenders find past accomplices for another round of offenses*
3. Gang continuity	*Gangs persistence more likely when they have a hangout*
4. New accomplices recruited	*New youths go to hangout, join in a car theft*

---

very fine features of the local outdoor environment, even taking into account different times of day.[19]

Most interesting is to classify outdoor metropolitan space by how it can be used for crime. We might distinguish outdoor spaces near buildings from those that are less convenient. Some urban spaces were once designed for entirely private uses, then abandoned. After abandonment, uninvited people could easily enter. Other urban spaces were designed for legitimate informal use, but that role was lost. For example, many urban parks became places to avoid.

It is possible to identify and classify spaces by how they are *actually* used by people. Some spaces are not used at all. Others are used for transit only. Others spaces host outdoor behavior settings, with recurrent convergences among people. After determining whether an outdoor behavior setting is present, we can examine whether it is hospitable to open crime. Look for these *good* signs:

> Mothers take children there.
>
> Females go there as often as males.
>
> Elderly people are not afraid to go there.
>
> Workers eat lunch or drink coffee there.

Look for these *bad* signs:

> People go through quickly, then get out.
>
> Drunk people hang out there.
>
> Young males dominate the setting.
>
> Syringes and beer bottles are littered there.
>
> Younger children won't play there.[20]

Additional features that make things worse:

> Proximity to offender residences and crime targets
>
> Concealment from outside notice
>
> Easy defense from unwanted intruders, such as police
>
> Shelter against the elements

Urban scholars have looked for other indicators of local crime problems, including broken glass, dog droppings, and litter on the ground.[21] Of course, some places are used differently by day and by night, or early in the day versus later. On the other hand, a public-access space will only be high in security if it welcomes people of all ages at all daylight hours, without letting the nighttime deposit too many discouraging cues. To understand crime, we must study the outdoor and in-between spaces, as well as other areas of easy public access.

Vacancy Problem Varies Greatly Among Cities

American cities vary greatly in how many of their structures are abandoned. Professors Ann Bowman and Michael Pagano have studied the issue and compiled data on abandonment. For Exhibit 5.5, I picked a dozen cities from that book to show how much they vary. You can see that several cities have almost no abandoned buildings, while old eastern cities, such as Philadelphia and Baltimore, have many abandoned buildings.

Crime opportunities are especially severe when abandonment spans contiguous or proximate properties. Philadelphia has suffered from that problem, perhaps more than any American city. The city not only keeps track of many abandoned sites,[22] but also delineates (with case studies) four types of abandonment:

a. Scattered vacant structures and lots

b. A declining neighborhood commercial strip

c. Mixed-use industrial area containing vacant land and buildings

d. Multiple contiguous commercial lots and deteriorated commercial structures[23]

Exhibit 5.5   Abandoned Structures per 1,000 Inhabitants, 12 Cities, United States, 1997–1998

City and State	Abandoned Structures per 1,000 Inhabitants
Philadelphia, Pennsylvania	36.5
Baltimore, Maryland	22.2
Kansas City, Missouri	11.3
Detroit, Michigan	9.7
Springfield, Missouri	7.4
Vallejo, California	5.0
San Antonio, Texas	2.7
Charlotte, North Carolina	2.2
San Diego, California	0.2
Chicago, Illinois	0.1
Reno, Nevada	0.1
Madison, Wisconsin	0.0

SOURCE: Appendix C in A. O'M. Bowman and M. A. Pagano, *Terra Incognita: Vacant Land and Urban Strategies* (Washington, DC: Georgetown University Press, 2004).

All four of these are important, but the last item on the list might be the most significant of all. Numerous contiguous abandoned lots and structures allow a connective crime habitat to develop (see Chapter 7), enabling the sorts of crime settings discussed in Chapter 6.

To be sure, vacant sites are not all suitable for crime. Some are inaccessible or dangerous for offenders. Some lots are too steep or full of junk or weeds to be used, even for crime. Some buildings are falling apart. Offenders, too, can be picky.

Abandonment is intricately related to the cost of urban land. When that cost is high, no property will remain abandoned for long. But when the cost of land is very low, it does not pay to replenish and rebuild, so it can easily remain idle for years, even decades. If the expanse of abandoned land is great, the process feeds on itself, removing incentives to bring the area back to life.

In recent years, American cities have enjoyed a revaluation of their land. This has created new incentives to fix up and replace homes and to reoccupy space. The consequence has been a reversal of abandonment in many parts of many cities. This is a good example of how economic processes impinge on crime in a direct fashion.

Unsupervised Places in General

If you look back at the crime triangle, offenders first to need to escape supervision, something can happen easily anywhere in a modern metropolis. Next they need to find targets that are not well tended, also relatively common in a modern society. Third, they need to find places that are unsupervised. Such places are especially concentrated in some parts of town, making it very vulnerable to crime.

That's why the *third* side of the crime triangle is so important for explaining crime differences within a city. Such areas have especially high crime levels because they lack sufficient place managers. That happens because

- most of its homes are not owner occupied, and renters are less likely to supervise places;
- most of its rental homes are occupied by short-term residents, with less stake in the future and less tendency to supervise places;[24]
- many of its residential properties are substantially or entirely abandoned, hence have no supervision at all; and
- it has many empty lots, also unsupervised.

On the other hand, a modern society leaves many middle-class residential areas empty during the daytime, when many people are at work. So we should not overstate the share of crime that occurs on the other side of the tracks.

Why Settings Are Abandoned

Many people are quick to appropriate *good things* to their own account, but quickly disown something *bad*. In recent years, famous baseball players have hit landmark home runs; occasionally a valuable ball drops into an abandoned building. Suddenly the owner realizes that the building is his.[25]

In a modern metropolis (following Oscar Newman),[26] there is much public space that everybody "owns," but perhaps nobody looks after. There is semipublic space drawing some supervision. Semiprivate space is monitored to a greater extent. Private space tends to be monitored the most. But these distinctions apply to supervision, not ownership. Some privately owned space is highly public in access. Some privately owned space is abandoned and therefore subject to criminal use. Even in occupied places, the owner can live away and look away.

Perhaps we should recast the life cycle in similar terms. A young child is under private control and kept in private or semiprivate settings. An aging child increasingly enters semipublic and public space. That gives more opportunity to become an offender, target, or accessory to crime. It also leaves an uncomfortable interlude during which youths are supported by parents, but not under their control. Teenagers spend a lot of time in these places, and we might ask ourselves whether those who have ceased managing space are assisting crime.

Familiarity Sometimes Increases Crime

From traditional sociology, we learn that "anonymity fosters crime." That idea is derived from such classical sources as Emile Durkheim (1858–1917) and Georg Simmel (1858–1918).[27] I see supervision as a very tangible process. It's easier to supervise and control familiar people. You know who they are and where to find them. If you are a threat to them, they will know it.[28]

If familiarity *tends* to reduce crime, that is not always the case. Sometimes *offenders* supervise their opponents, preventing interference with their own crimes, or even finding suitable victims among them. Familiarity strengthens whoever is in the stronger position.

a. When crime's adversaries have the upper hand, familiarity with potential offenders reduces their ability to commit crime.

b. When offenders have an upper hand, their familiarity with crime's adversaries helps them violate laws even more.

Exhibit 5.6 illustrates this point. Local area A shows a few active offenders, outnumbered by other residents. The offenders have to be careful. In a normal neighborhood, familiar faces can be identified and subject to criminal complaint and informal pressure. In these settings, the offender is in a weak position, and must commit crime through anonymity and stealth.

Local area B depicts a high ratio of active offenders to others, assisted by abandoned properties. When a local area has lost its basic controls, offenders gain the upper hand. Familiarity then helps the offender identify and punish anybody who does not comply with his wishes. Offenders figure out whom to bully and intimidate, and how to retaliate if turned in.

Exhibit 5.6   Familiarity and Crime

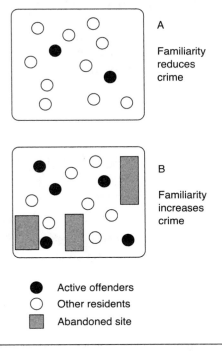

A

Familiarity
reduces
crime

B

Familiarity
increases
crime

● Active offenders
○ Other residents
▨ Abandoned site

That's why very dangerous areas are not necessarily characterized by total anonymity—quite the contrary. It's especially difficult for place managers to prevent crime under these circumstances.[29] This is quite consistent with Professor John Eck's recognition that drug dealers can dominate their vicinity, a topic for the next chapter. In addition, offenders can prevent noncrime activities from regaining ground.

Crime does best when both principles of familiarity apply in close proximity. Imagine one local area where offenders have the upper hand *next to* another area where these offenders can act anonymously. This combination helps offenders find victims who do not recognize them, then retreat to a place they can dominate.

Overview

To prevent crime, society has to supervise people, places, and things. Even when supervision covers a good part of the day, offenders might find the right time for crime. Many people interested in crime control fail to consider how difficult and expensive it may be to supervise a place completely.

Unfortunately, some places are largely abandoned. As a general rule, abandonment enhances crime by enabling anonymous intrusions. But when abandonment widens, crime can take over an area, thriving without anonymity, or even helping offenders to supervise to their own illegal advantage. That produces the thick crime habitat discussed in Chapter 7. It's interesting to see how crime can gain a larger foothold.

Central Points, Chapter 5

1. A handler supervises an offender; a guardian looks after a target; and a place manager protects a place or setting. All three forms of supervision tend to reduce crime.

2. Settings are most secure if their supervision covers more time and space.

3. Abandoned sites not only shelter crime inside and nearby, but also nurture crime in the larger area.

4. Some parts of a metropolis are largely unsupervised, thus quite suitable for crime.

Exercises

1. What tangible features of a local environment will keep teenagers out of trouble?

2. Describe a specific abandoned property that could well contribute to crime.

3. For a college campus you know, describe which places are best supervised, and which ones not.

4. Compare two public places, one safe and one unsafe. Count the number of women, children, and elderly people present at each.

Notes

1. Quoted in *The Columbia World of Quotations* (New York: Columbia University Press, 1996).

2. Line spoken by Lord Illingworth, in *A Woman of No Importance* (1893), act 3.

3. Quoted in *The Columbia World of Quotations* (New York: Columbia University Press, 1996).

4. Speaking of Los Angeles, but the point applies to many places. Quoted in *Simpson's Contemporary Quotations* (New York: Houghton Mifflin, 1988).

5. Legendary baseball quotation; Keeler (né: William Henry Keeler) (1972–1923) was inducted into the Baseball Hall of Fame in 1939. Quoted in P. Dickson, *Baseball's Greatest Quotations* (New York: Walker Books, 1991). Available from http://www.baseball-reference.com/, then search for Keeler (accessed October 21, 2005).

6. This advice is borrowed from personal conversation with Paul Brantingham, June 1995.

7. J. E. Eck and J. Wartell, "Improving the Management of Rental Properties With Drug Problems: A Randomized Experiment," in L. G. Mazerolle and J. Roehl, eds., *Civil Remedies and Crime Prevention* (Monsey, NY: Criminal Justice Press, 1998) (Volume 9 in *Crime Prevention Studies* series).

8. We could call the outer one the "control triangle."

9. Quoted in various versions, including The Free Library, available from http://wilde.thefreelibrary.com (accessed September 9, 2005).

10. Shoplifting might be an exception, since it already has widespread participation, but at low rates per person.

11. In addition, informal supervision by bystanders is easier to carry out in some places than others. It is debatable whether supervision against crime requires substantial motivation, or whether those with tangential responsibility can still discourage crime to some extent.

12. R. V. Clarke and P. Mayhew, "Preventing Crime in Parking Lots: What We Know and What We Need to Know," in M. Felson and R. Peiser, eds., *Reducing Crime Through Real Estate Development and Management* (Washington, DC: Urban Land Institute, 1998).

13. Not everybody agrees that abandoned buildings play an important role in crime. See W. Spelman, "Abandoned Buildings: Magnets for Crime?" *Journal of Criminal Justice* 21 (1993): 481–495. I am convinced his point should be taken seriously, but not that he is right. Most likely, abandoned sites create crime in the vicinity more than inside the building.

14. M. B. Robinson, "Accessible Targets, but Not Advisable Ones: The Role of Accessibility in Student Apartment Burglary," *Journal of Security Administration* 21 (1998): 28–44. Also see M. B. Robinson and C. E. Robinson, "Environmental Characteristics Associated With Residential Burglaries of Student Apartment Complexes," *Environment and Behavior* 29 (1997): 657–675.

15. I am indebted to Professor Ken Pease, who inspired this paragraph.

16. See J. H. Ratcliffe, "The Hotspot Matrix: A Framework for the Spatio-temporal Targeting of Crime Reduction," *Police Practice and Research* 5 (2004): 5–23.

17. This is a difficult topic to study, given the lack of consistent national indicators and local upgrading of information. Many statistics neglect abandoned lots without buildings.

Also, many buildings are no longer listed because they are too far gone or out of use. See T. G. Byrne, "The Area Five Abandoned Buildings Project" (n.d.), Center for Problem-oriented Policing, http://www.popcenter.org (accessed September 3, 2005).

18. Injecting in outdoor settings or abandoned buildings is a specific risk factor for AIDS. See S. R. Friedman and others, "Risk Factors for Human Immunodeficiency Virus Seroconversion Among Out-of-treatment Drug Injectors in High and Low Seroprevalence Cities," *American Journal of Epidemiology* 142 (1995): 864–874. See also D. Buchanan and others, "Neighborhood Differences in Patterns of Syringe Access, Use, and Discard Among Injection Drug Users," *Journal of Urban Health* 80 (2003): 438–454.

19. Many crime maps use addresses recorded in police data. Unfortunately, the different corners of a city park do not have different addresses. Indeed, crimes in the park or along the street are coded to the nearest telephone or building. Global positioning is increasingly part of police data and can lead to what's needed—models of crime in unbounded places, especially the urban outdoors.

20. For primers on legitimate and illegitimate use of urban space, see
   a. P. L. Brantingham and P. J. Brantingham, "Nodes, Paths and Edges: Considerations on the Complexity of Crime and the Physical Environment," *Journal of Environmental Psychology* 13 (1993): 3–28.
   b. A. Coleman, *Utopia on Trial: Vision and Reality in Planned Housing* (London: Hilary Shipman, 1985).
   c. J. Jacobs, *Death and Life of Great American Cities* (New York: Random House, 1961).
   d. O. Newman, *Defensible Space: Crime Prevention Through Urban Design* (New York: Macmillan, 1972).

21. See prior endnote.

22. Philadelphia Police Department, *Abandoned Property Report* (n.d.), http://www.ppdonline.org/rpts/rpts_abanprop_frm.php (accessed September 3, 2005). The Philadelphia Department of Planning website allows local people to add an abandoned property to the city's database. Citizens can tell the city exactly what places are used for prostitution and drug crimes. But most of this database was created after it was already too late.

23. Philadelphia City Planning Commission, *Vacant Land in Philadelphia* (1995), http://www.philaplanning.org/plans/vls.pdf (accessed September 3, 2005).

24. The first two points are dealt with at greater length in my prior book, M. Felson, *Crime and Everyday Life,* 3rd ed. (Thousand Oaks, CA: Sage, 2002).

25. See P. Finkelman, "Fugitive Baseballs and Abandoned Property: Who Owns the Home Rule Ball?" *Cardozo Law Review* 23 (2002): 1609–1633.

26. O. Newman, cited in endnote 20.

27. See
   a. E. Durkheim, *Suicide: A Study in Sociology,* trans. J. A. Spaulding and G. Simpson (New York: The Free Press, 1951). Original edition published 1897. Students who know French might note small translation errors, such as false cognates.
   b. G. Simmel, *The Sociology of Georg Simmel,* trans. K. Wolff (New York: The Free Press, 1950).
      I have turned the point around, speaking of "familiarity" rather than "anonymity." The latter term has too many extra social and psychological connotations.

28. However, strangers will stand out, a topic taken up in the chapters on foraging.

29. Some offenders might even intimidate handlers, e.g., by scaring their own family members to stop interfering with their crimes. As for guardians, they will have to fight to keep their property in a setting such as this.

In the stream of life, few things are perceived clearly because few things stay put.

—Yi-Fu Tuan[1]

There is a certain degree of temptation which will overcome any virtue.

—Samuel Johnson[2]

If we think about the obvious long enough, it dissolves.

—Mason Cooley[3]

Seek simplicity, and distrust it.

—Alfred North Whitehead[4]

I have set the village against the largest dimensions of time and place.

—Thornton Wilder[5]

6

Crime Settings

To understand any single crime incident, we must look beyond it. All offenders need to draw upon a larger society and its tangible resources. Thieves cannot survive in isolation, stealing from one another. Theft depends on goods to steal, a way to steal them, and a method to transfer them afterward. Even violent crimes depend on ordinary activities and settings, going beyond one offender or one incident. The prime building block for everyday life is the behavior setting—and so it is for crime.[6]

Behavior Settings Defined and Explained

During the 1950s, a psychologist named Roger Barker carried out field research in a small Kansas town. Guided by observations, he divided the town into hundreds of "behavior settings," considering what people did, where they did it, when, and with whom.[7] For example, he located a school history class, street corner, gas station, church cellar, and softball game— each activity in town. Barker tallied the time spent in each setting and considered how a setting persisted or changed.

Work and active leisure take place in behavior settings. It's also interesting that *informal* behaviors occur in particular settings—we might call them hangouts. Thus behavior settings help us discover a hidden structure for daily activities, even those that *seem* to be random and disorganized.

Behavior settings help make sense of the dynamics of everyday life for three reasons:

- One location can harbor *multiple* behavior settings at different hours.
- A behavior setting that closes up today recurs tomorrow. That introduces *regularity* into what seem to be unstructured activities—such as youths hanging out on an informal basis.
- *Even if the roster of participants changes entirely*, the behavior setting itself recurs.

Thus a behavior setting helps us find the structure of an informal activity, without requiring that exactly the same people be there every time. With Barker's approach, we can study the boys standing on the corner, watching all the girls go by. Going beyond Barker's work, we can explain several types of criminogenic setting. Before doing so, let's consider what such a setting does to evoke crime.

Cues Favorable to Crime

Public settings are not essential for every convergence that leads toward crime. Youths who already know each other can set up a crime from anywhere, or by telecommunication. Thefts and other crimes can occur even though a setting does not invite crime. But settings are important for crime to sustain itself and grow in abundance. The essential question to ask ourselves is what cues a setting emits—what signals it sends to potential offenders and others who influence whether a crime occurs. *Some settings emit an excess of cues favorable to crime over cues unfavorable to crime.* High crime areas have many settings emitting such cues.

Recall from the previous chapter that crime has three stages—the prelude, the incident, and the aftermath. We can divide criminogenic settings and their cues into the same three categories. Some settings make it highly suitable for offenders to converge. Others make it highly suitable for offenders to carry out criminal acts. Private settings assist offenders who already know each other. Public settings help them widen their net of illegal action, while exposing them to attacks by other offenders and by police.

In addition, conventional settings vary greatly in the intensity of crime-relevant cues. *Every* setting of daily life emits cues about itself. Some cues are irrelevant to crime. Some cues say to avoid crime here. Some settings emit cues that tell potential offenders to proceed with a crime. Certain settings are especially likely to emit cues that evoke a criminal response then and there, or soon thereafter. A good crime target, the absence of a guardian against a crime, easy access and egress—these are the hallmarks of a setting that evokes crime. Criminogenic signals are sent out by a subset of daily behavior settings. A few settings stimulate diverse types of crime, but other settings give off signals evoking specialized crimes. Thus a cash register is suitable for theft or robbery, a store's floor is best for shoplifting, and the storeroom entices employee theft. A cavernous commercial area invites all three.

Offender Convergence Settings

Crime theorists often focus on criminogenic information transmitted years before a crime occurs. Unfortunately, with a long span of time between transmission and crime, we cannot verify that A causes B. It's much more practical to specify crime cues emitted just before the crime event, or leading to a crime later on that same day. Any setting of everyday life *could* be the site of a crime; but certain types of setting are *especially* likely to emit criminogenic cues. The bad news is that some settings produce so much crime. The good news is that removing a few settings can reduce crime greatly.

Many criminogenic settings have fully legitimate purposes. Often people go to bars or other public places just to be social. As William H. Whyte explained, "What attracts people most . . . is other people."[8] Yet socializing sometimes fosters criminal behavior and can even lead to specialized settings dominated by offenders.

The Brantinghams discovered that crimes cluster around a local McDonald's restaurant, and around a local tough bar.[9] Offenders had found good hangouts. More generally, an *offender convergence setting* helps set the stage for criminal acts. Offenders can go there shortly before committing a crime, to find accomplices or to gain information leading directly to the crime. For example, an offender can learn whose home is empty and what business is easy to break into.

Youths often meet in informal but persistent settings, such as street corners, a hall in school, somebody's apartment, or other hangouts, including bars, fast-food restaurants, video parlors, parks, and street corners. In Japan, marginal youths often hang out in pachinko parlors (where legal gambling occurs). In the early 20th century, pool halls in the United States were offender hangouts, often enough that local regulation was common. For example, the state of Michigan gives local units of government the authority to regulate billiard and pool halls—the male hangouts of a century ago.[10] The most common regulations have to do with hours of operation and minimum age of entry.

As a result, underage youths need either to convert legitimate convergence settings to illicit purposes, or to find exclusive illicit settings in the interstices of daily life. (I will consider later in the chapter how abandoned sites can fill this role.) Interestingly, offender convergence settings require security and privacy. Totally public places might not be suitable if they expose offenders to interference from police, parents, or others. That's why offenders tend to prefer settings that meet their special needs in the prelude to a crime.[11]

Metropolitan areas often contain specialized offender convergence settings. In some of these settings, co-offenders find one another rather easily. An offender convergence setting provides crime structure and continuity—*despite instabilities among individuals, groups, or networks.* Even if specific participants change, the criminogenic setting can persist. In such settings, likely offenders

- have substantial time for informal, unstructured activity;
- are exposed to crime opportunities on the spot;
- can find accomplices for crime at nearby times and places; and
- are largely insulated from adults or from others who would interfere.

Neither special instigators nor innocents need to be distinguished, since anybody spending time in these settings might transmit as well as receive criminogenic information.[12] A frequent motivation for entering such settings is to socialize, with criminogenic information transmitted only in passing. Thus the boys converge in the park just to talk, but also cook up some vandalism.

But some offenders enter convergence settings, such as a tough bar, with crime in mind.[13] I suspect that many places where offenders linger combine these functions.

The main point is that some settings facilitate criminal action, whatever the type, however inadvertently, and regardless of the initial reasons that people have entered. Three definitions help us think about settings that especially foster crime:

Offender convergence settings are places that set the stage for crime by assembling accomplices and getting an illicit process started.[14]

Intoxication settings are places where offenders can drink beyond a minimal level, facilitating subsequent crimes.

Illicit-trade settings permit buyers and sellers of illicit goods and services to transact business.

I do not deny that the same place could serve all three purposes, but still we should keep these purposes separate in our minds.

Intoxication Settings

In creating crime, alcohol abuse is almost certainly the greater culprit than illicit drugs. Alcohol is more likely to generate fights and attacks and to remove inhibitions for ordinary offending.[15] It plays a tremendous role in interpersonal violence, but also helps many offenders gain the courage to break into houses, shoplift, vandalize, or carry out a robbery. Many crimes are more directly associated with alcohol, including public drunkenness and drunk driving, underage drinking, and serving alcohol to a minor. More interesting is that many crimes can be traced, within the hour, to specific settings where people drank too much.

One of the most interesting research developments has gone largely unnoticed by criminologists. The *last-drink survey* asks an arrested offender with alcohol on his breath where he had his last drink. The best last-drink surveys are found in New Zealand, where they inquire about specific bars and make the results known.[16] That way they can put pressure on bars to stop serving people already drunk, even closing some of them permanently.

Excess drinking on college campuses is a perennial problem, but it only receives attention in years when a bad incident gets media coverage. Some universities or university towns in the United States conduct last-drink surveys among students. The last-drink survey in the United States apparently began at the University of Delaware,[17] but the same idea was applied elsewhere. For example, San Diego State University gathered data on 2,160 drunk driving incidents in San Diego County, to determine where offenders had the last drink.[18] Some 41 percent had their last drink in a bar, and 35 percent in a private restaurant. The remaining 24 percent was distributed over diverse locations, with only 3 percent having the last drink inside a vehicle before arrest.

Interestingly, some drinking settings foster drunkenness—especially drinking in automobiles or bars. Indeed, spending time in intoxication settings predicts crime participation, including drunkenness, more accurately than social or demographic characteristics.[19]

Professor James Roberts carried out important dissertation research on heavy-drinking bars in Hoboken, New Jersey, and the New Jersey shores. In some settings, secondary servers—such as barmaids—sold drinks independently from trays. Thus the bartender lost control over who ingested how much alcohol. In other settings, the bar personnel were themselves drinking on the job—contrary to state law—in full view of patrons. Not all people who get drunk in these settings commit crimes afterward, yet I can't believe they all go home with a designated driver whose veins are free of alcohol.

American alcohol studies and last-drink surveys are not usually used as a tool for crime prevention, since the worst bars are not usually publicized. However, sometimes the media get hold of the data on the worst bars and put it in public view—after which the public becomes irate and something gets done.

Illicit-Trade Settings

Not all illicit trades involve the same types of settings, and not all actors have the same preferences. Professor John Eck of the University of Cincinnati offers us important insights on drug transaction places. He starts his classic article as follows:

> Pity the plight of the retail drug dealer. He has valuable drugs that he wants to sell. He also may have some cash from previous sales. He wants to make more sales. But if he approaches a possible customer he may be approaching a cop, a person working for cops, or somebody who is ready to take his drugs and cash by force. Our dealer must protect himself while contacting customers and making sales.
>
> Consider the plight of the active retail drug buyer. She has cash and maybe other valuables. If she approaches the possible seller to make a buy, she may find that she is dealing with a cop, or somebody who wants to take her money

but provide no drugs. Our customer must protect herself while contacting sellers and making purchases.[20]

Professor Eck notes that drug dealers and buyers make their trades using either social networks (based on prior acquaintance) or routine activities. If they use social networks, they are not dependent on special settings, and are more secure. But the use of networks restricts the number of customers a seller can find easily, and limits the buyer to just a few sellers.

That's why drug trades often rely on settings where routine activities bring more opportunities for drug exchanges. That makes it possible for strangers to exchange illicit drugs. The best drug sales areas are those where both buyer and seller already conduct legitimate routine activities. Drug markets using the routine activity solution have four geographic characteristics:

1. Sellers try to stay at specific places, or to move very short distances.

2. Place managers—those controlling settings for legitimate purposes—have tremendous impact on drug sales.

3. Illicit markets are located on arterial routes or near where lots of legitimate activities occur.

4. This kind of drug market can be large and serve many people.

For example, outdoor drug markets tend to spread many more illicit drugs to a wider clientele. But the best drug vendors often locate in small apartment buildings with no apartment manager and no locked gates. Sometimes drugs are openly sold through windows, from or to cars, or via "runners" who transfer the product and money, or using "touts" who draw customers into or toward the sales settings. The point is that open drug sales widen the market for the seller, and enable recruitment of new drug abusers.

Such drug-sale settings are highly vulnerable to police action, environmental design, and civil abatement—the use of civil and administrative law to influence property owners to remove illegal activities. Rana Sampson contributed an important pamphlet on preventing drug dealing from privately owned apartments. She combined what she learned at Harvard Law School, and as an undercover narcotics officer, with a review of academic literature and police experience. Officials can be surprisingly effective in reducing these drug-trade settings. Alex Harocopos and Mike Hough have shown how similar principles can help interfere with open-air drug markets.[21] It is increasingly evident that removing these settings can undermine illicit sales for the long run.

Some illicit trades can involve two settings. Illicit prostitutes might solicit on the street, then take the customer to a sex hotel, a wooded area, or an abandoned building. Both customer and prostitute are vulnerable to attack as they go from one setting to the other.

Fencing of stolen goods is an illicit trade, too. The burglar or thief goes to another setting afterward to trade booty for money—sometimes for drugs. On the way he is vulnerable to attacks by police and other offenders. There's good reason for offenders to want a suitable setting for crime's aftermath and to minimize the time and distance traveled when vulnerable.

Spaces, Places, and Settings

It's sometimes confusing that three crime-relevant words overlap:

> *Space:* a vague word referring to locations that may or may not be for human use.
>
> *Place:* a location clearly for human use that may or may not be recurrent.
>
> *Setting:* a location for recurrent use, for a particular activity, at known times.

Setting is just a short way to say behavior setting. It is the most precise of these three words. Spaces and places have an order to them that can help us understand crime.

Spaces where people don't go
Spaces people go by
Spaces people go through
Places where people stop briefly
Places where people remain for a while
   on the way to somewhere else   Degree of
Small destinations   Organization
Large destinations[22]

Going down the list, human organization increases its impact. Crime rises at the third step, where human involvement is sufficient to create crime exposure, but place managers are absent. At the end of the list, large destinations have plenty of place managers, but they might not recognize who belongs there and who does not.

The list helps us explain some surprises. Many of us think of an American downtown area as less secure than suburban shopping areas, but that's not the case. The reason is neither offenders nor victims go downtown often enough.[23]

A university or college is a large destination for students, professors, and staff. Large destinations attract not only local people but visitors from outside the area. They are often large, programmed, and compelling. A home is a small destination, even though it is very important for the person living there. A campus bar might be a destination or a temporary stop. A campus path is something you go through, without stopping—so it's a space, not a place. A hill on the side of the path is a place to go by. A cliff is where people don't go, unless they are rock climbers. Then it might become a destination.

Crime *might* occur in any of these spaces, but we can expect major differences. Personal robberies are most likely to occur where people go through or stop briefly, but not in places where more people remain. No crime is likely where people don't go, but it can be very risky to traverse spaces where nobody lingers. Destinations small and large vary by the hour and day in their activities and risks. That's why we need to specify settings by time and activity, in order to understand risk.

The first half of this chapter defined behavior settings, then considered how some settings foster crime, or even invite it. The rest of this chapter looks beyond a single crime setting, allowing the rest of the book to elaborate on how crime fits into a larger system.

Crime Fills in the Gaps

Crime takes advantage of the gaps between conventional behavior settings. A car thief works the parking lot while other people are at work. A robber finds a straggler walking home from the bus. After discovering three empty homes in a row, the burglar breaks into the one in the middle. Of course, we must go beyond Barker's work to determine this causal sequence for crime. Here is the simple logic:

- Most behavior settings are occupied by conventional activities.
- But not all convenient locations are always occupied by conventional activities.
- Offenders sometimes take these places over for their own purposes.
- Public action can sometimes thwart these takeovers.[24]

Removing criminogenic behavior settings can have an immediate impact. Society can quickly diminish crime by providing fewer places to get drunk, find co-offenders, trade stolen goods, or carry out illegal actions with impunity. Thus behavior settings help us explain crime in immediate terms. This is not a theory of socialization or acculturation. If that were the case, removal of behavior settings would only reduce crime slowly over a long period of time, as offenders age out.

Moreover, a community can interfere directly with specific settings that foster crime, without removing freedom. Liquor sales and bar regulations have done just that for many years. Building codes and the design of parks and public places can make more crime or less. We can learn specifically how settings transmit crime and what to do about it. As Samuel Johnson reminds us: "In so far as you approach temptation to a man; you do him an injury; and if he is overcome; you share his guilt."[25]

By understanding just how crime is transmitted, we can much better act to thwart it. Situational crime prevention, including crime prevention through environmental design, focuses on practical prevention by seeking to change tangible features of daily life. When this is done, crime opportunities decline, but not to zero.

Abandoned Settings, Revisited

Shaw and McKay included property abandonment as *one* feature of the delinquency area. I believe that they underestimated its importance. Abandoned properties were discussed in the previous chapter, but we can fill in some particulars. In abandoned places, the lack of supervision helps offenders

- find co-offenders,
- forage in nearby areas,
- stash stolen goods, and
- meet in order to dispose of the loot.

Of course, stashing can come before or after a crime. Drug dealers might stash contraband before the transaction, while thieves usually stash loot afterwards. After removing the money, offenders dispose of evidence. Chapter 17 considers how offenders minimize their risks by reducing "handling time." For example, well-managed stores remove hiding places where employees can stash goods stolen during the workday. But metropolitan neglect often makes it easier to carry out crime by offering it room to operate.

Behavior settings depend, of course, on spaces. These settings also vacate their spaces from time to time. A classroom is not always used for class, nor is a store always open. Metropolitan space and time are not entirely filled with legitimate behavior settings. The vacant slices of space and time are very important for understanding crime. Consider the following:

Paths from one building to another

Unused parts of buildings

Unused public or semipublic access areas

Temporarily abandoned spaces

Totally abandoned spaces—near where people go

Many offenders use the in-between areas, near where people go for legitimate purposes. Such areas help set up crimes then and there and in nearby times and places. For example, in-between areas are useful for consensual exchanges of illicit sex or contraband. Forcible rapists also can take advantage of interstitial areas; the offender tricks, lures, or forces a woman there, then attacks her.

This does not deny the diverse offenses occurring within conventional behavior settings. A shoplifter enters the store, counting on people to be occupied in buying and selling while he slips goods under his shirt. But many of these offenders rely on interstitial areas as staging grounds or places to stash the goods.

It is possible for boys to meet at a certain spot in the woods at a certain time each day to get drunk. That makes it a behavior setting—especially in mild climates or during mild seasons. But many offenses require shelter from the elements. Many offenses depend on access to a place with a roof overhead. Future chapters consider shady bars and other places that offenders use for their behavior settings. Fully or partly abandoned properties often prove useful for offender settings. They also remind us that a community can greatly reduce crime by reoccupying such properties.

Exhibit 6.1 depicts three buildings containing conventional settings, with paths between. Most people in the area are well aware of these conventional settings for work, shopping, and manufacturing. They might not notice the abandoned building or the offender setting behind it. The offenders use the obscure path for access to the more conventional area, and take advantage of the in-between area for crime. This might occur after dark, or in broad daylight but largely out of sight for the rest of the community.

An interesting implication emerges from Exhibit 6.1: Rich crime opportunities emerge when *active* work sites are next to *inactive* sites. The former provide crime targets, while the latter offer places for offenders to linger in between their raids. Active sites have known schedules, making it easy for offenders to pick the right time.

Moreover, widespread property abandonment provides offenders refuges from which they can intimidate local people, discouraging cooperation with authorities. If offenders can then act with impunity, any remaining supervision is undermined. Thus an area with half its space abandoned makes it easy to commit criminal acts in the other half. Supervision depends on

Exhibit 6.1   Crime Finds Its Spots

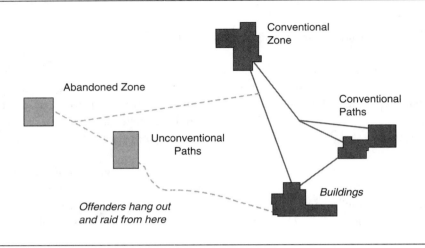

mutual protection among those supervising. If intimidation takes over, nobody wants to take the risk.

Crime Locations Can Be Dynamic

Seventy years ago, Shaw and McKay determined that crime neighborhoods were highly stable over time, in Chicago and several other American cities. Their student assistant, Solomon Kobrin, was a kindly man who was born in 1910 and died in 1996. He became a professor at the University of Southern California. My office was next to his for a few years while I was on that faculty. There Professor Leo Schuerman teamed up with Professor Kobrin to study crime profiles in Los Angeles neighborhoods from one census year to another.

Schuerman and Kobrin discovered that Los Angeles County crime neighborhoods were much more dynamic in the 1970s and 1980s than delinquency areas of the past.[26] They distinguished three distinct stages in crime neighborhoods: emerging, transitional, and enduring. In these terms, Shaw and McKay had only found delinquency areas in the enduring stage. But Schuerman and Kobrin learned that Los Angeles crime not only spread and shifted, but even receded in some places.

The dynamics of crime areas were confirmed by Robert J. Bursik, who found that—after World War II—the acceleration of suburbanization caused Chicago to undergo dramatic ecological changes.[27] The Schuerman-Kobrin discovery is consistent with urban shifts found in other metropolitan areas in recent decades.[28] Moreover, changes in crime also appeared among the street segments of Seattle over a 14-year period. Although Professor David Weisburd and collaborators found that most streets were rather stable in their crime levels, they also learned that certain street segments were responsible for most of the overall change in Seattle.[29] These dynamics present a new challenge for thinking about urban and metropolitan crime change.

Spreading Drug Markets

The spread of crime settings occurs in part because of abandonment, but also via open-air drug markets. When drugs are openly sold, buyers and sellers easily find one another. That makes it possible for total strangers or very casual acquaintances to make an illegal drug transaction. In particular, new drug users can be recruited without needing to know somebody. That helps drug-crime settings spread through metropolitan space.

Exhibit 6.2 depicts an area heavily impacted by drug-related crimes. Three types of settings are depicted: open-air drug markets (▢), homes of drug buyers (△), and locations for drug-related thefts, or other such crimes (●).[30] The area has five open-air drug markets. The diagram looks quite complex, and you cannot really tell from looking at it how this much crime arrived in this area. It's easy just to say this is "social disorganization"—but that's not a *real* answer.

Combining research with educated inferences, Professor George Rengert of Temple University has found a very good explanation of how such areas emerge: Ongoing drug-market areas generate more crime in adjacent neighborhoods, which then foster new drug markets. At first, the buyers from the initial area begin to commit crimes in the surrounding area, softening them up for worse problems later. Over time, new drug markets emerge in the vicinity of the first one. Then the drug buyers in these markets commit crimes even farther out, in order to pay for their drugs. The process can continue until a substantial portion of a city is dominated by drug crime. This has a clear policy implication: *do not concede* the worst and most overt drug market. If you make that mistake, crime will grow from there.[31]

Exhibit 6.3 shows *how* the drug situation in Exhibit 6.2 might emerge in a modern city. In Map A, the first open-air drug market takes the best location. At first, it serves a limited number of offenders, who commit a limited number of nearby crimes. Map B shows the growing number of offenders and drug-related thefts near the drug market, which itself grows—with additional sellers and additional sales per seller. (Don't count up the exact number of triangles and dots—they are just there to give you an idea.)

Exhibit 6.2   How Did This Happen?

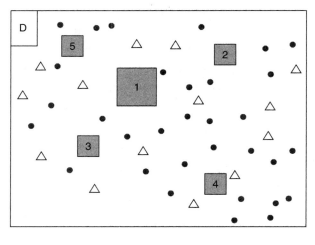

        Open-air drug market
    △   Drug buyer's home
    ●   Drug-related theft

As Map B indicates, this overt drug market helps soften up the edges around it. New drug users and new drug-related thefts occur in the surrounding area. Map C depicts the advent of a second drug market; drug users and drug crimes continue to grow in number and spread into surrounding space. If you go back to Exhibit 6.2, you will see (D) the original drug market and four other markets it helped generate, along with the proliferation of drug buyers and drug-related thefts.

By this simple and repetitive process, drug-related crime can spread widely.[32] It can lead to numerous overt drug markets, influencing a wide swath of urban space.[33] The next chapter further considers crime habitats that go beyond drug-related crime settings.

Overview

Every city, suburb, and town is a set of spaces, spanning time, with various behavior settings fitting among them. Some of these settings are legitimate and some are not. Among the illegitimate settings are those used for offender

Exhibit 6.3   How Drug Crime Spreads

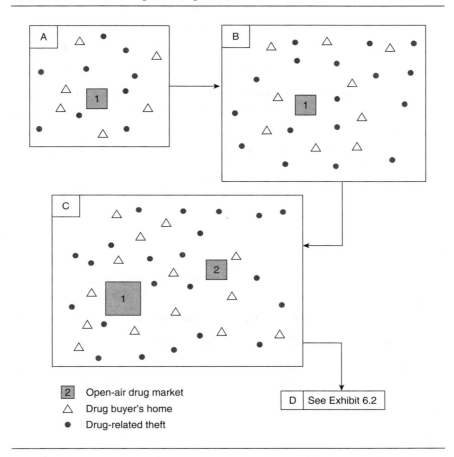

▣ 2	Open-air drug market
△	Drug buyer's home
●	Drug-related theft

D | See Exhibit 6.2

convergences and those especially dedicated to intoxication. As we proceed in this book, we will see that the line between legitimate and illegitimate settings is not always clear-cut.

Human settlements also include in-between areas, some of which are converted to criminal action. The interplay between offender settings and conventional settings and their proximity is important. Obscure paths between them can facilitate crime. Settings can send out cues that invite crime or discourage it. In general, crime is low in a setting where handlers supervise offenders, guardians monitor targets, and place managers look after the setting itself. Wherever likely offenders find suitable targets with handlers, guardians, and place managers distant, crime is likely to thrive.

Central Points, Chapter 6

1. Every city, town, or village can be divided into a multitude of recurrent "behavior settings," many of which are informal.

2. A behavior setting transcends and outlasts its specific participants.

3. Some settings induce offenders to hang out. That's where they can find accomplices and stage crimes in nearby times and places.

4. When drugs are openly sold, buyers and sellers easily find one another. That's why open-air drug markets spread crime and seed new drug markets in nearby areas.

5. Crime settings and opportunities can change a lot within the neighborhoods of a modern city.

Exercises

1. Does your state or local area regulate pool halls, bars, or other locations? Why?

2. Are there specific offender hangouts in a local area you know well?

3. What do you think makes a bar an offender hangout?

4. Do you know of an emerging crime area? Can you figure out why its crime rates might be growing?

Notes

1. Geographer, educator (1930–). Chapter 10 in *Passing Strange and Wonderful: Aesthetics, Nature, and Culture* (Washington, DC: Shearwater Books, 1993).

2. H. Bloom, ed., *James Boswell's Life of Samuel Johnson* (New York: Chelsea House, 1986).

3. U.S. aphorist (1927–). Quoted in *The Columbia World of Quotations* (New York: Columbia University Press, 1996).

4. Quoted in *The Viking Book of Aphorisms* (New York: Viking Press, 1966).

5. Writing about his play, *Our Town*, in the preface to *Three Plays: Our Town, The Skin of Our Teeth, The Matchmaker* (New York: Harper, 1998).

6. I use the terms "setting" and "behavior setting" interchangeably.

7. See

   a. R. G. Barker and H. F. Wright, *One Boy's Day* (New York: Harper & Row, 1951).

   b. R. Barker, *The Stream of Behavior* (Norwalk, CT: Appleton-Century-Crofts, 1963).

   c. R. G. Barker and P. V. Gump, eds., *Big School, Small School* (Palo Alto, CA: Stanford University Press, 1964).

d. R. G. Barker, *Ecological Psychology: Concepts and Methods for Studying the Environment of Human Behavior* (Palo Alto, CA: Stanford University Press, 1968).

e. R. G. Barker and P. Schoggen, *Qualities of Community Life: Methods of Measuring Environment and Behavior Applied to an American and an English Town* (San Francisco: Jossey-Bass, 1973).

f. For another classic perspective, see L. Ross and R. E. Nisbett, *The Person and the Situation* (New York: McGraw-Hill, 1991).

8. W. H. Whyte (1917–2003) was a leading expert in cities and how people moved about them. For his biography, publications list, and quotations, see the Project for Public Spaces, http://www.pps.org/info/placemakingtools/placemakers/wwhyte (accessed September 3, 2005). For a reading start, see A. Lafarge, ed., *The Essential William H. Whyte* (New York: Fordham University Press, 2000).

9. P. L. Brantingham and P. J. Brantingham, "Mobility, Notoriety, and Crime: A Study of Crime Patterns in Urban Nodal Points," *Journal of Environmental Systems* 11 (1982): 89–99.

10. P.A. 140, 1963.

11. We can apply Oscar Newman's distinction between public, semipublic, semiprivate, and private access. That distinction usually helps study how potential crime victims can protect themselves from outside offenders. But it also helps us understand how offenders protect themselves from police and other offenders. They seek to carve out their own private space for criminal consultation and perhaps illicit substance abuse. They also might find semiprivate space, using intimidation to thwart interferences. Later in this chapter, I discuss Professor John Eck's point that illicit drug traders combine public and private access in interesting ways.

12. Interestingly, criminogenic settings are often found within places considered conventional. For example, youths might gather a good deal of illicit information at school when teachers are out of earshot. A school contains washrooms, halls, parking lots, and unsupervised stairwells—any of these might provide a setting for criminogenic transmissions. School steps monitored at 2:30 p.m. might be poorly supervised at 3:30 p.m. and become highly suitable for finding co-offenders or otherwise sharing illicit information.

13. Following Professors Paul and Patricia Brantingham, we might call the former "convergence generators" from "convergence attractors."

14. I have developed these ideas at length in "The Process of Co-offending," in M. J. Smith and D. B. Cornish, eds., *Theory for Practice in Situational Crime Prevention* (Monsey, NY: Criminal Justice Press, 2003) (Volume 16 in *Crime Prevention Studies* series).

15. The link between alcohol and crime merits a whole book or several. I refer you to my favorite, H. L. Ross, *Confronting Drunk Driving: Social Policy for Saving Lives* (New Haven, CT: Yale University Press, 1992). Also see several pamphlets at the Center for Problem-oriented Policing, http://www.popcenter.org, especially the ones on Assaults in and Around Bars, Rave Parties, Disorderly Youth in Public Places, Underage Drinking, and Public Sexual Activity.

16. See Alcohol Healthwatch (New Zealand), "Last-Drink Survey" (n.d.). Available from Reducing Alcohol Related Harm, http://www.ahw.co.nz/ (accessed September 3, 2005). Also see Government of New Zealand, "Operative Regional Road Safety Plans, Target Area 6.1.10" (n.d.), http://www.ew.govt.nz/policyandplans/rspintro/rsp/ (accessed September 3, 2005).

17. See Building Responsibility Coalition, University of Delaware, http://www.udel.edu/brc/ (accessed September 3, 2005).

18. Also involved were the Responsibility Hospitality Coalition of San Diego and county DUI programs. Their report is available from East County Community Change Project, http://www.publicstrategies.org/east/data_index_pold_03.htm (accessed September 3, 2005). The original number of incidents was 2,349, but missing data reduced that number.

19. R. W. Snow and J. W. Landrum, "Drinking Locations and Frequency of Drunkenness Among Mississippi DUI Offenders," *American Journal of Drug and Alcohol Abuse* 12, no. 4 (1986): 389–402.

20. J. E. Eck, "A General Model of the Geography of Illicit Retail Marketplaces," in J. E. Eck and D. Weisburd, eds., *Crime Prevention Studies: Crime and Place,* vol. 4, pp. 67–93 (Monsey, NY: Criminal Justice Press).

21. R. Sampson, "Drug Dealing in Privately Owned Apartment Complexes" (2001), Center for Problem-oriented Policing, http://www.popcenter.org (accessed September 3, 2005). A. Harocopos and M. Hough, "Drug Dealing in Open-Air Markets" (2005), Center for Problem-oriented Policing, http://www.popcenter.org (accessed September 3, 2005). See also R. Sampson, "Advancing Problem-oriented Policing: Lessons From Dealing With Drug Markets," in J. Knutsson, ed., *Problem-oriented Policing: From Innovation to Mainstream* (Monsey, NY: Criminal Justice Press; and Cullompton, Devon, UK: Willan Press, 2003) (Volume 15 in *Crime Prevention Studies* series).

22. I have been influenced by J. S. Kayden, *Privately Owned Public Space: The New York City Experience* (New York: Wiley, 2000). Mr. Kayden is a lawyer, urban planner, and professor—affiliated with New York's Department of City Planning and the Harvard University Graduate School of Design. Mr. Kayden distinguishes among such spaces as

Neighborhood spaces that draw residents and employees from the local area for socializing, taking care of children, reading, and relaxing. Example: a small parklike area on the side of a building.

Destination space that attracts not only local people but visitors from outside the area. Such spaces are often large, programmed, and compelling. Example: the space in front of an international headquarters building.

Hiatus spaces that accommodate passing users briefly, but do not attract most people. Example: A few benches that people can sit on, with nothing more.

Circulation spaces that allow pedestrians easy transit. Example: an improved and convenient pedestrian path between two buildings.

Marginal spaces that lack satisfactory design, amenities, or aesthetic appeal. Examples: Barren expanses or strips, or spaces otherwise inhospitable to public use.

Mr. Kayden classified New York City's 503 privately owned public spaces as follows:

Neighborhood spaces	66
Destination spaces	15
Hiatus spaces	104
Circulation spaces	91
Marginal spaces	207

23. See R. B. Peiser and J. Xiong, "Crime and Town Centers: Are Downtowns More Dangerous Than Suburban Shopping Nodes?" *Journal of Real Estate Research* 25 (2003): 577–606.

24. This is not to deny that some of the same offenders will linger on after the community has removed crime settings. But they will have trouble maintaining their illicit efficiency.

25. H. Bloom, ed., *James Boswell's Life of Samuel Johnson* (New York: Chelsea House, 1986).

26. L. A. Schuerman and S. Kobrin, "Community Careers in Crime," in A. Reiss and M. Tonry, eds., *Communities and Crime* (Chicago: University of Chicago Press, 1986) (Volume 8 in *Crime and Justice: An Annual Review of Research,* a series).

27. R. J. Bursik, Jr., "Ecological Stability and the Dynamics of Delinquency," in A. Reiss and M. Tonry, eds., *Communities and Crime* (Chicago: University of Chicago Press, 1986) (Volume 8 in *Crime and Justice: An Annual Review of Research,* a series).

28. For entry into this topic, see M. Kennedy and P. Leonard, "Dealing With Neighborhood Change: A Primer on Gentrification and Policy Choices," in *Cities and Suburbs*

(Washington, DC: Brookings Institution, 2005). Many papers deal with gentrification, and some relate such changes to crime. See S. C. McDonald, "Does Gentrification Affect Crime Rates?" in A. Reiss and M. Tonry, eds., *Communities and Crime* (Chicago: University of Chicago Press, 1986) (Volume 8 in *Crime and Justice: An Annual Review of Research,* a series).

29. D. Weisburd, C. Lum, and S.-M. Yang, "Criminal Careers of Places: A Longitudinal Study," Report to the National Institute of Justice (December 2004). Available from the National Criminal Justice Reference Service, http://www.ncjrs.org/pdffiles1/nij/grants/207824 .pdf (accessed October 21, 2005).

30. In this simplified portrayal, I understate the number of drug buyers and drug-related crimes, and am not specific about the time period. I do not go into the diverse crimes by which offenders might get money for drugs, e.g., robbery. But I still think my portrayal can help us think about reality. Note the map of drug markets in Harocopos and Hough, cited above. Imagine that map including smaller sales points, buyer residences, and offenses committed to help buy drugs.

31. Another way to put it: Don't use a *triage.* Go after the worst area first. It's worst for a reason, and it will spread crime elsewhere.

32. G. Rengert, *The Geography of Illegal Drugs* (Boulder, CO: Westview Press, 1996). Also see G. Rengert and others, "A Geographic Analysis of Illegal Drug Markets," in M. Natarajan and M. Hough, eds., *Illegal Drug Markets: From Research to Prevention Policy* (Monsey, NY: Criminal Justice Press, 2000) (Volume 11 in *Crime Prevention Studies* series).

33. Many readers will recognize that this could be a *fractal* process. Fractals are part theory, part description, part math, part programming, part art, and part replication of nature. A fractal shows us that (1) what looks complex can result from a simple process, repeated; (2) what looks erratic can be systematic, indeed, deterministic; and (3) that jagged processes can be understood.

I cannot now say whether drug-related crime spreads in a fractal fashion, literally speaking. Indeed, the next chapter explains other aspects of crime habitat that would complicate the process. But this conceptualization can help us think. See

    a. M. F. Barnsley, *Fractals Everywhere* (Cambridge, MA, and London: Academic Press, 1993).

    b. M. Batty and P. Longley, *Fractal Cities* (San Diego, CA, and London: Academic Press, 1994).

    c. B. B. Mandelbrot, *The Fractal Geometry of Nature,* updated and augmented ed. (New York: W. H. Freeman, 1983).

    d. D. Peak and M. Frame, *Chaos Under Control: The Art and Science of Complexity* (New York: W. H. Freeman, 1994).

[In] the biodiversity library, vast quantities of books are hidden, others are in storage waiting to be catalogued, while only a small proportion have been read.

—Andrew Beattie[1]

The natural habitat of the tongue is the left cheek.

—Red Smith[2]

Considering the havoc mankind has wreaked upon nature with deforesting, stripmining, and the destruction of animal habitat, it only seems fair that nature get some of its own back and teach us that there are forces greater than our own.

—James Wolcott[3]

He that will not apply new remedies must expect new evils; for time is the greatest innovator.

—Francis Bacon[4]

7

Crime Habitats

Crime naturally lives, grows, and reproduces in certain broad areas. These areas can be mapped, for a city, metropolis, or even a small nation. Such maps are not *precise* crime locations, but still help us understand its most hospitable terrain.[5] A crime habitat contains, at a minimum, several crime settings.

Ecologists use the term "habitat" to describe where an organism or activity usually finds its home. A "crime habitat"[6] provides crime's basic needs—a favorable landscape and suitable locale. But, in specifying a crime's habitat, we do not consider all its requirements, or the fine features of a very local setting.

Crime does not spread smoothly over its natural habitat, like mayonnaise on a sandwich. Nor does crime exist only in its best location. Still it is useful to figure out crime's habitats. To do so, we must not mix cause with effect. Crime does not *define* its own habitat.[7] A high local crime rate might tip us off, but only that. A burglary might occur outside its natural habitat, or burglars might not have discovered or fully exploited a natural burglary habitat. The sociophysical features that invite burglary define its habitat, not the crime itself.

Specific Crime Habitats

A *specific* crime habitat invites a particular type of crime over a certain area. For example, a residential burglary habitat is conducive mainly to *that* crime. Here are some specific crime habitats in local areas:

- The University of Illinois at Urbana-Champaign provides an excellent habitat for bicycle theft. This pancake of a campus is dotted with bicycle racks, often hidden by hedges. These are linked by a system of bicycle lanes, so it is easy to steal a bike and be on your way.
- Hoboken, New Jersey, packs in many heavy-drinking bars, generating drunken conflicts—some involving college students.
- Many shopping malls are designed with wide exits from each store, providing an excellent habitat for shoplifting.
- Newark, New Jersey, has a huge airport, serving New York City. Its vast parking lots provide excellent habitat for auto theft.

Some specific crime habitats cover a wider region, or even a small nation:

- Alleys are found behind Chicago-area houses, creating a habitat for residential burglaries.
- The Netherlands provides prime habitat for bicycle theft. This small,[8] flat, nation is packed with bicycles and bicyclists.
- Densely populated Taiwan offers a natural habitat for theft of motorbikes. They are parked throughout Taiwanese cities, and seldom locked very carefully.
- Los Angeles provides an excellent habitat for graffiti. Its boulevards and freeways are lined with stucco walls, easy to paint. The worst artist can reach a vast audience.

- People park on the street in Stockholm, Sweden, risking theft of cars and car parts. But Stockholm is not a good habitat for residential burglary. Its apartment buildings are packed together, with few back and rear entries.

A specific crime habitat fosters one type of crime and can cover a whole region. A generic crime habitat covers less space but fosters a more problems where it is found.

Generic Crime Habitats

A generic crime habitat fosters many different crime types at a high rate, in a noticeable area. Such an area might be as small as a single high-crime neighborhood or as large as a good chunk of a big city.[9] Consider the tough part of town, with its greater number and diversity of crime settings. That's where offenders can act more blatantly. They might even control buildings and territory for their own illicit purposes. A generic crime habitat can often be recognized by an abundance of settings where offenders converge, intoxication is permitted, and illegal drugs are bought and sold openly. Even worse, a generic crime habitat can become self-sustaining. This chapter seeks to understand how that happens.

Three Types of Generic Crime Habitat

Generic crime habitat takes three forms:

    a. Discrete edges
    b. Connected edges
    c. Thick crime habitat[10]

The Brantinghams helped isolate the most basic form of generic crime habitat—the edge located between two communities.[11] Discrete edges can occur in normal cities under normal conditions but still invite a good deal of crime.

Discrete Edges Between Two Communities

Exhibit 7.1a depicts two neighborhoods with an edge between. Edges have special security problems, since offenders from both sides can go there

Exhibit 7.1   Three Types of Generic Crime Habitat

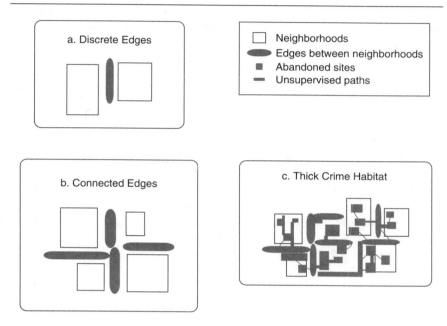

easily to commit crimes, then leave with relative impunity. Yet edges also draw victims, since many food stores, parks, parking spots, and other amenities are located between neighborhoods. For example, it's often easier to steal from cars parked *between* two neighborhoods.

Connected Edges

When edges are interconnected by a motorized transport system, crime risks are enhanced. Exhibit 7.1b displays four neighborhoods, with interconnected edges between them. That allows offenders to roam more freely among the edges. Both mass transit and automobiles can assist this process. Youths with access to automobiles can easily become offenders and victims—a problem not present in the Shaw and McKay era, when crime problems were more localized. Modern connectivity helps offenders and victims to range farther, allows illegal markets to serve a wider area, and for crime to spread in new ways. Even the word "local" takes on a larger meaning.

This chapter has already discussed specific crime habitats and introduced generic crime habitats. It has described three categories of generic habitats, and introduced edges and their connections. The rest of the chapter elaborates on thick crime habitat, explaining how crime can become dominant and even luxuriant.

Thick Crime Habitat

Abandoned sites add dramatically to crime's "edge factor." A multitude of abandoned properties creates an expanse of unsupervised space. That makes it possible for offenders to move freely, even on foot, and to return to home ground with the loot. The interconnection of abandoned sites and nearby edges produces a *thick crime habitat*. Exhibit 7.1c depicts such a habitat, and gives you an idea why its offenders can gain a strong local foothold.

Physical Nature of Thick Crime Habitat

Compared to more narrow crime habitats, thick crime habitat helps offenders

- move more freely,
- commit a greater variety of crimes, and
- recover from setbacks.

Thus thick crime habitat makes crime a more pernicious problem. These three physical processes occur in larger nature, too.

Natural Example 1: Human Lungs: If your lungs were spread out flat, the surface could cover an entire tennis court. Lungs have a tremendous number of interior folds. These folds help oxygen transfer much more easily into the blood.[12] For exactly the same reason, interior folds within a neighborhood allow offenders many more spots to enter and exit as they commit crimes. As you can see in Exhibit 7.1c, the interior folds of thick crime habitat create suitable physical conditions for numerous unsupervised movements.

Natural Example 2: Forest Fragmentation: Some species can only live in thick forests. Ecologists have warned that forest fragmentation destroys their habitat. That reduces biodiversity.[13] Even species that can live in an isolated forest have a problem: When a local colony dies out, it cannot easily be repopulated if forests are fragmented. However, thick and connected forests increase biodiversity and help species bounce back after they have been disrupted.

Thick crime habitat also makes possible greater diversity—that is, more forms of crime. To be sure, family violence and small-scale drug sales among acquaintances might occur anywhere. But blatant and repeated street violence and overt drug dealing normally require thick crime habitat. Even though a narrow crime habitat can still be dangerous, a thick crime habitat is worse. It not only produces more diverse crimes but also helps offenders recover from setbacks.

Crime Recovery in Thick Crime Habitat

Recovery is "crime's ability to bounce back, after interferences." Obvious interferences include situational crime prevention, police crackdowns, and problem-oriented policing. In thick crime habitat, the means of recovery are present, so interferences against crime might not succeed. It is important for such efforts to be well conceived. To quote Professor Michael S. Scott of the University of Wisconsin, a former police chief,

> Poorly planned, ill-conceived, and improperly managed crackdowns, intended merely as a show of police force and resolve, can create more problems than they solve. But carefully planned crackdowns, well supported by prior problem analysis, implemented with other responses to ensure longer-term gains, and conducted in a way that maintains public support and safeguards civil rights, can be an important and effective part of police strategies regarding a range of crime and disorder problems.[14]

That same principle could be applied to situational prevention or other efforts, especially in very-high-crime areas, where illegal action can be resilient.

In more normal circumstances, crime annoys but does not destroy legitimate business and community life. The latter has the upper hand, so that arrest of even a few local people might lead crime to decline noticeably. But in the case of thick crime habitat, crime is more dominant, having destroyed much of the local noncrime habitat. That's why crime gains and keeps its foothold in some places, and is not as easily jarred loose. There crime is resilient, excepting those cases where communities use situational prevention, problem-oriented policing, and environmental design, with a clear head for interfering with crime's recovery.

Policy Implications

Ecological experience points toward a three-part strategy to contain crime's growth:

- Make sure that a narrow crime habitat does not thicken.
- Make sure that two narrow crime habitats do not grow together.
- Try to fragment thick crime habitats that already exist.

This strategy can reduce crime's biodiversity and interfere with crime's recovery, while making it harder for offenders to move about for illicit purposes.

Thick Crime Habitat and Displacement

When offenders are denied a given crime environment, they sometimes displace their illicit efforts to some other time, place, or activity. The displacement hypothesis is very important. It implies that crime prevention efforts will fail overall, simply pushing crime from here to there. Empirical research increasingly finds that displacement does not happen as often as was once believed, that crime prevented here does not usually or automatically reestablish itself.[15] As a consequence, experts are more confident than ever that crime prevention is a feasible activity.

Fragmentation informs the issue of displacement. In highly fragmented crime habitats, crime prevention efforts are very unlikely to produce displacement. When crime is uprooted, it cannot easily recolonize if its habitat is fragmented. On the other hand, a high degree of connectivity makes it easier for offenders to shift gears, finding new targets, methods, times, or places. Even then, offenders might have to settle for inferior opportunities if the best ones have been denied.

Thick Crime Habitat and Community Pathology

Crime can occur as a normal feature of community life, without unbounded harm. Many normal youths get into some trouble during teenage years, then grow out of it. Even among adults, crime can exist within bounds.

A "healthy" community is not a utopia. It is home to flawed human beings, many of whom break laws. Such a community can adjust to change, dealing with its problems. Its youths stay out of trouble until 12 or 13 years of age, and flirt with danger for a few years. Some of them die in traffic accidents, some are badly injured, but most survive. Some go on to worse crimes, but most do not. Transgressions are largely handled—as they should be—away from the public eye. Burglaries and car thefts are undeniable, but the community quickly recovers precisely because it drives crime underground. Violence is episodic and scattered, not coalescing or escalating very far most of the time. Drug abuse occurs in private places, and sales are among acquaintances and friends. Sexual misconduct lurks in private places. Drunkenness is confined within families, leaving the rest of the community alone. Nonpathological crime occurs mostly in the edge areas between communities, in entertainment districts, or in particular moments when local people find an opportunity.

A healthy community is defined not by human perfection but rather by an ability to *manage* human imperfections. Such management prevents crime from preempting daily life. Thus crime lives in harmony with noncriminal activities. While crime harms particular individuals, families, or businesses, the community as a whole suffers rather little.

Thick Habitat and the Virulent Growth of Crime

Thick crime habitat makes it possible for crime to become virulent. In its virulent form, criminal activity *attaches, invades, colonizes,* and *poisons* conventional activities and the physical structures on which they rely.[16] Specifically,

- Crime *attaches* to particular settings, becoming overt and ongoing. Offenders can then act largely *with impunity.*
- Illegal activity *colonizes* nearby areas.
- Illegal activity *poisons* remaining legal activities, causing jobs and commerce to move away.[17]

Crime virulence has far-reaching impact—enabling crime habitats to widen greatly and nurture additional crime.

Overview

Crime's harms can grow in nasty progression, from

1. scattered crimes in an otherwise normal area, to

2. a specific crime habitat, to

3. an edge area providing generic crime habitat, to

4. thick crime habitat, and finally to

5. the virulent growth of crime.

In the first two steps, crime is a problem but not a general pathology. In the third step, most local people can still live in safety, except when they enter the danger zone. But the fourth step becomes truly pathological for local people, who cannot really escape ongoing crime risk. The fifth step is the worst, since it spreads a local problem beyond the local area, even wiping out a whole side of the city.

Crime truly becomes pathological by taking over terrain and by driving out an appreciable number of legitimate activities. The harmony between crime and its larger world evaporates. As this happens, teenagers coalesce and take over territory from parental control, turning it to widespread illicit purposes. The nastier teenagers can force the others to conform to illegal acts. Crime experimentation once began at ages 12 or 13, but now starts at age 10 or younger. Crime participation once faded at ages 16 or 17, but now persists into the 20s and beyond. The pathology of crime is most pronounced when adult offenders have seized a large swath of metropolitan space for their own illicit uses. In short, crime grows from a local annoyance into a pathological form of community life.

Central Points, Chapter 7

1. A specific crime habitat encourages one type of crime. A generic crime habitat fosters many types of crime.

2. Generic crime habitat develops along the edges between two neighborhoods.

3. Numerous abandoned sites produce a thick crime habitat, encouraging crime to diversify and spread.

4. Crime is pathological when it begins to drive out legitimate activities.

5. A healthy community is not crime-free, but it manages and contains crime, adjusting to it and preventing it from gaining the upper hand.

Exercises

1. Pick one crime, then describe its specific crime habitat.

2. Describe a place where crime is substantial, but out of sight.

3. Describe one abandoned site that contributes to crime.

4. Compare two cities (or towns) that foster different types of crime.

Notes

1. *Biodiversity: Australia's Living Wealth* (Sydney: Reed Books, 1995).

2. Quoted in *Simpson's Contemporary Quotations* (New York: Houghton Mifflin, 1988).

3. Birth date unknown, still living and writing, college dropout, author, contributing editor to *Vanity Fair*, contributor to the *Village Voice, Harper's*, and *New York* magazines. From his webpage, http://jameswolcott.com/archives/2004/09/an_ignoble_conf.php (accessed October 23, 2005).

4. Renaissance writer (1561–1626). "On Innovation," II, XXIV, in *Essays, Civil and Moral*. A volume included in the Harvard Classics (Cambridge, MA: Harvard University Press, 1909–1914).

5. Of course, some crimes easily occur wherever there are people, so there's not much point in mapping them. Other crimes are located in cyberspace, requiring a different type of map.

6. The word "habitat" is singular when we mean the type of habitat, but we can also refer to specific habitats as plural.

7. "Social disorganization" often mixes together the physical features of the local area with its crime rates. I argue against doing so. But not all scholars agree with me. For an exploration of this issue, see K. J. Rice and W. R. Smith, "Socioecological Models of Automotive Theft: Integrating Routine Activity and Social Disorganization Approaches." *Journal of Research in Crime and Delinquency* 39 (2002): 304–336. That paper could be interpreted in terms of specific or general crime habitat, but probably is closer to the latter.

8. Of course, the Netherlands gets larger when you have to bicycle its length. Relativity is part of all our judgments about crime and people involved in it.

9. It is sloppy to attribute diverse crimes to whole regions or nations. Some people claim that the American South has a "subculture of violence," ignoring the vast variations within regions. Others attribute violence to America, ignoring the fact that most violent crime rates are just as high in Europe. We should always be careful when discussing generic crime habitats. I am even uncomfortable referring to a whole side of town as dangerous, without considering its very local variations.

10. In the *Art of War* (~600–500 BC), Sun Tzu distinguishes nine types of terrain, including light terrain permitting shallow penetration of enemy territory, traversable terrain that both sides go through without much contention, and contentious terrain—intermediate areas that can be occupied by either side. Perhaps we need to distinguish edge habitats that facilitate property crime, those where gangs fight with one another, and those where police and offenders encounter one another. See Sun Tzu, *Art of War*, trans. R. D. Sawyer (Boulder, CO: Westview Press, 1994).

11. The Brantinghams also considered the edges of an offender's awareness space, a topic taken up later in this book. Edges can also be found among three or more communities, another topic taken up later in this book. References to the Brantinghams' works are scattered throughout this book.

12. T. Petty, "Pulmonary Health; The Normal Lung; The Magnificent Lungs" (n.d.), National Emphysema Foundation, http://emphysemafoundation.org/PulmonaryHealth.aspx.

13. This issue goes back to a classic work, R. H. MacArthur and E. O. Wilson, *The Theory of Island Biogeography* (Princeton, NJ: Princeton University Press, 1967). That work proposed the equilibrium theory of island biogeography, relating number of species to island

size and isolation. But fragmented habitats are not always the same as islands, surrounded by ocean hostile to land animals.

14. M. S. Scott, "The Benefits and Consequences of Police Crackdowns," Center for Problem-oriented Policing, http://www.popcenter.org (accessed September 3, 2005).

15. On the displacement issue, see

    a. R. Barr and K. Pease, "Crime Placement, Displacement, and Deflection," in M. Tonry and N. Morris, eds., *Crime and Justice: An Annual Review of Research* (Chicago: University of Chicago Press, 1990) (Volume 12 in *Crime and Justice: An Annual Review of Research,* a series).

    b. R. V. Clarke, ed., *Situational Crime Prevention: Successful Case Studies,* 2nd ed. (Albany, NY: Harrow and Heston, 1997).

    c. R. V. Clarke, "Hot Products," Police Research Series Paper 112, British Home Office, http://www.homeoffice.gov.uk/rds/prgpdfs/fprs112.pdf (accessed September 3, 2005).

    d. J. E. Eck, "The Threat of Crime Displacement," in *Criminal Justice Abstract* 25 (1993): 527–546.

    e. R. B. P. Hesseling, "Displacement: A Review of the Empirical Literature," in *Crime Prevention Studies* (Monsey, NY: Criminal Justice Press, 1994) (Volume 3 in *Crime Prevention Studies* series).

    f. S. Town, "Practical Tools: Crime Displacement Paper" (n.d.), British Home Office, Crime Reduction Centre, http://www.crimereduction.co.uk/skills10.htm#disp (accessed September 3, 2005).

16. Scientists will recognize four features of virulence: adhesion, invasion, colonization, and toxicity. Although crime is not a chemical process, I do not intend this as a metaphor. Criminal behavior carries out the same or similar processes.

17. The reverse impact of crime on economic conditions is an important topic. See R. M. McGahey, "Economic Conditions, Neighborhood Organization, and Urban Crime," in A. Reiss and M. Tonry, eds., *Communities and Crime* (Chicago: University of Chicago Press, 1987) (Volume 8 in *Crime and Justice: An Annual Review of Research,* a series).

The true, strong and sound mind is the mind that can embrace equally great things and small.

—Samuel Johnson[1]

Living next to you [the United States] is . . . like sleeping with an elephant. No matter how friendly and even-tempered is the beast, if I can call it that, one is affected by every twitch and grunt.

—Pierre Trudeau[2]

Nature uses only the longest threads to weave her patterns, so each small piece of her fabric reveals the organization of the entire tapestry.

—Richard P. Feynman[3]

Great fleas have little fleas upon their backs to bite 'em And little fleas have lesser fleas, and so ad infinitum.

—Augustus de Morgan[4]

8

Crime Niches

Crime's niche includes more than its habitat. A crime niche consists of *all aspects* of a crime's existence that enable it to survive and grow. Thus a niche goes beyond particular places or territories. Auto theft has an international niche, since cars are manufactured for a world market and sent here, there, and everywhere. A *crime niche* includes features that meet the crime's total requirements—its timing,[5] physical conditions, geomorphology, longitude, latitude, weather, climate, built environment, manufacturing, history, how it gets to targets and evades guardians, and how it uses its habitat. Thus the niche for bicycle theft includes the manufacture and styling of bikes and the tools to steal them, the local market for stolen bikes, the methods that a thief uses to remove the bicycle, the customers for the stolen bicycle or bicycle parts, and more. The concept of niche gives your mind a hunting license—encouraging you to figure out many aspects of life that contribute to each type of crime. But that does not mean you should include what's far-fetched. Instead, you should think of the particular resources that a crime usually needs, and whether those resources are provided or not.

The niche concept helps us build a universal crime science. Nations with different laws, crime rates, and crime mixes can still have some similar crime niches. For example, "the nighttime theft of parts from older cars parked near homes" transcends national boundaries and local legal systems. Crime's official categories often fail to capture the details of its requirements. The next chapter considers how niches overlap, leading to competition. For now, the niche concept helps us reach beyond legal names for criminal acts.

Crimes With the Same Name but Different Niches

No two crimes can persist with *exactly* the same niche, but many crimes can have *similar* niches.[6] Some crimes *seem* to be similar, but their different niches tell us otherwise—as you shall see. Law books often use the same name for crimes that have very different niche requirements. Different timing, locations, makes, models, and modus operandi—these are telltale signs of different niches.

Here are six types of auto theft, with comments about their different niche requirements:

Specific Auto-Theft Type	Varying Niche Requirements
Joyriding	Audience during the trip
Parts stripping	Tools and a parts receiver
Personal transportation	Place to hide car from notice
Insurance fraud	Paperwork, fake witnesses
Vehicle export	Transport method, customers
Stealing car for another crime	Avoiding notice at beginning and end

Cars five years old are better for stripping parts, since many need repairs. But joy riders prefer flashier models, and those stealing for export pick luxury cars. For personal transport, a thief might pick the easiest car to break into where he needs one, while a car used for another crime is usually speedy and easy to maneuver.

I have only begun to capture the niche variations in auto theft. Parts stripping alone has many variations. Some parts strippers take only the mirrors, for example; others the modern car's operating computer, while others take anything they can get. Some thieves or their customers use stolen parts to restore a crashed vehicle to legal status. Others use stolen parts in the normal stream of car repairs. Each type of car theft has a somewhat different niche, that is, different requirements.

Burglars on foot have different niches from those who use vehicles. Drug markets differentiate too. Some cater to customers in cars and others to pedestrians; some to younger users, others to those older. Johannes Knutsson of the National Police Academy, Norway, reports that closing an outdoor market in Stockholm lessened the illicit drug usage at younger ages; in contrast, older drug offenders were able to find dealers using personal contacts. In general, we should not lump together crimes solely because they have the same legal name. Crimes with the *same* legal name can have very *different* niches. Crimes with *different* names can have very *similar* niches. Consider purse snatching and street robbery, which are treated differently in law and crime statistics, but are very close to the same reality and have about the same niche. As we think of crimes in terms of their niches, a lot of issues start to clarify. But clarity requires that we be more specific about what each crime requires.

Hot Products and a Larger System

A good way to understand crime niches is to consider what gets stolen, when, where, how, and why. Professor Ronald V. Clarke's important work, *Hot Products,* tells you a good deal.[7] The acronym CRAVED sums it up. Most stolen products are[8]

C oncealable

R emovable

A vailable

V aluable

E njoyable

D isposable

These six features of the crime target are part of a larger sociophysical system, as Exhibit 8.1 indicates. Jewelry is easily concealed by a thief because it is usually small, yet still has substantial market value. Mass-produced items are similar or identical in color or style, hence it is not easy to tell what's stolen. Condoms are stolen with pleasure in mind. Electronic goods are often quite easy to fence. Cash is easiest of all, meeting all six criteria, and proving most useful in the larger system. However, that was not the case all through history. In the past, money consisted of heavy metals or stones, and promissory notes were made out only to particular persons. Even during my lifetime, the Soviet system had special rubles that were given only to Communist Party officials and were not worth stealing. Their bulky and malfunctioning consumer goods also tended to discourage theft.[9]

These six components—concealable, removable, available, valuable, enjoyable, and disposable—are normally applied to property for theft. But a small shift in grammar helps us apply the concepts to violent crime, too. A violent offender often must conceal his approach and withdrawal. He selects available targets of violence—one problem for victims of family violence is their easy availability. He values some targets for attack, by his own criteria. He might enjoy a violent attack on someone else. He wants to dispose of evidence of the attack. Not all property or violent offenses involve all six dimensions. But any community that makes all six easy for offenders can expect a high crime rate. For such a community provides offenses the niches they need.

Crime's Fundamental Niche

The term "niche" can be applied in two different ways:

The *fundamental niche* refers to resources that offenders *could* use for a given crime under ideal conditions.[10]

The *realized niche* consists only of those resources offenders have *actually* used for the crime in question.

Crime's fundamental niche assumes no interference by the criminal justice system or contravention by citizens or circumstances. Drug abuse would have a much greater niche if abusers never got arrested, sick, impoverished, or thwarted by police or citizens. A crime's realized niche is always smaller than its fundamental niche.

Even insects, the most successful organisms on earth, cannot have it all. They have predators, and cannot find every morsel. The distinction between

Exhibit 8.1   Products Thieves Crave, With Implications

Acronym	Six Factors in Theft	Examples*	Physical Implications	System Implications
C	Concealable	Jewelry	Easy to put under shirt	Market value is high despite small size
R	Removable	Burglars take more cigarettes than shoplifters	Offender can only carry so much	Cars and a little more time required to carry off bulkier loot
A	Available	Mass-produced goods	Cannot easily tell what is stolen and what is not	Manufacturing identical styles and common colors assists crime
V	Valuable	Parts to cars five years old	Cars face physical wear and tear	Replacement parts have a market
E	Enjoyable	Condoms	Goal is to use up the loot and discard	Natural sexual urge feeds criminal actions
D	Disposable	Electronic goods	Want to unload loot quickly and nearby	Widespread market for used goods
Multiple Benefits		Cash	Easy to take, move, and dispense	Convertible to whatever you want

*In real life, each example combines more than one criterion.

a fundamental niche and a realized niche helps us sort out certain dimensions of crime change. Increasing crime could tell us two very different things:

1. Crime's *fundamental niche* has widened, and somebody has taken advantage; or

2. Its *realized niche* has taken up a greater share of the unchanged fundamental niche.

It's simpler to think of crime's fundamental niche as the "opportunity for crime." It's simpler to think of crime's realized niche as the part that offenders actually exploit. The goal of crime prevention is to minimize both fundamental and realized niches.

Crime Changes in Four Ways

A crime rate can change in four basic ways:

Ecological Term:	In Simpler Words:
A fundamental niche widens.	A crime opportunity expands.
A fundamental niche shrinks.	A crime opportunity shrinks.
A realized niche widens.	Offenders seize upon crime opportunities.
A realized niche shrinks.	Offenders neglect or avoid existing crime opportunities.

Thus crime change follows some general rules of nature, even though simpler words can explain such change. The following sections offer examples.

Crime Opportunities Sometimes Expand

The expansion of the female labor force participation rates during the 1970s and 1980s in the United States and Europe made it much easier for burglars to enter homes during daytime. The use of plastics and lightweight aluminum in consumer products made them much easier to steal. These are examples of how crime opportunity expanded. That fits the larger natural process of *niche widening*. In sum, certain changes in larger society provide more resources for a given crime to occur, expanding crime opportunities as an unintended side effect. In both cases, the niche widens.

Crime Opportunities Sometimes Shrink

Sometimes a change in larger society shrinks a crime opportunity as an unintended side effect. At other times, people shrink crime opportunities intentionally. In the first case, the opportunity to commit a crime declines or even disappears. The virtual disappearance of safecracking reflects the declining availability of safes that could be cracked.[11] The opportunity to steal horses declined with the shrinking number of horses used in everyday life in a modern society.

Then there's the second case, where people deliberately shrink crime opportunity. For example, by assembling better car locks, people shrink the opportunity to steal them. Fundamental niches contain the resources by which crime must live. *Situational prevention can deny those resources* by reworking local conditions (such as unsupervised places) or national conditions (such as how cars are made).[12]

Offenders Might Seize More Crime Opportunities

Crime can also increase when offenders learn about existing crime opportunities and how to exploit them. The increase in daytime residential burglary did not occur immediately, perhaps because potential burglars were finding out their new crime opportunities. Similarly, car theft depends on trials and errors, as youths learn how to tamper with the locks and as the word spreads about how to do it. The growth of Internet crime reflects an expansion of its fundamental niche, as offenders widen their horizons. It took some time before offenders took advantage of these Internet crime opportunities. The realized niche widened as offenders learned their greater potential, filling more of their fundamental niche for crime. A realized niche can grow in many ways. A drug dealer might find new customers within the same fundamental niche, or the old customers might increase their purchases, or police might get tired of trying to stop them.

Offenders Avoid or Neglect Crime Opportunities

Conventional policing ignores the fundamental niche entirely, as it tries to apprehend and punish individuals. That's sometimes frustrating to individual officers. But police sometimes can get offenders to *avoid* existing crime opportunities. In so doing, they can shrink crime's realized niche.

Independent of police action, offenders can be underachievers. They sometimes neglect crime targets or underestimate what they might do. They could be too lazy to go after targets that take too much effort. Situational crime prevention keeps that in mind, reducing crime's realized niche after it has already shrunk the fundamental niche.

The first half of this chapter explained crime's niches and how they can help us transcend its legal categories. It showed that different crime targets have different niches. It showed how crime grows or shrinks according to its fundamental and realized niches. The remainder of the chapter shows that niches serve to sort out some important issues about crime, including its root causes.

Niches Help Us Clarify

The distinction between fundamental niche and realized niche helps us sort out some basic issues about how crime changes.

Clarifying Crime's Root Causes

Conventional police efforts, citizen interferences with crime, and social prevention have a common general method—to reduce realized niches, while disregarding the fundamental niches for crime. In contrast, situational crime prevention and problem-oriented policing seek first to reduce fundamental niches for criminal action by denying crime's specific resources and habitats upon which they depend. *These newer methods address the "root causes" of crime by seeking to shrink the tangible substrate upon which crime feeds.* In contrast, certain social policies wrongly claim to be addressing the root causes of crime. That misconception is based on the assumption that a very general motivation is crime's root cause. But unfocused and intangible concepts are antithetical to scientific thinking. If general motivation has anything to do with crime, its role would be through shrinking the realized niche, not crime's fundamental niche.

Clarifying City Change in Crime

In a smaller city, the arrest of a single burglary ring can shrink the realized niche, leaving a larger portion of the fundamental niche untapped. In contrast, larger cities have so many crime opportunities that it is much harder to shrink the realized niche through arrest or interference with a group of people. I suggest that

- as city size increases, crime's fundamental niche grows even faster; and
- as city size increases, crime's realized niche takes on a greater share of the fundamental niche.

This is just a fancy way to say that cities provide extra-high-crime opportunity and that city offenders take extra advantage of that extra opportunity. It's just too hard in a city for police action to interfere with offenders.

Clarifying the Role of Community Development

Some people talk about reducing crime through "community development."[13] Do such efforts reduce crime's fundamental niche or realized niche? Of course, the answer lies in what "community development" means, exactly, and in specifying particular crimes affected. If community development removes specific resources that make specific crimes possible, it removes fundamental niches for crime. The distinction between fundamental niche and realized niche helps us ask a better question, and perhaps come up with answers.

I believe that offenders exploit new crime niches more quickly than society learns to protect these niches. If my assumption is correct, the realized niche will rise fairly quickly to take advantage of expansions in the fundamental niche. As offenders discover these new opportunities, they give the larger community a shock for which it is hardly prepared. But well-publicized crime controls often rely on nitpicking, leaving the fundamental crime niches untouched. I don't mean to imply that all reductions in realized niches are unjustifiable or ineffective. But often these efforts are expensive, and with a high cost of labor they might not succeed for long.

That's why society can often do best by reducing the fundamental niches for criminal activities—through situational prevention and problem-oriented policing. Then it can be confident in its crime prevention. Ask yourself whether a local crime intervention nibbles at the realized niche or seeks to shrink the fundamental niche. Both are legitimate efforts, but they are not the same.[14]

Often crime change occurs in this sequence:

1. A basic change in technology or community leads to a fairly sudden growth in crime's fundamental niche. *Example:* Light television sets were marketed around 1960.

2. Crime lags somewhat, but is reasonably quick to fill this niche. *Example:* Television thefts accelerated around 1963.

3. Crime prevention counters the crime wave by nitpicking at the realized niche, without shrinking the fundamental niche. *Example:* Police made more arrests, and juvenile courts tried to reform delinquents.

4. Society shrinks the fundamental niche, whether by intention or accident. *Example:* The fence value of stolen television sets declined with market saturation.

In effect, crime rates tend to rise more quickly than they fall. Situational crime prevention is a set of efforts to speed up the response by shrinking fundamental niches for different types of crime. Sometimes crime is a response to the *growth* of something legitimate, such as the spread of small television sets. But crime can also grow in response to the *shrinkage* of certain legitimate activities.

Crime Fills a Vacuum

One of the most interesting concepts is *niche packing*—the tendency for coexisting activities to fill the available "space" along important niche dimensions. Crime abhors a vacuum. A new drug dealer seeks a corner not yet controlled by counterparts. If car sales are fully claimed, the new dealer seeks sales to those on foot. It may be a crime to sell on the street without a license, but crime applies the laws of business.[15] In central cities with pedestrian traffic, offenders do not wait to get a license before selling things. Thus Manhattan street corners have illegal vendors, San Francisco tourist areas house numerous panhandlers, and metro stations in many cities are used by a variety of entertainers and hucksters.

Not only does one crime fill the vacuum left by another, but illegal activities pack niches left open by legal activities. Professor Johannes Knutsson has studied illegal taxicabs in a Norwegian city[16] (the same phenomenon is found in American cities and other parts of Europe). When legal cabs do not pick up customers in a given area, or will not take them to a dangerous or remote place, illegal taxis might fill in. In American cities, unlicensed bars sometimes take over the after-hours period when legal bars are not allowed to operate.[17] Similarly, illegal street vendors just outside normal establishments try to sell different goods from the licensed stores. By avoiding direct competition, they hope the licensed stores might not complain about their presence.

One Crime Creates a Niche for Other Crimes

Sometimes different criminal and legal activities compete for resources. But at other times, one activity sets the stage for another—feeding its niche. Interestingly, some crimes feed other crimes. Several future chapters examine this point in detail, but let's consider now how an open-air drug market might contribute to nearby crimes.

Drawing on research by Dr. Rana Sampson, Exhibit 8.2 relates an open-air drug market in an apartment complex to some 22 crimes, annoyances, and other problems.[18] Note the links between the drug market and prostitution, auto break-ins, gang activity, graffiti, weapons violations, and violence. In addition, public annoyances—such as littering, speeding, trespassing, and traffic—are common side effects of an open-air drug market.[19]

Dr. Sampson also details numerous crimes, annoyances and problems related to an active local prostitution area. She considers not only prostitutes who loiter and trespass, but also pimps recruiting girls and extorting money

Exhibit 8.2   Larger Consequences of an Open-Air Drug Market*

Types of Consequences	Examples of Consequences
A. *Related to drugs directly*	Abandoned vehicles used as shooting galleries Drug use in alley beside property
B. *Related to getting money for drugs*	Auto break-ins nearby streets by drug users Auto thefts on nearby streets by drug users Commercial break-ins to enable drug purchases Possession of and trafficking in stolen property Prostitution around the corner Residential break-ins to enable drug purchases Robbery of passersby or nearby stores
C. *Related to drug market control*	Gang activity for control of market Graffiti establishing ownership of drug market Weapons violations, including gun possession, trafficking
D. *Violence*	Assaults by and between those purchasing drugs Drive-by shootings by competing drug dealers Robbery of dealers
E. *Annoyances*	Littering, including drug paraphernalia and used condoms Loitering at apartment complex Public drinking Public urination by drug buyers Speeding vehicles to and from drug market Trespassing on apartment complex grounds Unwanted additional foot, car, and bicycle traffic

*Applies to an open-air drug market in an apartment complex.

SOURCE: Adapted from Figure 1 in R. Sampson, "Advancing Problem-Oriented Policing: Lessons From Dealing With Drug Markets," in J. Knutsson, ed., *Problem-Oriented Policing: From Innovation to Mainstream* (Monsey, NY: Criminal Justice Press, 2003) (Volume 15 in *Crime Prevention Studies* series). Reprinted with permission from Criminal Justice Press. The author also lists "other violent crime, including homicide" and "parking problems caused by drug buyers."

from them. Often a drug market supplies nearby prostitutes, and drug use occurs in the alley near the prostitution market. Violent acts include assaults on prostitutes, rapes by johns, and attacks on them by pimps, as well as prostitutes attacking johns. Prostitution markets commonly bring forth littering (including drug paraphernalia and condoms), public urination, and unwanted foot and car traffic. In addition, visiting johns harass local women. Don't forget that prostitution spreads sexual diseases, including AIDS. We readily see that any given crime might be linked to other criminal activities, as well as to legitimate activities and unpleasant activities that are not necessarily illegal.

Overview

A crime's niche includes features that meet all the crime's requirements—from climate to transport system to a door easy to break. Each specific crime has a somewhat different niche. Even crimes with the same legal name might differ in their niches.

Theft works best for goods that are concealable, removable, available, valuable, enjoyable, and disposable. That's why we must consider what items are easy to steal and worth the risk. An offender might not realize all the niche requirements as he grabs the loot. But those requirements are there, nonetheless.

Central Points, Chapter 8

1. A crime's niche includes features that meet its total requirements, of human and nonhuman origin.

2. The most likely crime targets are concealable, removable, available, valuable, enjoyable, and disposable.

3. Each crime type has a fundamental niche, not fully realized.

4. Situational prevention and problem-oriented policing intentionally shrink crime's fundamental niche. In that sense, they attack the root causes of crime.

5. One crime can create a niche for other crimes.

Exercises

1. Name four niche requirements for auto-parts theft.

2. Consider winters far from the equator. Which crime niches do these winters create? Which do they shrink?

3. Name one minor crime that leads to more serious crimes. Explain how.

4. What does a college campus do for crime in its vicinity?

Notes

1. Quoted in *Bartlett's Familiar Quotations,* 10th ed. (Boston: Little, Brown, 1919).

2. Canadian prime minister, 1968–1984 (lived 1919–2000), speaking about the United States of America in a speech to the National Press Club, March 1969. Quoted in *Simpson's Contemporary Quotations* (New York: Houghton Mifflin, 1988).

3. This quotation is attributed to Feynman. See Wikipedia quotation website, http://en.wikiquote.org/wiki/Richard_Feynman.

4. British mathematician (1806–1871). *A Budget of Paradoxes* (New York: Dover, 1954). Original edition published 1872.

5. Ecologists are not consistent in dividing up the features of habitat and niche. For greater clarity, I define habitat to cover fewer features and give niche a longer list of coverage. In particular, the times favorable to a crime are best considered part of its niche.

6. According to the *competitive exclusion principle,* two species cannot compete indefinitely for the same limiting resource. Thus they cannot over time maintain exactly the same niche. Offenders are not always competing for targets, so this might not be the best explanation for niches to differentiate. But it remains sensible to use different niches to define different crimes.

7. R. V. Clarke, "Hot Products," Police Research Series Paper 112, British Home Office, http://www.homeoffice.gov.uk/rds/prgpdfs/fprs112.pdf (accessed September 3, 2005).

8. CRAVED is a substantial improvement on my earlier acronym VIVA, which considered a product's value, inertia, visibility, and access—all four affecting likelihood of a crime.

9. For a wonderful source on Soviet society, including crime, see the work of an outstanding journalist, Hedrick Smith, *The Russians* (New York: Quadrangle–New York Times Books, 1976). Do not confuse this with his sequel, *The New Russians.*

10. Our usual concept of the "opportunity for crime" is close to the "fundamental niche." The latter term is more precise than the word "opportunity," and links crime ecology to a larger scientific world. It also forces some discipline on thinking. The "fundamental niche for theft" challenges you to make a good list of specifics.

11. Work by Professor Maurice Cusson at the University of Montreal has told us a good deal about how crime shrinks. See M. Cusson and P. Pinsonneault, "The Decision to Give Up Crime," in R. V. Clarke and D. B. Cornish, *The Reasoning Criminal: Rational Choice Perspectives on Offending* (New York: Springer-Verlag, 1986). Also see M. Cusson, *Le Croissance et Decroissance du Crime* (Paris: Presses Universitaires de France, 1990).

12. Of course, situational prevention can also attack crime's realized niche by making crime more risky. But we usually think of police action as performing that role.

13. X. S. Briggs, E. J. Mueller, and M. Sullivan, *From Neighborhood to Community: Evidence on the Social Effects of Community Development* (New York: Community Development Research Center, 1997).

14. I admit that this distinction is sometimes relative. Thus effective policing might accomplish a reduction in both types of niche.

15. For a more general approach along these lines, see M. Sullivan, *Getting Paid: Youth Crime and Work in the Inner City* (Ithaca, NY: Cornell University Press, 1989).

16. See J. Knutsson and K.-E. Sovik, "Gypsy Cabs in Tonsberg—a Case for Problem Oriented Policing" (2004), Center for Problem-oriented Policing, http://www.popcenter.org/Library/ConferencePapers2004/GypsyCabs.pdf (accessed September 3, 2005).

17. This fits under the rubric of commensalism, as discussed in Chapter 14.

18. R. Sampson, "Advancing Problem-Oriented Policing: Lessons From Dealing With Drug Markets," in J. Knutsson, ed., *Problem-Oriented Policing: From Innovation to Mainstream* (Monsey, NY: Criminal Justice Press, 2003) (Volume 15 in *Crime Prevention Studies* series). Also see A. Harocopos and M. Hough, "Drug Dealing in Open-Air Markets" (2005), Center for Problem-Oriented Policing, http://www.popcenter.org (accessed September 3, 2005).

19. Note the book by B. A. Jacobs, *Robbing Drug Dealers: Violence Beyond the Law* (Piscataway, NJ: Transaction, 2000).

All, all is theft, all is unceasing and rigorous competition in nature; the desire to make off with the substance of others is the foremost—the most legitimate—passion nature has bred into us . . . and, without doubt, the most agreeable one.

—Marquis de Sade[1]

Do not hold the delusion that your advancement is accomplished by crushing others.

—Marcus Tullius Cicero[2]

When a show fails to destroy the competition—and it can fail while attracting 20 million viewers—it is itself destroyed.

—Les Brown[3]

Forget your opponents; always play against par.

—Sam Snead[4]

9

Crime Competition

From an ecologist's viewpoint competition occurs when organisms *in the same community* seek the same limiting resource. This resource may be prey, water, light, nutrients, nest sites, crime targets, control over space, or anything else that is scarce or limited.[5] We often call this a zero-sum situation, since a benefit to one party occurs only at the expense of the other party.

Competition is important for crime, since offenders sometimes compete with one another, or with legal activities.

Types of Competition

Ecologists distinguish two types of competition.[6] *Exploitative competition* means that competitors are using the same scarce resources, to the disadvantage of one another. For example, proximate prostitutes might compete for the same customers, to mutual disadvantage.[7] *Interference competition* occurs when some offenders interfere with the foraging or life processes of others, perhaps by cornering some part of the habitat. Some niches are intrinsically so localized that they afford little room to share. A well-known urban scheme in many nations is the rudimentary protection gang, "helping" you by watching your car, but vandalizing the car if you do not pay. Given the incentive to drive out competitors, protection gangs often end up in violent competition for turf.

Even though a drug dealer is not competing with a prostitute in services provided, he might push her away from the best corner to enhance his own sales or reduce his own risk of police interference. Whereas exploitative competition does not always exclude the loser, interference competition generally forces one of the two competitors to get out.

Niche Overlap

Like every legal activity, every crime type occupies a particular niche. Each activity has *niche requirements*. Thus street robbery needs to find victims in settings that are otherwise abandoned. Commercial burglary requires businesses that are sometimes empty and easily accessible. Business needs to sell when people will buy, then close up and go home. But how do these niches relate?

To begin, different niche requirements tend to coexist in the same area. This is called *niche differentiation*. Street robbery and commercial burglary might occur in the same neighborhood, while differing in timing, weapons use, confrontation, risk, booty, and on many other niche dimensions. Perhaps an employee pilfers from the stockroom while the manager is in the other room juggling the accounts. Their niches differ, and they need not interact in a criminal sense. If you look ahead to my proposed crime taxonomy (Chapter 21), the first level distinguishes crimes by the path the offender uses to get to the target—physical, organizational, or electronic. In general, these paths define very different crime niches. Such niche differentiation normally prevents these three types of crime from interfering with one another. Perhaps the ideal criminal would have his own lucrative niche with no other offenders intruding.

Niche overlap means that two or more activities compete for the same resources. Youths who offer to "protect" your car do not want other youths to intrude into their territory. Public officials collecting bribes do not want to share the loot with too many others. Prostitutes and drug dealers sometimes vie for the same corners, interfering with each other's marketing plans. Sometimes niche overlap is a very local concept, but at other times it looks beyond any given corner. We must ask ourselves when and where heroin and cocaine have *overlapping niches*.

Often one crime fills illegal gaps left unfilled by another—*niche complementarity*. For example, residential burglary takes advantage of daytime absences, while commercial burglary favors night and weekends. But the booty from both might end up with the same fence, so their niches are not entirely independent. Clearly, some crime niches are better than others, and some offenders try to claim them first.

Limiting Conflicts

Competition is greatest when niche overlap is the most extreme. For example, a highly competitive situation exists between two outdoor drug dealers selling the same drug, from the same park, to the same type of customers. Competition can also exist between legitimate and illicit activities. Licensed stores are often quite hostile to unlicensed street vendors, urging police to arrest them or drive them away. This hostility is most common if the street vendors offer the same goods at lower prices, paying no taxes or license fees. Many street vendors limit themselves to the sorts of goods that licensed stores do not sell, thus minimizing conflict with merchants and demands for police intervention. That makes their relationship more commensal than competitive.

Two purveyors of illicit commodities can minimize direct competition and increase their own safety by selling at different times and places to different types of customers. Those whose niches overlap only in part might feel less competition and avoid mutual attacks, especially if they have a positive mutual gain on some other dimension. Thus one person sells methamphetamine, another sells heroin; both sell some marihuana on the side, while trading security tips.

The competitive exclusion principle states that, "Two species cannot coexist for long if their niches are identical." We can thus expect that two criminal activities with identical niches will enter into competition of some sort. On the other hand, two criminal activities with overlapping niches often coexist yet compete to some extent. Consider marihuana and heroin, whose niches overlap but are clearly not identical. The growth of heroin sales might not drive marihuana sales down. On the other hand, some hard drugs might have similar niches and hence compete for customers. In places with strong drug markets, different drug dealers overlap in their niche for selling drugs and hence must compete for customers. However, many drug dealers sell diverse drugs in order to improve their competitive advantage.[8] Each of these points can be resolved with a combination of empirical research and an eye for ecological niches.

Organized Crime as Resource Partitioning

Sometimes coexistence of activities occurs through *resource partitioning*, allowing several parties to coexist, using the same limiting resource. Those that share the same habitat and have similar needs frequently use resources in somewhat different ways to avoid direct competition, at least for part of the limiting resource. In restaurants, waitresses divide up the tables or take turns with customers who tip well. Taxicabs wait in queues. Similar rules apply to illegal activities. Those selling sex from bars work out arrangements about who sits where, gets a first introduction, or has priority for a new customer. Those selling various illegal goods and services in the same park can make similar arrangements in order to minimize direct competition and avoid hostilities. A substantial component of organized crime might better be understood as resource partitioning rather than formal organizations or social networks.

Organized Crime Abhors Competition

Adam Smith explained that all business people hate competition and try very hard to control their markets.[9] Organized criminals have found one way to accomplish that. They drive out legal competitors. They form a coalition among themselves to sell certain goods or services. They divide up territories, within which each has a monopoly. So long as their agreements hold, they can live peacefully among themselves, using violence only against rival criminals and legal competitors.

If several criminals divide up a market among themselves, their cooperation is an alternative to fighting. They have agreed to restrain the market to mutual advantage. Each offender gains a monopoly in his sector, and can command a higher price. Through cooperation, they can reduce further danger. In construction or other services, they cooperate to rig bids or make sure only one of them bids on each job. They might use violence *against outsiders* to preserve their monopoly. But their goal is to minimize violence *within* their group. Resource partitioning explains why. Of course, one of them might get too greedy.

Very Local Interference

In 300 BC, Theophrastus noted that the chickpea (a.k.a. garbanzo bean) destroys nearby weeds. A good gardener knows that sunflowers, wormwoods, sagebrush, and other plants accomplish that, too. In botany, this is called *allelopathy,* a process by which one plant drives others away.[10] Community processes can also have negative side effects on crime, often inadvertently. For example, a small or tiny business can inhibit nearby crime as a secondary effect. Street peddlers have a good view of the street, helping to discourage robberies and thefts. In other cases, crime inhibition through legitimate activities is quite deliberate. Local governments can impede drug sales or muggings in an urban park by establishing an outdoor café inside the park or adjacent to it. Increasing pedestrian flows on the street or through a parking area can inadvertently thwart the plans of a street robber, or passersby can scare off a would-be burglar.

Crime prevention depends on natural surveillance and supervision by place managers. The crime triangle in Exhibit 5.1 explained the role of place managers in security. Natural surveillance is accomplished by

- designing better settings,
- managing settings well, and
- making sure nearby activities are satisfactory.

Crime Prevention Through Environmental Design (CPTED) is a set of techniques for designing better settings.[11] Managing these settings depends on a combination of individual and organizational efforts. But natural surveillance also depends on people likely to look beyond the hedges or through the windows. *That in turn depends on activities proximate to the area of potential insecurity.* Nearby activities are satisfactory if there is sufficient work and residential life to make the area secure.

Overview

Crime competes for its position in the sun. That fact gives us a handle on prevention. Professors Tim Crowe and Diane Zahm have stated what I call the Crowe-Zahm mixing principle:

Place safe activities in unsafe locations and unsafe activities in safe locations.[12]

The logic of this principle is to use safe locations to help supervise or contain unsafe activities, also taking advantage of safe activities to influence unsafe locations for the better. Safe activities include normal business, such as buying apples and flowers, and socializing while sober. Unsafe activities include young males getting drunk or a customer taking out a wallet where someone can easily grab it and run. Safe locations include those with substantial visibility. Unsafe locations include those that are obscured or abandoned. Accordingly, some businesses secrete guardians against crime, who provide natural surveillance and thus tend to poison criminal activities. Not only small legitimate businesses but even street vendors can provide additional "eyes on the street," enhancing security. Janitors, doormen, small business owners, and receptionists not only secure their own places but also enhance security on the streets in front.

Offenders, too, drive other activities away. Those acting legally often wish to avoid living, working, or walking in their vicinity. In the last chapter I discussed how some offenders want the protection of legal activities, but many offenders prefer to dominate their location. A drug sales area does better if the buyers can attract sellers at all times and with nobody to call police or otherwise interfere. We are only beginning to understand the secondary effects of criminal and legal activities on one another.[13] Many of these effects are inadvertent. Yet crime prevention specialists are increasingly realizing how they can install legitimate activities to inhibit crime growth.

Central Points, Chapter 9

1. Offenders sometimes compete with one another, or with legal activities. That competition includes using the same scarce resources or interfering with the foraging or life processes of others by cornering a part of the habitat.

2. Yet different crimes can coexist in the same area, avoiding competition.

3. Many offenders try to stay out of each other's way, dividing up crime opportunities among them.

4. Often one activity drives another way. For example, some legitimate businesses drive out crime, often without planning it.

Exercises

1. Name a crime activity you think competes with a legitimate activity. What makes you think so?

2. When would nearby drug dealers have to compete with one another? When not?

3. Strictly for avoiding crime victimization, name a business that would make a safe neighbor. Then name one you would rather not live next to.

Notes

1. French author (1740–1814). Quoted in *The Columbia World of Quotations* (New York: Columbia University Press, 1996).
2. Widely attributed. Cicero listed six basic human mistakes:
   a. The delusion that personal gain is made by crushing others
   b. The tendency to worry about things that cannot be changed or corrected
   c. Insisting that a thing is impossible because we cannot accomplish it
   d. Refusing to set aside trivial preferences
   e. Neglecting development and refinement of the mind, and not acquiring the habit of reading and studying
   f. Attempting to compel others to believe and live as we do
3. Quoted in *Simpson's Contemporary Quotations* (New York: Houghton Mifflin, 1988).
4. Famous golfer (1912–2002). Quotation widely attributed to him.
5. In contrast, the economist allows a broader market that could span the entire earth. For example, the wholesale price of illicit drugs on two continents is related. Thus ecologists and economists have a common interest in scarcity, but ecologists are more likely to focus on the spatiotemporal features and local tangible aspects of that scarcity. Both professions rest on a common assumption: One competitor's gain is the other's loss.
6. For a glossary, see EverythingBio.com, http://www.everythingbio.com.
7. This does not deny that a cluster of similar offenders might attract customers to the area, for mutual benefit.
8. See important work by G. F. Rengert, *The Geography of Illegal Drugs* (Boulder, CO: Westview Press, 1996). See also G. F. Rengert, J. H. Ratcliffe, and S. Chakrovorty, eds., *Policing Illegal Drug Markets: Geographic Approaches to Crime Reduction* (Monsey, NY: Criminal Justice Press, forthcoming).
9. A. Smith, *An Inquiry Into the Nature and Causes of the Wealth of Nations* (1776). Available from Edwin Cannan Library of Economics and Liberty, http://www.econlib.org/library/Smith/smWN1.html (accessed September 4, 2005).
10. This is another form of *amensalism*, explained later in this book.

11. See Crowe and Zahm, next endnote. Also see
    a. S. E. Michael, R. B. Hull, and D. Zahm, "Environmental Factors Influencing Auto Burglary: A Case Study," *Environment and Behavior* 33, no. 3 (2001): 368–388.
    b. D. Zahm, "Security by Design," in P. Knox and P. Ozolins, eds., *Design Professionals and the Built Environment* (Chichester, UK: John Wiley and Sons, 2000).
    c. D. Zahm, "Architecture, Landscape Architecture, Planning, and Crime," in C. D. Bryant, ed., *Encyclopedia of Criminology and Deviant Behavior* (Philadelphia: Brunner-Routledge, 2001).
    d. D. Zahm, *Designing Safer Communities: A Crime Prevention Through Environmental Design Handbook* (Washington, DC: National Crime Prevention Council, 1997).
    e. P. J. Brantingham and P. L. Brantingham, *Patterns in Crime* (New York: Macmillan, 1984).
    f. P. J. Brantingham and P. L. Brantingham, eds., *Environmental Criminology* (Prospect Heights, IL: Waveland, 1991).
    g. P. J. Brantingham and P. L. Brantingham, "Surveying Campus Crime: What Can Be Done to Reduce Crime and Fear?" *Security Journal* 5, no. 8 (1994): 160–171.
    h. P. J. Brantingham and P. L. Brantingham, "Environmental Criminology: From Theory to Urban Planning Practice," *Studies on Crime and Crime Prevention* 7, no. 1 (1998): 31–60.
    i. T. D. Crowe, *Crime Prevention Through Environmental Design: Applications of Architectural Design and Space Management Concepts* (Boston: Butterworth-Heinemann, 1991).
    j. B. Poyner, *Design Against Crime: Beyond Defensible Space* (London/Boston: Butterworths, 1983).
12. T. D. Crowe and D. L. Zahm, "Crime Prevention Through Environmental Design," *Land Development*, Fall (1994): 22–27. Available from the Center for Problem-oriented Policing, http://www.popcenter.org/Responses/Supplemental_Material/streetclosures/Crowe& Zahm_1994.pdf (accessed September 4, 2005).
13. See R. J. Sampson and S. Raudenbush, "Disorder in Urban Neighborhoods—Does It Lead to Crime?" Research Brief (Washington, DC: U.S. Department of Justice, National Institute of Justice, 2001). Available from William James Hall at Harvard University, http://www.wjh.harvard.edu/soc/faculty/sampson/2001.4_NIJ.pdf; also from the National Criminal Justice Reference Service, http://www.ncjrs.gov/pdffiles1/nij/186049.pdf (both accessed September 4, 2005). See also R. Peiser, "Crime and Real Estate: Unhappy Bedfellows," in M. Felson and R. Peiser, eds., *Reducing Crime Through Real Estate Development and Management* (Washington, DC: The Urban Land Institute, 1998).

Man is an animal who more than any other can adapt himself to all climates and circumstances.

—Henry David Thoreau[1]

Those who can see value only in tradition, or versions of it, deny man's ability to adapt to changing circumstances.

—Stephen Bayley[2]

It is not the strongest of the species that survives, nor the most intelligent; it is the one that is most adaptable to change.

—Charles Darwin[3]

It is common sense to take a method and try it. If it fails, admit it frankly and try another. But, above all, try something.

—Franklin D. Roosevelt[4]

10

Crime Adaptation

The human appendix is a useless organ that sometimes gets infected.[5] Nature spews out accidents by the billions, and is *very imperfect* at keeping what's useful and getting rid of what isn't. Otherwise we all would be healthy and crime would disappear.

On the other hand, living things must adapt or suffer the consequences of not doing so. Most human adaptation occurs nongenetically. Many of our tools for adapting to the world can also harm us.[6] A self-service store saves consumers money, but also facilitates shoplifting. A gun empowers police as well as offenders. Neither security nor crime can win out completely. To quote Montaigne, "Not being able to control events, I control myself; and I adapt myself to them, if they do not adapt themselves to me."[7] The average thief tries to do the same as the philosopher.

The challenge to crime ecology is to figure out the clumsy adaptation process that is so much a part of our imperfect lives. Sometimes offenders are inventive, other times they steal a car that's out of gas. Some people find a good hiding place, but others put the jewels in the cookie jar, not realizing it's a bad idea. If we know how crime and offenders adapt, perhaps we can help the rest of society keep pace.

Trials and Errors

As I was beginning to write this book, Stephen Jay Gould—the great author-scientist—died of metastasized cancer. He explained how rough and crude the Darwinian process is, and how many trials and errors are needed for it to have its impact. In the case of plants and animals, these errors are carried out through trillions of genetic mutations, without clear direction.[8] Yet "the fact that something is secondary in its origin doesn't mean it's unimportant in its consequences."[9]

In the case of offenders and those trying to stop them, daily experience includes a certain amount of fiddling about and probing. Not every act is fully "rational," adaptive, or progressive. Both offenders and those seeking security engage in a "trials and errors" process. They try this and try that. They experiment, explore, diversify, and copy one another. In the process, they discover some ways to get what they want, since life selects and rewards some behaviors more than others. While all of these actors might engage in reasoning, yet they often stumble, bumble, and err. Various participants in crime might gain ground or lose it. Or they bump into a crime opportunity they are not even seeking. Even when one offender imitates another, he explores whom to imitate and hence continues the trials and errors process. Thus, willy-nilly, crime and security adapt to one another and to forces bigger than both.

Adaptation may be a powerful force, but it does not usually move in one direction. That was the error of "social Darwinism," which claimed that society always got better. People do not seem to become more perfect, nor does the offender evolve toward brilliance. Indeed, during the 1970s and 1980s, crime increased mainly by becoming simpler,[10] taking advantage of new and easy opportunities.

Active offenders tend to be generalists rather than specialists, and for a good reason. Offenders thrive best by keeping their options open.[11] In contrast, those offenders with a single niche are highly vulnerable to losing that opportunity and being forced into a life of legality. To understand this point, contrast weekend prostitutes with a limited niche to more active prostitutes willing to move in search of new criminal opportunities. A London study found it easier to get the first group to stop.[12] But not all offenders quit easily.

Arms Race Between Offenders and Defenders

Crime and its prevention is a complex natural system. Crime participants seek to overcome the defenses of their adversaries by enhancing their abilities to attack. Thus the burglar fearing a counterattack carries along a weapon, just in case he needs it. If homeowners start using better locks, he brings a stronger crowbar with him.

Ecologists write about an arms race, namely an ecological struggle between predators and defenders. This has been ably applied to crime by Paul Ekblom, Professor at the Centre for Research in Designing Out Crime at the University of the Arts, London.[13] He explains that "Crime contends against crime prevention in a never-ending arms race, with move and counter-move driven by accelerating technological and social change."[14]

The purpose of Ekblom's comment is not to discourage crime prevention, but rather to encourage more foresight among those seeking to prevent crime. We must expect that offenders will try to overcome defenses by their intended victims, while devising defenses of their own against counterattacks. Situational crime prevention can still be effective, but it must be able to adapt to a changing environment.

Both offenders and victims of crime adapt to conditions.[15] Each side in this battle improves itself over time, adjusting to the other contender. Sometimes crime prevention improves better than crime; at other times criminal activities outstrip prevention. This helps explain why crime neither increases nor decreases forever.

The dynamic interplay between offender and guardian against crime is but one scene in the drama of crime adaptation. Offenders and those they worry are only a few of the persons who affect crime. Auto engineers in Detroit and Yokohama—by designing electronic keys—interfere with car theft in Walla Walla, Washington, and Grenoble, France. Yet the auto industry and its customers have too much going on to propel crime in a single direction at a steady pace.[16]

Take the example of suburbs in the United States. In the 1950s, suburbs helped people escape from crime risks in central cities. But in the 1960s, suburbs began to include more to steal and fewer people to prevent crime. Young people reached ages most suitable for crime participation, both as offenders and as victims. Suburbs, which had been beneficial against crime, began to suffer from the very automobiles that provided new crime targets and assisted offenders as well. Large suburban stores with few employees to look after merchandise suffered greater shoplifting. The growth of suburbs pushed the crime rate down before pushing it up.[17] Thus we see that crime adaptability is not unidirectional. Rather, criminal and countercriminal activities are in perpetual contention, both engaging in trials and errors, having successes and failures.[18] Sometimes one gains the upper hand in more cases than before; sometimes the trend goes the other way. As I explained on the first page of this book, bank burglars and safe manufacturers went back and forth, until the latter won their point.

Yet new products and procedures emerge in society with quite accidental but dramatic influences on crime. In the past half-century, the self-service store took over sales in modern societies for reasons having little to do with crime—their use of less labor and ability to deliver products more cheaply to people who own cars. But these stores created new niches for shoplifting. Automobiles became more and more popular for other transportation, but coincidentally offered new targets for theft. Electronic products became lighter in weight, also assisting crime. Electronic money placed less cash inside stores and homes, reducing robberies and burglaries, but electronic money provides new opportunities for fraud. Credit cards and the Internet enable people to engage in identity theft. Electronic mail opens the door for viruses and privacy invasions.[19] None of these changes in society was made with crime in mind. And so crime has its trends, its cycles, and its surprises.

Some Crime Changes Takes Decades or Longer

Professor Martin Killias of the University of Lausanne, Switzerland, helps us understand these changes in crime over decades and centuries. He defines "breaches" as

> sudden new opportunities for offending which opened as a result of changes in the technological or social environment. Such "breaches" often go unnoticed over extended periods of time. Once discovered, they provoke rapid increases in offences that usually provoke defensive actions aimed at curbing such developments.[20]

His article documents a succession of "breaches" that opened up during the course of history and which were regularly closed again after a certain period of time. Professor Killias extended my own thinking, known as the "routine activity approach," and I hope he will not mind my converting his comments to this historical sequence:

1. technology and organization change, altering everyday life;

2. offenders explore and find new opportunities to commit crime;

3. other offenders learn about these, by word of mouth or the media;

4. a dramatic crime wave follows;

5. in time, society reacts to the threat, closing the breaches; and

6. the crime wave fades away.

These adaptations take time. Exhibit 10.1 shows the broad sweep of crime change in Europe, from 1800 to 2000, as compiled by Professor Killias and others.[21] These dramatic changes reflect such changes as the spread of hard liquor in the earliest era and the use of guns in duels. In the modern world one finds a mass production of lightweight durables, easy to steal; the dispersion of activities away from family and household settings; the presence of women in public places; the spread of guns and automobiles. In time, modern society reduces its reliance on cash and some of its consumer goods become too common to be worth stealing.

This chapter has so far examined crime's adaptations, and its trials and errors process. It has considered the arms race between offenders and those seeking security. If other chapters show how crime can change quickly, the previous section explains that crime can shift very slowly, at least in the terms of one person's life. Now I consider several ways that social and community life change, affecting crime in the process.

Product Life Cycles and Crime

Professor Leroy Gould explained a general life cycle in theft of mass-produced items.[22] At first a product is too new to gain much interest from consumers or from thieves. After a product becomes increasingly popular, many people want it but not enough have it. That creates demand in the general public and among thieves. That's the period of greatest crime growth. Then the product becomes widely owned and not as widely stolen.

Exhibit 10.1   The Broad Sweep of European Crime Change, 1800–2000

"Crime Eras"				
Type of Crime	1800–1850	1850–1950	1950–1990	1990–2000
Homicide mortality	Doubled	Down 70% (men) / Stable (women)	Tripled (men) / Doubled (women)	Stable
Assault	Stable	Down 70%	Tripled	Up 80%
Robbery	Some increase	Stable	Quintupled	Stable
Theft	Doubled	Slow decrease	Quadrupled	Stable

*This table hides a lot. Its inconsistencies include nations and methods, and sometimes I infer to Europe evidence from only one or two nations.

SOURCE: Adapted from Table 1 in M. Killias, "The Opening and Closing of Breaches: A Theory on Crime Waves, Law Creation and Crime Prevention," *European Journal of Criminology* 3, no. 1 (2006): 11–31.

So it was with personal computers. At first they were for aficionados, so the general public would not buy or steal them. Then the product took off, more people knew how to use it, and many more people wanted one. Finally, personal computers reached saturation, and thefts declined.

If the price eventually declines, and demand is largely met, the item is hardly worth stealing. Car tape players, handheld calculators, and many other consumer goods went through this cycle or something like it. After the small television becomes very cheap, nobody wants to buy a used or stolen version, and no fence pays much if he cannot resell.

However, after saturation companies continue to develop their products, add new features, and interest people in buying upgrades. That can keep crime going, even in a saturated market. On the other hand, the top of the market probably is inclined to buy new goods with a warranty—no help to most thieves.

Crime spawned by changing technology and marketing of consumer goods is not usually confined to a single neighborhood. We need to figure out what's unique about any given area that makes its crime grow, diversify, and persist beyond any specific national crime wave.

How Mass Media Help Offenders Adapt

Scholars have never really sorted out whether the mass media "cause" crime.[23] Perhaps it makes more sense to ask whether mass media help offenders adapt to their environment. Perhaps the mass media inform *current* offenders, giving them new ideas about what to try, or ways to get to it. It is quite possible that the mass media enhance crime, not by creating motivation, but rather by encouraging illicit experimentation among those who already have crossed the line.[24] News coverage of prostitution areas might enhance business, drawing more customers or even inviting more providers. Professor Gloria Laycock has turned the tables by publicizing situational crime prevention measures, with measurable success in discouraging offenders.[25]

How Cities Help Offenders Adapt

Scholars also ask whether "urbanization causes crime." The question normally assumes that urban settings create crime motivation. Perhaps we should ask instead how cities make it easier for those already motivated for crime to adapt to circumstances. Nature does not place all its eggs in one basket. Diversification is a basic principle of adaptation. That's why crime is more resilient in a large city with many types of misbehavior, many customers for and suppliers of illicit drugs, etc. If conditions worsen for one crime, in a large city it is easier to do another.

If one crime opportunity is blocked in some urban settings, other illicit options are more readily available. On the other hand, suburban settings might provide fewer illicit options that replace those blocked. The general point for crime prevention is basic: enriching offender choices tends to keep crime going. Here is a simple model:

1. Most people experiment in life, sometimes contrary to law.

2. Most people fail in some of these experiments.

3. Even those who succeed might not find good chances to try again.

4. But those with plenty of alternatives can keep trying.

If this model is correct, a bad neighborhood does not work by creating bad people or bad motives. Rather, it helps experimenters succeed more or try more options. Having more crime opportunities might contribute to greater initiation of illicit acts; but more crime opportunities are probably most important because they invite *continued* experimentation and adaptation. That is, most people in most places experiment with things they are not supposed to do. But if at first they don't succeed, some locations help them try and try again.

Feedback to Offenders

Ideally, the environment should feed back to the offender in timely fashion the negative stimuli that discourage crime. But the timing of pleasure and pain from crime interferes with its control. In general, crime gives offenders definite and immediate pleasure, but the pain it gives them is slow and delayed. For example, drug abuse leads to a quick high; but its punishments are gradual and eventual. Official punishment for shoplifting depends on apprehension and more. When crime opportunities are rich, the trials and errors process might not teach offenders to be good for some time, if at all. Indeed, most offenders face more danger form one another than from the legal system.

Designing More Crime

In 2000, Paul Ekblom delivered an important lecture on designing out crime.[26] He explained how people sometimes design *more* of it. Ekblom defined the *four misses* of bad design—that is, four ways that design can enhance crime. Products and devices can be misappropriated, mistreated, mishandled, or misused. An example of a design *misappropriated* for illegal use is the traditional car lock, opened by a knob that is easy for a car thief to lasso and pull up. I've done it myself when I locked my keys in the car. Other products are naturally *mistreated,* such as the old telephone booths that invite vandalism. Other products are *mishandled*, such as somebody else's cell phone. Still other goods are *misused* for illegal purposes, such as airport luggage labels that a passing burglar reads to figure out who's left home.

In the past decade, merchants have distributed millions of discount coupons that can easily be faked, altered, and abused. Coupon fraud has become a billion-dollar enterprise—absent from crime statistics. This is a good example of designing more crime. A process is underway to design out the crime wave that was designed in.

Often good design against crime is also accidental. The London Underground has a different voltage in its lighting system than the rest of British society uses at home. This was done for noncrime reasons, but nobody wanted to steal their lighting.

Fortunately, after many decades of designing in crime, there has been some adaptation. Car locks in recent years have a better design to thwart easy theft. Public telephones have been placed on stands that discourage vandalism. More recently, cell phones have been programmed to thwart a thief's purposes.[27] And many luggage labels have a flap.

Professors Clarke and Newman have produced an entire book on redesigning products to reduce crime.[28]

Naïve Versus Clever Responses to Crime

Many responses to crime are quite naïve—not true adjustments but rather stabs in the dark. Here are a few examples of naïve prevention:

- Add cameras that nobody sees and screens that nobody watches.
- Create far more false alarms than real alarms.
- Put up a fence that healthy teenagers can easily climb over.
- Put up billboards against crime.
- Get prepubertal kids to promise sexual restraint.

More clever responses to crime include the following:

- Late 1800s: Milling the edges of coins so people could no longer chip off silver
- 1841: Canceling stamps so they can't be reused[29]
- Around 1849: Casting silver into 400-pound blocks to thwart bandits on horseback[30]
- 1991: Reprogramming the phones in the Port Authority Bus Terminal, New York City, to thwart long-distance phone fraud[31]
- Starting in my childhood: Shoe stores putting only the right shoe on display, with the left shoes out of public reach. There's no point in stealing under these conditions.
- Around 1993: Toughening bar glasses so they shatter into too many pieces to be effective as weapons[32]
- Around 1990: Using caller-ID; it began in New Jersey and spread around the United States. Identifying the caller, it led to a major decline in obscene and threatening phone calls.[33]
- Stores alternating the direction of hangers for expensive coats, so a thief cannot grab a bunch easily
- Creating shopping carts that immobilize if taken off the store's lot
- Creating self-service gasoline pumps that activate *after* payment
- Integrating hotel clothes hangers with the hanger rail

For automotive crime, some situational crime prevention efforts can be factory installed. Exhibit 10.2 offers 16 means to prevent seven auto crime problems. Many more ideas are found in the work of Professors Clarke and Newman, just cited. Note the variation in types of problems and response. There are many ways to prevent unauthorized use of a car—not just locks and alarms. Moreover, research is showing that many of these methods are working to reduce motor vehicle theft to much lower rates than many of us recall.

Exhibit 10.2   Multiple Techniques to Prevent Diverse Auto Crimes

Crime Problem	Device or Redesign
Assassination	Armor plating Ram bars
Illegal use of rental car	GPS locator to detect speeding
Theft of major parts	Parts marking, especially microdots Tamper-proof license plates
Theft from car	Dispersed sound systems Lockable gas caps Security-coded radios
Unauthorized use, joyriding	Alarms Better door locks Ignition locks Immobilizers Steering column locks
Truck speeding	Built-in "governors" that limit speed
Vandalism	Avoiding protruding ornaments Retractable aerials

SOURCE: These ideas are drawn from R. V. Clarke and G. Newman, "Modifying Criminogenic Products: What Role for Government?" in R. V. Clarke and G. Newman, eds., *Designing Out Crime From Products and Systems* (Monsey, NY: Criminal Justice Press, 2005) (Volume 18 in *Crime Prevention Studies* series).

Even thrill-seekers can sometimes be thwarted. Joyriders prefer to steal fast cars. Suppose such cars were manufactured with a special code required to go fast. Without that code, a joyrider would get no joy, even if he were able to steal the car itself. The owner would make sure not to give that code to the parking lot attendant, or to his nephew who borrows the car sometimes. I think these examples make my main point that crime prevention can be as resourceful as offenders, if it makes the effort.

Steps Backward

Not all gains against crime remain forever. Consider the remarkable decline in motorcycle and motorbike theft with the introduction and enforcement of helmet laws.[34] Having to wear helmets interferes with spontaneous theft. Unfortunately, manufacturers in some Asian countries have built motorbikes with a compartment to hold the helmet and a weak lock to protect it. The effect has been a new wave of thefts. Apparently, owners did not like to carry their helmets, and did not understand their crime vulnerability. You can see that adaptation can lead to more crime, not less. Let me predict that some car manufacturers will revert to cheap locks to cut costs, and that thieves will know what to do about it.

Overview

Arguably, human criminal tendencies are a constant, or at least do not vary as much as many people assume. What varies most is the human ability to adapt, both in creating crime and preventing it. This chapter has shown that crimes adapt in many ways to legitimate human activities, to other crimes, and to a larger world. Crime adaptation is highly imperfect, involving substantial trials and errors. Adaptation is not unidirectional, nor is it simple. Yet crime and security respond to feedback from the larger world. Offenders also adapt. They do best if they diversify, which is easier in urban settings. These concepts of ecology help us assemble diverse facts about crime, but also raise issues that will take time to resolve.

Central Points, Chapter 10

1. New products and procedures emerge in society with quite accidental influences on crime.

2. An arms race develops between crime and crime prevention processes, with neither one gaining the upper hand forever.

3. Situational crime prevention uses a great variety of crime prevention techniques, often making crime impossible or unlikely.

4. In general, crime gives offenders definite and immediate pleasure, but the pain it gives them is slow and delayed.

Exercises

1. Think of all the ways that a screwdriver helps offenders commit crime.

2. Walk by one business and one home. List the items on the premises that an offender could easily use as tools to carry out a crime.

3. Think of one *very* specific type of crime and a simple way to stop it.

Notes

1. U.S. philosopher, author, naturalist (1817–1862). "Walden," in *The Writings of Henry David Thoreau*, vol. 2 (Boston: Houghton Mifflin, 1906). Original edition published 1854.

2. British design critic (1951–). Quoted in *The Columbia World of Quotations* (New York: Columbia University Press, 1996).

3. Widely attributed to Darwin.

4. On the other hand, his distant cousin, Alice Roosevelt Longworth (1884–1980), daughter of President Teddy Roosevelt, was less than flattering. "[The New Deal] seems more like a pack of cards thrown helter skelter, some face up, some face down, and then snatched in a free-for-all by the players. . . ." Quoted in *The Columbia World of Quotations* (New York: Columbia University Press, 1996).

5. In writing this chapter, I was strongly influenced by the work of Stephen Jay Gould, the great paleontologist, evolutionist, science writer, and baseball fan, who recently died of metastasized cancer. See these books by S. J. Gould:

Bully for Brontosaurus (New York: Norton, 1991).

The Flamingo's Smile (New York: Norton, 1985).

Hen's Teeth and Horse's Toes (New York: Norton, 1983).

The Panda's Thumb (New York: Norton, 1980).

Ever Since Darwin (New York: Norton, 1977).

6. For example, sickle cells in the bloodstream of black Africans protects against malaria. But the United States rarely has malaria, so black Americans only get the bad side: sickle-cell anemia. Sickle cells have a balanced impact in Africa, killing some but saving others. In America, their impact is imbalanced.

7. French essayist (1533–1592. "Of Presumption," Book II, Chapter 17, *The Essays of Montaigne*, trans. E. J. Trechmann (New York & London: Oxford University Press, 1927).

8. Gould was very critical of how some people exaggerate adaptation, that is, overstate natural selection as a process of perfection. See S. J. Gould, "The Evolution of Life on Earth," *Scientific American* 271, no. 4 (1994): 62–69.

9. From discussion of Stephen Jay Gould with others. See Chapter 2 in J. Brockman, ed., *The Third Culture: Beyond the Scientific Revolution* (New York: Simon and Schuster, 1995).

10. Sophistication makes good newspaper articles, but crime and its prevention, alike, advance in simple ways. Computer information is mostly stolen after removing a password from someone's desk, the codebook from the trash, or some other unsophisticated method. The "professional burglar" learns what doors are easiest to kick in, and decides to look in the victim's cookie jar because that's where his mother hides her stash of jewelry, too. Even though crime probably becomes more diversified over time, it is not likely to become more skilled. Indeed, Professor Cusson at the University of Montreal has noted the "de-skilling of crime" in recent decades. See M. Cusson, *Croissance et Decroissance du Crime* (Paris: Presses Universitaires de France, 1990).

This is consistent with the easy thefts of consumer goods from unsupervised locations. As society changed, with women working and smaller households empty during the day, unskilled burglars found easier tasks. See also D. Walsh, "The Obsolescence of Crime Forms," in R. V. Clarke, ed., *Crime Prevention Studies* (Monsey, NY: Criminal Justice Press, 1994) (Volume 2 in *Crime Prevention Studies* series).

11. The versatility of offenders is considered in the chapters dealing with crime foraging. In addition, shady but legal activities provide offenders with diverse opportunities. Thus workers in shady bars or legal brothels might well have a former life of crime.

12. R. Matthews, "Developing More Effective Strategies for Curbing Prostitution," in R. Clarke, ed., *Situational Crime Prevention: Successful Case Studies,* 2nd ed. (Guilderland, NY: Harrow and Heston, 1997). Available from the Center for Problem-oriented Policing, www.popcenter.org (accessed November 5, 2005). See also M. S. Scott, "Street Prostitution" (Washington, DC: U.S. Department of Justice, 2002) (Problem-Oriented Guides for Police Series 2). Available from the Center for Problem-oriented Policing, www.popcenter.org (accessed November 5, 2005).

13. See
   a. P. Ekblom, "Can We Make Crime Prevention Adaptive by Learning From Other Evolutionary Struggles?" *Studies on Crime and Crime Prevention* 8 (1998): 27–51. Available from http://www.e-doca.net/Resources/Articles/Can%20we%20make% 20crime%20prevention%20adaptive.pdf (accessed September 9, 2005).
   b. P. Ekblom, "Gearing Up Against Crime: A Dynamic Framework to Help Designers Keep Up With the Adaptive Criminal in a Changing World," *International Journal of Risk, Security and Crime Prevention* 214 (1997): 249–265. Available from http://www.homeoffice.gov.uk/rds/pdfs/risk.pdf (accessed September 4, 2005).
   c. P. Ekblom, "Future Crime Prevention—A 'Mindset Kit' for the Seriously Foresighted" (2000). Available from UK Foresight Programme, www.foresight .gov.uk (accessed November 15, 2005).

14. See item c. in previous endnote.

15. Ecologists have sometimes debated about which is more important, the *individual* adapting to the larger environment, or the *population* engaged in the same process. I suspect that neither side can be dismissed. Each corn plant must find the sun amid the crowd, but the population of corn plants must survive the insects that gnaw at them all.

16. Ecologists sometimes argue whether adaptation is holistic for the human species or mainly for individual organisms. Perhaps these two forces develop in tandem and even in conflict. What is good for one is sometimes good for all, sometimes bad for all. What is good for all is sometimes bad for one. The interplay of these forces in a complex world includes crime within a highly imperfect adaptive process.

17. Nor did all types of suburbs display the same crime patterns. For example, those containing shopping malls experienced a disproportionate share of crime.

18. The word "trials" is plural for a reason. First, the pressures of life are not in a single direction toward a single end through a single route. Second, it includes not only the paths consciously attempted by an intelligent being, but also those routes taken without forethought. Third, it includes the trials imposed on individual organisms by larger nature. This triple meaning captures the nature of environmental adversity and the need to respond to it. And

so it is with crime. The offender who tries the same offense once more might encounter environmental resistance, failure, and a need to shift gears. If he tries a new criminal act or a different method, he might succeed or fail, and still need to shift. The person who seeks to prevent crime will also have to make adjustments over time.

19. See G. Newman and R. V. Clarke, *Superhighway Robbery: Preventing E-commerce Crime* (Cullompton, Devon, UK: Willan, 2003).

20. M. Killias, "The Opening and Closing of Breaches: A Theory on Crime Waves, Law Creation and Crime Prevention," *European Journal of Criminology* 3, no. 1 (2006): 11–31.

21. Note that:
   a. Eras differ greatly: Robbery quintupled from 1950 to 1990, while assault declined dramatically from 1850 to 1950.
   b. A single crime category experiences major shifts: Theft doubled in one "era," slowly decreased in the next, then quadrupled, and was stable in the most recent period.
   c. Some eras have a general crime wave: In 1950–1990, each type of crime increased greatly.
   d. Related crimes do not always go together: In the earliest period, homicide doubled, while assault was stable. In the latest period, homicide was stable, but assault increased 70 percent.
   e. Men and women do not always change together: The 1850–1950 decline in homicide mortality applied to males only.

22. L. C. Gould, "The Changing Structure of Property Crime in an Affluent Society," *Social Forces* 48 (1969): 50–59.

23. For a review, see J. Tedeschi and R. B. Felson, *Violence, Aggression and Coercive Action* (Washington, DC: APA Books, 1994).

24. But even after a person has an illicit idea from the media, the larger environment is usually the source of opportunities, rewards, and punishments. That environment need not provide the crime opportunities at all. Or if it provides an illegal chance, it might also confront the offender with less pleasure than pain for taking that chance. In some cases, the mass media might provide not only ideas for what to try, but also direct rewards. A few crimes receive tremendous media attention, and can thus feed the notoriety and vanity of the offender. In the case of terrorism, publicity becomes the means to scare people or even the end itself. In order to understand the uneven interplay between crime and the mass media, we need to know the type of offender, the circumstances, and the offender's goals.

25. See G. Laycock, "Operation Identification, or the Power of Publicity," *Security Journal* 2 (1991). Reprinted in R. V. Clarke, ed., *Situational Crime Prevention: Successful Case Studies* (Albany, NY: Harrow and Heston, 1991).

26. P. Ekblom, "Less Crime, by Design," lecture at Royal Society of Arts, October 2000. Available from the European Designing Out Crime Association, http://www.e-doca .net/Resources/Lectures/Less%20Crime%20by%20Design.htm#thinking_thief (accessed September 4, 2005).

27. On the cell phone abuse, see R. V. Clarke, R. Kemper, and L. Wyckof, "Controlling Cell Phone Fraud in the U.S.: Lessons for the U.K. Foresight Prevention Initiative," *Security Journal* 14 (2005): 7–22. Also see M. Natarajan, R. V. Clarke, and B. D. Johnson, "Telephones as Facilitators of Drug Dealing: A Research Agenda," *European Journal of Criminal Policy and Research* 3 (2005): 137–154.

28. R. V. Clarke and G. Newman, eds., *Designing Out Crime from Products and Systems* (Monsey, NY: Criminal Justice Press, 2005) (Volume 18 in *Crime Prevention Studies* series).

29. For these two examples, see Ekblom in prior endnote.

30. See G. S. Bajpa, *Crime Reduction Through Situational Crime Prevention: A Study in the United Kingdom,* report conducted as Visiting Commonwealth Fellow, Department of Criminology, University of Leicester, UK (2004). Available from Dr. Bajpa's website, http://forensic.to/webhome/drgsbajpai/ (accessed September 5, 2005). I am indebted to Professor Ken Pease for informing me of this point.

31. G. Bichler and R. V. Clarke, "Eliminating Pay Phone Toll Fraud at the Port Authority Bus Terminal in Manhattan," in R. V. Clarke, ed., *Preventing Mass Transit Crime* (Monsey, NY: Criminal Justice Press, 1996) (Volume 6 in *Crime Prevention Studies* series). Also see Clarke and Newman, work cited in endnote 27.

32. See

    a. J. P. Shepherd, and others, "Risk of Occupational Glass Injury in Bar Staff," *Injury* 25 (1994): 219–220.

    b. J. P. Shepherd, R. H. Hugget, and G. Kidner, "Impact Resistance of Bar Glasses," *Journal of Trauma* 35 (1993): 936–938.

    c. C. L. Davey, R. Cooper, and M. Press, *Design Against Crime Case Studies* (Salford, UK: The Design Policy Partnership, University of Salford and Sheffield Hallam University, 2002).

33. R. V. Clarke, "Deterring Obscene Phone Callers: The New Jersey Experience," in R. V. Clarke, ed., *Situational Crime Prevention: Successful Case Studies* (Albany, NY: Harrow and Heston, 1992).

34. P. Mayhew, R. V. Clarke, and D. Elliott, "Motorcycle Theft, Helmet Legislation and Displacement," *Howard Journal of Criminal Justice* 28 (1989): 1–8. See also B. Webb, "Steering Column Locks and Motor Vehicle Theft: Evaluations From Three Countries," in R. V. Clarke, ed., *Crime Prevention Studies* (Monsey, NY: Criminal Justice Press, 1994) (Volume 2 in *Crime Prevention Studies* series). Available from the Center for Problem-oriented Policing, http://www.popcenter.org/Library/CrimePrevention/Volume%2002/04webb.pdf (accessed September 4, 2005).

PART III

Crime's Relationships

Life did not take over the globe by combat, but by networking.

—Lynn Margulis and Dorion Sagan[1]

The two most engaging powers of an author are to make new things familiar, and familiar things new.

—Samuel Johnson[2]

. . . like the famous family of trapeze artists, they have jobs requiring a strong measure of interdependence. They also have a very long way to fall.

—Gwenda Blair[3]

. . . to live together for a period, and then go our separate ways.

—President John F. Kennedy[4]

11

Crime Symbiosis

The linkages between a crime and its settings, habitat, niches, and ecosystem are not simply abstractions. These linkages involve tangible flows of resources between offenders and a larger world. Some of these resources are entirely impersonal—such as the moonlight that illuminates a rear door, making it easier to break in. But other resources are quite personal, indeed, leading us to discuss crime symbioses. In Greek, symbiosis literally means, "living together." More specifically, *crime symbiosis is a close and prolonged relationship between two parties, providing illicit benefit to at least one of them.*[5]

Symbiosis is more focused when preceded by an article or pronoun, such as "a" symbiosis, "this" symbiosis, or "that" symbiosis. For example, a particular drug dealer and her particular customers might have a symbiotic relationship. But when the word "symbiosis" stands alone, it implies a *general* form of interdependence, such as the symbiosis between many drug sellers and drug buyers. Symbioses take many forms, as we see in this chapter and those following.

A criminal cannot survive without the sun in the sky, but we do not call that a symbiosis. Nor is a grave robber symbiotic with the cadaver he digs up, for symbioses link *living* things to one another. We cannot brush aside crime symbioses with nonhuman species. Marihuana cultivators and game poachers relate symbiotically to plants and animals, respectively. Cattle rustlers are symbionts[6] with the cattle they steal. This is not just a crime of the cowboy days. In a *Washington Post* story (April 11, 2004), Rene Sanchez reported that the high-protein diets in the United States have led to a resurgence of cattle rustling across the western prairie. But most crime symbioses are between human parties, as we shall see.

Symbiosis, Legitimate or Not

A criminal activity can be symbiotic not only with other criminal activities, but also with fully legitimate activities or with marginal activities. Exhibit 11.1 offers examples of all three. Two criminal activities are often symbiotic, such as burglars trading information about their targets. Offenders can be linked in illegal chains of assistance, finding out from others about a diverse set of buyers for stolen goods, or what the police are up to. Professor Pierre Tremblay of the University of Montreal calls our attention to the mutual assistance of offenders before, during, and after a given offense.[7] From interviewing offenders, he has discovered significant and varied assistance, especially for adult offenders with ongoing involvement in crime.

Crime symbioses with fully legitimate activities are also common. Consider legitimate law firms holding money in trust for their clients. Sometimes a lawyer within such a firm steals some of that money for himself. His illegal activity is symbiotic with his legal activity. Another example is the interplay between stolen car parts and the legal car parts market.[8] A very different example is the late-night restaurant that lives off sales to local prostitutes and drug dealers, never touching crime directly.

Exhibit 11.1   Crime Symbiosis in Three Directions

Crime Is Symbiotic With	Examples	
Another criminal activity	Burglars help each other find victims.	A drug addict feeds off shoplifting.
A marginal or dubious activity	A legal prostitute sells illegal drugs.	An hourly hotel houses illegal prostitutes.
A fully legitimate activity	A lawyer nibbles from a trust account.	A restaurant welcomes local drug dealers.

Professors Paul and Patricia Brantingham at Simon Fraser University refer to certain locations as crime generators and criminal attractors.[9] High schools routinely relate to drug use and attract drug dealers, despite "drug free school zone" policies.[10] Potential drug traders take advantage of check-cashing stores, bars, liquor stores, drug-treatment centers and homeless shelters—all common locations for drug markets. Crime can even be symbiotic with police stations, since officers park their civilian cars just outside, leaving easy theft targets for long periods.

Remarkable stories have come to light about legitimate organizations or persons fostering marginal or illegal activities. Professors, police officers, and others in respectable positions have been revealed as owners of buildings or businesses with shady or illegal components. Oral histories indicate that the U.S. military has sanctioned houses of ill repute during various wars, not widely known back home.[11]

Dr. Mike Sutton of the British Home Office is an expert on the fencing of stolen goods through legitimate outlets.[12] Many stolen goods are sold in pubs, secondhand stores, pawn shops,[13] and flea markets. In modern society, Internet sales increasingly facilitate the effort to unload stolen goods on non-participants in crime. The general linkages between illegitimate and legitimate activities are quite widespread. Professors Gloria Laycock and Barry Webb of the University College, London, have brought to our attention how legal outlets for used car parts absorb stolen parts, to the benefit of auto thieves.[14] Taking advantage of the symbiotic relationship between illegal and legal activities, authorities have sometimes learned to monitor body shops or used part outlets.[15]

Hence knowing crime's symbioses is very important for crime control. If we know how crimes feed on one another, and upon legal activities, we can also know how to choke off some of their essential nutrients.

This chapter neglects two types of symbiosis relevant to crime but not directly involving offenders. Legitimate activities can form symbiotic links to thwart crime. Thus two merchants can cooperate in looking out for check fraudsters. Legitimate and marginal activities can also cooperate. Thus a shady bar might assist police under certain circumstances in return for police protection in extreme situations, even though the bar works with offenders under other circumstances. Complex chains of symbiosis are part of life in the tough city. Next we turn to the interplay between overt crime and shady activities that are not quite criminal—the most interesting category of symbiosis.

Crime and Marginal Activities

The Dutch language has an excellent word that we don't have in English—*gedogen*. It means something like "to tolerate." It refers to activities that are not exactly legal and not exactly illegal. The Dutch are famous for tolerating prostitution and soft drugs. But let's not kid ourselves—most American authorities allow these law violations and look the other way, even if they pretend to do something. The Dutch don't pretend.

Legality and acceptance have at least four blends:

1. Illegal and despised

2. Illegal but tolerated

3. Legal but disliked

4. Legal and acceptable

Examples vary from place to place. Urban areas are usually more likely to look the other way compared to small towns. Nonresidential areas are usually more tolerant than residential areas. Child prostitution is illegal and despised in most places. In American cities, unobtrusive prostitution by women 18 and over is often tolerated, despite the fact that it's illegal. In European nations, such prostitution is disliked but often legal. In most nations, going to school is legal and acceptable. Of course, it's all a matter of degree.

My point is that some activities are legal but disliked by the public. We can call these marginal activities.[16] Because they are disliked, they are often carried out by unsavory characters, or located in dubious places. That's what's interesting.

Criminal activities often interact with marginal activities—those legal activities that are strongly disapproved by society or large segments of it (see Exhibit 11.1). For example, a society that legalizes prostitution often continues to hold it in some disdain. A legal but shady activity can still become embroiled in other activities that are clearly illegal, such as

- intimidation to take over the sex business,
- hiring underage prostitutes,
- illegal importing or recruiting of prostitutes, or
- selling illegal drugs to legal sex customers.[17]

Although the United States generally bans prostitution, most states permit sexually stimulating shows. While disapproved by large segments of the community, these shows have a substantial clientele, providing legal entrée for some illegal prostitutes to find customers. Local areas vary by how far they allow sex shows to go, but that does not mean establishments remain on the legal side of that line. Shady establishments paid mostly in cash can easily evade taxes. In short, shady activities often have symbiotic relationships with crime itself. Even in the Netherlands, careful public regulation of prostitution has not prevented its infiltration by organized crime.[18]

Legal gambling provides another example of how sometimes legal activities are still marginal and linked to crime. In Japan, pachinko parlors offer legal gambling,[19] but are often owned and managed by organized criminals known as yakuza. In the United States, legal casinos for most of the history of Las Vegas were involved with organized crime. Even in recent years, after organized criminals lost their substantial control of casinos, employees and management have probably continued to skim cash off the top, evading taxes in so doing.

Sometimes different persons carry out the marginal versus the illegal activities, in symbiotic proximity. At other times, the very same persons mix marginal and illicit activities. Thus an exotic dancer or barmaid uses a legal role (in a seedy establishment) to solicit illegally for sex or to sell illicit drugs. Women who age out of prostitution find a second career assisting prostitution or serving drinks in seedy establishments. In most modern nations, it is now legal to sell sexually explicit materials involving adults to other adults; nonetheless, organized criminals can become involved in pornography's production, distribution, or sale. Places or websites selling pornography legally can also be linked to outlets for prostitution or other illegal sex encounters. In addition, illegal sales to minors can easily supplement the profits of an otherwise legal pornography business.

The Crime and Misconduct Commission in Queensland, Australia, recognizes links between shady and illegal activities. It studied adult entertainment, ranging from striptease to sexually explicit performances.[20] Sometimes legal activities were not linked to illegal activities, but other times the link was found. Sometimes exotic dancers and owners of adult entertainment businesses were involved. In a small number of cases, illicit drugs were also connected to these businesses. Even though this Australian state licenses some brothels, the majority of prostitutes operate outside the legal framework. You can readily see that legalizing prostitution on paper does not necessarily bring it under state control.

Any embarrassing behavior, even if it is legal, must normally be concealed from somebody. That exposes the actor to blackmail, shakedowns, and conflicts with others. Offenders can take illegal advantage of customers ashamed to call police. Thus it might be rather safe to rob a customer purchasing embarrassing but legal goods or services.

On the other hand, an empirical study in Charlotte, North Carolina, finds that adult businesses do not enhance crime in the vicinity.[21] Andrew Ryder, an urban expert, notes that adult entertainment areas have changed their character in recent years.[22] We should not assume that all vice in all forms contributes to crime or is symbiotic with it. That's an empirical question.

Perhaps alcohol consumption offers the strongest symbioses between legal and illegal activity. *Legal* bars can act *illegally* in many ways, including serving drinks to those underage or persons already drunk. Legal bars can continue providing drinks after hours. They can set people up for drunk driving. They can foster drug violations and other offenses, on site or in nearby times and places. The links between alcohol and crime are manifold, again reminding us that legal and illegal activities are intricately intertwined. Yet well-managed drinking establishments avoid causing problems and might even contribute to the stability and security of an area. At the other extreme, some bars cross an invisible line, becoming rather direct crime participants.

Despite the exceptions and nuances, we cannot deny the general conclusion: Crime and shady activities draw from one another. Owners and employees of shady bars or pubs can make good money from bad behaviors. They might avoid violating the letter of the law themselves, but make a living helping others do just that. It's quite a challenge to explore the complex web of relationships among criminal activities, shady activities, and legitimate activities.

Three Types of Symbiosis

To classify crime interdependence, first ask these two questions:

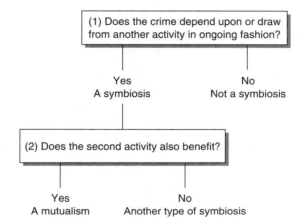

These two questions help us understand interdependence in nature, including the world of crime. The ecological literature offers three basic types of symbiosis, based on how the counterpart is affected:

- *Mutualism:* both parties benefit
- *Parasitism:* first party benefits, but the counterpart is harmed
- Forms of passive assistance, where one party benefits from the other, without helping or harming it much[23]

Exhibit 11.2 sums six interdependencies, including these three forms of symbiosis. This exhibit can help readers avoid getting lost in the following chapters as they deal with these types of interdependence.[24] We shall also need to be more precise about what it means for one activity to depend on another.

Getting Specific About Crime Symbiosis

To understand a crime symbiosis, we should specify exactly what benefit one party draws from another. We say, for short, "The drug dealer and drug buyer have a symbiotic relationship." But what we really mean is that a person *in the role of* drug dealer has such a relationship. Even more precisely,

Exhibit 11.2   Six Forms of Crime Interdependence

		Counterpart (Y)		
		Benefit +	Harm −	Neither 0
First Party (X)	+	*Mutualism* (X) sells drugs to (Y).	*Parasitism* (X) repeatedly steals small items from store (Y).	*Passive Assistance* (X) uses (Y) to reach illegal customers.
	−		*Competition* Prostitutes (X) and (Y) compete for clients.	*Amensalism* Public drunks (X) drive away customers for drug dealer (Y).
	0			*Neutralism* Auto thief (X) and shoplifter (Y) coexist.

NOTE: Italics designate symbioses.

we mean that the drug buyer needs to get his drugs from the dealer, who benefits by being paid.

Perhaps this dealer interacts in one way with the drug buyer, another way with his supplier, a third way while shoplifting the next day, a fourth way in giving his girlfriend a stolen ring, a fifth way in using ill-gotten money to buy beer for friends, and a sixth way in making a dramatic contribution in church on Sunday. He is really a person occupying different roles, only one of which is "a drug dealer."[25] This is not unique to crime. A panda interacts one way with the bamboo on which it feeds, another way with its mate, and a third way with offspring. Human symbionts diversify their sustenance patterns; and so it is with offenders. A person can act simultaneously in legal and illegal roles. A taxi driver carries contraband along with a legitimate passenger. A cashier has sticky fingers while performing legitimate duties.[26]

A person cannot be self-symbiotic. Symbioses can only occur *between organisms*, such as people or organizations. Yet we speak of symbioses in three ways:

Most precise: "Once a day the taxi driver drops off some drugs for a dealer he knows."

Less precise: "The taxi driver and drug dealer are symbiotic."

Least precise: "Transportation activities and drug dealing are symbiotic."

We have to be specific, but sometimes it's easier to use the middle statement for shorthand.[27]

Of course, shorthand terms can get us into trouble. Compare the shorthand words "pimp" and "madam"—both associated with prostitution. A pimp procures customers for a prostitute, while a madam runs a brothel. We think of the first as male and the second as female. But sometimes a female acts as a pimp or a male acts like a madam. These words interfere with research by prejudicing the results. We have to figure out exactly who does what, without letting the words become blinders.

Crime Symbiosis and Organizations

An organization is more than an office building with chairs and tables. Every organization, including every bar, hotel, or university, can be considered alive, and thus can be involved symbiotically in crime.[28] The seven special requirements of life, presented in Chapter 2, apply to every college or university. It has an organized structure, an ability to adapt, a metabolism, moving activities, and a potential for growth. It responds to stimuli. A college or university can even reproduce by spawning new departments and research projects, hiring new people, inducting new students, and building new campuses.

Modern organizations have definite property boundaries. They have symbiotic relationships with employees, customers, and others. Offenders form symbioses with an organization, or use its facilities to abuse others. So we must study symbioses not only among persons but also between persons and organizations.

Why Crime Symbiosis Develops and Persists

Much of human life is organized and ongoing, and so it is with crime. The same counterparts in crime might continue their relationships over a period of time. Sometimes it is easier to exploit the same or similar victims rather than search for another. New crime targets are not always easy to discover. Often it is easier to buy drugs from the same seller or otherwise continue criminal linkages. It is sometimes expedient for an offender to find specific environmental niches that make crime easier to repeat over time. Thus offenders devise relatively stable or ongoing criminal relationships with others, or exploit those relationships that already exist. If offenders had no criminal symbioses, they would surely develop some. History offers us a parallel: Hunting and gathering societies evolved into planting and cultivating societies in order to assure their food supply. Some offenders prefer an ongoing source of criminal sustenance.

Yet it is sometimes easier for offenders to find a new crime target every time. Societies filled with cars easy to steal or steal from, or stores with unsupervised goods, provide offenders what they need without requiring symbioses. It does not always make sense to go back to the same victims, who might be ready for the next attempt. Communities with drug corners make it easy for participants in drug sales to find each other without specific symbioses between a specific buyer and seller.[29] Anonymity has its benefit when carrying out crime, so offenders have reasons to avoid relationships. Offenders must consider the benefits and dangers of working with one another over time; and students of crime need to study why some offenders find ongoing crime relationships, while others do not. In any case, crime symbiosis remains an important topic.

Few People per Crime Symbiosis

In the simplest case, symbioses involve two parties, such as the accomplices in a burglary, or the bank robber and his lookout. Research on co-offenders finds that youths seldom carry out their crimes in groups larger than two or three, while adult offenders prefer to commit crimes alone or with one other. Even members of large gangs commit most of their actual crimes in small groups.[30] We can stretch the term "symbiosis" to include three youths cooperating simultaneously in a burglary. But when the number of parties gets larger, several distinct but related symbioses are probably underway.

Remote Crime Symbioses

Eagles, vultures, and other large birds can spot their prey from 3,000 or 4,000 meters. Sharks and homing pigeons apparently respond to and navigate by the earth's magnetic field, enabling them to go vast distances, converging symbiotically without requiring constant contact. With modern communications technology, humans have caught up with and surpassed other species in the ability to communicate over vast distances. These advances make more remote symbioses possible. Many modern drug transactions are arranged via cell phone and the Internet. Prostitutes and customers find one another in similar fashion. New criminal uses of the Internet seem to emerge every day.[31] Some symbiotic crimes occur without any face-to-face contact whatever. For example, child pornography rings can develop as providers and consumers become aware of one another through Internet contacts, but need no personal contact at all to exchange or deliver.

Settings That Mix Everything

Washington Square Park in New York City mixes a variety of legal, shady, and illegal activities. Their relative strength and the openness of illegal activities depend on what's happening in city government, the level of complaints, who's the mayor at the time, and whether the newspapers are looking.

A more interesting mix of legal, shady, and illegal activities is found in very large nightclubs and dance clubs in certain large cities.[32] In these settings, illegal activities can be camouflaged within shady activities, within legal activities. The line between one and the other is itself murky. Officials have sometimes interfered with these symbioses. Professor Ross Homel and his colleagues at Griffiths University in Australia have figured out a number of policy efforts that have successfully reduced violence and other crime on Australia's Gold Coast.[33]

So far this chapter has introduced the concept of symbiosis and its application to crime. I have explained in particular that criminal activities are often symbiotic with legitimate and marginal activities. Now I turn to the types of crime symbiosis, and how we should *think* about crime symbiosis.

Interdependence Is Not Always Pure and Simple

Karl Popper noted that "Science may be described as the art of systematic over-simplification."[34]

Types of symbiosis are just categories to help us think. Real life complicates symbiosis (and other interdependencies) by mixing up categories. Consider the drug dealer who stands outside a liquor store. If the dealer and store owner draw customers for one another, it is mutualism. If the store loses money bit by bit while the drug dealer gains, this is parasitism. If the offender takes advantage of the traffic, but neither helps nor harms the store's sales, then commensalism is present. If the dealer and owner are in a zero-sum situation, then competition is underway (a nonsymbiotic form of interdependence).[35] The predominant form of relationship might vary by hour, by store, by drug dealer, and in the judgment of the parties involved. Ultimately it is an empirical question how much one form of interdependence occurs in contrast to another. For tangible evidence, we can observe how close dealers stand to the door and how often the store owners try to chase them away. Perhaps the issue is one of quantity. A few inadvertent prostitutes do not necessarily interfere with the train or bus station. But a good station manager does not tolerate drunk people hanging around or prostitutes soliciting openly. The upcoming chapters further explore how certain criminal acts depend on one another and on noncrime situations.

Symbioses also mix together at the community level. Consider vice districts in big cities. Some such districts combine prostitution, drugs, and legal adult businesses in the same area. To some extent, they benefit from one another—mutualism. But prostitutes compete among one another for the same customers and drug sellers compete among one another for the same buyers, while prostitutes *and* drug sellers compete with one another for the same corners or coveys.

If these offenders are completely competitive, why do they locate in the same area? Perhaps the city's abandonment of that district allows them all to fill the abandoned area. Or perhaps they fish at the same stream, such as the pedestrian traffic fanning out from a train station, or downtown workers leaving for home when the job is over. Even competing offenders might need each other for some purposes. A common vice area assists joint protection and general marketing. The public usually knows where the vice district is, and a customer does not have to be familiar with any particular prostitute or drug seller. Just going to the vicinity usually suffices. As the song says,

> You can get anything you want,
>
> at Alice's restaurant.[36]

Competing offenders can also alert one another about police interference or dangerous customers. Co-presence provides group security (see Chapters 18 and 19 on defenses). Moreover, different offenders purchase goods and services from one another, such as prostitutes who buy from drug dealers, even as they compete for corners. So you can see that symbioses in real life mix together.

Colossalism

Most of crime's interactions with other activities are small and local, but that is not always so. "Colossalism" refers to a huge activity that creates local crime niches at a large scale.[37]

Sometimes a very large organization tramples local environments, with tremendous consequences for crime. Introducing a huge military base can help create a massive illicit ecosystem. No more dramatic presence existed than the combination of Clark Air Force Base and the U.S. Naval Base at Subic Bay in the Philippines. One merchant marine captain described Magsaysay Drive in Olongapo City as

> a collection of nightclubs, bars, brothels, and associated businesses that rivals any red light district in the world. When you leave the tranquility of the port and the Naval Base, you are assaulted by "shore pilots" and money changers at the gate . . . I remember taking a photo of a "V.D. Clinic" with many smiling women waiving from the doors and windows.[38]

Nostalgic webpages produced by former service personnel document the wide-open scene, with some 500 bars hosting prostitution. In 1992 (after a political change in the Philippines and the serious volcanic eruption of Mount Pinatubo) the U.S. government closed these two military bases. This sent a shockwave through the local crime scene, removing important niches for prostitution, child prostitution, sex slavery, robbery, theft, assault, and ancillary crimes.

Not all colossalism is as big as that. A major urban renewal project can crush the local crime community or the local ability to control crime, or both.[39] Often construction sites generate very high rates of theft, ranging from tools and equipment to appliances awaiting installation.

The arrival as well as departure of something huge can have a major impact on crime—with little direct impact on itself. The impact of the colossus is sometimes good, and sometimes bad, but always tremendous. Its variations do not allow me to classify it within a single cell of Exhibit 11.1. We can readily see that crime niches can be created or destroyed on a large scale. But some crime niches are destroyed on a small scale, among families.

Family, Crime, and Complex Symbiosis

Links between family life and crime are a topic of long and important discussion. Professor Travis Hirschi explained that attachments to family and involvement with family activities provide social control, discouraging crime participation by youths.[40] Professors Gottfredson and Hirschi attributed acquisition of self-control to preschool years.[41] Family researchers find that simple supervision is an important inhibitor of crime participation.[42]

Yet it is not easy to study family effects on crime, perhaps because the family itself is such an elaborate web of interdependence. A single family can produce an extremely complex array of crime interdependencies:

Family mutualism: Two siblings trade stolen goods.

Family parasitism: A younger child nibbles money from his mother's purse, while his teenage brother siphons off his father's liquor. The oldest siblings go to college and send home the bills.

Family passive assistance: Mother picks up her son after his thefts are completed.

Family competition: Two siblings fight over limited resources.[43]

Family neutralism: A brother and a sister avoid interference with one another's illegal behaviors.

To detail the family web of activities as linked to crime, I would have to write another book.

Crime Can Be Close but Not Closely Related

Sometimes a crime participant and a proximate counterpart have no direct impact on one another. This is called *neutralism.* Consider the shoplifter inside the store and the auto thief outside. Their offenses do not interact or have any direct interdependence. On the other hand, they are so close and have sufficient indirect association that they deserve their own category. The store generates crime opportunities for both, so their crimes are not totally unrelated. Henry Wadsworth Longfellow's poem tells of

Ships that pass in the night, and speak to each other in passing,

Only a signal shown and a distant voice in the darkness . . .[44]

Sometimes offenders in the same area communicate even less.

We cannot ignore neutralism, for we need to be aware that nearby criminal acts are not always intertwined. Consider drug sales in the park. In some cases, the sellers have taken over an urban park and driven out legitimate activities. But in other cases a few quiet sellers leave everybody else alone. Birds sing, children swing, elderly ladies chat, somebody sells cotton candy, enjoying the spring weather while one or two guys sell marihuana. We need to distinguish those offenders who are content with this arrangement from those who insist on taking over the territory. I recall the single beggar in Park Slope, Brooklyn, who sat down between two stores and politely put out his hat. The community left him alone. On the other hand, panhandlers who are numerous, aggressive, or in motion interfere with others.

Neutralism occurs because some offenders need little space and make few demands on other offenders, and even leave legitimate activities unbothered. Quiet thieves or dealers minimize their intrusions and can coexist with the community. A call girl with a discreet apartment and referrals can work quietly, unlike a flagrant streetwalker.

The "broken windows" theory of policing brings the issue of neutralism to the fore.[45] The policy recommendation is to prevent minor crimes from growing within the community, lest they feed into much more serious community crime problems later. Often that works, but not always.

When the New York City subway system deployed better turnstiles, fewer people jumped over to ride for free. After that, robberies within the subway system declined noticeably.[46] But not all small offenses have consequences for major offenses. Subway officials learned to reduce graffiti painting greatly, an important accomplishment in its own right.[47] But this success had no larger impact on other offenses in the system. In ecological terms, graffiti has a neutral relationship to other subway crimes—but not a neutral relationship to the larger community that it defaces, or its quality of life.[48] We cannot assume that all minor crime is directly linked to all major crime, or that all legitimate and illegitimate activities are clearly intertwined. In studying crime, it is very important, indeed, to find out which proximate offenses have a special impact on one another and which do not. It is fascinating to note that some very distant activities are interdependent, while some very proximate activities are largely insulated from one another.

Overview

Crime symbioses involve counterparts in relationships that must benefit at least one. These counterparts can include organizations as well as individuals, involved in various illegal, legitimate, or shady activities. Crime symbioses usually involve very few persons at once, but complex and compounded crime symbioses are possible. Numerous criminal activities depend tangibly and literally upon other activities. Without these relationships, some crimes could not thrive and others would not exist at all. Society can sometimes reduce crime significantly by tampering with its symbiotic requirements.

Central Points, Chapter 11

1. One type of crime can be symbiotic with another. It can also be symbiotic with conventional activities and legal but marginal activities.

2. Crime symbioses can develop with high schools, universities, check-cashing stores, bars, liquor stores, drug-treatment centers, homeless shelters, public housing, and police stations.

3. Even lone offenders might depend on symbiotic relationships to unload the stolen goods.

4. Sometimes the offender draws benefits from others, neither helping nor harming them in the process.

Exercises

1. What symbioses assist underage drinking?

2. How can a drinking establishment be symbiotic with criminal activity?

3. Some local thefts need relationships, and others do not. Give an example of each.

4. "Many city police departments transfer officers frequently from one neighborhood to another." Explain this policy, using the concept of symbiosis.

Notes

1. *Microcosmos: Four Billion Years of Evolution From Our Microbial Ancestors* (New York: Summit Books, 1986).

2. It is possible that the above and common version of this quotation is really a paraphrase of the author. In Johnson's *Lives of the Poets*, discussing Alexander Pope's poem, *The Rape of the Lock*, Johnson wrote,

> In this work are exhibited in a very high degree the two most engaging powers of an author: new things are made familiar, and familiar things are made new.

That was tracked down by Dr. Mardy Grothe of www.chiasmus.com (accessed September 8, 2005). Inquire online for Johnson's *Lives of the Poets* (London: George Bell and Sons, 1890). Your best bet is probably Project Gutenberg, which has online access at no charge, http://www.gutenberg.org/etext/9823.

3. Speaking about *Newsweek* editors, quoted in *Simpson's Contemporary Quotations,* (New York: Houghton Mifflin, 1988).

4. When asked to comment on the press in general, news conference, May 9, 1962. *Public Papers of the Presidents of the United States: John F. Kennedy, 1962* (Washington, DC: U.S. Government Printing Office, 1962).

5. We can refer to the underlying principle of symbiosis in the singular, while describing different forms as "symbioses." Symbiosis sometimes refers to generic relationships. For

example, the tick feeds off the dog. But ticks will bite any warm-blooded animal they can find. For crime symbiosis, we usually refer to ongoing relationships rather than fleeting ones.

6. Two spellings are found in the ecological literature, "symbiont" and "symbiant."

7. P. Tremblay, "Searching for Suitable Co-offenders," in R. V. Clarke and M. Felson, eds., *Routine Activity and Rational Choice* (New Brunswick, NJ: Transaction Books, 1993) (Volume 5 in *Advances in Criminological Theory,* a series).

8. See F. Gant and P. Grabowsky, "The Stolen Vehicle Parts Market," *Trends and Issues* 251 (Canberra, Australia: Australian Institute of Criminology, 2001).

9. P. L. Brantingham and P. J. Brantingham, "Criminality of Place: Crime Generators and Crime Attractors," *European Journal of Criminal Policy and Research* 3 (1995): 5–26.

10. G. G. Rengert and S. Chakravorty, "Illegal Drug Sales and Drug Free School Zones," paper presented at the annual meeting of the Association of American Geographers, Chicago, March 1995. See also G. F. Rengert, *The Geography of Illegal Drugs* (Boulder, CO: Westview Press, 1996); and D. W. Roncek and A. Lobosco, "The Effect of High Schools on Crime in Their Neighborhoods," *Social Science Quarterly* 64 (1983): 598–613.

11. See
    a. Interview with William M. Coleman # 4700.0942, Harry Williams Center for Oral History, http://www.lib.lsu.edu/special/williams/ (accessed September 4, 2005).
    b. S. Sturdevant and B. Stotlsfuz, *Let the Good Times Roll: The Sale of Women's Sexual Labor Around U.S. Military Bases in the Philippines, Okinawa and the Southern Part of Korea* (Berkeley: University of California Press, 1991).
    c. P. Jones, "The U.S. Military and the Growth of Prostitution in Southeast Asia," working paper, Division of Social and Behavioral Sciences, John Brown University, Siloam Springs, Arkansas, 2004. Available from http://www.jbu.edu/academics/sbs/faculty/Navy%20and%20Asia.pdf (accessed September 4, 2005).

12. See M. Sutton, "Handling Stolen Goods and Theft: A Market Reduction Approach" (London: British Home Office, 1998) (Home Office Research Study 178). See also M. Sutton, J. Schneider, and S. Hetherington, "Tackling Theft With the Market Reduction Approach" (London: British Home Office, 2001) (Crime Reduction Research Series Paper 8). Available from http://www.homeoffice.gov.uk/rds/prgpdfs/crrs08.pdf (accessed September 4, 2005).

13. Professor Ronald V. Clarke argues that pawn shops are less significant for fencing than previously thought. I suggest that their importance will vary greatly by local conditions.

14. B. Webb and G. Laycock, "Tackling Car Crime: The Nature and Extent of the Problem" (London: British Home Office, 1992) (Crime Prevention Unit Paper 32).

15. See F. Gant and P. Grabowsky, "The Stolen Vehicle Parts Market," *Trends and Issues* 251 (Canberra, Australia: Australian Institute of Criminology, 2001).

16. Illegal but tolerated activities are also marginal in a sense, but I do not deal with that issue here.

17. See
    a. J. S. Albanese, D. K. Das, and A. Verma, eds., *Organized Crime: World Perspectives* (Upper Saddle River, NJ: Prentice Hall, 2003).
    b. J. O. Finckenauer and E. Waring, *Russian Mafia in America* (Boston: Northeastern University Press, 1998).
    c. J. B. Jacobs, C. Panarella, and J. Worthington, *Busting the Mob: United States v. Cosa Nostra* (New York: New York University Press, 1994).
    d. J. B. Jacobs with C. Friel and R. Radick, *Gotham Unbound: How New York City Was Liberated From the Grip of Organized Crime* (New York: New York University Press, 1999).

18. C. Brants, "The Fine Art of Regulated Tolerance: Prostitution in Amsterdam," *Journal of Law and Society* 25, no. 4 (1998): 621–635.

19. See work by Professor Ichiro Tanioka, including I. Tanioka, *Pachinko and Japanese Society* (Institute of Amusement Industries, Osaka University of Commerce, Osaka, Japan, 2000) (Publication Series 2).

20. See *Regulating Adult Entertainment: A Review of the Live Adult Entertainment Industry in Queensland* (Queensland, Australia: Crime and Misconduct Commission, 2004). Available from http://www.cmc.qld.gov.au/ (accessed September 4, 2005).

21. D. Linz and others, "An Examination of the Assumption That Adult Businesses Are Associated With Crime in Surrounding Areas: A Secondary Effects Study in Charlotte, North Carolina," *Law and Society Review* 38 (2004): 69–104.

22. A. Ryder, "The Changing Nature of Adult Entertainment Districts: Between a Rock and a Hard Place or Going From Strength to Strength?" *Urban Studies* 41 (2004): 1659–1686.

23. This includes *commensalism*, with one party using the unused food of the other; and *aegism*, with one party drawing protection from its counterpart. I deal with these issues in Chapter 14.

24. However, amensalism is considered in Chapter 8 instead, since it fits better with a discussion of niches.

25. Social scientists vary in their use of the word "role." It can refer to identities, expectations, actual behaviors, or some combination of these. It is common to use the word only for legitimate behaviors connected to some position in society. By that definition, an illegitimate role is an oxymoron. The essential benefit of the word is that it segments an individual's behaviors and positions. Thus it becomes useful to consider various roles someone plays in crime, whether or not any given role is legitimate by the rules of society or anybody within it.

26. This is consistent with Hawley's notion of symbiotic roles, but it is better stated in terms of activities. Crime may feed on only one legitimate activity connected with the role of cashier. The cashier's other duties, such as helping customers find the items they are seeking, need not be criminogenic at all. Moreover, the word "role" usually refers to the conventional and assigned responsibilities, not the violations carried out in the process. The use of these words has evolved over the years. Hawley uses the word "symbiosis" to mean acting in the same role, but used "commensalisms" for acting in different roles. Today, the word "symbiosis" is used more broadly to incorporate commensalisms.

27. The third statement is quite vague, especially if it stands alone. It also invites people to confuse food chains and symbioses. Many legitimate activities and crime activities are linked in chains, even if most links are not in direct symbiosis.

28. The words "organization" and "organism" share the Greek root, *organon*, which means an instrument. This further justifies treating organizations as living entities.

29. For more on outdoor drug sales, see B. A. Jacobs, *Dealing Crack: The Social World of Streetcorner Selling* (Boston: Northeastern University Press, 1999).

30. Chapter 20 reviews the research of Professor Malcolm W. Klein, relevant to this point.

31. See G. Newman and R. V. Clarke, *Superhighway Robbery: Preventing E-commerce Crime* (Cullomptom, Devon, UK: Willan, 2003).

32. See F. Measham, J. Aldridge, and H. Parker, *Dancing on Drugs: Risk, Health and Hedonism in the British Club Scene* (London: Free Association Books, 2000). Also see M. S. Scott, "Rave Parties" (2002), Center for Problem-oriented Policing, http://www.popcenter.org (accessed September 5, 2005).

33. See R. Homel and J. Clark, "The Prediction and Prevention of Violence in Pubs and Clubs," in R. V. Clarke, ed., *Crime Prevention Studies* (New York: Harrow and Heston, 1994) (Volume 3 in *Crime Prevention Studies* series). Also see R. Homel and others, "Preventing Alcohol-related Crime Through Community Action: The Surfers Paradise Safety Action Project," in R. Homel, ed., *Policing for Prevention: Reducing Crime, Public Intoxication and Injury* (Monsey, NY: Criminal Justice Press, 1997) (Volume 7 in *Crime Prevention Studies* series).

34. Anglo-Austrian philosopher (1902–1994). Quoted in "Karl Popper" (n.d.), Wikipedia Encyclopedia, http://en.wikipedia.org/wiki/Karl_Raimund_Popper (accessed November 9, 2005).

35. To the extent this is for protection, it reflects epizoism, a topic discussed in Chapter 15.

36. Arlo Guthrie, *Alice's Restaurant* (song) (West Chester, PA: Appleseed Music, 1967).

37. The term colossal comes from the *Colossus* of Rhodes, a huge building built by the Greeks in 304 BC. The word "colossalism" is somewhat dubious. I have to take personal responsibility for using it to understand crime.

38. Captain John McDonnell LLC and Internet Guide to Freighter Travel http://www.geocities.com/freighterman.geo/subic_bay.html (accessed September 3, 2005). See also P. Jones, "The U.S. Military and the Growth of Prostitution in Southeast Asia," working paper, Division of Social and Behavioral Sciences, John Brown University, Siloam Springs, Arkansas, 2004. Available from http://www.jbu.edu/academics/sbs/faculty/Navy%20and%20Asia.pdf (accessed September 4, 2005).

39. Although much of the construction impact on crime is unplanned, that is not always the case. The total reconstruction of the Times Square area in New York City at the end of the 20th century deliberately destroyed niches for prostitution, robbery, and theft, even though that was not the only goal of development.

40. T. Hirschi, *Causes of Delinquency* (Berkeley: University of California Press, 1969).

41. M. Gottfredson and T. Hirschi, *A General Theory of Crime* (Palo Alto, CA: Stanford University Press, 1990).

42. For a pragmatic discussion of parental interference, see T. Hirschi, "Family," in J. Q. Wilson and J. Petersilia, eds., *Crime* (San Francisco: Institute for Contemporary Studies, 1995). More recent inquiry into supervision as it discourages delinquency is found in M. Warr, "Making Delinquent Friends: Adult Supervision and Children's Affiliations," *Criminology* 41, no. 1 (2005): 77–106

43. On sibling rivalry, See J. Tedeschi and R. B. Felson, *Violence, Aggression and Coercive Action* (Washington, DC: APA, 1994).

44. U.S. poet (1807–1882). Quoted in *Bartlett's Familiar Quotations,* 10th ed. (Boston: Little, Brown, 1919).

45. G. L. Kelling and C. M. Coles, *Fixing Broken Windows: Restoring Order and Reducing Crime in Our Communities* (New York: Martin Kessler Books, 1996).

46. R. R. Weidner, "Target-hardening at a New York City Subway Station: Decreased Fare Evasion—At What Price?" in R. V. Clarke, ed., *Preventing Mass Transit Crime* (Monsey, NY: Criminal Justice Press, 1996) (Volume 6 in *Crime Prevention Studies* series).

47. This reduced fear, increased usage, enhanced revenues, and created a better environment. For an account, see M. Sloan Howitt and George Kelling, "Subway Graffiti in New York City: 'Gettin' Up' vs. 'Meanin' It and Cleanin' It,'" in R. V. Clarke, *Situational Crime Prevention: Successful Case Studies,* 2nd ed. (New York: Harrow and Heston, 1997).

48. For a review of situational prevention in subway settings, see N. G. LaVigne, "Visibility and Vigilance: Metro's Situational Approach to Preventing Subway Crime" (November 1997). Available from the National Criminal Justice Reference Service, http://www.ncjrs.gov/pdffiles/166372.pdf (accessed September 4, 2005).

The web of our life is of a mingled yarn, good and ill together.

—William Shakespeare[1]

This town [Chicago] was built by great men who demanded that drunk-ards and harlots be arrested, while charging them rent until the cops arrived.

—Mike Royko[2]

Making the simple complicated is commonplace; making the compli-cated simple, awesomely simple, that's creativity.

—Charles Mingus[3]

For the mistress, there is the pleasure of having and exerting power over a man who is powerful himself. For the wife, there is the title, the social status and the money. And for the man himself, there is the satisfaction of having his needs met by two women. In the Washington Affair there is something for everyone.

—Sally Quinn[4]

12

Crime Mutualism

Criminal activities gain from one another and from noncriminal activi-ties.[5] Activities can grow, survive, or reproduce at a higher rate in the presence of one another. A crime mutualism means that both parties relate with *net benefit*. Like so many ecological concepts, mutualism is morally neutral. Bees and trees, prostitute and john, grocer and customer, mother and child—both parties in all four pairs gain something from their relationship.[6] So long as they relate in different roles, each with net benefit, they can be considered mutualists.[7]

Net Benefit, Rightly Understood

A "net benefit," does not mean that crime is beneficial in all respects and forever. Yet both the offender and counterpart mostly get what they want for a while. The illicit buyer secures the drugs; the seller receives the money. The buyer of sex services gets an orgasm; the prostitute is paid for providing it. The burglar and the fence trade booty for cash. The illegal gambler bribes the dishonest policeman, but gets to stay in business.[8]

A mutualism does not need to be an intense relationship.[9] Even if encounters are brief, participants can gain repeated benefits over time. This does not deny that crime mutualists face dangerous exposures. An illicit counterpart serves his purposes now, but might attack him later, or even kill him. A setting for drug deals is itself risky. Lightning eventually strikes those who keep standing briefly in storms.[10] Yet many costs of crime mutualisms occur incrementally. The substance abuser is happy for a while, but his health declines in time.

A mutualism can shift quickly. Suppose that a youth buys marihuana and is quickly arrested by a nearby police officer. At this point, another mutualism could develop between the youth and the police: the apprehended offender often incriminates his former partners in crime, trading forbidden knowledge for official leniency. Thus a mutualism implies ongoing cooperation, but not forever.

Variety in Mutualisms

Diverse forms of mutualism can develop between criminals and police. Some forms of organized crime pay ongoing bribes to police in return for informal permission to operate outside the law. But not all ongoing police relationships with offenders are corrupt. Many police maintain legitimately polite relationships in order to keep tabs on their quarry. Police also need to receive tips, and might allow minor offending to continue in return for assistance in combating something worse. Some minor offenders even cooperate when being arrested, hoping to receive a good word higher up the line or to be let free, perhaps trading some information in the process.

The interplay of legal and illegal activity is fascinating. Offenders buy things at the store, like everybody else.[11] But some legal businesses depend on their local felons. A restaurant serving mostly legal customers during the daytime might depend substantially on drug dealers and buyers as the sky darkens. Many small businesses with slim profits stay afloat by legally serving illicit clients, including the local prostitutes, pimps, and johns. During the cleanup of Times Square in New York, some small businesses complained because local criminals were their main customers.[12] A hotel within view of my office in Newark, owned by a leading citizen in town, is the local center for drugs and prostitution. Clearly this hotel is sustained by its criminal activities. But that is not always the case with crime mutualisms.

Do Offenders Depend on Mutualisms?

The concept of "crime opportunity" has a good history. But the term hides some important variations. When we say that crime opportunity is missing, what do we really mean? Do we wish to imply that crime cannot exist there? Or do we mean to say that it can exist but at a lower rate?

The ecologists help us out with a useful distinction, based on what's really possible. *Obligate mutualisms* are essential for survival. Apples are in trouble without honeybees.[13] The yucca plant and yucca moth would go extinct without each other. Neither prostitutes nor johns can perform their criminal part without the other. *Facultative mutualisms* are less limiting. Several species can pollinate wheat, and the wind delivers many seeds. Perhaps a bar with plenty of other customers has a facultative mutualism with its resident prostitutes. But certain bars have obligate mutualisms with prostitutes, and would go out of business without them.[14]

An advanced heroin addict risks death without her drugs. If dealers are few, the relationship becomes one of survival. But death is not the only issue. An illicit *activity* can die or fade if one of its providers is removed. Consider a small town with very limited access to illicit drugs, not near a major city or highway. If the local dealer is sent to jail, the local drug abusers might well desist. Even in an urban area with multiple suppliers of illicit goods or services, not all customers know them or are willing to take risks seeking them. Thus obligate mutualisms are found despite the presence of many suppliers.

An open-air drug market skirts that requirement. A drug sale there takes but a moment and does not depend on strong ties.[15] Mere recognition of a counterpart suffices, and that might be why some customers go there. That gives public officials an interesting chance to thwart certain illicit drug sales. Professor Johannes Knutsson studied the police crackdown against public drug dealing in an urban park in Stockholm.[16] Afterward, older and established drug users continued to exchange drugs through private ties, using their homes. But younger and newer drug users depended on open-air markets that were no longer available. In time, the drug-abusing population got older because the younger generation was unable to replenish it.

A stunning finding by Professors Robert Langworthy and James LeBeau illustrates this point in another way.[17] Police in some American cities set up sting operations to catch offenders in the act. In this case, local police created a storefront establishment to buy stolen auto parts, arresting the sellers. *The net effect was to enhance auto parts theft on nearby streets.* I would turn this result around to infer that many people would not steal auto parts without at least a minimal relationship to a local fence. With a more dependable illicit relationship, auto theft rates tend to rise.

Sometimes a crime mutualist has a strategic position, facilitating the crime opportunity for several others. When that's the case, its removal can impair a good deal of crime. Thus mutualisms provide tremendous opportunities for both crime and its prevention. The prior statement is especially true for obligate mutualisms. But many criminal mutualisms are somewhere in-between—neither totally obligatory nor fully free. Those more marginal in their criminal participation are especially apt to move away from it upon losing their easy opportunities to fence goods or buy drugs.

How Mutualists Help

Crime mutualists help each other in three ways:

1. exchanging resources,

2. stopping mutual enemies, and

3. spreading and reproducing crime.[18]

Exchanging resources is the best known form of mutualism in crime and nature (see Exhibit 12.1). One person sells contraband and the other buys. One offers information about what to steal, and other reciprocates. Perhaps the most famous counterpart in nature is the relationship between legumes and soil bacteria. The latter can fix nitrogen gas, feeding the legumes, which provide food to the bacteria in exchange.

Right outside my window, a large and spiny holly bush helps the small birds in the vicinity hide from their larger enemies. A defensive mutualism is also found between some gangs and drug dealers,[19] against their mutual

Exhibit 12.1   Three Functions of Crime Mutualism

Function of Mutualism	Examples in Nature	Crime Examples
1. Exchange resources	Legumes and nitrogen-fixing bacteria	Drug buyer and drug seller
2. Stop mutual enemies	Bush whose pollen is spread by small birds that hide there to avoid predators	Gangs and drug dealers against police
3. Spread and reproduce	Bees spreading pollen for flowers as they gather nectar	A newspaper includes thinly disguised advertisements for prostitutes. Both sides make money on the deal.

enemy, the police, or against rival criminals. A pack of toughs walking around has a defensive mutualism (but Chapter 20 argues that a juvenile gang works rather differently). Some businesses have formed defensive mutualisms with organized crime in order to thwart their unions.

The true story of the birds and the bees is that they help *other* species reproduce by spreading their pollen or other seeds. The dispersers nurture themselves in the process. Dispersion is an important feature of crime. Outdoor drug marketers help each other disperse drug-taking to new users. Legal dating services help initiate new prostitutes or help continuing prostitutes find new customers.[20]

If you look back to Exhibit 4.3, you can learn a lot about crime mutualism from Professor Howard Parker's research on how young Britons obtain illicit drugs.[21] As indicated, many youths obtain their drugs indirectly through friends and acquaintances. Thus the lives of average youths are often interwoven with crime, to varying degrees and in diverse ways.

Mutualisms and Residence

Two mutualists can live rather independently, convening mainly for crime purposes. Other mutualists live one inside the other.[22] Consider a house of prostitution within a building, whose owner draws profit in exchange for letting it be. Some crime mutualists are in-between, more or less cohabiting. Thus a student drug dealer might in student apartments, very close to his customers. Public housing includes illegal providers in mutual relationship with close neighbors.

In general, close living among mutual offenders makes it more difficult to thwart their criminal association. Consider the house of prostitution with resident prostitutes versus a massage parlor with employees who come and go. In the latter case, outside influences come to play, drawing the prostitutes toward legal activities or alternative illegal ones. In the former case, residence might impair the exit from an illegal situation. Authorities probably find it more difficult to break criminal links that are reinforced by cohabitation.

Perhaps that is why one finds laws on houses of prostitution are longer and more detailed than laws about other forms. The legal code of Canada distinguishes between procuring someone to have illicit intercourse, getting someone to move into a house of prostitution for that purpose, concealing someone inside such a house, getting a person into Canada for that purpose, directing an immigrant into such a house, and more.[23] As a general rule, crime policy should focus on particular settings that have been converted to ongoing crime use. Even if a vice is legal, its settings become a policy matter, since many people are involved.

This chapter has already given you a foundation for thinking about crime mutualism. It has not only explained what mutualism is, but the basic varieties found. Now I consider how we draw the line between mutualism and other interdependencies, and how mutualism can become elaborate.

Co-Offending Not Necessarily Mutualism

If accomplice relationships are *too* fleeting and unstable, they cannot be considered mutualisms.[24] But what about two burglars who continue to work together? If they perform the same tasks, they have no mutualism because they are in the same role. Suppose that one crime participant performs an entirely different role, such as driving the stolen goods away for the others? If this division of labor continues, the mutualism definition might fit. But ecology's categories are just words to help us study life; they are not life itself.

Close Calls

Some crime mutualisms are close calls because at least one party can deny knowing anything. The landlord for an illegal activity benefits from the rent and may be well aware. But he or she may try to deny that knowledge. Legal codes try to ensnare these mutualists. Consider Canada's legal code; its prostitution law includes

> anyone who "as owner, landlord, lessor, tenant, occupier, agent or otherwise having charge or control of any place, knowingly permits the place or any part thereof to be let or used for the purposes of a common bawdy-house. . . ."[25]

If arrested, you can expect these folks to deny knowledge.

Conspiracy Not Necessarily Mutualism

Most criminal conspiracies are probably a good deal less complex than movies and television shows portraying them. A criminal conspiracy includes multiple actors jointly engaging in concerted criminal activity. Conspiracy laws might require that conspirators agree to, plan, facilitate, assist, or promote crimes together. A criminal conspiracy can be, but is not necessarily, a crime mutualism. If a conspiracy involves preparation for a single offense, it makes no sense to call it mutualism. If the same conspirators continue over time, and their roles differentiate, a mutualism exists.

Sometimes the rules designed to protect against crime pave the way for criminal conspiracies. Many companies have a simple requirement that all checks over a certain amount (e.g., $500) must carry two authorized signatures in order to be valid. Such a rule interferes with single offenders who wish to write unauthorized checks. Now they need either to forge the other signature or to conspire with the other signatory. Usually, forcing offenders to form mutualisms will narrow their crime opportunities. That does not prevent crime mutualisms from developing and elaborating in some cases.

Lichens and Organized Crime

Beatrix Potter (1866–1943) is remembered well for her books about Peter Rabbit, but she was also the first person to draw, study, and explain lichens as the symbiotic association of two different organisms.[26] Someone else presented her paper on April 1, 1897, at the Linnaean Society of London, since women were banned from attendance.

Perhaps we can call lichens a *multiflow mutualism*. A sandwich with fungus on the outside and algae as filling, the lichens attach to logs, rocks, or walls. The fungus protects the algae, keeps it from drying out, absorbs nutrients for it, and performs photosynthesis for it. In return, algae produce various sugars and oxygen to nourish the fungus, and more.[27]

Organized crime is very much like this. Scholars have long rejected the exaggerated media image of corporatized criminals.[28] They have searched for alternative models of organized crime. A common scholarly approach is to define organized crime as a network, rather than an organization. The network approach probably works best when illegal commodities are passed along in a chain.

That will not account for certain types of racketeering. Rackets are complex and ongoing ties between organized crime and businesses or unions that are legitimate in other respects.[29] Rackets require ongoing criminal cooperation that a network model cannot account for. That's where Beatrix Potter, the naturalist, helps, as you shall see.

Most unions are not involved with mobsters. But the International Brotherhood of Teamsters—America's huge union for trucking industries—had a long history of mob involvement.[30] Its membership peaked at 2.3 million workers, but it is about half that size today. With the support of other unions, the federal government made a concerted effort to break its link to organized crime.[31]

The American labor movement began in a violent environment. To avoid unionization, many businesses hired thugs to attack union organizers or strikers. Unions initially fought back with their own people, but some unions turned the tables by hiring their own thugs. Labor racketeers learned to play both sides of the fence, forging "sweetheart deals" with companies, gaining union compliance in weak contracts. Some labor leaders began to use violence to destroy opponents within the union. Mobsters had something to offer—violence, blackmail, bribery, and sex favors. They were tied in with corrupt politicians and judges. And they could get officials into compromising situations, since mobsters knew their vices.

Corrupt unions had some resources to trade, too. Through strikes or slowdowns, a union could put a business out of commission, not always for the benefit of their members. At its peak, the Teamsters Union could stop or slow down shipments of about anything, anywhere in America, pressuring businesses severely. Teamsters could hire mobsters as union officials, asking little or no work in return. Most importantly, the Teamsters controlled a multibillion-dollar pension fund, easily converted to dubious purposes, including giving pensions to mobsters and loaning them vast amounts of money to build Las Vegas casinos.[32]

Racketeering is a general term for the interplay between organized crime and otherwise legitimate organizations. Businesses can also be involved in

Exhibit 12.2   Racketeering as a Multiflow Mutualism

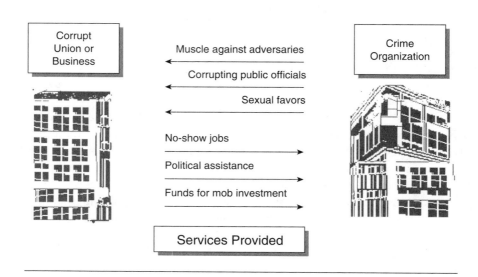

racketeering. Certain industries have especially been known for this—garbage collection, jukeboxes, casinos, trucking, construction, warehousing, and more. I suggest that business or union racketeering is best understood in terms of multiflow mutualism, as depicted in Exhibit 12.2. Modeled after the Teamsters Union case, this exhibit depicts six flows of resources between other organizations and "the Mob." (Very often, both unions and businesses are involved in the same racket with organized crime, so we might imagine a chart with three boxes, with various resources flowing among them.)

Lichens are most remarkable for their ability to survive where other organisms cannot. Some forms of organized crime have also developed the ability to extract an illicit living, often for many people, from what at first glance is far from fertile ground, and to keep it going for generations.

This does not mean that organized criminal activity is monolithic. Consider the chain of heroin distribution. The growth of the plants might be diffuse, while processing is more centralized. Some drug wholesalers distribute drugs in large shipments from central places. As packets get smaller, the level of organization declines, with drugs reaching a multitude of end-consumers. In contrast, local production and distribution of designer drugs or homegrown marihuana might never involve large organization. In addition, crime within legitimate organizations takes on a vast variety of forms. Such offenses can be directed against employees, customers, clients, patients, one's own organization, another organization, or the general public.[33] Some white-collar crimes are carried out alone, while others involve partners or even elaborate conspiracies. Once more the variety of criminal life is impressive.

How Organized Are They, Really?

Writer George Will jokes that "Football combines two of the worst things in American life. It is violence punctuated by committee meetings."[34] Unlike football players, an important reason to commit crime is to avoid conventional responsibilities, hence to avoid meetings. To assess the degree of criminal organization, ask yourself these questions, in this order:

1. *How long* does each illegal act really take?

2. *How many* persons carry it out simultaneously?

3. Does the illegal act stand alone, or within a *chain* of illegal actions?

4. Do the *same persons* repeat illegal acts together?

5. Are these joint repetitions *numerous*?

6. Is their criminal cooperation *formalized* in a crime organization?

7. Does that formal crime organization last a *long time*?

8. Do participants have a lot of meetings?

Imagine two guys spending a minute together stealing some cash. They each take their share and split. If, however, they break into a house and need to resell the booty, they must interact either with a fence or a legal market. Perhaps they expand their cooperation slightly, working together a few times on crime. Perhaps they bring someone else in occasionally, then repeatedly. If they begin to trade crime tips with others, their span widens. And so it goes. You can readily see that criminal organization can fall well short of its televised image.[35] Crimes can themselves be organized rather simply yet can take advantage of complexities in the organizations around them.

To complicate crime's organization, many illegal acts are mixed in with legal ones. Much marihuana is smoked during a simple party after the potato chips are gone. While victims are tied up in an office meeting, a thief goes from desk to desk stealing purses. Perhaps he has a single helper. We can see that criminal cooperation is important but often simpler than meets the eye.

Overview

Many criminal "needs" cannot easily be met alone, and criminals can only thrive or even exist because of mutualism. Not all illicit drugs grow locally. Some require refinement or manufacturing beyond ordinary skills and equipment. Selling stolen goods might require cooperation with others. Security from other offenders or police can depend on mutual assistance. Finding customers for illegal goods or services depends on advertising in legal outlets or locating illicit activities in legitimate places. Crime mutualisms, primitive or advanced, help offenders solve problems, giving them extra crime opportunities.

Central Points, Chapter 12

1. With a mutualistic offense, both parties must gain a net benefit, at least for a while.

2. Crime mutualists can exchange resources, help each other against their adversaries, or assist in the growth or spread of illegal activity.

3. Police and offenders can form a mutualism, sometimes assisting enforcement. Other times, it's corrupt.

4. Even legitimate businesses can develop mutual ties to offenders.

5. Racketeering is a form of complex mutualism, akin to lichens.

Exercises

1. Should two crime mutualists trust each other?

2. How might a mutualism *begin* legally before going the other way?

3. Name a government civil service position that invites mutualistic crime. Then name a business position that does the same.

4. Look up a historical public scandal. What mutualisms developed?

Notes

1. *All's Well That Ends Well*, act IV, scene iii.
2. "Speaking of Chicago," *Chicago Daily News*, December 21, 1976.
3. Widely attributed to this great jazz musician (1922–1979).
4. Quoted by Ben Bradlee in *A Good Life: Newspapering and Other Adventures* (New York: Simon and Schuster, 1996).

5. It makes some sense to distinguish direct mutualisms from indirect mutualisms, where the latter involve chains of association or exchange. Markets for illicit commodities depend largely on indirect mutualisms. Such markets are largely neglected in the current book, but that does not mean they are unimportant.

6. Two parties to a mutualism are not necessarily equal. A drug-dependent buyer might be outflanked by a nondependent drug seller.

7. To understand more about mutualisms, see A. J. Beattie, *The Evolutionary Ecology of Ant-Plant Mutualisms* (Cambridge, UK, and New York: Cambridge University Press, 1985). See also C. B. Miller, *Biological Oceanography* (Oxford, UK: Blackwell, 2003).

8. "Mutualist" is a noun referring to parties in a mutualism. I use this word only occasionally because it does not sound right to me.

9. A prostitute has a clear mutualism with repeat customers, but one-time customers lack such an ongoing relationship. For convenience we can classify such sales of illegal goods and services as mutualisms, even if not all customers are repeaters. Nonrepeaters might send other customers, too. In the end, mutualism becomes a matter of degree. Mutualism differs greatly by the time span of interdependence. A mother and child depend on one another for a very long number of years. A call girl might develop an ongoing relationship with a customer, at least for a while. A street prostitute has a mutual relationship with diverse customers, but no relationship with any one of them. A personal drug dealer might maintain certain customers over a longer period, but those buying drugs on the street might go to the same corner rather than the same person.

10. Note the binomial theorem. If you are rather sure something will not happen to you in one trial, you can be much less sure it will not happen over many trials.

11. Some market relations are more tailored to crime. Some offenders buy large amounts of legal drugs that they reduce for illicit use. Still their business might be scarcely noted given the larger sales volume.

12. For an old account of New York's Times Square, see O. Coombs, "The Roughest Bar in Town," *New York Magazine*, December 1, 1980. This was discovered in light of the work reported in M. Felson and others, 1996, "Redesigning Hell: Preventing Crime and Disorder at the Port Authority Bus Terminal," in R. Clarke, ed., *Preventing Mass Transit Crime* (Monsey, NY: Criminal Justice Press, 1996) (Volume 6 in *Crime Prevention Studies* series). Available from the Center for Problem-oriented Policing, http://www.popcenter.org/Library/CrimePrevention/Volume%2006/01%20Felson.pdf (accessed September 8, 2005).

13. Pollination is, of course, more complex. See C. Westerkamp and G. Gottsberger, "Diversity Pays in Crop Pollination," *Crop Science* 40 (2000): 1209–1222. Available from SCI Journals Online, http://intl-crop.scijournals.org/cgi/content/full/40/5/1209 (accessed September 4, 2005).

14. A tavern that benefits from prostitution may have a mutualistic relationship with it. But if a tavern shelters some prostitutes without making appreciable money from them, its relationship can be called passive assistance.

15. For more on the geography of drug sales, see J. E. Eck, *Drug Markets and Drug Places: A Case-Control Study of the Spatial Structure of Illicit Drug Dealing* (doctoral dissertation, University of Maryland, 1994). See also G. F. Rengert, *The Geography of Illegal Drugs* (Boulder, CO: Westview Press, 1996).

16. See

a. J. Knutsson, "Restoring Public Order in a City Park," in R. Homel, ed., *Policing for Prevention: Reducing Crime, Public Intoxication and Injury* (Monsey, NY: Criminal Justice Press, 1997) (Volume 7 in *Crime Prevention Studies* series).

b. J. Knutsson, "Swedish Drug Markets and Drugs Policy," in M. Natarajan and M. Hough, eds., *Illegal Drug Markets: From Research to Prevention Policy* (Monsey, NY: Criminal Justice Press, 2000) (Volume 11 in *Crime Prevention Studies* series).

c. A. Harocopos and M. Hough, "Drug Dealing in Open-Air Markets" (2005), Center for Problem-oriented Policing, http://www.popcenter.org (accessed September 4, 2005).

17. See:
   a. R. Langworthy, "Do Stings Control Crime? An Evaluation of a Police Fencing Operation," *Justice Quarterly* 6 (1989): 27–45.
   b. R. Langworthy and J. LeBeau, "The Spatial Evolution of a Sting Clientele," *Journal of Criminal Justice* 20 (1992): 135–146.
   c. J. LeBeau and R. Langworthy, "The Spatial Distribution of Sting Targets," *Journal of Criminal Justice* 20 (1992): 541–551.

18. Other terms found in the ecological literature: trophic mutualism, mycorrhizal mutualism, defensive mutualism, and dispersive mutualism. See H. F. Howe and J. Smallwood, "Ecology of Seed Dispersal," *Annual Review of Ecology and Systematics* 13 (1982): 201–228. Also see J. S. Clark, "Seed Dispersal Near and Far: Patterns Across Temperate and Tropical Forests," *Ecology* 80 (1982): 1475–1494.

19. For an exploration of how gangs and drug sales relate, see C. L. Maxson, *Street Gangs and Drug Sales in Two Suburban Cities* (Washington, DC: U.S. Department of Justice, 1995) (National Institute of Justice, Research in Brief). Also see M. W. Klein, *The American Street Gang: Its Nature, Prevention and Control* (Oxford, UK: Oxford University Press, 1995).

20. The crime taxonomy proposed in Chapter 21 reflects these diverse forms of communication, helping offenders get to their targets.

21. H. Parker, "How Young Britons Obtain Their Drugs: Drug Transactions at the Point of Consumption," in M. Natarajan and M. Hough, eds., *Illegal Drug Markets: From Research to Prevention Policy* (Monsey, NY: Criminal Justice Press, 2000) (Volume 11 in *Crime Prevention Studies* series). See also H. Parker and others, *Illegal Leisure: The Normalisation of Adolescent Recreational Drug Use* (London: Aldrich, 1998).

22. Some ecologists use the word "inhabitation," but I have decided to avoid it.

23. *Criminal Code*, RSC 1985, c. C-46, s. 212 (2). Available from the Canada Department of Justice, http://laws.justice.gc.ca/en/C-46/ (accessed September 4, 2005).

24. Even rudimentary and fleeting relationships among offenders require some cooperation, concurrence, and sense of reciprocal benefit. Normally, we do not code these as mutualisms because the relationships are too brief and most are not repeated.

25. *Criminal Code*, RSC 1985, c. C-46, s. 210 (2). See endnote 23, above.

26. N. Gilpatrick, "The Secret Life of Beatrix Potter," *Natural History* 81, no. 10 (1972): 38–109. See also websites on her work as a naturalist, such as that at the American Physiological Society, http://www.the-aps.org/education/k12curric/pdf/potter.pdf (accessed September 4, 2005).

27. See website *Nearctica*, founded by Dr. Robert W. Poole and Dr. Patricia Gentili, http://www.nearctica.com/ecology/pops/mutual.htm#lichen (accessed September 4, 2005).

28. Perhaps the organized notion of a mafia fits reality better in other nations than in the United States.

29. Sometimes the words "rackets," "racketeer," and "racketeering" are used for simpler forms of crime. I prefer to use these terms in distinction to simpler forms of organized crime. Yet I do not want to push the assumption of complexity too far.

30. Although I have offered an American example in these pages, many other nations have complex webs of corruption. On Italian corruption, see D. della Porta and A. Vannucci, *Corrupt Exchanges: Actors, Resources, and Mechanisms of Political Corruption* (New York: Aldine de Gruyter, 1999). Concerning Taiwanese corruption, see K.-L. Chin, *Heijin: Organized Crime, Business, and Politics in Taiwan* (Armonk, NY: M. E. Sharpe, 2003).

31. See
   a. D. S. Witwer, *Corruption and Reform in the Teamsters Union, 1898 to 1991* (dissertation, Brown University, 1994).
   b. R. James and E. D. James, *Hoffa and the Teamsters: A Study of Union Power* (Princeton, NJ: Van Nostrand, 1965).
   c. J. B. Jacobs, C. Panarella, and J. Worthington, *Busting the Mob: United States v. Cosa Nostra* (New York: New York University Press, 1994).

d.   J. B. Jacobs with C. Friel and R. Radick, *Gotham Unbound: How New York City Was Liberated From the Grip of Organized Crime* (New York: New York University Press, 1999).

32. Office of the Independent Hearing Officer, Laborers' International Union of North America, *In Re Trusteeship Proceeding of Local 1001 (Chicago, Illinois), Complaint for Trusteeship.* Available from Illinois Police & Sheriff's News, www.ipsn.org/local_1001/complaint.htm (accessed September 4, 2005).

33. See Exhibit 7.2 in M. Felson, *Crime and Everyday Life*, 3rd ed. (Thousand Oaks, CA: Sage, 2002). Also see D. O. Friedrichs, *Trusted Criminals: White Collar Crime in Contemporary Society* (Belmont, CA: Wadsworth, 2004).

34. *Famous Football Quotations,* http://home.att.net/~quotesabout/football.html (accessed October 26, 2005).

35. For a review, see H. Abadinsky, *Organized Crime*, 7th ed. (Belmont, CA: Wadsworth, 2003).

The Democrat is a cannibal—they have to live off each other—while the Republicans, why, they live off the Democrats.

—Will Rogers[1]

Shear your sheep, don't skin them.

—Latin Proverb

Imprudence relies on luck, prudence on method. That gives prudence less edge than it expects.

—Mason Cooley[2]

We must plant the sea and herd its animals using the sea as farmers instead of hunters. That is what civilization is all about—farming instead of hunting.

—Jacques Cousteau[3]

One cannot jump out of a burning building gradually.

—Mason Cooley[4]

13

Crime Parasitism

Every exploitative crime has a clear victim. In some cases, exploitation becomes an ongoing relationship, hence symbiotic. Parasitism is a *particular* form of symbiosis, and the term should be used carefully.[5]

A parasite lives *over time* at the expense of its *specific* host.[6] The parasite and host are closely associated, one gaining from the other.[7] The parasite harms the host a little at a time, without killing it, or only kills it in slow motion. The flea gains sustenance by drinking the dog's blood, but the dog survives each little bite. That allows the parasite to exploit its host over a longer period.[8]

A good example of crime parasitism is the repeat shoplifter who drains the same store blouse by blouse. A given individual, family, household, or organization can be repeatedly victimized and slowly harmed, recovering to be victimized again. The crime host provides the parasite ongoing resources, helping the crime to recur. I remind the reader: this is not a metaphor! I intend the word "parasitism" literally, since some types of crime exact from victims a little at a time.

If you only consider crimes one by one, you will miss how they fit into a larger system. A set of minor crimes in repetition can bleed the victim, with major consequences. The concept of parasitism helps explain this. Crime prevention can be more effective if it figures out these relationships among crimes and proceeds to interfere more systematically. Of course, offenders have a way to avoid notice and interference.

A crime parasite generally lives in close or ongoing contact with his host. Even a violent parasite uses force a bit at a time in order to prolong the benefit. He avoids challenging the host to a life and death struggle and tries not to provoke resistance or investigation. A property-crime parasite also avoids undue attention. A crime parasite does best by drawing ongoing, illicit sustenance in small amounts, minimizing risk and making sure he can come back for more. Crime parasitism fits the larger natural category, *social parasitism*. Social parasites take advantage of the behavior or social structure of another organism.[9] Crime parasites vary widely in how they do this, as we shall see.

Family Violence Can Be Parasitism

Family violence typically fits this profile: A stronger family member repeatedly injures a weaker counterpart. It is a form of parasitic crime if it takes advantage bit by bit. A violent husband or boyfriend might harm a woman enough for intimidation and control, while avoiding injuries that require major medical or police attention. A parent who abuses a child does so incrementally, often avoiding injuries obvious to outsiders. This is one way that some family violence stays under the radar screen.

At young ages, a stronger sibling hits the weaker sibling too obviously, drawing parental reaction. In time a family bully learns to modulate the abuse, avoiding obvious injuries that would secure parental intervention. An older brother can learn to bully wisely, drawing no blood, inflicting temporary pain as needed to extract benefits in smaller steps.[10]

The Prudent Crime Parasite

By definition, a parasite must not harm the host too much, too fast. But how much and how fast? The "prudent social parasite" hypothesis states that a parasite minimizes its impact on its host in order to take advantage for longer.[11] More aggressive parasites tend to be *less* successful than those who are prudent. Mason Cooley, the aphorist, explains: "Prudence does not make people happy; it merely deprives them of the excitement of being constantly in trouble."[12]

Perhaps some offenders consider how much time remains to milk their victims. If time is short, a crime parasite probably becomes more aggressive. If they think they have plenty of time to keep taking what they want, they might be more prudent in taking a little at a time. Perhaps temporary employee thieves tend to grab, while long-term employee thieves are more likely to nibble.

Parasitic offenders do not always predict perfectly what they can get away with. Sometimes others figure out what's happening and act to stop them. Sometimes victims have had enough. And sometimes the crime parasite overdoes it.

Can Crime Parasites Control Themselves?

In the world of crime, prudence is not always likely, or even possible. To understand why, it's important to distinguish single from multiple parasites. Perhaps a restaurant has to deal with pilfering by a single waitress, while a large store probably faces many shoplifters.

As a general rule, single parasites have slow impact, while multiple parasites can inflict severe and rapid harm. Numerous independent parasites cannot easily modulate their overall harm, and might destroy the source of nutrient for all. I recall a university department whose photocopier was heavily abused to meet personal needs. The offenders were unable to coordinate their nibbling, so they overworked and destroyed the machine. A new copier was then installed and monitored more carefully.

An individual crime parasite can also lose control and undermine his niche. Perhaps the offender begins with small nibbles, becomes too greedy, then loses the crime opportunity or even destroys the host. Pilfering employees can easily bankrupt a small business with a slim profit margin. Many offenders lack sufficient self-control to resist demanding more, in time undermining their own positions.

This helps us understand why parasitic crime against business works best if it becomes somewhat organized. If *every local thief or thug* extracts what he wants from local businesses, the amounts will rise to an intolerable level. But a more modulated illegal process can last much longer.[13] This point applies not only to repeated thefts, but also ongoing extortion—using force or threats. (Note the discussion of niches and resource partitioning in Chapters 8 and 9.)

Yet nature provides success stories of very aggressive parasites. The cuckoo lays its egg in the nest of the host, letting the other bird raise its offspring. (I discuss brood parasitism later in this chapter.) The invading infant monopolizes the food and kills the nest-mates. The cuckoo can find a new host for its next round, so its aggressive parasitism is not fatal to itself. Some aggressive criminal parasites also overfeed, then move on. Perhaps they would be more successful if they could modulate their own criminal instincts.

Parasitism and Repeat Victimization

Consider repeat victimization—a research and crime-prevention topic studied by Professors Ken Pease, Graham Farrell, and other scholars.[14] All crime parasitism requires repeat victimization, but not all repeat victimization requires crime parasitism. When *entirely different* offenders harm the same victim, that's not parasitism. But if the same offender harms the same victim bit by bit, parasitism is in play. If a purely harmful offender selects an entirely new and unrelated target every time, this is predation, not parasitism. If an offender attacks the same person or organization, or its property, this is full parasitism. There are also some in-between cases.[15]

Sometimes the host does not even know that a parasite is present. Many businesses are sloppy or slow about taking inventory. If they don't know what's supposed to be on the shelf, how can they spot theft in time? How can they figure out who is doing it? In some cases, those taking inventory are the very employees who are stealing. A restaurant can easily lose a cup of sugar here, a hamburger there. You can see how the same offender keeps drawing benefits from the same victim.

In retail trade, the term "shrinkage" covers missing goods, but often cannot pinpoint why they are missing it. Shrinkage mixes together

- Theft by insiders
- Shoplifting and other theft by outsiders
- Bookkeeping errors
- Foods spoiled or clothing torn
- Items that are lost in the system
- Items missing from the warehouse[16]

Companies don't usually know how much shrinkage comes from one or the other. That makes it easy for crime parasitism to take hold. Even if the organization knows they are losing to theft, they might not be able to pinpoint who is doing it.[17]

Sometimes the victim knows who is stealing, but is unable or disinclined to do anything about it. Many organizations tolerate pilfering when the known costs of enforcement exceed the apparent benefits of stopping the crime.[18] Perhaps an organization considers economic and political problems, media attention, embarrassment, and reprisals. I specifically know of two organizations that remained silent about pilfering by an employee who brought in more money than he stole. In other cases, an apprehended parasitic offender is too troublesome or costly to arrest and prosecute. Minor shoplifters are often let loose.[19] By nibbling a small amount at a time, a parasitic offender can stay largely under the radar and persist.

As I noted in Chapter 3, important research in Britain and Australia has developed and studied the "near repeat hypothesis."[20] This states that homogeneous dwellings near one another will tend to have similarly high risk of burglary. Near repeats can be seen as parasitism if the same offenders go back to roughly the same or very similar victims. How then do we classify near repeats by different offenders on different targets? I refer this back to committee.

At the other extreme, the lion eats the lamb once and does not repeat with that particular lamb. The same is true of the human murder, but we usually classify occasional repeats with the same target (e.g., attempted murder) as predatory offenses, not parasitism. Many less serious offenses are predatory, too. For example, many a robber avoids returning to the same store, and others steal here, there, and everywhere. There is nothing to prevent the same offender from using a predatory strategy with some of his crimes, while maintaining a parasitic link to a few easy targets.

Parasites and Bullies

Bullying is a special case of crime parasitism.[21] Some bullies repeatedly demand small amounts of money from the whipping boy. Other bullies gain attention or power over the whipping boy, using force and intimidation without seeking monetary gain. Often bullies are noisy and overt, displaying dominance to others for additional advantage beyond the whipping boy alone. Yet some violent parasitism employs surreptitious threats and occasional demonstrations of violence rather than repeated noisy attacks.

Stalking and sexual pestering are akin to bullying and can often be understood as parasitism. The offender repeatedly bothers the victim, making small demands or intrusions each time, but creating an ongoing problem, greater than the sum of the parts.

The first half of this chapter explains the fundamentals of crime parasitism—including what it does for the offender. It shows that some basic crime issues—family crime, bullying, and repeat victimization—can be better understood in larger ecological terms. Now I turn to additional crime forms that make more sense in terms of parasitism.

Parasitism Takes Interesting Forms

As in larger nature, crime parasitism takes many interesting forms helping us make sense of various criminal behaviors.

Parasitic Blackmail

A one-time blackmailer for a large amount is not a parasite. In contrast, the parasitic blackmailer demands more modest payments repeatedly. Perhaps the offender has gained sordid information about the victim and threatens to reveal it to wife, employer, or community. The victim could be an individual or a company whose profits would suffer or whose executives would be embarrassed. Even the threat to spread falsehoods can harm those who have public positions to protect, so they may decide to pay.[22]

Hush Money

Not all hush money is paid because someone demanded it. In September of 1972, White House operatives gave $220,000 to the convicted "plumbers"—the people who broke into the opposing Democrats' headquarters in the Watergate building in Washington. This money purchased their silence about White House involvement in their burglary. In November 1972, President Nixon defeated George McGovern in the election, carrying 49 of 50 states. Soon after the Watergate scandal began to unravel and the hush money became public. President Nixon was the only president in history forced to resign from office. These events were chronicled in the 1976 movie, *All the President's Men,* starring Robert Redford and Dustin Hoffman. The hush money was apparently initiated from the White House, so this was neither blackmail nor parasitism. But once you start paying somebody off, it is not always easy to extract yourself. Bribing someone voluntarily starts you down a slippery slope toward their extorting you. Perhaps the Watergate burglars had already turned the tables on the White House, or would have sooner or later.

Child Abandonment as Brood Parasitism

Brood parasitism is a prolonged effort to get others to raise your offspring for you. For example, the cowbird deposits its own eggs in the nest of another for free incubation. Child abandonment by humans is akin to brood parasitism, for the parent is seeking to get others to do the job. Drug addicts are known to turn their children over to grandparents or other relatives. Others turn their children over to state agencies, adoption, or foster parents. One parent abandoning a child to the other parent is perhaps brood parasitism, especially if child support payments are evaded.[23] We should distinguish wholesale abandonment from altruistic abandonment, since in the latter the parent seeks a better life for the children. Welfare fraud is not brood parasitism, since the fraudster uses her own nest. There are many ways that humans, as individuals or organizations, get others to take over their chores.[24]

Urban Annoyances Interpreted as Parasitism

A few aggressive panhandlers bother tourists at particular corners in central San Francisco.[25] But the most creative beggars are found in Manhattan, many giving you a clever line. Some of them follow you until you give them money. During the 1990s, a small number of "squeegee men" in New York City would corner an intersection, then pester different motorists who stopped there, insisting on washing their windshields for a fee.

Are repeat public annoyances parasitic? Professor Robert C. Ellickson of Yale University has written of street nuisances, including panhandling, as follows: "The harms stemming from a chronic street nuisance, trivial to any one pedestrian at any instant, can mount to severe aggravation. As hours pass into days and weeks, the total annoyance accumulates."[26]

Absent an ongoing relationship between one panhandler and one giver, this is not strict parasitism. Yet many ecologists see fleas as parasites and dogs as hosts—even without a one-flea, one-dog relationship.[27]

Parasites Taking Turns

Youths demanding small amounts to "watch your car and keep it safe" shift from one car owner to another, and take turns doing so. Similarly, a few bullies might take turns with the same victim or a few similar victims. These are *loosely* parasitic crimes that do not fit the strict definition. Even though these youths have only rudimentary organization, we can readily imagine that they would age into more elaborate forms of organized extortion.

Parasitic Enslavement

In slavery days in the United States, slaveholders branded their slaves to perpetuate control.[28] Slavery is the ultimate parasitism, since the slaveholder comes back not only to the same victims but also their children and children's children.[29]

The human species was not the first to enslave. Slave-making ants, many of them small and red, are found in the United States,[30] on both sides of the Mason-Dixon Line. Several ant species belonging to the genus *Polergus* can only survive by taking slaves. The female enters a nest of the host species, kills the rightful queen, and enslaves the remaining ants. The new master ant groups the eggs and larvae by age. Her slave ants keep raiding colonies of the host species for eggs that hatch into new slaves.[31]

Human slavery has been legal and illegal, depending on time and place. Throughout history winning armies have enslaved the losers. Although the great religions eventually moved toward reform, slavery was taken for granted in the Old Testament,[32] New Testament,[33] and Qur'an.[34] The slaveholders in the United States prior to Emancipation had the law on their side.

With today's world largely hostile to slavery, the modern enslaver normally must conceal the slave. Yet open human slavery still seems to exist. Human rights activists detail circumstances in Sudan, where slave making is linked to civil war.[35]

False Imprisonment

We might ask ourselves whether false conviction and imprisonment constitute illegal slave making, especially if a public official knowingly lies to lock somebody up. This classification is more difficult if an official has arrested someone who is definitely guilty, based on evidence that cannot be legally admitted. Some officials have been tempted to use illegal means to assure conviction. Many enslavers excuse what they do, saying their victims deserve it, and sometimes they have a case. But breaking criminal law to punish somebody else raises serious issues.

Improper Prisoners of War

Defending armies have historically enslaved their defeated invaders, who started the war. The Geneva Accords ban these excuses among modern warring nations, but permit prisoners of war under specific conditions. Soldiers from nations who participated in the Geneva Accords have legal rights, but many nations are not parties. Nor are there Geneva protections for secret agents, combatants out of uniform, or private armies seeking to overthrow governments. Such issues arise about prisoners taken from ongoing wars in Iraq and Afghanistan. However, many nations—including the United States—have their own legal requirements to keep prisoners of war from eventuating into victims of false imprisonment or other parasitic abuses.

Prison Abuses

Abuses of prisoners of war can occur, even when the victorious army has a clear policy against it. In civilian prisons, it is not uncommon for prisoners to abuse weaker prisoners on an ongoing basis. Some prisoners make sex slaves of other prisoners. Some guards abuse prisoners for sex or other reasons. Although not widely reported, these problems are also present in juvenile homes, which have to worry about one or more boys raping a weaker boy, or even raping counselors.

Kidnapping and Sex Slavery

Kidnapping is a form of temporary slavery, with varying motives. If the goal is a single ransom payment, control will not last long. But some kidnappers are more interested in sex than money. Sex slavery is parasitism; the enslaver keeps the victim for the next sexual episode. Enslavers treat their victims even worse if they are in a hurry. Short-term sex slavery reduces the incentive to take even moderate care of the slave.

Perhaps the most common form of sex slavery is connected with prostitution.[36] Although not all prostitutes are captives, sometimes that is the case. Some brothels rely on sex slaves to service their customers.[37] Although they will probably seek to maintain the slaves' health for some months, the premium on youth and the ability to find new sex slaves erodes the incentive to treat the current ones well. Today's sex slavery probably does not extend to the next generation, but young children of prostitutes might be caught in a bind similar to that of their mothers.

False Claims of Sex Slavery

It makes some people feel better to declare that all prostitutes are forced to do what they do, perhaps by a pimp or by organized crime. This raises an interesting (but by no means new) controversy. Professor Jo Doezema of the Institute of Development studies at the University of Sussex, UK, questions whether most prostitutes from abroad are sex slaves.[38] The same issue applies to domestic prostitutes, who can easily learn to sell sex by their own decision, without outside cajoling and without any pimp at all.

Professor Julie Cwikel, Head of Ben Gurion University's Center for Women's Health Studies, interviewed 55 Israeli brothel workers.[39] Only 10 reported having been sold against their wishes. Only six engaged in sex work against their own volition. Three-quarters knew before leaving their country of origin that they were heading into prostitution. The remainder said they decided to become prostitutes after arrival, except for two who said it was against their will. Many ethnographic studies of prostitutes ask similar questions.[40] My point is not to deny the problems that prostitutes have, including extortion. But I doubt that slavery is the main issue in prostitution.

Control of Animals and Cruelty Toward Them

In most societies, human control of animals is a normal and legal source of food. Humans control cattle with barbed wire and brand them to prevent theft and to recover them in case of escape. Animal rights activists might consider caged birds, zoos, cattle pens, and chicken coops as a form of slavery for human benefit. But even free-range chickens have a very limited bill of rights. Vegetarians who milk their flocks without slaughter are still social parasites in ecological terms. Hindu culture officially protects cattle from cruelty, but still tethers them for work and milk.

Of course, domesticated animals would generally not live at all without human sponsorship. Dogs and cats do especially well in prosperous nations, where they are well fed with no chores to do. Most often pet ownership is a form of mutualism, but in some cases it has parasitic overtones. Although household pets are under control—in a sense, enslaved—their mistreatment or neglect is a criminal offense in many jurisdictions.

Dogfighting and cockfighting are good examples of enslavement of animals for human purposes. Although legal in some societies, these practices are illegal in most of the United States. There are some rural jurisdictions that look the other way, in effect permitting cockfights. The fights not only collect admission fees, but encourage substantial betting. I personally knew someone in a rural county of the United States who raised and fought cocks. He showed me his animals and the steel spurs that he attached to their claws to maximize harm to their adversaries. They would fight one-on-one, until one died. Sometimes the winner would die, too, soon after the fight. Of course, the purse goes to the human owner. The parasitic relationship continues, but only for a cock that keeps winning and survives its injuries to fight another day.

Gladiators

Roman circuses carried this concept back to human victims, forcing gladiators to fight to the death in the Roman Coliseum, to entertain the crowd. This was legal in its era, but was banned when Christianity took over in Rome.

Interestingly, a single ecological category includes cowbirds, slave-making ants, slaveholders, sex-slave kidnappers, shepherds, chicken-keeping vegetarians, Roman emperors, and organic farmers with free-range chickens. Only some of these activities are illegal, but all remind us that parasitism is intrinsic to many features of human life, crime included.

The Offender as Host

One offender can be a parasite with another offender a host. Here are a few examples:

- One offender discovers another's racket, then extorts a share of the loot in exchange for silence.
- A local gang offers protection to a small-time drug dealer, but rakes off a share of the profits.
- A corrupt policeman extracts a weekly bribe for letting an illegal business continue.[41]
- A Chinatown gang draws routine payments from cash-only Chinese restaurants, knowing they don't pay taxes.[42]
- A pimp draws ongoing gains from unwilling prostitutes.

We should distinguish "parasitic pimps" from "service-oriented pimps," who provide protection and assistance to prostitutes who pay them willingly. However, mutualism can shift to parasitism if the more powerful party continues to demand a commission, while phasing out services.

It is quite clear that many offenders are themselves in weak positions, subject to criminal victimization on an ongoing basis. Some ecologists use the word *kleptoparasite* to describe animals that steal food from another who has just obtained it. Bald eagles are very inclined to do this, and large predators (such as lions) are capable of the same. It is all too easy for powerful and armed offenders to wait until a prostitute or a male hustler has made some illicit money, then seize it—well aware of their victims' reluctance to seek police assistance. And so the web of crime is woven.

Organizations as Parasites or Hosts

Consider these crimes:

- A nursing home employee repeatedly abuses a patient.
- A bartender nips whiskey from the boss, jigger by jigger.

These are parasitic offenses within an organizational setting.

Organizational routines are very favorable for parasitic crime. Not only the organization itself, but also an employee, client, or interacting organization,[43] can serve as parasite or host. In each case, the offender takes advantage of ongoing social processes. Exhibit 13.1 offers a four-by-four matrix of parasitic crime within an organizational setting. These categories can handle employee pilferage, workplace bullying, embezzling pensions, harvesting other employees' wallets, janitors stealing at night, and a variety of accounting frauds.

Ecologists distinguish external from internal parasites (ectoparasites vs. endoparasites). For example, head lice attack people from outside and remain there, while tapeworms live within the stomach. This distinction is not much use for studying parasitic crime against individuals, but is very useful when organizations are involved. We might think of ongoing shoplifters as external parasites, while pilfering employees are internal parasites. The external-internal distinction can apply to businesses, schools, universities, or other units. That distinction is reflected in common language by the terms "outside job" and "inside job."[44] In crime as in nature, the strategies of outsiders and insiders can differ. The outsider usually avoids spending much time in the presence of the victim, while the insider takes advantage of ongoing presence to find just the right moments for extracting booty.[45] Of course, hybrid forms exist: sometimes an outsider has inside knowledge, or makes a devil's deal with an insider.[46] Clearly, the organizational context is well suited for parasitic crime in many directions.

Host Specificity and Susceptibility

Students of crime have long realized that some people are victim prone. Are they prone to attack by different offenders or the same ones? A *susceptible*

Exhibit 13.1 Parasitic Crime and Organizations

	The Parasite			
	(1) Employees	(2) Customers, Clients, Patients	(3) This Organization	(4) Other Organizations
The Host (1) Employees	Bullying co-workers	Harvesting wallets from offices	Nibbling at pension funds	Swiping by cleaning service
(2) Customers, clients, patients	Mistreating patients	Swiping from the lockers	Adding hidden charges	Embellishing by outside billing service
(3) This organization	Nipping whiskey from the bar	Shoplifting	Juggling accounts between units	Overbilling suppliers
(4) other organizations	Shorting the deliveries	Pilfering from delivery trucks	Evading taxes	Shifting costs to another contractor

NOTE: Many of the offenses above have nonparasitic forms, too.

host provides an environment meeting the parasite's needs. Hosts are not the only ones who "specialize." For most predatory crime, offenders are generalists. But crime parasitism, by definition, implies specialization. An ongoing relationship of parasite with host depends on a rather specific ability to intrude. A cashier might be able to steal small change from the till, but that does not provide entrée to the warehouse. The lawyer can misuse a trust fund under his own supervision, but not all trust funds. Some bank fraudsters take only a tiny bit from each account, thus concealing the ongoing parasitism. But they might have access only to certain types of accounts. As we learn more about the specificity of crime parasites and their hosts, perhaps we will better know how to thwart them.

Even powerful organizations have parasitic weaknesses. Retail establishments have huge warehouses and sales floors, both difficult to watch. Casinos have vast amounts of cash, and customers with open wallets. Other environments are *resistant* to parasites. Businesses with a simple and complete paper trail, frequent inventorying and auditing are far less susceptible to parasitism.

Additional Offender Vulnerability

All humans are subject to nature's anatomical parasites, but offenders often take more risks and have worse health, making them even more susceptible.[47] Prostitutes suffer high rates of infection from sexually transmitted diseases. These include AIDS, chlamydia, cold sores, genital herpes, genital warts, genital human papillomavirus, gonorrhea, hepatitis B and C, pelvic inflammatory disease, syphilis, and frequent yeast infections. Many of these infections compound one another. For example, the AIDS virus can enter the human body more easily through sores resulting from other diseases. In many nations, legal prostitutes undergo health inspections to control parasitic diseases. Of course, these parasites do not pay any heed to whether an activity has been legalized, and prostitutes can be infected between inspections. Drug abusers are susceptible to many infections, too. Crime's ecosystem links active offenders to illicit contacts with the rest of the population, increasing their risks of dangerous infections. This helps infections spread among offenders, between offenders and participants in shady activities, and among the general population.

Interestingly, criminal activities expose offenders to a vast chain of bioenvironmental risks. Many offenders have far less to worry about from official punishment than from the diseases they contract and enhance, before, during, and after incarceration.[48]

Overview

The vocabulary of crime includes many verbs with parasitic implication, including badger, bite, blackmail, exact, and squeeze. It also includes such nouns as protection, racket, payoff, payola, and shakedown. These terms offer very little precision for studying how a parasite imposes upon a host. Future studies of parasitism should consider the demands on the host along several dimensions. Are the demands even or erratic? How much do they take at a time? How much harm is done by each? Does the parasite underestimate or overestimate the capacity of the host? How long can the host survive? Does a prolonged relationship expose the parasite to detection or counteraction? Which criminal parasites move faster? Which are more prudent, and why? These empirical questions need to be answered before we can understand crime parasitism in full.

Crime parasitism is an important topic. Without an ongoing relationship, crime's harms are somewhat dissipated in the larger community. Yet, many offenses are parasitic in a literal sense, concentrating their harms among a few. Repeat victimization and bullying often reflect parasitic relationships. Some parasites operate within organizations, others from outside, and still others with no relationship at all to organizations.

Over time, a high-crime area develops a tangle of parasitic crime relationships. Gangs badger drug dealers. Bigger gangsters pester smaller ones. Pimps require a tithe from prostitutes. Toughs shake down businesses. Bullies find whipping boys. Cops exact bribes. Youths ask protection payments from car owners. The destructive power of crime parasitisms could well exceed the local impact of more obvious criminal actions.

Central Points, Chapter 13

1. Crime parasitism harms the same victim a little at a time, without killing it.

2. The prudent crime parasite stays under the radar screen and avoids overdoing it. But in reality, many offenders become greedy, undermining their own crime positions.

3. Parasitism helps us understand and classify some offenses that are otherwise difficult to place.

4. Offenders are themselves highly susceptible to parasitic offenders.

Exercises

1. What crime parasitisms might develop at a standard high school?

2. What crime parasitisms might develop at a standard workplace?

3. If you go into business, what three rules would you follow to minimize pilfering?

Notes

1. U.S. humorist (1879–1935). Quoted in *The Columbia World of Quotations* (New York: Columbia University Press, 1996).

2. Quoted in *The Columbia World of Quotations* (New York: Columbia University Press, 1996).

3. French ocean explorer (1910–1997), coinventor of the aqualung, which made scuba diving possible. Quoted in *Simpson's Contemporary Quotations* (New York: Houghton-Mifflin, 1998).

4. Quoted in *The Columbia World of Quotations* (New York: Columbia University Press, 1996).

5. The relationship among the three terms is depicted in Exhibit C, Appendix B.

6. The word "host" is standard in the literature on parasites, so I continue to use it.

7. However, the close association is not always symmetrical. A repeat shoplifter may know the store well, but the store might not know him. A repeat burglar might operate incognito.

8. For more on parasitisms, see A. O. Bush and others, *Parasitism: The Diversity and Ecology of Animal Parasites* (Cambridge, UK, and New York: Cambridge University Press, 2001). Also see C. Combes, *Parasitism: The Ecology and Evolution of Intimate Interactions* (Chicago: University of Chicago Press, 2001).

9. In contrast, "anatomical parasites" take advantage of the bodily structure or shape of another plant or animal, or any of its parts, extracting benefit for themselves. For example, most viruses attach to specific "receptor sites" on the host cell's surface. This term does not apply very well to crime. But some offenders take ongoing advantage of both social and physical features of their hosts. Thus an offender keeps stealing from an office located in a remote part of its building, or a dock that is easily accessed.

10. For more on sibling rivalry, see R. B. Felson, "Aggression and Violence Between Siblings," *Social Psychology Quarterly* 46 (1983): 271–285. Also see K. L. Hoffman and J. N. Edwards, "An Integrated Theoretical Model of Sibling Violence and Abuse," *Journal of Family Violence* 19 (2004):185–200.

11. J. F. Hare and T. M. Alloway, "Prudent Protomognathus and Despotic Leptothorax Duloticus: Differential Costs of Ant Slavery," *Proceedings of the National Academy of Sciences* 98 (October 9, 2001): 12093–12096. Available from PubMed Central, http://www.pubmedcentral.nih.gov/articlerender.fcgi?artid=59828 (accessed September 4, 2005).

12. Quoted in *The Columbia World of Quotations* (New York: Columbia University Press, 1996).

13. A few pages hence, you will see more on Chinatown extortion. See also K. Konrad and S. Skaperdas, "Extortion," *Economica* 65, no. 260 (1998): 461–477.

14. On the repeat victimization literature, see Chapter 3, including endnote 35.

15. Exhibit D in Appendix B helps sort out the distinction between parasitism and predation, along with the "close calls." Note the link to "near repeat" victimizations discussed in other chapters.

16. Shrinkage also includes items that never were there, due to vendor fraud; some vendors pretend they did not receive the goods, then insist on undeserved credit.

17. Parasitic crime provides wonderful opportunities for using certain English verb forms. These include the

> present simple continuous (e.g., is stealing),
> present perfect continuous (e.g., has been stealing),
> past simple continuous (e.g., was stealing), and
> past perfect continuous (e.g., had been stealing).

18. Of course, real costs of pilfering are probably greater than apparent costs. See Dennis Challinger, "The Realities of Crime Against Business," paper presented at the Crime Against Business Conference, Melbourne, Australia, June 18–19, 1998. Available from the Australian Institute of Criminology, http://www.aic.gov.au/conferences/cab/challinger.html (accessed September 4, 2005). See also Ronald V. Clarke, "Shoplifting" (2003), Center for Problem-oriented Policing, http://www.popcenter.org (accessed September 4, 2005).

19. But exposing a shoplifter to management might prevent a return to that store and thus reduce parasitic crime. This is a good example of how lame enforcement can sometimes do some good.

20. On near repeat victimizations, see Chapter 3, endnote 36.

21. See R. Sampson, "Bullying in Schools" (2002), Center for Problem-oriented Policing, www.popcenter.org (accessed September 4, 2005).

22. Most *legal* negotiations involve acceptable pressure by one side against the other. If somebody crashes carelessly into my car, I push his insurance company to pay me for my losses. He has some cards in his hand—the cost (to me) of suing in time and money. I have some cards in my hand—his costs and the extra damages he might have to pay later. Normally our lawyers haggle and get an early settlement, and that's it. But sometimes legal haggling involves something more dubious. In the United States, the legal system fosters a form of blackmail against the wealthy or corporate offenders, who have to balance

> a.   their civil liability (in large amounts of money),
> b.   their criminal liability (including imprisonment), and
> c.   their public ruination via mass media.
> A clever negotiator can leverage b. and c. to get more money through a.

23. These human schemes go beyond parasitism, and will require additional classifications in the future.

24. Derelict property is also abandoned. Laws often prohibit such abandonment, and it is sometimes criminalized.

25. For more on panhandling, see Mike Scott, "Panhandling" (2002), Center for Problem-oriented Policing, http://www.popcenter.org (accessed September 4, 2005).

26. R. C. Ellickson, "Controlling Chronic Misconduct in City Spaces: Of Panhandlers, Skid Rows, and Public-space Zoning," *Yale Law Journal* 105 (1996): 1165–1248.

27. See Exhibit D in Appendix B.

28. See R. Netz, *Barbed Wire: An Ecology of Modernity* (Middletown, CT: Wesleyan University Press, 2005).

29. In some places, however, children of slaves are released.

30. See K. S. Hedlund, "Ants of North America" (n.d.). Available from the author's website, http://www.cs.unc.edu/~hedlund (accessed September 4, 2005). Slave-making ants are found elsewhere, too. See the website of Professor Tom Alloway's course on animal behavior at the University of Toronto, http://www.erin.utoronto.ca/~w3psy252f/ (accessed

September 4, 2005). Also see review of this issue in B. Hölldobler and E. O. Wilson, *The Ants* (Cambridge, MA: Harvard University Press, 1990), pp. 452–464.

31. Joan M. Herbers and Susanne Foitzik spent some years studying ant slave colonies near Albany, New York, and White Sulphur Springs, West Virginia. See S. Foitzik and J. M. Herbers, "Colony Structure of a Slave-Making Ant. II. Frequency of Slave Raids and Impact on the Host Population," *Evolution* 55 (2001): 316. Also see S. Foitzik and J. M. Herbers, "Coevolution in Host-Parasite Systems: Behavioural Strategies of Slave-Making Ants and Their Hosts," *Proceedings of the Royal Society of London.* B-268 (June 7, 2001): 1139.

32. Example: "Then Abimelech brought sheep and cattle and male and female slaves and gave them to Abraham, and he returned Sarah his wife to him." *Genesis* 20:14. Sometimes the key word is translated as "servants," but there are too many other biblical references to deny the presence of slavery as a matter of course.

33. "Slaves, in all things obey those who are your masters on earth, not with external service, as those who *merely* please men, but with sincerity of heart, fearing the Lord." *Colossians* 3:22. Again, the word is sometimes translated as "servants," but there's too much other evidence that this was about slavery.

34. The instruction is to "restrain their carnal desire (save with their wives and slave-girls, for these are lawful to them; he that lusts after other than these is a transgressor). *Ladders* 70:8–70:38. See the two endnotes above on Old and New Testaments.

35. Human Rights Watch, "Slavery and Slave Redemption in the Sudan," Human Rights Watch Backgrounder, *Human Rights News*, March 2002 and March 1999. Available from Human Rights Watch, http://www.hrw.org/backgrounder/africa/sudanupdate.htm (accessed September 4, 2005).

36. For this perspective, see
   a. K. Bales, *Disposable People: New Slavery in the Global Economy* (Berkeley: University of California Press, 1999).
   b. J. Chuang, "Redirecting the Debate Over Trafficking in Women: Definitions, Paradigms, and Contexts," *Harvard Human Rights Journal* 11 (1998). Available from the Harvard Human Rights Journal, http://www.law.harvard.edu/students/orgs/hrj/ (accessed September 8, 2005).
   c. D. M. Hughes, "The 'Natasha Trade': Transnational Sex Trafficking," *National Institute of Justice Journal,* January 2001. Available from the National Institute of Justice Journal, http://www.ojp.usdoj.gov/nij/journals/jr000246.htm (accessed September 8, 2005).
   d. J. Salt and J. Stein, "Migration as a Business: The Case of Trafficking," *International Migration* 35 (1997): 467–491.

37. Sometimes the slavery takes on intermediate forms. Prostitutes may be free to leave but lack passport, identification, money, knowledge of the local language, or means of survival. We should not overestimate sex slavery, since most prostitutes probably have probably chosen their work. But that does not disprove the existence of sex slavery, to one extent or another.

38. J. Doezema, "Loose Women or Lost Women? The Re-Emergence of the Myth of 'White Slavery' in Contemporary Discourses of 'Trafficking in Women,'" *Gender Issues* 18 (2000): 23–50.

39. J. Cwikel, K. Illan, and B. Chudakov, "Women Brothel Workers and Occupational Health Risks," *Journal of Epidemiology and Community Health* 57 (2003): 809–815.

40. See, for example, T. Sanders, *Sex Work: A Risky Business.* Cullompton, Devon, UK: Willan, 2004). She considers such topics as "keeping safe," "dodging cops," "secrets and lies," and "choice, risk, and selling sex."

41. We have to decide whether the police officer is conferring a benefit or creating a cost. The former implies mutualism, and the latter parasitism. It is an empirical question whether the offender really needs the corrupt police officer's assistance.

42. For more on Chinese gangs, see K. Chin, *Chinatown Gangs: Extortion, Enterprise and Ethnicity* (New York: Oxford University Press, 1996).

43. A modern economy brings with it vast interdependencies among different organizations, including subsidiaries, contractors, subcontractors, and organizations simply purchasing goods or services from one another. All of these interdependencies give opportunities for criminal parasitism. The ecologist's distinction between ectoparasites and endoparasites can no longer capture these proliferating varieties of crime, some of which have come to light amidst recent exposés of corporate crime. For example, securities frauds occur when one organization plunders the resources of another that it controls. Companies that hire other companies to manage their assets might discover too late that a parasitic crime is underway. Interorganizational parasitism is an important part of modern white-collar crime, and an open field for future ecological analysis.

44. The Brantinghams (cited many times in these pages) distinguish outsider crime from insider crime with respect to neighborhoods as well. This idea is similar, but does not usually refer to parasitic crime in its literal sense.

45. Sometimes the distinction between outsider and insider is confusing. Mimicry is an important natural pattern in which one species imitates another in looks, smell, or behavior, usually for defensive purposes (as subsequent chapters consider). A specialized form is *Wasmannian mimicry*, where one species resembles its host in order to live within the same nest or structure. Several beetles so closely resemble ants that the ants do not understand they are being tricked into providing sustenance to outsiders. I recall a fake university student who stole scores of computers from the campus over a period of two years before he was caught.

46. There is a substantial overlap between these criminal examples and white-collar crime. But customers who commit crimes in an organizational context are not all white-collar offenders. Many of these crimes occur in blue-collar organizations or roles as well. I offer an extensive discussion of white-collar crime in Chapter 7 of M. Felson, *Crime and Everyday Life*, 3rd ed. (Thousand Oaks, CA: Sage, 2002). I argue that such crime should be renamed "crimes of specialized access," and should include crime by all employees, regardless of their social status or organizational position. That definition does not exclude clients, customers, and patients committing crimes via organizations.

47. Many papers link crime to risky and unhealthy behaviors. For a start,
   a. H. Siegal and others, "Under the Influence: Risky Sexual Behavior and Substance Abuse Among Driving Under the Influence Offenders," *Sexually Transmitted Diseases* 26 (1999): 87–92.
   b. M. Junger, R. West, and R. Timman, "Crime and Risky Behavior in Traffic: An Example of Cross-Situational Consistency," *Journal of Research in Crime and Delinquency* 38 (2001): 439–459.
   c. A. Vazsonyi and others, "An Empirical Test of a General Theory of Crime: A Four-Nation Comparative Study of Self-Control and the Prediction of Deviance," *Journal of Research in Crime and Delinquency* 38 (2001): 91–131.
   d. M. Junger, P. van der Heijden, and K. Keane, "Interrelated Harms: Examining the Associations Between Victimizations, Accidents, and Criminal Behavior," *Injury Control and Safety Promotion* 8 (2001): 13–28.

48. Prisons are probably not good for health, but neither is a criminal lifestyle outside of prison. See
   a. C. Coffey and others, "Mortality in Young Offenders: Retrospective Cohort Study," *British Medical Journal* 326 (2003): 1064–1066.
   b. D. P. Farrington, "Crime and Physical Health: Illness, Injuries, Accidents and Offending in the Cambridge Study," *Criminal Behavior and Mental Health* 5 (1995): 261–278.

c. H. Stattin and A. Romelsjo, "Adult Mortality in the Light of Criminality, Substance Abuse, and Behavioural and Family-Risk Factors in Adolescence," *Criminal Behavior and Mental Health* 5 (1995): 279–311.

d. C. A. Yaeger and D. O. Lewis, "Mortality in a Group of Formerly Incarcerated Juvenile Delinquents," *American Journal of Psychiatry* 147 (1990): 612–614.

e. A. Oyefeso and others, "Drug Abuse–Related Mortality: A Study of Teenage Addicts Over a 20-Year Period," *Social Psychiatry and Psychiatric Epidemiology* 34 (1999): 437–441.

If you want to deserve Hell, you need only stay in bed. The world is iniquity; if you accept it, you are an accomplice, if you change it you are an executioner.

—Jean-Paul Sartre[1]

The accomplice to the crime of corruption is frequently our own indifference.

—Bess Myerson[2]

. . . knowingly harboring, concealing or aiding any person who has committed a felony . . . with intent that such person shall avoid or escape from arrest, trial, conviction or punishment for such felony.

—Kansas Criminal Code[3]

Some stories are hard to see, generally, because the clues are hidden or disguised.

—Ben Bradlee[4]

14

Passive Assistance

A modern society does not imprison Mother for giving chicken soup to her delinquent son.[5] Nor does society arrest the bus driver for delivering a youth to where he commits a crime. A city does not close a huge hotel simply for bringing local prostitutes their customers. This chapter calls to your attention some of crime's indirect features that remain very important. This is a general issue in the study of nature. Weeds grow best amidst the flowers, and crime draws resources from those who seem not to be involved. We can call this *passive assistance.*

Passive assistance is a matter of degree. When a sex-oriented newspaper *survives* from advertising prostitution, that's a mutualism. In contrast, a large city newspaper might have only a *few* advertisements assisting prostitutes. Its relationship to prostitution is incidental. Many parents help their children carry out crimes, unintentionally and inexplicitly. Of course, passive assistance is still very important, especially to the offender. It occurs in three forms:

Passive Communication: Helping an offender transfer information to allure victims or reach co-offenders

Passive Feeding: When one offender picks up what's left by another

Passive Shielding: When an offender finds others to shield his illegal acts

The last of the three is a bit more complicated, so I discuss it later.

Passive Communication

The angler fish has a remarkable bacterium inside it that lights up to attract its prey. The lighting process is called *bacterial bioluminsescence.*[6] It shows us that one organism can provide important communication services to another.

For many crimes, especially illegal exchanges, communication is very important. Buyers and sellers of illegal goods or services cannot always find one another easily on their own. Even after illicit buyers or sellers know each other, they might lack fixed addresses, or live where their counterparts do not wish to go, or wish to conceal their own locations. That's why they might rely on other activities to make their illegal contacts feasible or efficient. Offenders often employ conventional communication systems to find their targets without direct physical contact.

In many large cities around the world, prostitution communicates with flyers left beside public telephones. The telephone company, by providing these locations, offers passive communication supporting prostitution.

In addition, many prostitutes draw customers via suggestive advertisements in classified sections of large daily newspapers, in telephone books, or other advertising places.[7] These particular ads might be a small part of the overall revenues. Nightlife newspapers publish rather obvious advertisements for illegal prostitutes, gaining legal revenue and extra circulation in return.

Passive communication assists other crimes, too. Weeklies advertise used products, providing a means for thieves to distribute their booty under a legal guise. The Internet provides many means for circulating illicit drugs and sex, and enabling pedophiles to make their first contacts, or even setting up meetings leading to statutory or forcible rape. A mutualism occurs when a communications company makes a lot of money (compared to its overall profits) providing services to one or more criminal enterprises. But if its relative profits from crime are small, its services to crime are incidental for itself, but very important for crime.

Feeding Off the Scraps

Hyenas clean up what's left after the lion feeds. Then the insects come along to get the rest. An egret eats insects dislodged as cattle graze in the field. The clown fish harmlessly eats the sea anemone's leftovers. Accordingly, many criminals feed off the scraps of legal activities or of other offenders. This process is called *commensalism*.[8] The word's broad meaning is a symbiosis in which one organism gains benefit feeding with another, without harming or helping it. Commensalisms usually involve one organism consuming the unused food of the other—eating the scraps.[9] Many criminal activities feed of the scraps of other crime, and of legal activities as well.

Consider the less attractive street prostitutes, who try to find leftover customers after the more attractive girls have already been picked up. Even if they share some of the same strolls with the more attractive girls, the second or third choices are not really competitors. Similarly, the weaker drug dealers sell the less profitable drugs on the worst corners to the less suitable customers—after the most powerful offenders have carved out the best niches for themselves.

Illegal activities sometimes feed off scraps from *legal* activities, too. I discussed niche packing in an earlier chapter. Illegal taxicabs take over the routes and times that licensed taxis hate. Illegal after-hours bars open up in some American cities after the legal closing times. Illegal street vendors find niches abandoned by licensed merchants.

Crime can also be commensal with *shady* activities—legal but déclassé. This point helps us understand why legalizing sex sales cannot necessarily gain control over the problem. Even though legal brothels can be regulated to some extent, unlicensed prostitutes cater to leftover customers, including those who want to pay less, prefer someone underage, or do not want to use condoms.[10] These customers can go to an unlicensed house, or find an illegal prostitute in a street or bar. Illegal prostitution can benefit by locating in shady areas, or drawing surplus customers from legal establishments in the vicinity. It's not so easy to legalize vice when offenders find a way to feed off its scraps.

Passive Shielding

Passive shielding occurs when a nonoffender shields an offender, with little gain or loss from the crime. I learned about this form of interdependence from ocean biologists, who call this *aegism*.[11] "Shielding" includes helping the offender to

- move about,
- find quick refuge, or
- find shelter.

Sometimes a legal activity keeps using a setting that is also available for illegal activities. Other times a legal activity has abandoned a setting completely, after which offenders take over for their purposes. Exhibit 14.1 explains these methods, pairing crime examples with examples from the ocean.

Exhibit 14.1   Shielding Crime in Four Ways

Helping the Offender	In the Ocean	In the World of Crime
1. *Move about*[1]	The barnacle attaches to the whale.	Mass transit helps offenders get around.
2. *Find quick refuge*[2]	Coral fish retreats into the coral reef.	Cavernous public housing provides offenders refuge.
3. *Find shelter in a site still used*[3]	Harmless bacteria live inside the fish.	Offenders solicit inside train stations.
4. *Find shelter in an abandoned site*[4]	The hermit crab moves into abandoned shells.	Drug abusers move into abandoned buildings.

1. phoresis, 2. epizoism, 3. inquilinis, 4. endoecism.

- Just as the barnacle attaches to the whale for transport, so offenders get around by mass transit and asking lifts from parents.
- Just as the coral fish uses the reef for refuge, so offenders retreat into public housing complexes to evade police or other dangers.
- All too often, offenders find shelter inside existing behavior settings, like bacteria in the belly of a fish.
- Offenders also use abandoned buildings and lots for illegal purposes—a topic discussed at length in several earlier chapters.

These forms of shielding are considered in the next few sections.

Providing Offenders Transport

One of the main necessities for crime is the need to get to the target. (I explain this point in Chapter 21, which proposes a taxonomy for crime.) Mass transit systems in cities provide offenders a means to travel to their crime sites and home again afterward, often carrying the loot. Citizens and researchers alike have considered whether a new transit system or even a single new station will expose local residents to additional risks of incursions by outside offenders. For example, offenders using the New York subway system to commit their offenses usually made short trips within the same borough.[12] Perhaps transit systems help nearby areas trade offenders, increasing overall crime without necessarily endangering one area in particular. Any longer trips to commit crime usually had a destination near Times Square. Clearly the Central Business District (CBD) provides extra attractions for crime. The same can be said of the Central Entertainment District (CED), which attracts a younger crowd, often after dark, infusing alcohol into the bloodstreams of many visitors. The transport system makes these areas accessible for those from other stations to commit crimes. But does the system transport offending to residential stations? Professor Christopher M. Sedelmaier[13] found that an extended light-rail system in New Jersey had no impact on crime rates in the vicinity. On the other hand, research in Vancouver, British Columbia, showed that some young offenders took the monorail to particular stations to carry out offenses nearby.[14] These offenders were interested in the shopping mall and the cars parked between the transit stop and mall itself.

Even private transport can assist crime without intending to do so. Louise Biron found that middle-class teenage burglars in Montreal would call their mothers for a lift home with the loot.[15] Others use taxis to go home or ride with friends. Knowingly or not, those providing offenders with transportation play a role in criminal acts, even without receiving benefits or booty.[16]

We might consider Internet systems as a form of transport, assisting criminal movement toward their targets. Much more needs to be known about how legal activities shield illegal behaviors.

Providing Offenders Refuge

Drug sales might occur on the perimeter of public housing projects of central cities in the United States. This location fits the basic principle observed in nature, for sellers can retreat into the urban reef in case of danger from police or other predators. I have heard police officers from Newark, New Jersey, complain that they are unable to corner and arrest offenders who easily retreat within a local public housing complex and its nearby streets.

This is not a new problem. During the 19th and early 20th centuries, New York's Chinatown was a labyrinth of tiny rooms, stairs, corridors, and businesses that provided refuge for those involved in illegal drugs and prostitution. Impenetrable to outsiders, including police, Chinatown housed certain types of crime in the true sense of a coral reef.

In 1838, Charles Dickens portrayed the crime-ridden "rookeries of London," where Fagin and his gang preyed on their victims two centuries ago. In 1850, Thomas Beames described the area

> like an honeycomb, perforated by a number of courts and blind alleys, *cul de sacs*, without any outlet other than the entrance. Here were the lowest lodging houses in London, inhabited by the various classes of thieves common to large cities. . . .[17]

Beames specifically referred to the "haunts" and "lurking places."

Although most social accounts of crime-saturated areas emphasize their poverty and depravity, the ecological paradigm reminds us to study the settings, activities, and the opportunities they afford for offenders to gain refuge. Bear in mind that these lurking places are not entirely dead construction, since people live and work there. Some industrial areas are abandoned during off-hours (when they are available for crime use), but occupied at other times. Even totally abandoned locations were probably once used for legitimate purposes. (See the prior discussions of abandoned sites in several early chapters.)

The concept of refuge can be applied not only to offenders but also to the victims of their predations. Professors Bonnie Fisher and Jack Nasar have done just that, noting that the worse environments for pedestrians deny them a sense of refuge.[18] A challenge for urban designers and architects is to provide refuge for likely victims of crime, without providing refuge for the offenders, too.

Providing Offenders Shelter

Students of urban crime have long known that prostitutes, drug dealers, and gangs often commandeer abandoned urban properties for their own purposes. Even businesses that are still in operation during the day are often emptied at night, giving way for criminal use. Thus a junkyard houses criminal activities at night and on weekends. A school parking lot becomes an off-hours place for a gang to gather. A city park becomes the hangout for a local gang during certain hours. Any legitimate activity with a limited schedule can provide shelter to criminal activity operating on another— usually later—schedule.[19] I believe that the "delinquency areas" emphasized by urban ecologists, Shaw and McKay, exist largely because they have a particular type of ecosystem, providing offenders refuge and shelter.

Urban train stations can shelter illegal activity, including drug sales, prostitution, and scams. Some stations are sufficiently cavernous to assist offenders wishing to hide from police. A bar or tavern is a living business but might also provide a home for offenders who do not necessarily buy more beer than anybody else.[20] A mapping study by Professors Paul and Patricia Brantingham found that property crimes were closely related to the location of a local bar. Drinking establishments can provide ongoing shelter for prostitutes, drug dealers, stolen-goods handlers, drunk drivers, and burglars. Of course, such sheltering can develop into mutual dependence.

The Brantinghams linked fast food restaurants to local criminal activities.[21] Some drug dealers make illegal exchanges within fast food restaurants, or at least meet for that purpose. Malls provide shelter and nurture to offenders who quietly sell illegal commodities or commit other crimes without necessarily harming the mall itself.[22]

College dormitories can provide a home for underage drinking, marihuana smoking, bicycle-fencing operations, and various other offenses. Even well-organized group homes for juveniles can provide shelter for assaults and rapes. Hospitals make it easy for some of their employees to assault or steal from patients. Prisons house a good deal of crime among prisoners, sometimes involving staff as victims or offenders. Although secondary-school crime takes place mostly after school and off the premises, schools are often enough used for illegal actions inside, too.[23]

Racetracks frequently provide a home to pickpockets, who take advantage of flowing cash and episodic distractions. Unlike the pickpocket feeding off a crowded street, the racetrack pickpocket finds shelter within an ongoing activity. If these offenders begin to harm the racetrack itself, parasitism takes over. One form of symbiosis often gives way to another. A challenge in studying crime symbioses is to figure out these sequences and turning points.

Some apartment buildings are especially hospitable to illegal activities. John Eck and Julie Wartell showed that improving management of rental properties could reduce the drug problems within. The point for now is that places that are not intrinsically criminal nonetheless might assist illegal activity.[24] Even private homes shelter crime. Intrafamily violence is often (but not always) carried out under the aegis of the home. Many a private home is the setting for smoking marihuana or more serious drug use, underage alcohol consumption, sexual assault, and more. Many a working parent provides inadvertent shelter for delinquent offspring and symbiotic friends. We need to ask ourselves when an establishment with criminal activity inside is linked to the activity as a mutualism, as a host to a parasite, or as a passive assistant. It is clear that nonparticipants provide crime substantial shelter.

Assisting Offenders in More Than One Way

Certain settings assist crime in very diverse ways. This section considers motels and a behemoth bus station.

Budget Motels and Criminal Activities

Karin Schmerler, a public safety analyst at Chula Vista Police Department in California, carried out an excellent study of crime and disorder at local budget motels and what can be done about it.[25] As she explained,

> The very nature of overnight lodging makes it conducive to crime and disorder. Motels and hotels house people only temporarily, often in commercial areas with high crime rates. Because budget motels offer low rates, accept cash, and often have a relatively unrestricted environment, local residents with illicit or antisocial intentions find them particularly attractive. Drug sales, prostitution, loud parties, and other activities can be undertaken at motels, with less risk than at private residences. Motel guests have little motivation to report drug dealing and prostitution because they have no long-term stake in the motel. In addition, motel managers often have a limited opportunity to get to

know the backgrounds of the people on their premises. . . . Direct access to rooms allows problem guests and visitors to come and go without being seen by motel personnel.

Even smugglers use motels as they move illegal immigrants into the country.

Ms. Schmerler calculated "police calls per service per motel room per year" for each motel, including both chain and independent establishments. Exhibit 14.2 presents some of her results. In 2003, among independent motels, Tower Lodge had more than five calls for police service per room per year, more than 10 times higher than the Riviera Motel. Most of the motel chains generated less than one call to the police, per room per year. Motel 6 stood out among the chain motels as most likely to generate police activity. Three independent motels were quite a bit worse. The fewest calls were made about the Holiday Inn Express, a motel chain that advertises "no surprises."

How New York's Bus Terminal Assisted Crime

When it comes to assisting offenders, the most extreme case I know is New York City's Port Authority Bus Terminal. For decades it provided offenders a safe haven, as well as a place to find victims or partners in crime. Before it was reengineered, removing many crannies and corners, that terminal's perimeter areas served illicit purposes, while its lobbies were the site of illegal solicitations and lead-ins to predatory attacks.[26]

Indeed, New York's bus terminal combined several types of passive assistance for crime, inside the building, at the edges, or in nearby Times Square:

Communication—It helped sexual rule breakers make eye contact, signal one another, then arrange illicit liaisons elsewhere or inside.

Transport—It brought offenders to their targets via buses and subways.

Refuge—Offenders could linger just outside, with a chance to retreat into the bowels of the sprawling building.

Shelter amidst ongoing activities—Its on-premise activities included drug sales, drug use, prostitution, consensual nonpecuniary sex, thefts, personal attacks, and more.

Shelter in abandoned areas—The bus terminal left whole areas abandoned at night that offenders seized for their own purposes.

This combination of so many illegal activities harmed the building's reputation and revenue. So they moved in an excellent manager, who corrected the problems.

Exhibit 14.2   Calls for Police Service at 26 Local Motels, Chula Vista, California, 2003

Calls for Service per Room, per Year	Chain Motels	Independent Motels
More than 5.0	—	Tower Lodge
4.0 to 4.9	—	Big 7
		Etc. Motel
3.0 to 3.9	—	—
2.0 to 2.9	Motel 6	Highway Inn
		Early Californian
		El Primero
1.0 to 1.9	Rodeway Inn	Traveler Inn Suites
	Good Nite Inn	Palomar Motel
		Royal Vista Inn
		Palomar Inn
0.5 to 0.9	Days Inn	Harborview
	Vagabond Inn	Bay Cities Motel
	Best Western A	Farmhouse Motel
	Best Western B	Avon Motel
		Travel Inn
Less than 0.5	La Quinta	Riviera Motel
	Ramada Inn	
	Holiday Inn Express	

SOURCE: Chula Vista Police Department, Chula Vista, California, http://www.hulavistapd.org/motels

Overview

Passive assistance poses questions for us all. Friends or family members might assist a burglar's transport or offer refuge to an offender, without criminal guilt or moral turpitude. The mother who knows of her son's transgressions can hardly deny him his bed and breakfast. The high school provides a home for juvenile delinquents, but cannot throw them out without a good reason.

Many people and places shield and protect crime, knowingly or not, with uneven ability to intercede. We can see in this chapter even more that criminal activities are intricately related, in ongoing fashion, to legal features of life. I wonder how often I have assisted criminal action as I go about my daily life.

Central Points, Chapter 14

1. Many legitimate activities passively assist crime.

2. Offenders sometimes use legitimate activities to contact victims, accomplices, or partners in illegal exchanges.

3. Offenders sometimes use legitimate transportation facilities to get to crime scenes or to return home, or to commit criminal acts within those facilities.

4. Many places provide refuge for offenders who commit their crimes just outside. Other places provide direct shelter for illegal activities or for those who commit these activities.

Exercises

1. How might an airport assist crime?

2. What crimes depend on motorized transport?

3. How might a good mother assist her son's or daughter's delinquent acts?

4. How might a high school assist crime?

Notes

1. French novelist, dramatist, philosopher, political activist (1905–1980). Quoted in *The Columbia World of Quotations* (New York: Columbia University Press, 1996).

2. U.S. television figure, columnist, government official (1924–). Quoted in C. Safran, "Impeachment?" *Redbook*, April 1974.

3. *Kansas Criminal Code*, sec. 21–3812-a.

4. *A Good Life: Newspapering and Other Adventures* (New York: Simon and Schuster, 1996).

5. In Stalinist times, the suspicious Soviets were inclined to punish all of a suspect's family and associates, often with death.

6. For more on bacterial bioluminescence, see V. B. Meyer-Rochow, "Light of My Life: Messages in the Dark," *Biologist* (London) 48 (2001): 163. Also see the bioluminsence

webpage of the life sciences department of the University of California, Santa Barbara, http://www.lifesci.ucsb.edu/~biolum/ (accessed September 4, 2005). Bacterial bioluminescence is found in various other organisms. See V. Nunes-Halldorson and N. L. Duran, "Bioluminescent Bacteria: *Lux* Genes as Environmental Biosensors," *Brazilian Journal of Microbiology* 34 (June 2003): 91–96. Available from Scientific Electronic Library online, http://www.scielo.br/ (accessed September 4, 2005).

7.   When aegism takes an electronic form, especially using the Internet, we might call it *cyberaegism*—providing that the communications companies do not have a substantial benefit or cost. If offenders use the Internet to carry their illegal files, we might call that *cyberphoresis*. Cyberaegism overlaps the other categories.

8.   Latin for "together at the same table."

9.   For more on commensalism, see A. J. Bruce, "Shrimps and Prawns of Coral Reefs, With Special Reference to Commensalism," in O. A. Jones and R. Endean, eds., *Biology and Geology of Coral Reefs,* vol. 2, 37–94 (New York and London: Academic Press, 1973). Also see M. Barbour and others, *Terrestrial Plant Ecology* (Menlo Park, CA: Addison-Wesley Longman, 1998).

10.   For a review of the issues, see Crime and Misconduct Commission, Queensland, Australia, "Regulating Prostitution: An Evaluation of the Prostitution Act 1999 (Queensland)" (2004). Available from the Crime and Misconduct Commission, http://www.cmc.qld.gov.au/library/CMCWEBSITE/RegulatingProstitution.pdf (accessed September 4, 2005).

11.   This derives from the Greek word *aegis*, referring to the shield of Zeus. *Phoresis* comes from the Greek word *pherein*, to carry. *Epizoism* comes from the Greek words *epi* (outside) and *zoion* (animal). Epizoism is also called *epiphytism*. *Inquilinism* comes from the Latin *colere*, to live in. *Endoecism* comes from the Greek *endo*, within. Of course, there are plenty land examples of these symbioses. Many prairie mammals dig tunnels and dens that are later inhabited or even shared by other species. I did not use Jonah as an example of phoresis, since he did not gain much from the ride.

12.   Geographers call this a distance decay function. It takes on special properties in a system with discrete entries and exits.

13.   See C. M. Sedelmaier, *Railroaded: The Effects of a New Transport System on Local Crime Patterns* (dissertation, Rutgers University, 2003).

14.   P. J. Brantingham, P. Brantingham, and P. S. Wong, "How Public Transit Feeds Private Crime: Notes on the Vancouver 'Skytrain' Experience," *Security Journal* 2 (1991): 91–95.

15.   L. Biron and C. Ladouceur, "The Boy Next Door: Local Teen-age Burglars in Montreal," *Security Journal* 2 (1991): 200–204.

16.   Transportation is also relevant to the targets for crime. Trucks and other vehicles convey property targets toward offenders lying in wait. Transport systems, including streams of pedestrians on streets, bring targets toward offenders. In terms of relativity, a body at rest is in relative motion, so we can construe all convergences in terms of phoresis. But for simplicity, it is best to emphasize transport for offenders, not for their targets.

17.   In 1850, Thomas Beames wrote a classic work. See T. Beames, *The Rookeries of London* (London: F. Cass, 1970). Original edition published 1850.

18.   B. S. Fischer, and J. L. Nasar, "Fear of Crime in Relationship to Three Exterior Site Features: Prospect, Refuge and Escape," *Environment and Behavior* 24 (1992): 35–65.

19.   Sometimes we must use substantial judgment to apply ecological terms to crime. When studying marine biology or other animal topics, it is easy to distinguish endoecism from inquilinism. In the former case one animal resides inside the burrow of another. In the second case, an animal resides inside the body of the other. But when studying crime, we consider how crime finds its home within settings, such as homes, bars, hotels, motels, or schools. If these are abandoned or largely so, their use for illegal activities is best classified as endoecism. But if these settings continue to be active for legitimate purposes, inquilinism is the closer

classification. That's why timing of offender usage is an essential issue for understanding crime's aegism.

20. To be sure, some drinking establishments house prostitutes or drug dealers with explicit methods to share in their takings. That implies mutualism, not inquilinism.

21. P. C. Brantingham and P. L. Brantingham, "Mobility, Notoriety and Crime: A Study of Crime Patterns in Urban Nodal Points," *Journal of Environmental Systems* 11 (1982): 89–99.

22. When they get more overt, beginning to do harm to the mall, the inquilinism gives way to parasitism. For more on mall-related crime, see T. C. La Grange, "The Impact of Neighborhoods, Schools, and Malls on the Spatial Distribution of Property Damage," *Journal of Research in Crime and Delinquency* 36 (1999): 393–422.

Also see S. Phillips and R. Cochrane, "Crime and Nuisance in the Shopping Centre: A Case Study in Crime Prevention" (n.d.), British Home Office, http://www.homeoffice.gov.uk/rds/prgpdfs/fcpu16.pdf (accessed September 4, 2005). (Crime Prevention Unit Paper 16)

23. I have not placed a limit on inquilinism. Does the school really shelter crime if the offender does nothing more than think about it a few moments while at school? Should we limit this concept to crime carried out inside the school? As we learn more from ecologists and from our own experience in crime ecology, perhaps we will find our limits and clarify our organization.

24. J. Eck and J. Wartell, "Improving the Management of Rental Properties With Drug Problems: A Randomized Experiment," in L. G. Mazerolle and J. Roehl, eds., *Civil Remedies and Crime Prevention* (Monsey, NY: Criminal Justice Press, 1998) (Volume 9 of *Crime Prevention Studies* series).

25. See K. Schmerler, "Disorder at Budget Motels" (2005), Center for Problem-oriented Policing, http://www.popcenter.org (accessed September 4, 2005). See also motel guides at the Chula Vista Police Department, Chula Vista, California, http://www.chulavistapd.org/motels (accessed September 4, 2005).

26. See Chapter 12, endnote 12.

PART IV

Attack and Defense

A cunning fox cannot outsmart a skilled hunter.

—Chinese proverb

You have to be fast on your feet and adaptive or else a strategy is useless.

—Charles de Gaulle[1]

. . . under cover of darkness, and further concealed in a most cunning disguisement.

—Herman Melville[2]

I can always find a way to get my honey!

—Winnie the Pooh (A. A. Milne)[3]

15

Foraging Fundamentals

The giant panda eats just a few varieties of bamboo, moving on to a new habitat when these run out.[4] In contrast, omnivorous North American bears feed on a wide variety of berries, fruits, nuts, insects, grains, meat, and more. This helps us understand why the black bear tends to thrive, while the panda are diminishing in numbers.[5] It also helps us think about how offenders sustain their crime, and what we might do to stop them.

The topic of offender specialization has generated some confusion in the past. Some observers mistakenly divide offenders into two groups of specialists—violent and nonviolent offenders. True, some "property offenders" seldom use violence. But they tend to commit a wide variety of property offenses. Similarly, most "violent offenders" commit a diversity of crimes, the bulk of which are not violent. If the same offender burgles, shoplifts, grabs wallets, and strips cars, we can hardly call him a specialist.[6] One reason to diversify is to broaden one's access to crime opportunities. That is the essence of foraging. This chapter explores how offenders forage, and the next two chapters explore their broader strategies. Of course foraging is not universal.

Does a Given Crime Require Foraging at All?

Many crimes involve no foraging at all. Often an offender is in routine and close contact with the target. For example, violent aggression arises among couples with a sexual relationship, among friends and acquaintances, even among strangers whose activity space routinely overlaps. Employee theft often involves no search, since valuable property crosses in front of one's eyes without having to hunt for it. However, many valuable goods are shipped in plain boxes, requiring an employee to forage on the dock or in the storeroom in order to locate them precisely.[7]

Although offenders forage mostly in the physical world, they can also forage electronically or in files at the workplace.[8] Most of this chapter focuses on the first. But the other two are important precisely because they make foraging easy for some offenders. Someone in just the right position in an organization can find the crime targets with less effort and risk. Telephone foragers, such as obscene phone callers, can let their fingers do the walking. Internet foragers can mass mail messages in order to find people to trick. Information businesses are increasingly using software to stop this from happening. Future Internet charges will probably render widespread foraging too costly to offenders, who will decide it is not worth it.

Why Study Foraging?

Foraging is important for at least two reasons. First, it offers a handle on crime prevention. By forcing offenders to forage less efficiently, a community can lower its crime rate. Second, foraging helps us see how otherwise "unrelated" crimes fit a common pattern. A burglary now and shoplifting an hour from now might be part of the same foraging trip by the same offender.

Perhaps an offender has a general *foraging pattern* that goes beyond any one of his offenses. Third, crime foraging fits a larger human activity pattern. Perhaps burglars and shoplifters forage similarly. Fourth, victims and other crime participants forage too, as you shall see. Finally, foraging fits a larger pattern of nature. Foraging applies to many crimes and criminals, and is an essential feature of crime. This chapter examines some of the basic tactics of foraging, while the next two chapters consider broader strategic aspects. Foraging is an essential part of crime—and life itself—because it enhances opportunities.

Tactical Diversity

Satchel Paige might have been the greatest baseball pitcher in history. He pitched for the Negro leagues, and only entered the major leagues in middle age when the color bar was broken. He was also a colorful person. In his own words, "I use my single windup, my double windup, my triple windup, my hesitation windup, my no windup. I also use my step-n-pitch-it, my submariner, my sidearmer, and my bat dodger. Man's got to do what he's got to do."[9]

In nature, thousands of specific tactics are employed. Tactical diversity is part of hunting for food as well as foraging for crime targets.

Drawing from larger ecology, the diversity of foraging tactics fits three categories, listed in Exhibit 15.1. Like other living things, each offender has a *diet breadth*.[10] Perhaps a certain offender is willing to steal money, jewelry, and an occasional computer. Others steal only money, thus having a narrower diet breadth. If a given town offers little opportunity to sell stolen jewelry, diet breadth is narrowed and crime is less problematic. *Hunting method* includes a variety of methods for approaching, entering, and committing crimes.[11] Thus the same offender might break into buildings, steal from garages, and go into stores intending to shoplift, while using a variety of means for personal attacks. *Range* takes into account the trip to crime, and how far offenders wander off their known paths. Some offenders have wider diets and more varied hunting methods and broader ranges, and others are relatively narrow on all three dimensions.

Of course a population of offenders varies more than any individual within it. But one population is not the same as another. The thieves of Newark, New Jersey, might forage with greater diversity than the thieves of Cape May, a relatively small city at the southern end of the state.

Exhibit 15.1   Three Categories of Foraging Diversity

Categories	Foraging for Food	Foraging for Crime Targets	How Versatile Is the Average Offender?	How to Reduce the Offender's Options
1. Diet breadth	Diversity of food it consumes	Diversity of crime targets	Fairly versatile	Reduce suitable crime targets and crime benefits
2. Hunting method	How it captures quarry	Methods for overcoming victims	Fairly versatile	Reduce easy and low-risk crime options
3. Range	How widely it searches	Trips to crime locations	Not very versatile— sticks to known areas	Narrow the realm of insecure settings

The Average Foraging Thief

A *particular* offender tends to be rather versatile in diet breadth and perhaps hunting tactics. But he might still have preferences. The average thief would probably prefer cash, with jewelry and lightweight electronic items as a backup. But he is highly unlikely to steal bulky goods of little value per pound. Thus the diet breadth is limited, but not totally restricted.

Probably his greatest versatility applies to hunting method. He might break in. He might walk in. He would probably prefer to enter through an unlocked door, but still be willing to break in as a second choice.

He might take something outside. He might shoplift. He checks for unlocked cars, but also might break into locked cars. He treks over to the university, hoping to pick up a few wallets. Perhaps he uses a stolen credit card for a brief period. He takes the money to buy his drug of preference, then shifts to another drug if convenient. But an offender is probably the most restricted in foraging range. He commits crime in the areas he knows—from home to school or work to places of shopping and recreation. But he will depart from the normal path to some extent.

Why Offenders Do Best as Generalists

The giant panda can eat 25 varieties of bamboo if it has to, but first looks for its favorites. Theoretically, offenders should be generalists on all three dimensions to get the most out of crime. But foragers tend to be *practical*, even if a wider range is possible. Offenders are *relative generalists*, developing an operational diet breadth, method, and range, even if a wider range is possible. Although it is impractical for one person to commit all types of crime or to attack all targets, it is even less practical to limit oneself to a single crime specialty.[12]

The trials and errors nature of crime is highly consistent with foraging in diverse ways. Yet some offenders only attack those close to them, or only pilfer from their own employers. Of course, offenders who commit crimes very close to home also tend to act illegally elsewhere if they can.

Crime can be prevented by limiting foraging opportunities, or by making foraging more costly. The low-crime society makes offenders look long and hard for crime targets, or forces them to rely only on *occasional* crime opportunities. In contrast, a high-crime society makes foraging easy and compounds it with easy access without foraging, while providing many opportunities that help offenders extend their versatility. As Exhibit 15.1 indicates, designing secure processes and systems serves most to reduce diet breadth and hunting possibilities, while designing secure environments tends to lessen the offender's range.

We can expect the dynamics of crime opportunity to interact with those of foraging. If an offender's opportunities are suddenly lessened, he will probably *begin* by seeking alternatives. But if that does not work for him, he might have to restrict his efforts and reduce criminal action, or even abandon it.

Opportunities to Become More Versatile, or Less

Offenders who own a small truck can carry off a wider breadth of loot than those on foot. Those who have moved around are more familiar with different places, widening their ranges accordingly. Those who live in their cars also have a diffuse range. Consider John Allen Muhammad and Lee Boyd Malvo, accused of several sniper attacks in Virginia. They lived in the car and parked it in different places, thus confounding police trackers and crime geographers.

People living close to a subsistence level probably forage with less discrimination. That is, they are willing to eat anything. Human hunting and gathering societies do best when they forage with very open minds.[13] On the other hand, prosperity helps people become picky eaters, vegetarian or vegephobic.[14] A wealth of crime targets helps some offenders focus on their best targets. But do not push this too far, for many types of target can be grabbed if the opportunities are present.

Settings Rich in Crime Targets

A setting rich in crime targets will tend to

- draw more nonoffenders into crime,
- invite former offenders to return to the illicit fold,
- encourage occasional offenders to increase their participation, and
- make active offenders more efficient at what they are doing.

In the process, all of these offender *populations* have a greater variety of options, and will tend to become more versatile. On the other hand, an *individual* offender with a lucrative and easy source of illicit profit might limit himself to that. A white-collar offender with an excellent crime niche might not bother with other targets. Of course, most offenders—white-collar or not—lack a single niche that is repeatedly productive, and must generalize beyond a single crime opportunity.

Perhaps the greatest source of limitation on offending comes from the limitations on human movement. For example, offenders who reside in unconnected small towns have less diversity of crime targets available and limited chances to fence stolen goods. In parts of the world with few cars, this is much more the case. Isolation interferes with crime. It gives access to less variety of items to steal, fewer chances to fence goods, and perhaps a narrower range of intoxicants. Of course, modern transport systems help to overcome these limitations.

Crime Timing and Range

The weather and the seasons influence crime by constraining everyday routines of offenders as well as their targets. We can think of the daily range of offender activity as elastic, partly in response to environmental conditions and sustenance requirements. In pleasant weather, people range farther from home, where they are more likely to be offenders or targets of crime, while leaving the home and its contents unsupervised. Ranges vary not only with climate but also by weekday or weekend. Vacation periods also modify the range of activities, creating new crime opportunities not available during the rest of the year. Often that occurs in warm months, but many people take their trips when the home weather is most oppressive. Think about birds, whose usual range is not the same in summer and winter, and hungry birds might sometimes go where they are not expected at all.[15]

Crime Tactics Change With Targets

Offenders have found many means to scout or explore, as well as to grub, poke into, rifle through, rummage, ransack, root out, track down, ferret, or chase after their targets. Humans also diversify their tactics. The Haida Indians have historically used seven tactics to catch fish, including basket traps, dip nets, rakes, spears, stone traps, and weirs (fences), as well as hook and line. They varied these methods by type of fish,[16] a reminder that predatory methods are highly situational.

Modern auto thieves also use a variety of methods.[17] Some steal keys. Others find cars with keys in them. Others use key duplicates. Others jump-start the engine or thwart control systems. Others take a car at gunpoint or using strong-arm methods. Others steal car parts from immobile cars. Others take contents from unlocked cars. Others break in locked cars. This variety reflects also the purpose of auto theft. Those stealing a car for a few days are not inclined to wreck it, while those who want a 10-minute race wouldn't let that worry them.

Physical Capacities and Offender Tactics

Even before they go hunting, organisms differ in physical capacities, hence in predatory methods. Cats use their claws, short and powerful limbs, and stabilizing tails to make quick turns and sprints, using a grapple-and-slash method to kill. Birds have more powerful claws, excellent for ambushing, biting the neck or back, then carrying the carcass away to eat elsewhere. Canines pursue and bite, using powerful jaws and necks as well as long and sharp teeth.

Criminals must take into account their own heights, weights, and appearance vis-à-vis potential human targets or guardians. (See the maximum size rule in Chapter 17.) Thus the weaker offenders do best avoiding violent offenses, unless they find smaller victims, use power in numbers or weapons, or use surprise to enhance their attack. Weakness also affects property offending, with feeble burglars confined to smaller booty, unless they have stronger compatriots or automotive assistance. More adept offenders can climb over fences or jump upon fire escapes. Certain offenders are excellent at social life, finding accomplices to compensate for their own physical limitations. Some offenders have mastered the art of intimidation, instilling fear beyond their muscular capacities. Some have trusting faces or smooth voices that assist interpersonal deception, while others cannot win the confidence of anybody, and have to use brute force or utter stealth. Diverse personal traits can affect how each offender selects the type of crime to commit, as well as the particular target, setting, and range of illicit exploration.

So far in this chapter, I have explained when foraging occurs and does not. I have offered the basic categories of foraging, considering offender generality and specificity in these terms. Now I turn to the diverse tactics by which offenders seek out targets.

Basic Foraging Tactics

Serendipity is as applicable to stealing as it is to an afternoon in the library. Offenders are very likely to stumble upon crime opportunities. Conversely, their adversaries might chance upon them, interfering with their criminal acts when they least expect interference. Offenders vary in knowledge. Sometimes they know just where to go to find their crime targets. Sometimes they know rather little. Foraging offenders often have intermediate knowledge—with some idea where to look but not precise information.

Professor Kim Rossmo distinguishes four foraging styles by which offenders find victims. Some set out from home. (He calls these "hunters" in a narrow sense of that word.) A poacher sets out from elsewhere. A troller finds victims fortuitously while engaging in nonpredatory activities. A trapper abuses a job or other position, using subterfuge to get offenders where he can take advantage.[18] These distinctions are part of a larger foraging literature.

Hunting Versus Browsing

In general, hunting with low probability of success requires relatively large gains when success finally arrives. Lions find that the wildebeest usually gets away, but when they catch one they have a large dinner. Other animals live off higher success rates with smaller quarry. A whale sweeps up many small fish in its wake, allowing little chance of escape. Although the fox finds some large targets, it is more likely to consume insects casually, browsing rather than chasing. Accordingly, the petty shoplifter can be fairly sure to exit numerous stores with small items, and many a youth steals little items on the way home from school. Many offenders, while browsing for small items, hope on a good day to grab a rack of valuable leather coats. The wise merchant alternates the direction of hangers on the rack, so the coats lock when the thief tries to grab them all. If you wish to live in a more secure community, make your offenders work hard for their loot.

Ambush Versus Pursuit

Predators hunt in various ways. It is often economical to ambush their prey rather than to engage in a swift pursuit. Those attacking the weak, old, or sick might find a pursuit to be no particular problem, while attacks on the healthy require more stealth and surprise. The robber who finds a weak victim on an otherwise empty train platform can easily give chase. But attacking a healthy adult often requires ambush, weapons, or accomplices. In today's world, the healthy, young, and strong tend to take the most chances, underestimating what offenders might do to them.

Lying in Wait

The spider, after spinning its web, waits to trap its prey. It feels the vibrations along the web lines to determine when to act. As the Scottish poet James Thomson describes the spider,

> In eager watch he sits,
> O'erlooking all his waving snares around.[19]

Similarly, the alligator quietly waits until something edible happens by. The process is slow, but uses little energy and fits its cold-blooded metabolism. Human hunters use a variety of ground blinds, camouflage chairs, tree steps, and other devices. To quote one hunting website,

> Deer are creatures of habit. If unmolested, they follow the same routine, the same trails, day after day, shifting the pattern only because of weather conditions and the availability of food.[20]

Lying in wait and alluring sounds are part of the hunter's repertoire:

> The key to hunting [just before the breeding period] is to move your stand into doe activity areas. Funnels and travel corridors between bedding and feeding areas are excellent locations. It is during this time that doe bleats and tending buck grunts are highly effective. The art of horn rattling also works very well in some areas.

Survival activities themselves expose people and their property to criminal action. The lion lies in wait at the watering hole, knowing the gazelle must go there sooner or later. Similarly, the blitz rapist might wait around near women's rooms for the right moment to attack.[21] Human foragers take advantage of natural flows as their quarry goes about daily life. Many a human offender waits for targets. Offenders hang out on street corners and loiter around washrooms or on subway platforms. Others wait in shadows, doorsteps, or in stairwells. Illicit drug sellers linger in the park. Many offenders lack patience, but might be able to use this strategy by chatting among themselves, drinking, smoking, napping, coming and going, or finding something else to do.

Police, too, lie in wait seeking to arrest these and other offenders. A police stakeout is essentially a legal form of loitering. Police face problems similar to those of offenders. One of my students, an undercover agent, reported great difficulty doing stakeouts in low-crime neighborhoods. Watchful neighbors interfere with police work, just as they do with crime. In contrast, she had little trouble with stakeouts in a high-crime area, where nobody asks too many questions.

Unfortunately, the modern cell phone makes it easier to linger, pretending to be talking to someone while watching for the right moment to commit a crime.

The word "stalking" has come to mean the repeated and prolonged harassment or shadowing of a woman by an unwanted male admirer. Similarly, fans stalk celebrities, some in hopes of a glimpse, others for criminal purposes. But stalking in the predatory literature involves an effort to approach and attack prey for the kill. Foxes stalk their smaller and faster prey, such as rabbits.[22] The fox crouches low to the ground, moving quietly for the kill. Many offenders use parallel methods to make quick attacks on victims who would resist or escape if they know what was about to happen. If you hear the footsteps behind you for some time, you are probably safe. The footsteps you do not hear are the most dangerous.

Crime prevention through environmental design offers many methods to interfere with offenders stalking victims. Communities can locate women's washrooms away from telephones, light up suspicious areas, open up blind spots, and place legitimate businesses in areas formerly used for criminal approach. The point is to give offenders a smaller window of opportunity.

Testing for Targets

Although some animals are sure of their prey, in other cases, animal predation depends on testing. A wolf pack tests many animals before finally finding a sick, young, old, or wounded animal, or one that cannot run away.[23] Many burglary reports find that a door or window was tampered with, or a lock half-broken, without actual entry. Unsuccessful burglaries are very common, giving us reason to believe that testing for targets is a common feature of crime. Even robberies involve failed approaches, attempted pursuits, and withdrawals. Crimes vary in how much stealth they require, which is why not all offenses share the same habitat. In particular, crime habitats vary in how much they make offenders and offenses stand out or fade from view.

Social Foraging

Offender cooperation can contribute to crime at all stages. Such cooperation can take at least four aspects:

1. Preoffense cooperation

2. Co-foraging

3. Co-attack

4. Cooperation in the crime's aftermath

All four aspects are important, helping to explain social foraging.

Even a lion has difficulty overcoming an ox.[24] That's the reason for social foraging—a general ecological term for foraging in groups.[25] Some animal species forage alone; others forage in groups; and still others can forage either way. In general, group foraging is more common if the prey is bigger than the predator. Group foraging overcomes the predator's individual limitations. The disadvantage is that dinner must be shared, or the co-predators must fight over it. These rules apply to criminal foraging. Unarmed robbers tend to forage in small groups, while an armed robber, especially with a gun, can overcome the victim without accomplices.

The gain per lion declines as the group size gets too large, a principle that might also explain why human miscreants avoid committing crimes as a large group. Among lions, the optimal group size is two, but lions typically forage in groups that are larger than optimal, probably because other social factors enter in to the picture. Of course, the benefits of group size vary with circumstances. To rob everybody in the restaurant, one needs several well-armed accomplices.

Foraging patterns among birds vary by age,[26] and so it is with humans. Human teenage delinquents most often forage in small groups, usually in pairs, but larger groups are possible. The youngest teenage offenders are especially likely to commit crimes in groups. As offenders age into their 20s and beyond, they are more prone to lone offending.[27]

The social cooperation in offending is not highly structured as one might suspect (see Chapter 20 on street gangs). Those who forage alone this time might forage in a group next time, and vice versa. Juveniles tend not to commit their offenses with the same co-offenders from one occasion to the next. These offender inconsistencies are consistent with anthropological and archaeological reports that human hunter-gatherer groups range widely in size, and vary considerably throughout the year.[28]

The benefits of assisted foraging go beyond the size of the attack group alone. A nesting osprey notices when other birds return with food, then follows them.[29] Signaling opportunities for food is common enough among animal species. Of course, humans also share or trade knowledge. Professor Pierre Tremblay emphasizes information sharing among offenders before the onset of the offense, even if an offender acts alone to commit the crime.[30] Although social foraging can be quite elaborate in the animal world, we are only beginning to understand how it works in the world of crime.

Foraging Is Complicated by Other Activities

Foraging often occurs in conjunction with or conflict with other activities. That affects its safety and effectiveness.

Foraging in the Midst of Your Own Predators

While foraging, offenders must take into account their own adversaries. Many studies show that animals forage differently when their own predators are present or absent. Group predation alleviates risk by providing more allies to fight and assuring that not every animal needs to be vigilant; designated watchers can alert the group if danger is present, while more eyes are watching. Solitary hunting requires extra vigilance against the hunter's own enemies. Burglars, too, can avail themselves of lookouts against their opponents. Group thievery helps warn against police, guards, owners, or others who would turn them in or otherwise thwart their illicit efforts. Groups can better threaten opponents, even when conducting property crime. Thus nonviolent pickpocket teams can suddenly threaten violence if their quarry turns on them.

Attracting Mates, Attracting Predators

Attracting a reproductive partner is a fundamental requirement for a species to survive in the long run. Interestingly, this attraction process sometimes is at odds with basic and immediate survival, for the mating game exposes many organisms to substantial risk of being eaten.[31] Mating success requires an organism to advertise itself to attract a mate. Each member of the species seeks notoriety over its competitors in order to find a mate, in the process exposing itself to predators as well. Frog noises and bird songs, bright colors, and odors—all these attract mates and predators, alike. Male *Girardinichthys* fish with large fins not only attract females but also have trouble maneuvering and are more likely to be eaten by water snakes.[32] Human masculinity also has display characteristics that can attract females along with attacks by other males. Display often conflicts with safe offending, since concealment and machismo are largely incompatible. Some masculinity displays are targeted toward other males, in quest for status or power in the group or to convey threats for one's own future security. These displays can however evoke extra attacks. In addition, some offenders announce their own crimes to others as a form of masculinity display, also exposing themselves to extra risk of police notice.

Animals must balance the conflicting needs of reproduction and immediate survival. This is sometimes accomplished by maximizing attractiveness only during a curtailed mating season; the nonmating season is longer and security returns to top priority. For example, many bird species have bright feathers during mating season and toned-down feathers for the rest of the year. Birds have many mating systems: monogamy, polygamy, polyandry, and promiscuity.

The constant natural problem is to balance the need to reproduce against the risk of being eaten. Some herbivorous animals possess large penises and copulate quickly to reduce their risks while at it.[33] Spiny lobsters move into deeper waters during mating season, thus avoiding predators. However, for some species, reproduction is very risky indeed. Australian *Latrodectus* spiders participate in what's called sexual cannibalism. The male somersaults onto the female's fangs during copulation, with a two-thirds risk of being consumed in the process.[34]

Human Risks While Foraging for Sex

Like other organisms, humans forage for sex. Unlike other species, the human season for sex is expansive, exposing people to very high risk of predatory attack. Some of these victimizations are themselves sexual in nature, including forcible rape, statutory rape, and various forms of sexual assault. But nonsexual offenses also take advantage of sexual foraging. Most of their risks are connected with legal activities, such as going to bars, being out late, and socializing in university dormitories or student apartments.

The sexual urge is powerful, leading people to take substantial risks. That provides a chance for predators to lie in wait. Attracting a partner for sex conflicts with the desire to stay secure. Sex leads many people to go to risky places and engage in risky activities. The fact that people will risk their lives for sex has been demonstrated time and time again. A friend of mine, now deceased, survived the Warsaw ghetto and then the Polish experience of Nazi occupation. During that time the Nazis made it quite clear that they would shoot to kill any Pole seen on the street after curfew, and they did just that. But Poles still went out in search of sexual opportunities, and some died for it.

Risky foraging includes impersonal contacts with prostitutes, often leading to violence in one direction or the other.[35] Disapproved sexual alliances are especially prone to risky foraging. Some homosexual liaisons with strangers occur in settings where protections are few. Perpetrators of hate crimes are likely to go where they think they will find victims. "Gaybashers" foraging for homosexuals to attack are more likely to find them in places where homosexuals are themselves foraging for sexual liaisons. Probably the greatest dangers come from other homosexual foragers or male hustlers. When I was a student, a professor was murdered after picking up two young male strangers. Yet other homosexuals meet in relatively safe social settings.

Regardless of sexual orientation, human males are more dangerous than human females. This predicts that violence is *minimized* when females forage for other females. Violence is *maximized* when males forage for other males. Heterosexual foraging, then, produces *medium* risks relative to the two types of same-sex foraging.[36]

Foraging for sex generates nonviolent offenses, too. Many people out socializing come back to find the car stolen,[37] or go home to find the apartment burgled. And so the ongoing processes of life expose people to unwanted crime risks.

Age Focus of Sex Foraging and Crime Victimization

Humans spend decades with an interest in sexual intercourse, hence in attracting sex partners. Crime victimization can also occur at any age. But those in young adult ages often have not yet formed sexual unions and are especially prone to forage for sex. These ages are also highly vulnerable to crime victimization, in part because of sex foraging. Young adults are especially likely, in the interest of sex, to stay out late in social settings with high crime risk. Very large discos and bars catering to the young provide mating opportunities, assisting large numbers of young males and females to find one another within a relatively limited period of time. These settings can also set the stage for crime victimization, substance abuse, and fights. Legitimate and consensual mating opportunities also set the stage for sexual attacks on others in nearby times and places.

Sexual Prudishness and Foraging in Conventional Places

Men do not need a disco to forage for women. Judith Blake and associates[38] wrote a classic book about pregnancies 40 years ago in Jamaica. Jamaican mothers were then very prudish, and simply told their daughters to stay away from men, without any further details. Men kept on the lookout for young women going to market, trying to persuade them to go home with them. By about age 20, enough women would do so, many ending up pregnant. The point is that fully legitimate routine activities (in this case, simply going to market) can easily lead to risk of criminal victimization.

Various species have congregation sites for sexual liaisons. Among species whose females roam but whose males are restricted, the males congregate in *leks* for social courtship displays and fighting. The females of the species come to these sites, select a male, and leave the others unsatisfied. Human males range more widely, but human society has some techniques for concentrating females where males can find them. The university plays an important role. Traditionally, church socials and interfamily gatherings often served the purpose of bringing boy and girl together. Public plazas or *zocalos* in Spain and Hispano America served a similar purpose. In modern society, preliminaries to mating occur in high schools, bars, and other social places with parents absent or out of earshot. When there is a shortage of females in public settings, males must compete aggressively for their attentions. Human males might also display their wares in groups at parties and dances so that females can choose those they wish. But human males also display masculinity through excess drinking and physical prowess, sometimes leading to criminal action.

Overview

Foraging theory helps us find patterns among what seem to be discrete events. Each offender commits diverse crimes that seem to be unrelated, but in fact have a common foraging pattern. That pattern is part of larger nature.

Offenders use tactical diversity, but their repertoires are not unlimited. Offenders vary in diet breadth, hunting method, and range. They tend to be relative generalists, partly because they can find more targets that way. But they are more likely to limit themselves to a particular range with which they are familiar. And they do not go after absolutely every type of crime opportunity. Some offenders hunt for larger targets, while others browse for small items, and many combine these techniques. Many offenders also vary in whether they commit crimes alone or with others. Despite these variations, offenders are more consistent in how they forage than in how they violate the law.

Central Points, Chapter 15

1. It is usually impractical for one person to commit just one type of crime, and always impractical to commit all types of crime.

2. Offenders hunt and browse, and ambush and pursue, as well as lie in wait. Even such a "simple" crime as auto theft uses many specific tactics.

3. Those foraging for sex or other activities risk their own victimization.

4. Younger offenders are most likely to forage in groups.

Exercises

1. Why do you think juveniles are more likely than adults to commit crimes in groups?

2. List three human physical traits that help people forage for crime.

3. When and where are *you* most vulnerable to crime foragers?

4. How might offenders best forage among college students?

Notes

1. Widely attributed, not verified.

2. U.S. author (1819–1891). Quoted in *The Columbia World of Quotations* (New York: Columbia University Press, 1966).

3. A. A. Milne was the pseudonym of British author Ernest H. Shepard (1882–1956). *Winnie-the-Pooh* (New York: Dutton, 1926).

4. San Diego Zoo webpage, http://www.sandiegozoo.org/animalbytes/t-giant_panda .html (accessed September 4, 2005).

5. Another example is the wolf, which relies on meat but still can hunt caribou on the tundra, deer on the prairie, or mountain goats, or forest elk. "Hunting Techniques of the Gray Wolf" (n.d.), Alien Earth website, http://www.nibbleuniversity.com/websites/alienexplorer/ ecology/m191.html (accessed September 4, 2005).

6. The generality of misbehavior is better understood since Professors Gottfredson and Hirschi linked many missteps—legal or illegal—to a "low level of self-control." We need to approach this point with some subtlety. On the one hand, offenders seldom plan ahead more than an hour or two, and often just a few seconds. On the other hand, their choices usually make some short-term sense. Those with *too much* self-control will think more of the future and commit little crime. Those with no *self-control* at all can't even accomplish a simple crime. It takes a bit of self-control and some reasoning to forage efficiently. I have dealt with this issue in the first chapter of *Crime and Everyday Life*. See the appendix of the current book, too.

7. This might be called *parasitic foraging*, since the offender takes small amounts from the employer over time.

8. This point is relevant to the taxonomy presented in Chapter 21.

9. Quoted in the Baseball Almanac, http://www.baseball-almanac.com/quotes/quopaig .shtml (accessed September 4, 2005).

10. For more on diet optimization issues, see G. E. Belovsky, "Diet Optimization in a Generalist Herbivore: The Moose," *Theoretical Population Biology* 14 (1978): 105–134.

11. In the future, one should divide hunting methods into subcategories. The chapter on crime classification goes into this further, and future work should do more, still.

12. Because a crow eats about anything, people are reluctant to eat crow. But at least one website provides recipes: Crow Busters, http://www.crowbusters.com (accessed September 4, 2005). The meat can be frozen, marinated, or freshly prepared. You can see that the full range of possibilities is not normally executed.

13. See B. Winterhalder, "Diet Choice, Risk and Food Sharing in a Stochastic Environment," *Journal of Ethnobiology* 6 (1986): 205–223.

14. The word "vegephobic" has been used elsewhere. I cannot vouch for its scientific value, but see R. M. Wilcox, "Vegetable-Free Living" (2004), http://pw2.netcom.com/~rogermw/ vegetable/veg1.html (accessed September 4, 2005).

15. For example, see E. Levine, ed., *Bull's Birds of New York State* (Ithaca, NY: Cornell University Press, 1998). The first New York State bird book was by J. E. DeKay, *Zoology of New York; or the New York Fauna. Part 2: Birds* (New York: Appleton, 1844).

16. From the Saskatchewan Schools website, http://www.saskschools.ca/~avonlea2/ grass3/grade56/, click on "hunt" (accessed October 26, 2005).

17. T. Levesley and others, *Emerging Methods of Car Theft—Theft of Keys* (London: British Home Office Research, Development and Statistics Directorate, 2004) (British Home Office Findings 239).

18. For an introduction to Rossmo's contributions, see

   a. D. K. Rossmo, *Geographic Profiling* (Boca Raton, FL: CRC Press, 2000).

   b. R. M. Holmes and D. K. Rossmo, "Geography, Profiling, and Predatory Criminals," in R. M. Holmes and S. T. Holmes, eds., *Profiling Violent Crimes: An Investigative Tool,* 3rd ed. (Thousand Oaks, CA: Sage, 2002).

   c. D. K. Rossmo, "Geographic Profiling," in Q. C. Thurman and J. Zhao, eds., *Contemporary Policing: Controversies, Challenges, and Solutions* (Los Angeles: Roxbury, 2004).

   d. D. K. Rossmo, "Geographic Profiling as Problem Solving for Serial Crime," in Q. C. Thurman and J. D. Jamieson, eds., *Police Problem Solving* (Cincinnati, OH: Anderson, 2004).

   e. D. K. Rossmo, "Geographic Profiling Update," in J. H. Campbell and D. DeNevi, eds., *Profilers: Leading Investigators Take You Inside the Criminal Mind* (Amherst, NY: Prometheus Books, 2004).

19. Scottish poet (1700–1748), writing about the spider. Quoted in *The Columbia World of Quotations* (New York: Columbia University Press, 1996).

20. Whitetail World, http://www.kerrlake.com/deer/white5.htm (accessed September 4, 2005).

21. See J. LeBeau, "The Methods and Measures of Centrography and the Spatial Dynamics of Rape," *Journal of Quantitative Criminology* 3, no. 2 (1987): 125–141. See also J. LeBeau, "Four Case Studies Illustrating the Spatial-Temporal Analysis of Serial Rapists," *Police Studies* 15, no. 3 (1992): 124–145.

22. The fox information in this chapter is drawn from Liska's *EncycVulpedia,* http://mynarskiforest.purrsia.com/ev1con.htm (accessed September 4, 2005).

23. "Hunting Techniques of the Gray Wolf" (n.d.), Alien Earth website, http://www .nibbleuniversity.com/websites/alienexplorer/ecology/m191.html (accessed September 4, 2005).

24. "Lion: *Pantheo Leo*" (n.d.), The Nature-Wildlife Pages, http://www.nature-wildlife.com/liontxt.htm (accessed September 4, 2005).

25. The word "foraging" helps sort out the conflicting definitions for "co-offending." Most of the literature uses that term only for cooperation *during* the criminal act itself. But important theoretical and empirical work by Professor Pierre Tremblay of the University of Montreal includes cooperation before or after the offense as co-offending. See P. Tremblay, "Searching for Suitable Co-Offenders," in R. V. Clarke and M. Felson, eds., *Routine Activity & Rational Choice* (New Brunswick, NJ: Transaction Books, 1993) (Volume 5 in *Advances in Criminological Theory* series).

26. J. M. Wunderle, "Age-specific Foraging Proficiency in Birds," *Current Ornithology* 8 (1991): 273–324.

27. M. Warr, *Companions in Crime: The Social Aspects of Criminal Conduct* (Cambridge, UK, and New York: Cambridge University Press, 2002). A. J. Reiss, "Co-offending & Criminal Careers," in M. Tonry and N. Morris, eds., *Crime & Justice: An Annual Review of Research* (Chicago: University of Chicago Press, 1988) (Volume 10 in *Crime and Justice* series). Even animals tend to forage differently by age. Sometimes dominant adults displace juveniles, who must go to inferior foraging sites. Juveniles might be less proficient in searching, capturing, or handling prey. Nutritional requirements might differ, too. Researchers have not sorted out these alternative explanations. But foraging animals tend to make more complex movements, displaying more skill, as they age. Humans are not as likely to increase their skill as they age, probably due to the cumulative effects of substance abuse.

28. L. R. Binford, "Forty-seven Trips: A Case-Study in the Character of Archaeological Formation Process," in R. S. V. Wright, ed., *Stone Tools as Cultural Markers* (Canberra: Australian Institute of Aboriginal Studies, 1977).

29. E. P. Greene, "Information Transfer at Osprey Colonies: Individuals Discriminate between High and Low Quality Information," *Nature* 329 (1987): 239–241.

30. P. Tremblay, "Searching for Suitable Co-offenders," in R. V. Clarke and M. Felson, eds., *Routine Activity & Rational Choice* (New Brunswick, NJ: Transaction Books, 1993) (Volume 5 in *Advances in Criminological Theory* series).

31. G. Maier and others, "Is Mating of Copepods Associated with Increased Risk of Predation?" *Journal of Plankton Research* 22 (2000): 1977–1987.

32. C. M. Garcia, G. Jimenez, and B. Contreras, "Correlational Evidence for a Sexually Selected Handicap," *Behavioral Ecology and Sociobiology* 35 (1994): 253–259.

33. G. Yamada and others, "Differentiation, Cellular and Molecular Mechanisms of the External Genitalia," *Differentiation* 71 (2003): 445–460.

34. L. M. Forster, "The Stereotyped Behaviour of Sexual Cannibalism in *Latrodectus Hasselti* (Araneae, Theridiidae), the Australian Redback Spider," *Australian Journal of Zoology* 40 (1992): 1–11.

35. M. A. Monto, "Female Prostitution, Customers, and Violence," *Violence Against Women* 10 (2004): 160–188.

36. See R. B. Felson, *Violence and Gender Re-examined* (Washington, DC: APA, 2002).

37. M. Bromley and J. K. Cochran, "Auto Burglaries in an Entertainment District Hotspot: Applying the SARA Model in a Security Context," *Security Journal* 15 (2002): 63–72.

38. J. Blake, J. M. Stycos, and K. Davis, *Family Structure in Jamaica: The Social Context of Reproduction* (Glencoe, IL: Free Press, 1961).

The fox barks not when he would steal the lamb.

—William Shakespeare[1]

Thus the orb he roamed
With narrow search, and with inspection deep
Considered every creature, which of all
Most opportune might serve his wiles, and found
The serpent subtlest beast of all the field.

—John Milton[2]

Anybody can be good in the country; there are no temptations there.

—Oscar Wilde[3]

A search is a search, even if it happens to disclose nothing. . . .

—Antonin Scalia[4]

16

Foraging and Familiarity

A n employed college student knows well her home, classrooms, dormitory, the student cafeteria, her workplace, and her favorite recreation area. She moves among these locations often, and knows the routes well. She also might have explored around these places and along these routes. But she does not go everywhere. She has a limited individual awareness space, affecting where she goes—even when she breaks her exact routine.

The experiences of a college student going to class and offenders going to do a crime are connected, helping us piece together crime patterns. Alfred North Whitehead explained,

> The progress of Science consists in observing interconnections and in showing with a patient ingenuity that the events of this ever-shifting world are but examples of a few general relations, called laws. To see what is general in what is particular, and what is permanent in what is transitory, is the aim of scientific thought.[5]

Professors Paul and Patricia Brantingham devised crime pattern theory[6] to help explain where offenders go to commit their crimes. Like everybody, offenders go about normal everyday routines. Those routines give each individual an *awareness space*, that is, the places they know as they go about daily life. Someone's awareness space is based on particular nodes and paths. *Personal nodes* are the places that person routinely goes to and from.[7] *Personal paths* are the routes between these nodes. Accordingly, Exhibit 16.1 illustrates a person's awareness space, helping us understand where offenders look for their crime targets.[8] It depicts four personal nodes, the paths among them, and the personal edges of someone's awareness space. That space usually includes such nodes as home, school, workplace, and favorite bar. A person's paths are the narrow lines depicted. Most important, our offender's "awareness space" extends short and moderate distances off these paths and around these nodes. Offenders usually commit crimes within their routine awareness space, or close to it. In particular, offenders most often commit crimes along the edges of their routine nodes and paths. They explore these areas to find their targets.

Professor Kim Rossmo (of Texas State University) is an expert on the awareness space of serial offenders—who perform the same crime in a series of separate events. He has mapped series of murders, rapes, arsons, burglaries, and other offenses—in order to figure out where the suspect probably lives, works, goes to school, and hangs out.[9] Even very strange offenders usually repeat their crimes within an orderly awareness space and pick crime locations according to their routines. Professor Rossmo has combined his experience as a police officer with his knowledge of crime pattern theory to help find the culprit. Mapping just a half dozen serial offenses can lead to the offender's doorstep.

Exhibit 16.1   The Offender's Awareness Space

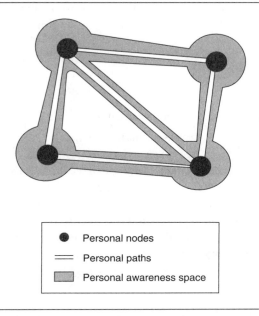

●	Personal nodes
═══	Personal paths
▨	Personal awareness space

Being Out of Place

Edges are the boundaries between two neighborhoods, such as a major street that divides one area from another. Some edges are extremely sharp, so that one side of the tracks is all high-rise buildings, and the other low-rises with different social groups living in each. This is important, since people might not cross certain edges, thus avoiding crime participation as offenders or victims. Other edges are not so sharp. For example, two neighborhoods that ease into one another might need to deal with offenders from both sides.

Exhibit 16.2 depicts four contiguous neighborhoods and the edges between them. It raises an issue: Where is crime likely to be highest? In general, we should expect crime to be highest in the edges between the neighborhoods—a, b, c, d, and e. But the last of these might be the least secure, since offenders from all four neighborhoods can easily get there, commit a crime, then slip back into their home territories.

Edges are not just residential. As a professor I do not really belong in a student bar, and students do not really belong in the faculty dining hall. People seem out of place if they go where they are not expected. Different social groups are relatively segregated for at least part of the day. Many boundaries divide up everyday life. Whether visible or not, these boundaries influence where we go and how people respond to us. In general, people are most comfortable, and perhaps most secure, among those they recognize

1. by name,
2. by face,   *in order of*
3. by role,   *declining*
4. as members of their own social category, and   *security*
5. as members of categories similar to theirs.[10]

Accordingly, the Brantinghams distinguish a local area's "insiders" from "outsiders."[11] *Insiders* "belong there"—whatever the reason—and can enter the area without drawing undue notice. *Outsiders* draw unwanted attention, interfering with their ability to commit a crime. In the course of a day, each of us probably changes from an insider to an outsider, then back again. Such changes affect our ability to commit crimes.

Exhibit 16.2   Where's the Offender Safest?

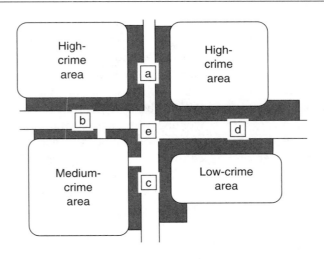

Four neighborhoods with different crime levels, and five different edges [a, b, c, d, and e]

▮▮▮ Common edges

What Makes an Offender Conspicuous?

An offender generally prefers to be inconspicuous before, during, and after committing a crime. If he has the bad luck to be noticed, he would rather that nobody recognize his face or name. Often an offender can choose times, places, and offenses that avoid conspicuous risks to himself. Here's a six-step plan for an inconspicuous crime:

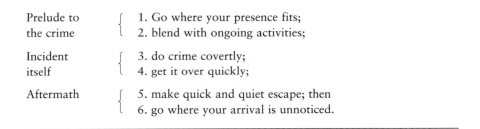

Prelude to the crime	{	1. Go where your presence fits; 2. blend with ongoing activities;
Incident itself	{	3. do crime covertly; 4. get it over quickly;
Aftermath	{	5. make quick and quiet escape; then 6. go where your arrival is unnoticed.

Some offenses are overt by definition, such as hitting an enemy or robbing a pedestrian. The latter is a conspicuous crime, since the offender must confront the victim directly. The victim, if facing a deadly weapon, usually gives up the money fast, but that is not always so. Offenders take the risk of direct confrontation because they expect the rewards to outweigh the risks.

In light of this chapter, we should reexamine the emphasis on violent vs. nonviolent crimes. It is more useful to distinguish overt from covert crimes. An overt crime involves direct confrontation, noise, and notice, even without violence against a person. It draws attention and looks abnormal in its setting. A covert crime is inconspicuous—unless the offender has bad luck or makes a mistake. Smashing a window that people will hear is an overt crime, despite its nonviolence. Although it is possible to poison someone covertly, most violent offenses are overt, and nonviolent offenses are more likely than not to be covert.

More About Insiders and Outsiders

Avoiding notice is more easily said than done. *Insiders* have an obvious reason to be there and do not seem out of place before or after they commit the crime. On the other hand, *outsiders* might well search for settings where they will be less conspicuous.[12] That's why insiders and outsiders are more likely

Exhibit 16.3   Overt and Covert Crimes Committed by Insiders and Outsiders

	Their Action Is:	
The Offenders:	*Covert*	*Overt*
Insiders	A Quiet local thefts	C Common fights
Outsiders	B Raiding parked cars	D Common robberies

to select different offenses, and to think differently about how overt they wish to be. Exhibit 16.3 sorts a few crime examples. A local theft is a covert crime by insiders. A common local fight is an overt crime by insiders. Outsiders are more likely to raid parked cars covertly, but to rob people overtly. Of course, there are many exceptions. Moreover, an insider this afternoon might commit a crime as an outsider this evening. In addition, in edge areas (discussed in earlier chapters), outsiders have a good chance to commit overt crimes without being recognized or drawing interference.

Offender Disadvantages

Exhibit 16.4 helps us discuss some of the main disadvantages for both insiders and outsiders, in the prelude to an incident, during the incident itself, and in the aftermath. Starting at the top, both insiders and outsiders have a lot of problems committing an overt crime. They are probably conspicuous before, during, and after the incident. Insiders who commit overt crimes have the additional problem that they are identifiable by name if exposed.[13]

For covert crimes, insiders can find their moment and remain inconspicuous at all three stages of a crime. In contrast, outsiders are too conspicuous beforehand and afterward, although they might conceal their actions during the incident itself. If exposed, the outsider at least can avoid being identified by name, and hope that any bystanders will provide a hazy description.[14] For covert crimes, the insider has a definite advantage before, during, and after the offense.

In general, a covert crime is not noticed until after the offender's trail is stone cold. Overt offenses are immediately obvious to adversaries, thus more likely to produce counterattacks or identification of offenders. On the other

Exhibit 16.4   Conspicuous Offending

| | | Offender Is Conspicuous | | | |
Types of Offending	Types of Offender	(1) Prelude	(2) During Incident	(3) Aftermath	If Exposed, Identifiable by Name
Overt	Insider	Δ	Δ	Δ	Δ
	Outsider	Δ	Δ	Δ	
Covert	Insider				Δ
	Outsider	Δ		Δ	

Δ Offender is conspicuous.

hand, some overt crimes continue because the victims and bystanders are intimidated, and unwilling to risk counteracting them.

More on Crime's Overtness

A crime can be overt to some people but hidden from others. For example, family violence is overt *within* the household, but might well be hidden from the outside world. Perhaps in the future we should distinguish crimes that are known

- only to a lone offender,
- only to co-offenders,
- also to offender friends and associates,
- only to the offender and his direct family victim,
- only to the offender and family members, or
- beyond one's personal circle.

Offenders might commit blatant offenses within a small circle of friends or family members, counting on them to keep quiet. But when more people know, an obvious crime becomes more of a problem for the offender. In general, it is not very easy to commit blatant crimes without drawing notice. But some offenders find just the right moment to do so. Even an occupied area is not supervised at every moment or in every part. Most offenses happen quickly. Thus an armed robbery is an overt crime, but it takes a few seconds to hand over the money. By the time the victim figures out what to do, the offender is already gone.

To understand this chapter fully, you should revisit the earlier chapters, where I discussed abandoned locations. Places that are very well supervised are generally unsuitable for any offenders. Places that are fairly well supervised are unsuitable for outsiders, but insiders might find the right moment. Urban places that are poorly supervised invite almost anybody to commit crime.[15] In general, the more a place is supervised, the less time the offender has to commit crime there. Of course, offenders who are able to intimidate local people can turn much of this around, acting almost with impunity. That's the ultimate breakdown in control. But even they must steer clear of drawing prolonged attention to their illegal acts.

An "ideal" location for preventing crime is fairly well supervised by local people most of the time. They can usually notice outsiders, discourage crime by insiders, and prevent local offenders from intimidating the neighborhood. Crime can still occur there, but the offender needs to be a little more clever.

The Tricky Offender

Overt crimes would seem to be a sign of courage, but that is not always so. In the words of William Blake, "The weak in courage is strong in cunning."[16] Sometimes offenders find covert ways to commit overt crimes.

Mimicry means that one species seeks to look like another. It normally refers to how potential prey can defend against predators (a topic considered in subsequent chapters). But predators can also mimic other species. Ecologists use the term *aggressive mimicry* to describe a technique for getting closer to unsuspecting prey by mimicking something innocuous or even desirable. Sometimes immobile predators use mimicry to bring their prey to them. For example, the frogfish uses a fleshy filament just above its lip to mimic the movements of a small organism, thus to lure its prey to the vicinity of its mouth. The hunter mentioned earlier used bleats and mating sounds to lure a buck.

Often offenders mimic legal behavior in order to carry out illegal acts. Thus a phony Santa Claus cheats people out of donations. Other offenders pretend to work for a utility or delivery company, or even claim to be police officers, in order to gain illicit access. Rapists have been known to dress like students or employees, or otherwise hide their purpose as they attract their quarry. Professor James LeBeau of Southern Illinois University has studied rapists and their methods. He distinguishes a blitz rape from a confidence rape.[17] In the latter case, offenders hide behind conventional roles, only to lurch forward when the victim cannot easily escape. Pedophiles often use a form of mimicry, approaching children as friends and helpers, rather than attacking in overt fashion. A *bludget* is a female thief who decoys her victims into alleys, usually by pretending to offer sex.

Sometimes offenders of one type mimic offenders of another form. Sometimes this involves no extra harm to others. Many prostitutes are actually male transvestites, using perfume (olfactory mimicry), along with various auditory, visual, and behavioral cues to find and fool customers, limiting their service to oral sex. In other cases, predatory offenders mimic consensual offenders. A fake prostitute turns out to be a robber (see the paragraph above). A fake customer mugs the prostitute or even murders her.[18] The standard operating procedure for fraudsters is to entice the victim with ill-gotten gains, only to turn the tables. For example, a con man promises to double your money in a shady enterprise, then disappears with your "investment."

Sometimes legal behavior *mimics* illegal acts. A fake "drug dealer" sells catnip to inexperienced customers, who think it's marihuana. Authorities can hardly arrest someone *pretending* to be a drug dealer. Police officers use illicit deceptions to make legal arrests, dressing like prostitutes or drug buyers in order to snag offenders. Undercover officers pose as convicts to lure cellmates to reveal information, and sting operations purchase stolen goods to incriminate thieves and burglars. Police also lure offenders to steal a car containing a hidden tracking device, or even to attack their person, with fellow officers hiding around the corner.

Although we normally think of camouflage as a defensive strategy, *aggressive camouflage* assists predators. The angler fish of the Sargasso Sea looks like seaweed. The Malaysian forest has a mantis that imitates an orchid petal. Costa Rica's assassin bug mimics a discarded termite body. Perhaps the ultimate is the death adder of the Australian desert. It looks like gravel while wiggling a tail to imitate a worm—a *combination* of aggressive camouflage and aggressive mimicry. Many a robber has hidden in the shadows, teamed with a prostitute to allure the victim.

A potential crime victim can be tricky, too. Many homeowners feel that they can dissuade burglars by leaving a light on. But burglars often see through these efforts, particularly if the light is always the same.

An experiment with the blue jay shows that it can learn to find its prey hidden against a background, if the deception is not too complex.[19] Perhaps one way to thwart offenders is to formulate a more complex deception. This argues that programming house lights to shift could be a successful strategy to thwart offenders. However, offenders tend to be more experienced than occasional victims, and have the advantage when it comes to deception and seeing through it.

Tactical Elaboration

Human criminal activity not only applies but also elaborates techniques found among nonhuman predators. Criminal action can combine several techniques, or can develop a single technique. Of course, a single criminal act is usually rather simple, but the population of such acts uses diverse methods. Here are 10 basic offender tactics, each with its own variants:

- *Conceal entirely:* Many offenders avoid confrontation entirely, seeking to conceal that a crime was ever committed. The bank official steals a tiny bit from each account, hoping to escape notice at all. A large organization might never discover what was stolen from its storeroom or sales floor, especially if products are plentiful.
- *Delay notice:* Some offenses will eventually be noticed, but the offender delays that time until his trail is cold as ice. The burglar who quietly breaks a basement window at the beginning of your vacation hopes not to be noticed until your return.
- *Surprise:* As mentioned earlier, many confrontational offenders surprise or startle their personal victims, providing no time to muster a defense. A quick purse snatcher is well on his way before others think to run after him, or even look back at his face.
- *Confound:* Offenders have learned to bewilder or distract their victims or targets, sometimes acting especially odd during the offense or especially normal in exiting. Whatever confounds opponents suits the offender's purposes.
- *Embarrass:* Victims or guardians are often embarrassed by a criminal act. That keeps them from interfering or reporting, or delays them in doing so. Sexual offenders benefit from their victim's embarrassment. Bank robbers sometimes force their victims to strip naked. A white-collar offender often escapes prosecution because it would make the victim look stupid.
- *Subdue:* Offenders use numbers, threats, weapons, nasty demeanors, or bull-like charges to subdue their personal victims and gain compliance. Even property offenders can subdue guardians against crime, preventing interference with their illicit actions.
- *Trap:* Offenders pick spots where victims are against a wall, or corner them so they have nowhere to go.
- *Overtake:* Offenders outrun or outflank their victims, making it easier to get victims to comply.
- *Control:* Offenders often seize or grab their victims to force or encourage compliance.
- *Quick injury:* Offenders knock over and incapacitate victims at the outset, stunning them and preventing resistance as the criminal act proceeds.

Even though property offending is relatively common, much of it can succeed with stealth alone. In contrast, violent offending generally must risk resistance, therefore requiring a larger repertoire of technique.

Overview

Arguably, a good majority of violent offenders conceal or delay notice of their offenses; or surprise, confound, embarrass, subdue, track, overtake, control, or quickly injure their quarry, or use combinations of these methods. If you look at the above list you will see that I have neglected the many stratagems used by con artists, usually for money but sometimes for sex. I have considered numerous variations in white-collar offending elsewhere.[20] Crime stratagems are very diverse, indeed.

Many offenders combine attack methods. In nature, multiple inflictions serve a purpose. A spider bites, inflicting mechanical damage but often injecting venom through hollow fangs. The robber not only throws a punch that hurts but also stuns the victim into compliance. The rapist combines implicit threat with promise not to harm.

Crime purposes are also subject to combination. A burglar takes the jewels but also rapes the resident. A jilted lover steals back the ring he gave her, taking her television while at it. A disgruntled employee steals to harm the hated boss, but keeps the money to throw a party. And so life pushes beyond the categories we give it.

Central Points, Chapter 16

1. Offenders usually commit crimes within their routine awareness space, or close to it. These are determined by personal nodes, the paths among them, and the edges of these locations.

2. It is easier to avoid notice if you belong somewhere. That helps commit a crime in secret. But outsiders have advantages for some types of crime, especially when they go to edge areas.

3. Overt crimes place additional burdens on an offender, requiring different tactics than covert crimes.

4. Some offenders rely on trickery and surprise, in various forms. Offenders might mimic legal behavior, or offer illegal goods and services in order to trick the buyer.

Exercises

1. What are the three main nodes that anchor your awareness space?

2. What edge area creates your greatest risk of crime victimization?

3. Describe a specific crime that requires trickery, and one that does not.

Notes

1. *Henry IV, Part Two,* act III, scene i.

2. British poet (1608–1674). Quoted in *The Columbia World of Quotations* (New York: Columbia University Press, 1996).

3. Chapter 19, *The Picture of Dorian Gray* (1890). Available from UpWord website, http://www.upword.com/wilde/dorgray.html (accessed September 9, 2005).

4. Associate justice, U.S. Supreme Court, in a majority opinion that refused to expand police powers to search or seize evidence that they suspect may be stolen, March 3, 1987. Quoted in *Simpson's Contemporary Quotations* (New York: Houghton-Mifflin, 1998).

5. *An Introduction to Mathematics* (London: Williams and Norgate, 1911).

6. The original classic paper is P. L. Brantingham and P. J. Brantingham, "Mobility, Notoriety, and Crime: A Study of Crime Patterns in Urban Nodal Points," *Journal of Environmental Systems* 11 (1982): 89–99. Many of their other papers are cited at various points in this book.

7. There are rough distinctions between "nodes," "nodal points," and the "areas around nodes." Perhaps it is easier to remember the room you go to, the building, and the campus as three parts of your awareness space.

8. I have used "personal nodes" instead of nodes to remind us that awareness space applies to an individual. The term "personal edges" is used for the same reason. The Brantinghams applied these terms to crime ideas originated by K. Lynch in *The Image of the City* (Cambridge: MIT Press, 1961). These ideas are also quite close to ecological theory, which distinguishes the following.

    1. *Nest:* Where you live.

    2. *Territory:* What you defend.

    3. *Home range:* Where you go routinely, without defending

Except for domestic violence, offenders tend to commit offenses within their home ranges, but beyond their own nests. Given the complexity of modern human life, we might wish to divide "home range" into three parts—a residential range, work (or school) range, and a leisure (and shopping) range.

In addition, when people are closer to their homes they are more likely to defend themselves and their families from crime, report crimes to police and demand police action, and assist others to prevent crime or thwart it.

Conversely, as people range farther from their territories, they are less likely to defend, report, or assist others against crime. These generalizations are reflected in crime victim surveys and crime rates. In addition, substantial unreported victimizations occur when people are on vacation. See tourist crime citations in Chapter 17, endnote 34.

9. D. K. Rossmo, "Place, Space, and Police Investigations: Hunting Serial Violent Criminals," in J. E. Eck and D. Weisburd, eds., *Crime and Place* (Monsey, NY: Criminal Justice Press, 1995) (Volume 4 in *Crime Prevention Studies* series).

10. Human suspicion of others is quite researchable. Eighty years ago, the concept of "social distance" was first studied by Emory S. Bogardus. He calculated a "social distance scale," asking people the same seven questions about dozens of different social groups. For example, he asked whites about the distance they felt toward black people. It's interesting to consider how much social distance transfers into suspicion. Of course, residents accept in their midst those from other social groups known by name, face, or role. See E. S. Bogardus, "Measuring Social Distances," *Journal of Applied Sociology* (later *Sociology and Social Research*) 9 (1925): 299–308. Available online from The Mead Project, Department of Sociology, Brock University, Canada, http://spartan.ac.brocku.ca/~lward/Bogardus/Bogardus_1925c.html (accessed September 9, 2005). See also R. E. Park, "The Concept of Social Distance as Applied to the Study of Racial Attitudes and Racial Relations," *Journal of Applied Sociology* (later *Sociology and Social Research*) 8 (1924): 339–344. See update by E. S. Bogardus, "A Social Distance Scale," *Sociology and Social Research* 17 (1933): 265–271.

11. See elaboration of the point in D. Beavon, P. L. Brantingham, and P. J. Brantingham, "The Influence of Street Networks on the Patterning of Property Offenses," in R. V. Clarke, ed., *Crime Prevention Studies* (Monsey, NY: Criminal Justice Press, 1994) (Volume 2 in *Crime Prevention Studies* series). Available from the Center for Problem-oriented Policing, http://www.popcenter.org (accessed September 4, 2005).

12. The same concept can be applied to an insider or outsider at work, in a college dormitory, or elsewhere.

13. Sometimes the offender is identified by residence or with a partial name or link. The point is that an insider can be found without much trouble if he has been recognized.

14. This chapter neglects forensic identification. I consider offenses unlikely to involve a crime laboratory.

15. For details on modus operandi for several offenses, see the Wikibooks Manual of Crime, http://en.wikibooks.org/wiki/The_Manual_of_Crime (accessed September 4, 2005).

16. British poet, painter, engraver (1757–1827). Quoted in *The Columbia World of Quotations* (New York: Columbia University Press, 1996).

17. Professor James LeBeau has distinguished types of rapists in terms of geographic motion and modus operandi. See

    a. J. LeBeau, "The Journey to Rape: Geographic Distances and the Rapist's Method of Approaching the Victim," *Journal of Police Sciences and Administration* 15 (2004): 129–136.

    b. J. LeBeau, "The Methods and Measures of Centrography and the Spatial Dynamics of Rape," *Journal of Quantitative Criminology* 3 (1987): 125–141.

18. Of course, people shift from one illicit role to another. Thus a real prostitute on Tuesday might be a fake prostitute on Wednesday, using the role to lure robbery victims.

19. T. A. Pietrewicz and A. C. Kamil, "Search Image Formation in the Blue Jay, *Cyanocittata Cristata,*" *Science* 204 (1979): 1332–1333.

20. Chapter 7 in M. Felson, *Crime and Everyday Life* (Thousand Oaks, CA: Sage, 2002).

Being with a woman all night never hurt no professional ballplayer. It's staying up all night looking for a woman that does him in.

—Casey Stengel[1]

When you go in search of honey you must expect to be stung by bees.

—Kenneth Kaunda[2]

Some plays just come out of me, just on instincts. I'll make a play and wonder, How did I do that?

—Roberto Alomar[3]

I can picture in my mind a world without war, a world without hate. And I can picture us attacking that world, because they'd never expect it.

—Jack Handey[4]

17

Strategic Foraging

Birds searching for worms and offenders looking for jewels have similar patterns. Ecologists describe such patterns using *optimal foraging theory*. The word "optimal" is not meant to imply that animals forage with perfection, or that foraging is genetically fixed, deterministic, or without intraspecies variance.[5] Indeed, animals learn from their parents and from their environment as they forage. Animals forage not just for food, but also for nesting places, flowers to pollinate, or mates. People forage for many legal and illegal purposes, including food, apartments, roommates, library books, parking spaces, websites, short-term sex, long-term partners, treasure, and diverse crime targets. The purpose of this chapter is to figure out some of the foraging regularities found among offenders.

Over the past 30 years, students of crime have learned more about how offenders seek and find crime targets. Paul and Patricia Brantingham (of Simon Fraser University in British Columbia, Canada), Ronald V. Clarke (Rutgers University), and Ken Pease (Huddersfield University in Britain) are founders of this approach. Indeed, the word "foraging" is used on occasion.[6] The purpose of this chapter is to make our knowledge of foraging somewhat more systematic.

Not only do students of crime learn from animal foraging, but science can borrow in the other direction. Dr. Martin R. Aidan (Director of the ReefQuest Center for Shark Research in Vancouver) and Dr. Neil Hammerschlag (of the Pew Institute for Ocean Science in Miami, Florida) have studied sharks as if they were serial criminals. They applied the offender tracking approach devised by Professor Kim Rossmo (Texas State University). The three of them produced a paper treating shark attacks as if a shark is a serial killer.[7]

Although individuals have some personal foraging styles, foraging theory transcends individuals. As a general rule, offenders tend to forage near their homes and other places they already know. For both shopping and shoplifting, people tend to go to familiar malls or stores nearby.

Crime Foraging and the Maximum Size Rule

Ecologists present foraging theory by starting with the simplest rules, fitting these to reality, then elaborating to accommodate new findings, and so on. Let's begin with the simplest strategic rule of all: Foraging animals are limited by the size of crucial body parts relative to their quarry. The *maximum size rule* tells us that, in general, no animal forages for something bigger than its head. It cannot eat something that it cannot take down and bite into, unless it has devised extra strategies.

In similar vein, a criminal will generally not forage for anything he cannot carry. Thus offenders face an initial limit on the weight and bulk of crime targets. An offender must also be able to overcome a human target in order to inflict violence upon it and to prevent it from doing so in return. The *maximum size rule* (or "size rule" for short) is just a point of departure, since there are often ways to push beyond this limit.

Exhibit 17.1   Crime Foraging Rules

(Starting With the Simplest)	Foraging Rule	Example
1	Size rule	Carry off jewels and small items of value
2	Extend your own capacities	Use weapons, vehicles, or accomplices
3	Minimize search time	Forage on the way home from school
4	Minimize handling time	Steal money—it's easier to deal with

Additional elaborations are summed up in Exhibit 17.1 and discussed in the following.

Extending Maximum Size

Animals devise methods to overcome the head-size rule. Group foraging helps animal takes down larger quarry. Strong teeth and jaws help tear a carcass into smaller pieces that can be eaten. Offenders, too, can reach beyond their own sizes. They can draw assistance from accomplices or use vehicles for removal of their booty. Research by Clarke and associates finds that offenders using pickup trucks steal large appliances from construction sites.[8] In contrast to inner-city burglars on foot, residential burglars often can steal larger items, using cars or trucks. Guns and other weapons help offenders inflict violent crimes on big guys, too.[9] Generally speaking, an offender must use extra foraging techniques to extend the physical limits of criminal acts. Exhibit 17.1 uses the term "extend your own capacities" to show how offenders push beyond the size rule. Even then the offender is limited by the size of truck or ability to load it, unload it, store the booty, or deliver force, etc.

Getting the Most While Searching for Booty

Ecologists call a foraging area a "patch." The route to get there is a "path," but you could also talk about highways, roads, trails, and backyards that offenders use when they need them. Living things forage along paths to get to the patches to eat.

In general, animals forage to maximize their energy gain for the time they spend. Krebs and his coresearchers experimented with a conveyer belt delivering worms to the chickadee, an intelligent bird. At first, these birds ate whatever worm came along. In time, a chickadee learned to wait for the whole worms.[10] Similarly, shoplifters and other thieves will pass up less valuable crime targets, favoring those worth more to them. Burglars rummage through a drawer, leaving items they think are less of value in search for those better.

Professor Clarke's work on "hot products" has elaborated offender preferences, by the acronym CRAVED (discussed in Chapter 8). It is interesting that squirrels, too, prefer food that is concealable, removable, available, valuable, enjoyable, and disposable. That's why they forage for acorns. That's also why they enjoy the luxury of eating from my bird feeder.[11]

Clarke notes that we can prevent criminal acts in three ways—by increasing crime's immediate risks, increasing crime's efforts, and decreasing crime's quick rewards. I took his advice to thwart the squirrels. A new bird-feeding device increased squirrel risks and difficulties, while decreasing their payoff per raid. Amateur squirrels no longer steal from me, and professionals get less. This is a good example of what crime policy intellectuals call "harm reduction."

As Exhibit 17.1 indicates, offenders seek to minimize search time. That's why removing easy targets can lead to real crime prevention. We know that foragers prefer nearby patches to those farther away. But they will travel farther to a patch richer in food than the one that is close. They also tend to stay longer if they have traveled farther. Researchers have found that chipmunks collecting nuts at more distant patches spend longer in each patch and take larger loads back to the burrow.[12] It is no surprise to us that criminals try to commit crimes near to home or where they are going anyway. But offenders will forage in patches somewhat farther away if additional booty makes it worth their while. And if they have traveled farther, they are inclined to stay longer and seek more booty to make the trip a success.

Important Strategy: Minimize Handling Time

Richardson and Verbeek[13] studied crows foraging for clams, noting that they left quite a few clams behind after going to the trouble to dig them up. We cannot easily interview crows, but we can infer that they left the smaller clams aside because, even at that point, these were not worth the effort to open. Ecologists have developed a *law of foraging*, easily adapted to studying crime:

$$Foraging\ Ratio = \frac{Illicit\ Gains}{Search\ Time + Handling\ Time}$$

Offenders seek to maximize their illicit gains relative to the sum of their search and handling time.[14] This rule tells us a lot, but does not tell us everything. For example, birds known as oyster catchers have trouble opening mussels at all, so they cannot simply pick the largest ones.[15]

This ratio gives us some insight into offenders, too. Offenders are unlikely to take loot that is too difficult to fence, or that requires too much time and energy to handle. Minimizing handling time is especially important because it's risky to be carrying the loot. Interestingly, the same principle might apply to stolen vehicles. The journey after crime in stolen autos is quite short, and vehicles tend to be abandoned rather near where they are taken.[16] If an offender drives a stolen car far, it should be a good car, worth the risk. If a burglar needs to drive 100 miles to unload the booty, it has to be worth the trouble. The offender also has to know how to fence the goods and where to do so. Handling time becomes an issue for quite diverse offenses, even for serial murderers who have to dispose of the bodies. As we learn more about offender foraging, we can elaborate this equation. But never lose sight of these fundamentals.

Indeed, the first parts of this chapter have applied the most basic strategic ideas of foraging to crime. The rest of the chapter further helps explain how offenders think and act as they search for targets.

Offenders Even Out Their Risks

Foragers are especially inclined to maximize their intake during certain periods. Thus pregnant mammals often are especially hungry and forage for more food. Hibernating bears maximize intake before hibernation begins, but not during. The tendency to maximize during certain periods affects risk taking. Yellow-eyed juncos and other foraging birds switch from risk-averse to risk-prone behavior as they are increasingly deprived of food.[17] Deer are more likely to come down the mountain and forage during daylight if they are hungry, but to lie low if they have enough to eat. This is congruent with informal police reports that drug abusers are more dangerous and take more risks when they are starved for drugs. Some offenders might take more risks in preparation for a party or holiday.

After discovering a flower with too little nectar, the bumblebee tends to avoid such flowers in the future. It tries to increase its average gain, but that's not its only issue. Professor Leslie Real at Indiana University conducted several experiments making nectar *unpredictable* for bumblebees.[18] Bees had a choice between (a) flowers that with a modest and dependable amount of nectar, and (b) other flowers with more nectar on average, but less dependability. Bees overwhelmingly preferred dependable gains to greater but undependable gains.

Although we think of offenders as risk-takers, they appear to pick targets on the safe side. They shoplift in poorly supervised stores when it is easiest to succeed. They rob the weakest victims with the fewest guardians near. Like animal predators selecting strays unprotected by the herd, robbers pick on homeless street people or stragglers at dusk, even if other victims might sometimes have more to offer up.[19]

Situational crime prevention relies on increasing risks and dangers for offenders in the immediate context of their crimes. Dr. Martin Gill's interviews with commercial robbers found that they pay relatively little attention to remote punishments, such as prison, but give a great deal of consideration to dependability and safety in their immediate crime situations.[20] Sometimes crime opportunities cannot be removed; but authorities can still disrupt crime significantly by making its environment undependable for offenders.

Learning, Innovating, and Standing Pat

What you learn should respond to how your environment changes.

a. If an environment changes too quickly and too much, past experience will not help you predict its future state, anyway. There's no point learning about it.

b. If your environment never changes at all, there's no point learning anything *new* about it.

c. If your environment is *rather* stable, but still changes, you should check every now and then to see if your opportunities have changed.

Many foraging environments fit (c). Perhaps that explains why foraging bumblebees select their flowers based on short-term memory. Accordingly, offenders who rely on short-term memory but allow themselves to resample their environment might fare better. No foraging pattern will work perfectly, since offenders do not always recognize crime opportunities, might not know correct travel times, or simply make mistakes. Many offenders stick to the old ways much of the time, but try something new every now and then, hoping to discover new crime opportunities. We should not expect offenders to be exactly the same every day, week, and month—even if they follow some general patterns.

Animals innovate more than many humans realize. Innovation is important for feeding and foraging, and may be seen as part of social learning. A new book, *Animal Innovation,* includes this story in its advertisement:

> In 1953 a young female Japanese macaque called Imo began washing sweet potatoes before eating them. . . . [P]otato washing gradually spread throughout the troop. When, three years after her first invention, Imo devised a second novel foraging behavior, that of separating wheat from sand by throwing mixed handfuls into water and scooping out the floating grains, she was almost instantly heralded around the world as a "monkey genius." Imo is probably the most celebrated of animal innovators. In fact, many animals will invent new behavior patterns, adjust established behaviors to a novel context, or respond to stresses in an appropriate and novel manner.[21]

Animal innovation is closely linked to social learning, reminding us again that foraging theory is not wedded to genetic determinism. But we must put innovation in perspective. Criminal offending mixes innovation and ordinary repetition, mostly the latter. Foragers avoid innovating most of the time, for that would increase their risks. Indeed, foraging theory implies that it is good to repeat oneself a good deal of the time, but not always. New searches are necessary not only to improve success, but also to overcome loss of old targets or the introduction of countermeasures.

We should not underestimate the value of randomness in foraging. It is less glorious than innovation, but it can accomplish some of the same things. Perhaps all animal brains contain some random moves for emergency use, to help surprise prey or to jump clear of predators. If God does not play dice with the universe, perhaps he hands us some dice to help us discover new possibilities.

Looking About

Foraging animals often have conflicting demands, including watching for predators, searching for mates, defending territories or nests, etc.[22] Sheep often feed during the hottest part of the day when their predators are least active.[23] They also seek good "escape terrain" with an unobstructed view of the surrounding area. For example, bighorn sheep favor steep and rocky terrain despite its lower quality of grass, and lambs even more so. They avoid tall vegetation for the same reason. The more time spent with head up scanning for predators, the less they can eat. Of course, sheep often forage in groups to help each other to scan for enemies.

Criminal offenders also seek unobstructed views, especially if they can obstruct views of themselves. Offenders sometimes lurk in shadows, allowing ill-designed lighting to blind their victims or those who might interfere with their attacks. Professors Jack Nasar and Bonnie Fisher[24] observed that poorly designed urban spaces help offenders find victims, who cannot easily see them coming or escape. We can readily see that crime foraging is subject to rules, but also has some surprises.

The pursuit of information is part of the foraging process. A forager acquiring information tends to stay longer than would be predicted by the direct gains alone. This has been confirmed for the downy woodpecker.[25] Some crime foragers also spend more time simply because they want to know more about their targets or the areas where they expect to find them.

Human hunters, like animal counterparts, often scout their quarry. They do so before, during, and after the legal hunting season. Before the season, experienced hunters learn how deer trails have changed, gathering data from local farmers and neighbors, and asking people to keep a lookout. During the season (or even before it), skilled hunters gather information as they hunt that can be used on the next outing:

> Half the battle is getting to know your quarry, where he sleeps, eats, and travels. If you find where a big buck is seen more than twice, my advice to you is to find out which direction and what time. Then proceed to find out as much about him as you can. Spend every available moment studying what you have learned about him. You will be surprised at what this will mean come hunting season.[26]

Criminal scouting can follow some of these rules, too. On off days, offenders can note where good targets can be found. They can trade information with friends, either co-offenders or nonoffenders who pass on information, anyway. As they forage today, they can make notes for tomorrow. None of these efforts needs to be vigorous or obstreperous. Given the ease with which ordinary crime is committed in a modern society, it should not require substantial scouting time.

Animal predators are well aware where their quarry forage, drink, bathe, and nest. Human hunters take this into account, too. The Division of

Wildlife of the Ohio Department of Natural Resources suggests how hunters should scout for squirrels by finding mature nut trees: "Oaks, hickories, and beechnuts are all desirable food for squirrels, so look for areas where these nuts are available, and check to see if there are 'cuttings' (shell pieces that indicate squirrels have been feeding here) in the area."[27] Efficient street robbers know where the drunks are.

Foraging in Space

Most foraging is not entirely random or undirected in space. Offenders tend to reuse many of the same strategies and return to the same hunting ground.

Search Paths

Search paths are the routes offenders take in foraging for their crime targets. Theoretically, an offender might forage by four basic methods, listed from the least to the most orderly:

1. Traveling randomly

2. Moving by various routes toward a specific area

3. Proceeding in a very general direction

4. Following a distinct and established route, repeatedly

Random search paths will surely miss a lot but might discover new opportunities. At the other extreme, repeating the same route makes the offender too predictable. Arguably, offenders do best to forage in a general direction, gaining some predictability in their targets without becoming too predictable for police or quarry.[28]

Very Local Foraging

Chapter 3 presented the "near repeat hypothesis," which states that similar and proximate homes have similarly high burglary rates. Apparently, these offenders forage similar targets to improve their chances for success. Sometimes these areas are very close, even within a few doors, but sometimes the area is larger. Researchers have confirmed "near repeats" for relevant settings, presenting a fruitful new area of study.

Foragers generally return to areas that proved to be productive. A forager does best by finding the right patch among many patches that vary in quality. Once an offender finds a good foraging area, why keep looking? Only after successes are disrupted, targets are depleted, or the offender's own predators are alerted, does it make sense to look elsewhere.

The Central-Place Foraging Strategy

In some ways, humans don't travel very differently from animals. Norway rats are central-place foragers, moving along paths from a central location to patches that contain food.[29] These rats note vertical landmarks and beacons. As paths got longer, rats follow them less. Beavers tend to forage around their lodges and squirrels around their trees. Each moves away from refuge to foraging area, then returns for security. Swallows also forage from central places.[30]

Professors Paul and Patricia Brantingham have for many years applied this concept to crime, explaining how most offenders forage near home, work, or school, or on routes around these places.[31] Dr. Kim Rossmo's serial-offender crime studies reflect the same principle. In the future, it would be most useful to learn how much central-place foraging occurs from familiarity and how much it reflects a wish to return to the refuge if problems occur.

This is closely related to the Brantinghams' concepts of nodes, paths, and edges, noted in earlier chapters. Most of us go to particular nodes in our daily lives—home, work, school, shopping, and recreation. Each of us is much more familiar with these nodes than with the rest of the metropolis. Even rural people know some towns better than others. People also know the paths they travel along to get to their routine nodes. But they might wander out a bit from the edges of the nodes and paths they know.

Offenders are most likely to commit crimes around the nodes and paths with which they are familiar. They also forage along the edges, returning to the areas they know afterward. An offender's quarry is at greater risk when the quarry is wandering into edge areas, especially the area that offenders know better than the quarry. Insiders have a distinct advantage over outsiders when committing criminal acts. That's why tourists are at great crime risk. It's also a reason that many local offenders can easily outflank police and security guards unfamiliar with the local area. Accordingly, we should always compare an offender's foraging territory to his nesting area. Offenders foraging away from home must weigh their decisions differently. Distance alters what they might gain, as well as their technical requirements for gaining it. In alien territory, local victims know more than the attackers, limiting the options available for the latter.

Victims too face different dangers from outsiders as opposed to insiders. Raids by outsiders can be dangerous and costly, interfering with security.

But at least one knows to suspect strangers, and is fairly sure they will depart when they are done. Insider offenders are still around after they commit their offenses. Of course, some places have to fear repeated raids by outsiders. The worst locations must fear both insider and outsider attacks on person and property, with no respite.

Foraging for Accomplices

Most juvenile offenses are carried out with accomplices, but not the same accomplices. Thus offenders who want accomplices must find new ones, usually of a similar age. Is this a foraging process? We are only beginning to learn about how this is done,[32] but perhaps urban offenders have a few places they look for social life, some of it leading to cooperative crime. Older offenders often act alone at the point of crime, but rely on accomplices beforehand to gain information and afterwards to unload stolen goods. Thus crime benefits, in one form or another, from accomplices. Perhaps we can think of older offenders as foraging for information that they use soon afterwards for crime purposes.

Crime is an age-segregated activity, with older offenders reluctant to accept the company of new youths as they reach crime-prone ages. Thus criminal activity has a natural tendency to die down, unless there is a way to replenish it. Replenishment in turn depends on offender convergence settings (hangouts), where offenders can find one another to arrange new offenses as opportunities emerge.[33]

Arguably, offender convergence settings occur mainly toward the interior of rich crime habitats, not on the edges. If this assumption is true, it explains why large, interconnected metropolitan systems assist co-offending. In contrast, small and isolated towns or neighborhood generate some crime, but provide offenders with more limited assistance in finding accomplices. Thus crime in smaller places does not become as luxuriant, diversified, or sustainable at high levels. None of this denies that crime exists in many places. It merely explains why habitat fragmentation forces criminal activity to start over more often than in settings with interconnected crime habitats.

Legal Activity Facilitates Foraging

Very often, legal activities make foraging easier. Employees, students, legitimate residents—all of these can go about their legal business and find crime targets in the process. Some positions are especially fruitful for foraging. Thus a delivery person has a legitimate reason to be traveling about neighborhoods or businesses, seeing crime opportunities in the process.

This is why it is often a mistake to assume that having a job or going to school prevents crime participation. A legitimate activity might reduce or increase crime opportunities. Thus a truck driver going from dock to dock has crime opportunities exceeding those of someone stuck at a desk, unless the desk provides entry to personal accounts, access to passwords, or a chance to trick people. A high school student on an open campus across from a shopping district has many more chances to forage for crime targets than another student on a closed campus quite distant from commercial locations.

Communities can interfere with the foraging of youths by channeling their activities into settings that truly minimize the opportunity to wander. But it is not automatically the case that legitimate roles provide such channeling.

Disrupted Foraging Routines

In general, crime follows the routines of the offenders and their victims. But routines can be disrupted, and crime can follow accordingly. Students away on spring break shift both their offending and victimization to other locations, sometimes beach resorts.[34] Their campus property becomes highly vulnerable to theft while they are gone, but perhaps less by student offenders. Vacation homes are very vulnerable when the season is over. Holiday spots often have a good deal of crime. But we need to know more about how vacationers forage as offenders, or how local offenders forage differently in holiday areas. Longer-term migration also influences crime. Those who just moved in are very vulnerable to burglary, as are vacated homes. Areas with many transients are very vulnerable. But do people forage differently there?

How and When Does the Offender Forage?

Many youths, for example, go out foraging for excitement of some sort, with no specific idea *where* that will lead. In the process, they end up committing a criminal act. Foraging is part of that act, even though they were not foraging for a particular target. Foraging for girls, for liquor, for noise, for nightlife, for excitement—these can lead to crime without clear intent.

We already know from rap sheets that most offenders are not specialists over time. But they might specialize on any given outing. Sometimes offenders

- discover crime targets by accident, not foraging at all;
- are out seeking very general fun or excitement, not thinking about crime;
- forage for unspecified crime opportunities;
- forage with one type of crime in mind, but find another; or
- have one type of crime in mind, and stick to it.

Most offenders do not plan far in advance,[35] so foraging decisions could be made rather soon before the criminal act. That does not minimize the importance of foraging decisions. Indeed, it is quite possible that offenders are more definite about their foraging than they are about their targets. Many burglars do not know quite what home they will enter, or what they will find there. But they do know they will probably go down this street and look around. We know that offenders make decisions, but at what stages in the foraging process does that happen? Which decisions are made precisely, and which are made with just a vague sense of criminal intent? The foraging perspective helps us ask some clear questions. It also shows how scientists have found some reasonable and verifiable answers.

Foraging for Illicit Commodities

Illegal markets do not always involve mutualisms between ongoing buyers and sellers. Sporadic sales often require some degree of foraging. In any large city one finds areas where people forage as buyers or sellers of drugs or illicit sex. Professor George Rengert of Temple University distinguishes local from regional drug markets.[36] In local drug markets, people who know or are acquainted make the drug deals. In regional drug markets, strangers have to find each other by some sort of search process. If drug sellers linger in known areas, they do not need to walk far, and others figure out where to find them. Media accounts of drug areas provide free advertising, telling new customers where to look. Like other offenders, drug-market foragers must consider search time, distance traveled, transaction time, risks, and dependability of the patch they forage.

All businesses need to be dependable for their customers. By disrupting drug-market locations, authorities can add to the uncertainty of buyers in search of sellers. Outdoor drug dealers congregate in certain spots to give their customers a dependable market. Similarly, some categories of prostitutes congregate on known blocks or in known bars because this reduces foraging time for them and for the buyers of their services. On the other hand, dependability also reduces foraging time for those robbers who take advantage of either prostitutes or their customers, and for police when they decide to crack down. Media can provide thinly disguised advertisements for prostitutes, thus creating a form of foraging that is ostensibly safer. A customer can forage through advertised listings of shady activities or suggestive addresses on the Internet, then make contact. The growth of these opportunities for buyers and sellers alike has exceeded the ability of police to keep track (see Chapter 14, on passive assistance).

Overview

Ecological theory and research on animal foraging can easily converse with the growing body of research on how offenders move toward their crime targets. Animal hunters, human hunters, and offenders have much in common. Foragers face limits in what they can carry, the time and effort they must devote, their uncertainty, the time it takes to find things out, and their risks at the hands of others. A foraging offender must try to avoid his own potential attackers—including police, but more often other offenders.

Central Points, Chapter 17

1. Not all crimes require foraging. But when foraging is required, offenders tend to forage near their homes and places they already know.

2. A criminal will generally not forage for anything he cannot carry or overcome physically, unless there is an alternative means to do so.

3. Accomplices and vehicles help offenders extend their reach.

4. Offenders try to minimize search and handling time, compared to their gains. Offenders will forage farther away for larger gains.

5. Offenders forage with neither total randomness nor total regularity.

Exercises

1. What crimes require long searches?

2. What crimes require more handling?

3. Use foraging theory to figure out your greatest vulnerability to crime.

4. What offenders do you think will take the greatest risks while foraging?

Notes

1. Quoted in R. Kiner, *Baseball Forever* (Chicago: Triumph Books, 2004).

2. Zambian politician, president (b. 1924). Quoted in *The Columbia World of Quotations* (New York: Columbia University Press, 1996).

3. Baseball player. Quoted in *Baseball World*, http://www.geocities.com/Colosseum/Park/1138/quotes/quotesa.html (accessed September 3, 2005).

4. *Deep Thoughts: An Inspiration for the Uninspired* (New York: Penguin, 1992).

5. A classic paper by Stephen J. Gould and Richard Lewontin in 1978 sent many biologists scurrying to explain variations in nature without making deterministic statements. See S. J. Gould and R. Lewontin, "The Spandrels of San Marco and the Panglossian Paradigm: A Critique of the Adaptationist Programme," *Proceedings of the Royal Society of London* 205 (1978): 581–598. See also R. J. Cowie, "Optimal Foraging in Great Tits, *Parus Major*," *Nature* 268 (1977): 137–139.

6. See

  a. P. J. Brantingham and P. L. Brantingham, "Crime Niches and Criminal Foraging in Patchy Environments: Anthropological Models in Crime Pattern Analysis," paper presented at the American Society of Criminology annual meeting, Toronto, November 1999.

  b. D. K. Rossmo, "Routine Activities and Foraging Theory: The Influence of Motivation on Size of Criminal Hunting Area," paper presented at the American Society of Criminology annual meeting, San Francisco, November 2000.

  c. R. Freeman, "The Supply of Youths to Crime," in S. Pozo, ed., *Exploring the Underground Economy* (Kalamazoo, MI: W.E. Upjohn Institute for Employment Research, 1996).

  d. P. Ekblom, see Chapter 10, endnote 13.

  e. W. K. Bickel, L. A. Giordano, and G. J. Badger, "Risk-sensitive Foraging Theory Elucidates Risky Choices Made by Heroin Addicts," *Addiction* 99 (2004): 855–861.

  f. Professors Ronald V. Clarke and Ken Pease do not normally use the word "foraging," but their work fits in, as I have indicated. Citations to their work are found throughout this book.

7. R. A. Martin, N. Hammerschlag, and K. Rossmo, "Application of Geographic Profiling to the Study of White Shark Predatory Behaviour at Seal Island, South Africa, *Nature*, forthcoming. See also Rossmo reference in endnote 31.

8. R. V. Clarke and H. Goldstein, "Reducing Theft at Construction Sites: Lessons From a Problem Oriented Project," in N. Tilley, ed., *Analysis for Crime Prevention* (Monsey, NY: Criminal Justice Press, 2002) (Volume 14 in *Crime Prevention Studies* series).

9. For an analysis of the size of offenders and violence, see R. B. Felson, "Big People Hit Little People: Sex Differences in Physical Power and Interpersonal Violence," *Criminology* 34 (1996): 433–452.

10. J. R. Krebs and others, "Optimal Prey Selection in the Great Tit," *Animal Behavior* 25 (1977): 30–38.

11. Perhaps this is a form of welfare fraud.

12. L.-A. Giraldeau and D. L. Kramer, "The Marginal Value Theorem: A Quantitative Test Using Load Size Variation in a Central Place Forager, the Eastern Chipmunk, *Tamias Striatus*," *Animal Behavior* 30 (1982):1036–1042.

13. H. Richardson and N. A. M. Verbeek, "Diet Selection and Energy Optimization by Northwestern Crows Feeding on Japanese Littleneck (*Corvus Caurinus*)," *Ecology* 67 (1987): 1219–1226.

14. Unlike general ecologists, I emphasize "gains" rather than energy. I also use the term, "foraging ratio" for current purposes.

15. A student of economics will quickly recognize "costs and benefits" as the idea behind the current chapter, and elsewhere in this book.

16. Y. Lu, "Getting Away With the Stolen Vehicle: An Investigation of Journey-After-Crime," *The Professional Geographer* 55 (2003): 422–433.

17. T. Caraco, S. Martindale, and T. S. Whitham, "An Empirical Demonstration of Risk-sensitive Foraging Preferences," *Animal Behaviour* 28 (1980): 820–830.

18. L. A. Real, "Paradox, Performance and the Architecture of Decision-making in Animals," *American Zoologist* 36 (1996): 518–529.

19. On the victimization of the homeless, see J. Hagan and B. McCarthy, *Mean Streets: Youth Crime and the Homeless* (New York: Cambridge University Press, 1998).

20. Note Martin Gill's studies of commercial robbery:
   a. M. L. Gill, *Commercial Robbery: Offenders' Perspectives on Security and Crime Prevention* (London: Blackstone, 2000)
   b. M. L. Gill, "The Craft of Robbers of Cash-in-Transit Vans: Crime Facilitators and the Entrepreneurial Approach," *International Journal of the Sociology of Law* 29 (2001): 277–291.

21. Spelling and punctuation are Americanized in this quotation. M. S. Reader and K. N. Laland, *Animal Innovation* (Oxford, UK: Oxford University Press, 2003).

22. S. Martindale, "Nest Defense and Central Place Foraging: A Model and Experiment," *Behavioral Ecology and Sociobiology* 10 (1982): 85–89.

23. R. Berkley, "Role of Predation Risk in Foraging Behavior" (n.d.), in Behave: Stories of Applied Animal Behavior, website created by members of a graduate foraging ecology class at the University of Idaho and Washington State University under the direction of Drs. Karen Launchbaugh and Lisa Shipley, http://www.cnr.uidaho.edu/range556/Appl_BEHAVE/projects/predation_and_foraging.html (accessed September 4, 2005).

24. B. S. Fischer and J. L. Nasar, "Fear of Crime in Relationship to Three Exterior Site Features: Prospect, Refuge and Escape," *Environment and Behavior* 24, no. 1 (1992): 135–165. They use the terms "prospect" and "refuge," and their work is highly relevant to the issues we are addressing here.

25. S. L. Lima, "Downy Woodpecker Foraging Behavior: Efficient Sampling in Simple Stochastic Environments," *Ecology* 65 (1984): 166–174.

26. "Whitetail World: Everything You Ever Wanted to Know and More About the Whitetail Deer" (n.d.), http://www.kerrlake.com/deer/WHITE5.HTM (accessed October 26, 2005).

27. Department of Natural Resources, Division of Wildlife, "Squirrel Hunting" (2005), www.dnr.ohio.gov/wildlife/hunting/SmallGameAndTrapping/squirrel.htm (accessed September 4, 2005).

28. See G. G. Rengert and J. Wasilchick, *Suburban Burglary* (Springfield, IL: Charles C Thomas, 1985).

29. J. P. Roche and W. Timberlake, "The Influence of Artificial Paths and Landmarks on the Foraging Behavior of Norway Rats," *Animal Learning & Behavior* 26 (1998): 76–84.

30. D. M. Bryant and A. K. Turner, "Central Place Foraging by Swallows: The Question of Load Size," *Animal Behavior* 30 (1982): 845–856.

31. See
   a. P. J. Brantingham and P. L. Brantingham, eds., *Environmental Criminology* (Prospect Heights, IL: Waveland, 1991).
   b. P. L. Brantingham and P. J. Brantingham, "Mobility, Notoriety and Crime: A Study in Crime Patterns of Urban Nodal Points," *Journal of Environmental Systems* 11 (1984): 89–99.
   c. P. L. Brantingham and P. J. Brantingham, "Nodes, Paths and Edges: Considerations on the Complexity of Crime and the Physical Environment," *Journal of Environmental Psychology* 13 (1993): 3–28.
   d. D. K. Rossmo, *Geographic Profiling* (Boca Raton, FL: CRC Press, 1999).

32. M. Warr, *Companions in Crime* (New York and Cambridge, UK: Cambridge University Press, 2002).

33. This issue is taken up again in Chapter 20.

34. See

    a. R. W. Glensor and K. J. Peak, "The Problem of Crimes Against Tourists" (2005), Center for Problem-oriented Policing, http://www.popcenter.org (accessed September 4, 2005).

    b. A. Pizam and Y. Mansfeld, eds., *Tourism, Crime, and International Security Issues* (Chichester, UK, and New York: Wiley, 1996).

    c. P. Stangeland, *The Crime Puzzle; Crime Patterns and Crime Displacement in Southern Spain* (Málaga, Spain: Gomez Ediciones, 1995).

35. See for example F. Feeney, "Robbers as Decision Makers," in D. Cornish and R. V. Clarke, eds., *The Reasoning Criminal* (New York: Springer-Verlag, 1986).

36. See Chapter 11, endnote 10, and Chapter 12, endnote 15.

In cases of defense 'tis best to weigh
The enemy more mighty than he seems.

—William Shakespeare[1]

There is always more spirit in attack than in defense.

—Titus Livius[2]

That general is skilful in attack whose opponent does not know what to defend; and he is skilful in defense whose opponent does not know what to attack.

—Sun Tzu[3]

If size did matter, the dinosaurs would still be alive.

—Wendelin Wiedeking[4]

18

Crime's First Defenses

Defenses are extremely important for crime. Victims seek to defend themselves against potential and actual offenders. Offenders must defend themselves against counterattack. Police must defend against offender attacks, and try to overcome offender defenses, too. Guardians against crime must consider the risk of offender retaliations or counterattacks before deciding whether to intervene or look the other way. Indeed, defense is an essential part of crime's offensive strategies and tactics, applying to violence and property crime and to all parties to criminal action. This chapter gives most attention to potential victims defending against crime. Yet offense and defense can quickly trade places, like the parry and thrust in fencing.

It is a mistake to think that defenses apply only to violent crimes, or are limited to direct personal resistance. Many defenses are built into human artifacts, such as locks on doors, alarms, passwords, cell phones that are defunct if stolen, or phones programmed to make local calls only. Manufactured security often requires managerial effort, too. Keys must be assigned and tracked; credit card photos must be checked; money must be counted.

Interestingly, some defenses against violence also apply to property crime. For example, physical intimidation can assist a property offender against adversaries. A 1984 experiment created fake shoplifting incidents, namely, stealing a bottle of wine in full view of a nearby customer. The researchers observed whether each bystander tried to turn in the apparent offender.[5] One of the "thieves" was 66 inches tall and 140 pounds in weight. The other was 72 inches tall and 255 pounds in weight. Bystanders were more willing to turn in the puny shoplifter than the physically imposing shoplifter. When they turned the latter man in, they usually waited until he had left the store. We can readily see that a fear of violent retaliation is not confined to violent crimes.

Nature presents us with a vast array of defenses relevant to crime.[6] *Primary defenses* apply prior to attack, usually before detecting the presence of an adversary. A defender uses *secondary defenses* after detecting a menacing situation. Although human defenses are quite elaborate, they still fit well the categories and subcategories devised by ecologists. This chapter applies primary defenses to crime. The next chapter applies secondary defenses to crime, then summarizes all 16 defenses in Exhibit 19.2. I subsume the nine primary defenses (Exhibit 18.1) under three headings. The potential target or victim can try to (A) hide, (B) dissuade, or (C) overwhelm or thwart potential attackers, without confrontation.

Avoidance

The simplest form of defense is avoidance. Whether by instinct or learning, animals are often aware of the habits of their predators, avoiding risky locations, times, and activities as best they can. Deer try to alleviate their hunger quickly, as darkness falls, continuing until the approach of dawn.

Exhibit 18.1   Nine Primary Defenses Applied to Crime (usually applied prior to detection by adversary)

	Defenses	*Examples*
A. Hide	1. Avoidance	Walk in safer areas, avoid certain persons
	2. Camouflage	Offender carrying a clipboard or dressing like a local student
B. Dissuade	3. Personal reputation[1]	Develop a tough reputation
	4. Batesian mimicry	Walk like a tough guy
	5. Müllerian mimicry[2]	Wear gang colors
	6. Warnings[3]	Put up a "dangerous dog" sign
C. Overwhelm	7. Physical defenses	Use locks, bolts, walls, armor
	8. Group defenses[4]	Walk in a pack, live in a compound
	9. Vigorous recovery	Let candy sales overcome thefts at the counter

1. Naturalists do not normally list this as a defense.

2. See Chapter 20.

3. Also called "aposematic patterns." See Chapter 20.

4. Discussed in Chapter 18. Pack defenses by gangs are discussed in Chapter 20.

They retire for the day if they can, to avoid being seen as they graze.[7] Animals also select their travel routes with safety in mind. The shortest way between two points may be a straight line, but many animals prefer crooked routes and indirect movement to evade predators. Ovenbirds use tortuous routes to search for prey where their own predators are active.[8] Indeed, many animals move in paths with many twists and turns, as do soldiers running through fire, or cowboys on television. Maybe a crow doesn't fly straight because it needs to avoid owls.

Experts in Vancouver, British Columbia, discovered that households are more secure from property crimes when located on street blocks with fewest streets turning into them. For example, cul-de-sacs provide a greater chance to avoid offenders and are generally safer than through streets.[9] Thus a powerful device against crime is to construct remote neighborhoods that allow people to avoid likely offenders.

Many potential crime victims seek to avoid risky locations, times, and activities. These "routine precautions" often include avoidance behavior.[10] Some suburbanites avoid their central cities at least partly for security reasons. Many people park their cars in supervised lots or on lighted streets. Others avoid public transit at night or otherwise seek to avoid risky situations. Local people often have a good sense of the texture of their local environments with respect to crime risk. They probably know which streets are safer or more dangerous, which places house addicts, and which side of the street is worse than the other. They can select a route to the store that is safer, even if marginally so. Many people living in high-crime areas try to carry out their daily business early, hiding inside as dark approaches. Avoidance in time and space is a standard category of biological defense against predators; no less is true of humans. On the other hand, research by Professor Wesley Skogan indicates that many crime victims in high-crime areas have very limited options to alter their routine activities for greater security.[11]

Remember offenders also have adversaries against whom they might have to defend. Trading or consuming drugs only among friends is a form of avoidance. Call girls who stick to known customers are also engaging in avoidance of additional customers, who might bring danger with their extra business. Burglary is a form of avoidance, compared to robbery and other crimes that are overt and confrontational.

If market prices for illegal commodities rise, sellers can avoid the worst dangers and pick the safest niches the same level of sales. But buyers will have to move to more dangerous niches to find the same price. If prices for illegal commodities drop, the sellers will have to move into more dangerous niches to make the same sales, while buyers can find their illegal commodities for the same price in a safer niche. To reverse the order of reasoning, risk level can entice buyers and sellers into or out of a niche, thereby affecting its prices. But avoidance has its limits for safe criminal behavior. Even a few known customers can be risky if they are drawn from dangerous populations or from those in dangerous circumstances or conditions of intoxication. Many offenders nonetheless have some sense of the variations in risk from different offending situations and might make choices accordingly. That provides an important tool for crime prevention, which often seeks to increase offender risks.

Police, too, must pay attention to the spatiotemporal aspects of their enforcement efforts and the dangers these produce. Police are supposed to take some risks to interfere with crime, but they are not expected to take inordinate risks. Most police are trained not to enter dangerous situations without backup from other officers, unless there is imminent threat to human life. In controlling riots and other extreme situations, police often decide to hold back. Nor can we rule out some police laying low until their retirement party comes along.

Potential guardians against crime also tend to remain inactive if danger lurks. Many bystanders look the other way or fail to call police. Many fear retaliations from offenders or even danger from the innocent parties in crime. In police states, most citizens are afraid of the police and do not wish to get involved with them, even in an innocent role. Avoidance is an important strategy for offenders, potential victims, and conceivable guardians against crime.

Camouflage[12]

Rather than running or hiding, many plants and animals have evolved camouflage to escape notice from predators or sometimes to assist their own predation. Two camouflage methods are observed in nature: Protective coloration and protective resemblance. Protective coloration means that an organism blends in with surroundings by adapting similar colors, blending patterns, reducing the contrast with the surroundings, disrupting normal body outlines, or hiding its eyes. Protective resemblance means adapting the look and motion of surrounding organisms. For example, sometimes an insect looks like a twig and moves like one, too. Some bugs seem like thorns, and butterflies like dead leaves. A Brazilian beetle folds up its legs and flops over to resemble bird droppings. Many mammals change from brown to white to brown and back to match the season.

The basic principle of camouflage is the ability to hide in plain sight.[13] That ability applies to crime as well. It includes adapting personal look, movement, and clothing; blending into a crowd; or like methods used by offenders to hide from adversaries or vice versa. Camouflage can enable an offender to approach a crime scene, to carry out the crime, or just to survive and escape unharmed, or some combination of this list. For potential victims, camouflage helps hide the target from the offender's notice. For police, camouflage makes it easier to observe a crime, apprehend an offender, carry out an investigation, or whatever is needed. Camouflage methods will vary greatly by type of crime and crime niche.

To facilitate a crime or avoid becoming a target of others, the offender disguises himself by blending in with the surrounding environments, activities, or persons. Crime-related camouflage uses nonhuman and human devices. Dark clothing at night can camouflage an attacker. A crowd of pedestrians, a bevy of employees entering in the morning or leaving in the evening, the turbulence of rush hour, a store full of customers, a large bar packed with drinkers, a college campus in the 10 minutes before class—all of these can camouflage illegal acts or offender approaches or exits. Many an offender has carried a clipboard or carried a briefcase in order to blend in with surroundings. Sellers or buyers of illegal goods or services often blend in with legitimate business transactions, avoiding notice and interference from bystanders.

Opera houses and concert halls in big cities must contend with well-dressed thieves stealing purses. Lee Harvey Oswald entered a movie theatre after shooting President Kennedy, hoping to elude police. Perhaps had he done a better job blending in, he might have remained free from custody, and avoided being shot himself.

Not only offenders, but also potential crime victims use camouflage. Shoppers leave their new purchases in the car, covered with something unattractive, then return to the mall. People place valuables in cookie jars or otherwise try to make them inconspicuous. Detectives use camouflage by wearing conventional clothes and driving unmarked cars. But camouflage can fail if all detective cars are the same model, easily noticed by offenders. Even uniformed police sit in cars that look like ordinary cars until it is too late for the speeder.

A substantial amount of white-collar crime is intrinsically camouflaged. Illegal transactions are buried in a thousand identical forms and transmitted in the usual way. Clerks look, dress, and act like the others as they steal something from the bank or the customer. Camouflage is the most common primary defense in nature. But is it the most common form of defense by offenders and by victims? This is the kind of empirical question raised by linking the study of crime to the larger field of ecology.

So far, I have explained how potential victims hide, sometimes in plain sight. Now I turn to four methods by which they dissuade others from attack, by means of personal reputation, two types of mimicry, and warnings.

Personal Reputation and Dominance

I have already discussed pecking orders based on physical prowess. That topic also has implications for an individual's defense. Although personal reputation for toughness is not normally listed as a defense, it can clearly be an advantage to some youths in some circumstances to carry about a reputation for physical toughness and prowess. A nasty personal reputation helps an offender intimidate others. Without intimidation, an offender risks being turned in if he is recognized going to the scene of a crime, doing the crime, or leaving the scene. With intimidation, any witnesses might go mute. Thus intimidation widens greatly the span and circumstances for committing a successful crime. However, that reputation does not work well outside the sphere where one is known or beyond oneself or one's immediate associates. In Chapter 20 I consider how the street gang extends the ability to intimidate beyond one individual's nasty reputation.

Mimicry and Crime

The coral snake (*Micrurus fulvius tenere*) is an extremely dangerous viper common in Florida, Arizona, and southward into Latin America. It is not likely to attack people, but when it bites it holds on tight, injecting as much venom as possible and doing tremendous destruction to the nervous system of the victim. Its bright and gaudy colors have generated several mimics. For example, the scarlet king snake (*Lampropeltis triangulum*) is often called the "false coral snake" because it has similar colors and patterns. The latter snake is not venomous at all. But it benefits from looking almost like the coral snake, scaring off potential predators. Of course, some beasts must really be obnoxious, or there would be nothing to mimic. Chapter 20 explains that a form of mimicry is extremely important for street gangs. But first, consider a more common form of mimicry.[14]

Batesian Mimicry

In 1852, British naturalist Henry Walter Bates discovered two similarly marked families of Brazilian forest butterflies. One was poisonous to birds. The other resembled the poisonous one and thus managed to survive despite being well worthy of a meal. Via Batesian mimicry, organisms gain protection from predators by imitating a poisonous or obnoxious species. The three participants in mimicry are the *model,* the *mimic,* and the *dupe.* The model is what's mimicked. The mimic appears and acts like the model. The dupe is the one who falls for it. The coral snake is the model for the scarlet king snake, with its potential predators the dupes. Many other examples are found in nature, including the Costa Rican moth larvae whose *derrière* resembles a tiny viper, a South American cricket that looks like a wasp, a grasshopper that mimics the ferocious tiger beetle, clear-wing moths that look like wasps, and cockroaches portraying themselves to be ladybird beetles whose blood is poison. Ecologists sometimes distinguish mimicry of taste, mannerisms, looks, and other features of targets that attract or repel predators. Various terms are sometimes added, such as "speed mimicry," for a slow organism that resembles one that is fast moving, discouraging predators before they can find out the truth.

Consider Professor Ronald Clarke's three crime prevention methods: making crime targets less attractive, more risky, and more difficult for offenders. All three can be accomplished in reality, but also by trick. A valuable target can be made to look plain; an easy target can be made to appear risky or difficult. Thus a very suitable crime target mimics an unsuitable target. We can make an expensive computer look very ordinary from the outside, convincing potential thieves to leave it alone. We can make a store appear more risky for shoplifting by using fake video cameras. We can make a window appear more difficult to climb into with plastic bars that look like steel.[15]

Mimicry is just the opposite of camouflage. With camouflage, the defender takes steps to blend in, incognito. With mimicry, the defender seeks a public display, covering up the reality with flaunted fakery. Whereas camouflage provides security by seeking to look ordinary, mimicry achieves the same goal by displaying a relatively specific image sure to be recognized and avoided. A form of false advertising, mimicry applies quite well among *Homo sapiens*.

Human Deception

Professor Diego Gambetta at the University of Oxford notes that humans are second to none in mimicry.[16] Unlike other organisms, they can play the game intentionally and strategically rather than through natural selection. Unlike other species, humans use mimicry mainly amongst themselves.

Professor Gambetta considers how people use mimicry to gain advantages, small and large. He gives examples of youths passing themselves off as older, to buy alcohol, cigarettes, or adult magazines; and of older people claiming younger age to obtain student discounts. He discusses Russians forging Jewish ancestry in order to emigrate. After War II, Nazis pretended to be Jewish to escape Allied troops, and Jews have pretended to be Christians to escape the Nazis. In America, light-skinned blacks have passed for white to escape discrimination. Men have pretended to be gay to avoid being drafted into the army. Males have mimicked females and females, males. I know some southern whites who mimic Yankees, and some northerners who pass themselves off in the other direction. Interestingly, people will mimic high or low status, depending on their goals—sometimes breaking laws in the process.

Mimicking Masculinity

Natural mimicry applies at least four techniques. Flies use auditory mimicry, beating their wings to sound like buzzing bees. Various insects use olfactory mimicry, smelling like wasps to scare off enemies. Visual mimicry assists innocuous insects that take on the color and shape of bees. Behavioral mimicry takes many forms. Some animals fly around like an aggressive species to scare off predators. It is common among primates to puff up the chest and shoulders to give an appearance of toughness. Sometimes crime participants fake toughness as a secondary defense, after detecting the approach of or attack by an adversary. But many displays of toughness are used as primary defense, too.

Mimicry is used by all participants in the crime process, including victims, offenders, and police. Offenders convey toughness to gain compliance from victims but also to prevent counterattacks or interference. People seek to enhance their own security by mimicking those who are more masculine than themselves (although they sometimes calculate wrong, challenging adversaries and enticing extra attacks). Methods include the following:

Auditory mimicry. Speaking with a deeper voice to mimic those who are stronger or more developed physically

Olfactory mimicry. Making perspiration obvious

Visual mimicry. Standing tall, holding up shoulders, puffing out chests, wearing extra layers of clothing to suggest more muscle than is really there

Behavioral mimicry. Walking like toughs

Some offenders use toy guns to mimic those with real ones. Others use tattoos, gang insignia, or aggressive postures to simulate toughness in order to gain compliance from victims or avoid counterattacks.

Police convey masculine strength to gain compliance and prevent attacks on themselves, although more subtle methods sometimes gain greater compliance from suspects. One police official in Scandinavia told me he much prefers female officers, who use their heads to gain compliance, avoiding masculine displays.

Those with cash on hand might actively mimic someone low in income and empty of pocket. Some potential crime victims mimic offenders in order to thwart attack. Indeed, juvenile gang membership is in part an effort to mimic criminal toughness in order to scare off attackers, as discussed in Chapter 20.

Warnings

Warnings are common in nature, as means to repel adversaries. Repulsion occurs through smell, taste, and sound, often using sight as a warning. Skunks are repulsive in smell but conspicuous to the eye. The monarch butterfly tastes bad but looks bright and beautiful so you can't miss it. But sight is not the only means of warning. Once while hiking in rattlesnake country, I heard a good rattle, but decided not to investigate the exact location. Warnings and warning devices are common methods for discouraging offenders. Obvious examples are electrified fences, guard dogs, and burglar alarms. Warnings can also take a polite and sophisticated form, such as welcoming known shoplifters as they enter your store, and asking them too many friendly questions—until they leave. Warnings are sometimes deceptive, such as fake alarm signs, and other times are used as secondary defenses after the adversary is detected.

I have discussed six methods of defense under two headings: hiding and dissuading. Now I examine three means by which defenders seek to overwhelm their attackers.

Physical Defenses[17]

Although situational crime prevention often employs physical defenses against crime, plants and animals have done so for millennia. Professor Graham Farrell has already written about the long ecological history of physical defenses, many of which have parallels with crime prevention.[18] Vegan dinosaurs had bony heads, armor plating, and plated body shields to deflect blows. Each bony back plate on the *Saltasaurus* was bigger than a person's head. Dinosaurs also had a leathery skin that predators could not easily penetrate, as well as nasty spikes for attack and counterattack. Modern turtles and crustaceans rely on hard shells to keep out intruders. Eye placement is another morphological defense against attack. Many animals have eyes on their sides or recessed for security.

Plants, too, depend greatly on physical defenses for their survival. Not only do they use many thorns and spines, but a vast variety of other security devices. Milkweed plants have a sticky white sap that interferes with predators. Although many cactus needles are formidable, many have small and pliable needles that penetrate your hand in a thousand places and tell you not to come back. Other plants have hairy structures inhospitable to insects. Indeed, textures are extremely important for interfering with plant adversaries. Some grasses and horsetails have slippery silica coatings. Some leaves are tough and stringy, difficult to digest, or difficult to grasp.

Many natural physical defense strategies are also applied to crime prevention. Depending on climate, homeowners plant thorn bushes or cactus to keep intruders away from windows. In Mexico, old walls were constructed with a spine of broken glass pieces on top. Some businesses leave mud or oil near their rear entries to discourage trespassers. Many college dormitories and other settings use protective films to make windows harder to smash and enter. Graffiti prevention often includes surfaces too slippery to take on paint or too rough to display it clearly. CDs were originally sold in small packs easily stolen, but merchants later sold them in larger packages not as easily slipped under shirts or blouses. Clearly, crime prevention efforts include not only variety but also often physical creativity.

Of course, the physical route from the offender to the crime target can have many layers and steps. Various physical obstacles can be placed along that route (Chapter 21 incorporates this point into a crime taxonomy). A property can be hard to find, then hard to enter, then its buildings either secured or confusing, then its particular targets bolted down. Indeed, the very construction of towns initially occurred as physical defenses against marauding robbers. Of course, people not only find safety in construction and hardware but also with one another.

Group Defenses[19]

For protection, many species travel and linger in groups, for two main reasons: (1) Although individuals at the edges face greater relative risk of attack, the larger group in the center is relatively more secure, and (2) as group size increases, per capita risk becomes diluted.

Group defenses serve a third purpose: groups provide more eyes and increase vigilance. Among animals, herd vigilance is probably instinctive; but group security is not automatic among humans. It depends on common identities, interests, and localism. Professor Ronald V. Clarke points out that, in situations of diffuse responsibility, group vigilance is weak.[20] This is consistent with social psychological research on bystander ambiguity and inaction in the wake of crime.[21] Clarke is very much in favor of *assigning clear responsibility to particular employees* in order to maximize security.

The great architect-intellectual, Oscar Newman, was well aware that people take most responsibility for their own property, and areas adjacent to it.[22] That's why he wished to design buildings and facilities that maximize private and semiprivate space, while minimizing public and semipublic space. He also urged construction of "communities of interest," for people at the same stage in the life cycle.[23] For example, when families with small children share the same neighborhood, they are more likely to be vigilant as a group. Accordingly, Professors Paul and Patricia Brantingham report that housing for the elderly is safest with more units and a recreation room on the first floor, allowing the group to watch the door.[24]

Some people make a point of traveling in groups for protection, especially at night.[25] Such groups usually consist of people with personal ties. In crowds of people, those in the center are more secure from purse snatching and other attacks than those at the edges. Even going out in pairs is a form of group defense. When offenders seek crime targets in the crowds leaving a sporting event, going home after work, or exiting public transit stations, they usually prefer stragglers.[26] Offenders cannot always be sure that no one in a crowd will stop them.

Some people think of community-watch or block-watch programs as forms of group defense. However, these methods are notorious for their failure to prevent crime. Lacking direct daily contact, a watch "organization" is largely imaginary, with nothing but a sign issuing an empty threat. In general group defenses among humans depend upon supporting social ties and a physical environment to enhance control of space. "Gated communities" can create another illusion, especially if nobody watches the gate or notices incursions.

Research by Professor C. Ray Jeffery found that student apartments at Florida State were most vulnerable to burglary if they were at the edge of the campus complex, while those in the middle were more secure.[27] Perhaps interior security derives in part from group defenses.

These defenses depend upon keeping social relationships intact. Herbert Gans's classic book, *The Urban Villagers*,[28] describes how a homogeneous urban neighborhood was bulldozed to produce a less secure environment. A similar theme is found in Jane Jacobs's classic work, *Death and Life of Great American Cities*. The essential point is that urban design and policy affect the ability of a human population to use group defenses for their own security.

Offenders, too, can use group defenses. They move as a group not only to intimidate victims, but also to discourage counterattacks by victims, police, angry neighbors, or other groups of offenders. Some "gangs" of pickpockets operate with only one or two offenders directly involved in any given incident, but with larger numbers nearby for security—in case a victim counters.

Police also use group defenses. In the 19th and early 20th centuries, officers walked together in packs for their own safety. Perhaps officers with the lowest seniority were forced to travel on the outside of the herd. The motorized police departments of the modern era for many years assigned two officers per car; but rising labor costs and widening suburban territory have left that policy behind.

Vigorous Recovery

The starfish very much irritated fishermen by preying on their oysters. The fishermen thought they could solve their problem by tearing the starfish in half and throwing the pieces back into the ocean. The fishermen were only making matters worse, since torn starfish simply regenerate lost arms and multiply. Many plants and animals deal with adversaries simply through vigor, tolerance, outgrowing damage, or replacing damaged tissues.

Perhaps the best example of vigorous recovery is putting the candy near the checkout counter. True, more people will steal, but still more people buy it. If the extra sales more than offset the extra thefts, the store ends up ahead.[29]

Crime victims do not do as well as starfish, but they generally recover from crimes. Many crimes are small in their impact. Many with a larger impact are far from fatal and, especially under prosperous conditions, the economy can outgrow crime. Insurance provides a means for spreading risks and hence a defense against crime. Many stores build into their prices losses to shoplifting and employee theft. Stores often cut their labor force, increasing shoplifting but reducing costs, too.

Vigorous recovery has a very interesting application to policing. Without admitting this publicly, many police feel they have little or no impact on local crime. I believe they can have much more impact than they believe, but that's not the point. If they believe in the vigorous recovery of crime, they feel less incentive to be energetic police officers. Similarly, citizens underestimate their own potential impact on crime prevention, and are more likely to be apathetic or to put their efforts into the wrong types of prevention. Unfortunately, many crime victims rely on vigorous recovery rather than taking action to prevent crime itself. Hence vigorous recovery protects criminal activity that could be thwarted.

Overview

Perhaps one of the problems with crime prevention is that so many people do not understand the importance of multiple defenses. They rely too much on locks, neglecting other methods. Paul Ekblom reminds us that nature usually relies on multiple defenses:

> It's rare for living things to rely on passive armour-plate protection alone. Plants have toxins and irritant hairs. Armoured animals like the dinosaurs have often supplemented their defenses with actively-wielded bony horns, clubs or spikes.[30]

By drawing on more than one of the defenses discussed in this chapter, we can help reduce crime risk in many settings. This chapter has identified numerous primary defenses, namely, protections against crime that avoid confrontation with attackers in the first place. Included are methods for hiding—avoidance and camouflage. Attackers are also dissuaded by personal reputation, mimicry, and warnings before spotting their quarry. Attackers can also be thwarted or overwhelmed by physical defenses, group defenses, or rigorous recovery.

What happens *after* the predator discovers the prey?

Central Points, Chapter 18

1. Physical defenses and group defenses are well-known security techniques.

2. Potential victims often avoid offenders or use various forms of camouflage.

3. Mimicry helps offenders appear more dangerous to adversaries than reality dictates.

4. Vigorous recovery allows crime victims to keep ahead of offenders.

Exercises

1. Have you ever avoided particular places to protect yourself from crime?

2. Taking care for your own safety, drive through a fairly high-crime street around 9 a.m., mapping which houses and businesses have bars on front windows and doors and which do not.

3. Go to the website of the Highway Loss Data Institute, http://www.hwysafety .org/. What two-door cars create more theft loss? What are the better models to buy?

Notes

1. *Henry V*, act II, scene iv.

2. Roman historian (59 BC–17 AD). Quoted in *The Columbia World of Quotations* (New York: Columbia University Press, 1996).

3. Chinese general (6th–5th century BC). Chapter 6, axiom 9 in J. Clavell, ed., *The Art of War* (Seattle: Clearbridge, 1981).

4. CEO of Porsche. Quote widely attributed, but not confirmed.

5. F. Fedler and B. Pryor, "An Equity Theory Explanation of Bystanders' Reactions to Shoplifting," *Psychological Reports* 56 (1984): 746. Also see D. J. Steffensmeier and R. R. Steffensmeier, "Who Reports Shoplifters? Research Continuities and Further Developments," *International Journal of Criminology and Penology* 1 (1977): 79–95. The latter found that shoplifter appearance had an impact. In particular, straight-laced shoppers were more likely to report a "hippie" shoplifter. This is actually quite an interesting future research topic, for it mixes two dimensions: anathema and fear. Perhaps an offender is most likely to be arrested for a minor crime if disliked but not feared.

6. See such references as these:

    a. M. Edmunds, *Defense in Animals* (Essex, UK: Longman, 1974).

b. M. E. Feder and G. V. Lauder, eds., *Predator Prey Relationships: Perspectives and Approaches From the Study of Lower Vertebrates* (Chicago: University of Chicago Press, 1986).

c. H. W. Greene, "Defensive Tail Display in Snakes and Amphibians," *Journal of Herpetology* 7 (1973): 43–61.

d. H. W. Greene and R. W. McDiarmid, "Coral Snake Mimicry: Does It Occur?" *Science* 213 (1981): 1207–1212.

e. D. Owen, *Camouflage and Mimicry* (Chicago: University of Chicago Press, 1980).

f. C. F. D. Rocha, "The Set of Defense Mechanisms in a Tropical Sand Lizard (*Liolaemus Lutzae*) of Southeastern Brazil," *Ciencia y Cultura* 45 (1993): 116–122.

g. J. M. Savage and J. B. Slowinsky, "The Colouration of the Venomous Coral Snakes (Family *Elapidae*) and Their Mimics (Families *Aniliidae* and *Colubridae*)," *Biological Journal of the Linnaean Society* 45 (1992): 235–254.

h. W. Wickler, *Mimicry in Plants and Animals* (New York: McGraw-Hill, 1968).

i. G. R. Zug, *Herpetology: An Introductory Biology of Amphibians and Reptiles* (San Diego, CA: Academic Press, 1993).

7. Whitetail World, http://www.kerrlake.com/deer/white5.htm (accessed September 4, 2005).

8. R. Zach and J. B. Falls, "Foraging and Territoriality of Male Ovenbirds in a Heterogeneous Habitat," *Journal of Animal Ecology* 48 (1979): 33–52.

9. See D. Beavon, P. L. Brantingham, and P. J. Brantingham, "The Influence of Street Networks on the Patterning of Property Offenses," in R. V. Clarke, ed., *Crime Prevention Studies* (Monsey, NY: Criminal Justice Press, 1994) (Volume 2 in *Crime Prevention Studies* series). The original idea was found in an unpublished manuscript. Also see R. H. Ewing, *Traffic Calming: The State of the Practice* (Washington, DC: Institute of Transportation Engineers, 1999).

10. M. Felson and R. V. Clarke, "Routine Precautions, Criminology, and Crime Prevention," in Hugh Barlow, ed., *Crime and Public Policy: Putting Theory to Work* (Boulder, CO: Westview Press, 1997).

11. W. G. Skogan, *Disorder and Decline: Crime and the Spiral of Decay in American Neighborhoods* (New York: Free Press, 1990).

12. Also called "crypsis."

13. My wife hides the holiday candy in obvious places, where I don't notice it.

14. Ecologists also consider "aggressive mimicry," a technique for getting closer to unsuspecting prey by mimicking something innocuous or even desirable. This type of mimicry does not fit perfectly under defenses, and is instead considered in the chapter dealing with crime foraging.

15. Ecologists sometimes use terms such as "aposematic mimicry" or "Mertensian mimicry." More commonly, these are subsumed under Batesian mimicry. I have avoided using these terms, but the point that mimicry uses varied methods is well taken.

16. D. Gambetta, "Deceptive Mimicry in Humans," in S. Hurley and N. Chater, eds., *Perspectives on Imitation: From Neuroscience to Social Science*, vol. 2: Imitation, Human Development and Culture (Cambridge: MIT Press, 2005). Also see D. Gambetta, *Crimes and Signs: Cracking the Codes of the Underworld* (Princeton, NJ: Princeton University Press, 2005).

17. Sometimes called "structural defenses" or "morphological defenses."

18. G. Farrell, "Crime Prevention," in C. Bryant, ed., *Encyclopedia of Criminology and Deviant Behavior* (New York: Taylor and Francis, 2000).

19. Group defenses, symbiotic protection, and social defenses are very close to one another. As crime ecology develops, perhaps these distinctions will become more vivid. I decided not to merge the terms under one concept for now, but that option should be considered in the future.

20. R. V. Clarke, *Situational Crime Prevention: Successful Case Studies* (Monsey, NY: Criminal Justice Press, 1992).

21. See J. A. Piliavin and H. Charng, "Altruism: A Review of Recent Theory and Research," *Annual Review of Sociology* 16 (1990): 27–65.

22. O. Newman, *Defensible Space* (New York: Macmillan, 1992).

23. O. Newman, *Community of Interest* (New York: Anchor, 1981).

24. Personal communication from the Brantinghams. I have explored these issues in M. Felson, "Those Who Discourage Crime," in J. E. Eck and D. Weisburd, eds., *Crime and Place* (Monsey, NY: Criminal Justice Press, 1995) (Volume 4 in *Crime Prevention Studies* series).

25. Of course, group defenses can backfire. Groups of youths at nighttime parties are sometimes more likely to clash than individuals. No defense is absolute.

26. Offenders are also more likely to attack cars on peripheral streets or the edges of parking lots and structures. But a parking lot is not a group defense, especially given its high risk.

27. Note his classic work founding what's now known as CPTED: C. J. Jeffery, *Crime Prevention Through Environmental Design* (Beverly Hills, CA: Sage, 1971).

28. H. Gans, *The Urban Villagers* (New York: Free Press of Glencoe, 1962).

29. However, Dennis Challinger explains that stores underestimate their losses to theft, including the cost of replacing what's stolen. See D. Challinger, "Will Crime Prevention Ever Be a Business Priority?" in M. Felson and R. V. Clarke, eds., *Business and Crime Prevention* (Monsey, NY: Criminal Justice Press, 1997).

30. See P. Ekblom, "Less Crime, by Design," lecture at the Royal Society of Arts, London, October 11, 2000. Available from the European Designing Out Crime Association, http://www.e-doca.net/Resources/Lectures/Less%20Crime%20by%20Design.htm (accessed October 26, 2005).

We must all hang together, or most assuredly we shall all hang separately.

—Benjamin Franklin[1]

He ate the dormouse, else it was he.

—Ben Jonson[2]

Always forgive your enemies; nothing annoys them so much.

—Oscar Wilde[3]

If you can't say something good about someone, sit right here by me.

—Alice Roosevelt Longworth[4]

19

The Last Line of Defense

It makes sense to employ primary defenses whenever possible. At the very least, we should not design settings that make crime easy, then try to offset the initial mistakes. But do not brush aside secondary defenses. A high percentage of criminal acts are attempted but not completed. The offender's failure often reflects secondary defenses—those employed after detecting the approach or attack by an adversary. A number of these defenses are common in nature, as we shall see in this chapter. Suppose a burglar hears an alarm sound, and then leaves with less loot. The secondary defense gained partial success.

Exhibit 19.1   Seven Secondary Defenses Applied to Crime (usually applied after detection by adversary)

Categories	Defenses	Examples
	10.[1] Move away from adversary	Cross street to avoid adversary
	11. Communicate ability to escape	Walk with certainty, display health
D. Discourage	12. Distractions, feigns, and startles	Feign poverty
	13. Symbiotic protection	Walk toward security office
E. Oppose	14. Chemical and weapon defenses	Mace, guns, and knives
	15. Sudden weaponry	Tae kwon do
	16. Emergency social defenses	"Circle the wagons"

1. Numbering continued from Exhibit 18.1, p. 281.

Not only do secondary defenses have an impact on a particular criminal act, but also they might discourage illegal action at future times and places. Secondary defenses also apply to offenders themselves, who devise methods for self-protection against retaliation or counterattack. Moreover, police use secondary defenses for their own security as they carry out the law enforcement process.

The ability to intimidate has value at many stages of the crime process.[5] But some unique and diverse secondary defenses are found in nature and apply quite well to crime participants. The seven secondary defenses are summarized in Exhibit 19.1, and organized into two categories: discouraging the adversary, and opposing him.

Movement Away From Adversary

Upon detection, not all living things wait for the fight. When a scallop is about to be eaten by a starfish, it shoots out a stream of water, propelling itself to safety. Some birds institute an erratic flight pattern as soon as they perceive an aerial predator. Fighter jets and football linebackers also use that method. Deer, rabbits, and many other animals retreat to nearby brush. Some victims use sheer speed to escape from likely offenders they have detected. These movements away from the adversary do not have to be fast, and sometimes that is counterproductive. Many adversaries respond to those running away, so it is best for the quarry to ooze out of the scene.[6]

Movements away from adversaries bring to light the significance of the habitat. Some habitats favor one party in the crime process over the others in escaping danger to themselves. Offenders do best to commit crimes in places where they are more familiar and their victims less so. That helps explain why vacationers and those from another part of town make such excellent victims for local offenders. In addition, the local offender's knowledge of the local area gives him a distinct advantage over police officers from outside. Teenage offenders on foot can easily elude middle-aged officers, stuck in their cars, and only half-familiar with the texture of the local turf.

Communicating the Ability to Escape

Upon detecting adversaries, some animals send *pursuit-deterrence signals*. This tells the adversary that its presence is known but that the quarry is too fast to catch. The skylark sings when it senses danger, saving trouble for both itself and its predator. The song says, "I know you're there. I'm too fast for you. Don't waste your time." In modern society, a driver might rev up his motor to tell an approaching adversary he is ready to go. Perhaps running in place with track shoes visible conveys a sense of speed. An attacker usually needs to surprise a speedy victim.

Distractions, Feigns, and Startles

Nature offers three methods for putting off adversaries: a distraction display, a startle display, and feigning death. A *distraction display* draws adversaries away from oneself or whatever one is protecting. Birds commonly make noises to distract predators away from their nest, protecting offspring. Distraction has many roles in crime, too. Leaving his car to continue shopping, a shopper displays goods of no interest to a thief as a distraction from the others. A pickpocket has an accomplice distract the victim, not only to carry out the crime but also to impair a counterattack. Drug dealers noting police arrival make motions to draw them away from their stash. Police use loud noises to distract offenders, seeking to protect themselves as they carry out raids.

A *startle display* scares away the attacker. The stick insect suddenly flashes its wings, kicks its legs, and makes spastic motions. The sea slug makes a spectacular display, uncoiling a large rolled tentacle, and then pointing it at its enemy. One of my very attractive nieces, to ward off aggressive strangers, learned to make a face like Medusa.

Feigning death is how the opossum convinces predators to lose interest. "Playing 'possum" has helped some humans escape human mass murderers, including massacres by invading armies. On a less dramatic scale, witnesses to a crime, fearing retaliation, sometimes feign slumber, drunkenness, or lack of awareness. People living in dangerous areas quickly learn to avert their eyes and escape attention. Like an octopus that changes color and skin texture to match the surroundings, some people melt into the background when they sense danger. Arguably, distractions, feigns, and startles deliver more protection than guns, knives, and karate.

Symbiotic Defenses

Wrens nest near wasps, letting the latter scare off their predators. I have heard people express satisfaction that, "My neighborhood is controlled by organized crime, and they don't tolerate burglars." Whether or not their report is true, it expresses a general notion that those who are otherwise obnoxious can serve a positive purpose, at least on some occasions. More generally, targets of crime hope that, after the adversary has detected them, relationships to others can help discourage an attack. A safe house can assist avoiding family violence. One can walk toward the security office or police station or into the housing compound where neighbors, friends, or relatives provide cover. One can exclaim, *"If you touch me, my big brother George will come get you."* Of course, more direct defenses exist as well.

I have discussed four means by which potential victims discourage their attackers. Next, I consider three methods for quick opposition upon attack.

Chemical and Weapon Defenses

If all else fails, the impending victim needs to do something fast. Animals use chemical defenses to deal with predators that have ignored their prior warning signs. The squid, octopus, and cuttlefish have an ink sack near the end of their digestive tract to use as a defense. A squid discharges the contents of the sack and then turns pale, confusing its pursuer.

During the 1970s, some urban Americans began to carry chemical defenses, such as mace, tear gas, or pepper spray. Police officers also use chemical defenses, from a small can to control a single suspect to a tear-gas grenade for scattering crowds. Human weapons technology seems intentional and sophisticated, but still delivers crude harm. A wasp is more accurate, without collateral damage.[7]

Sudden Weaponry

When detected or pursued, a harmless animal might suddenly mimic a dangerous model. It might flatten the head or body and open its mouth wide like a snake. It might hiss, vibrate its tail like a rattler, or imitate an owl. The porcupine fish swallows water to inflate its body, causing the spines along its body to become erect. The surgeonfish has a razor-sharp retractable spine on either side of its tail that it pops out when it's in danger. Humans also pull out weapons when threatened, hoping to scare off attackers. Masculinity displays can also be called forth in times of danger. I have seen people square shoulders and snarl when feeling danger from other people. The surge of adrenalin can enhance one's ability to strike back, letting one's adversary know it.

Emergency Social Defenses

Chapter 18 spoke of group defenses, but groups are not much use if they aren't there when you need them. After an adversary spots his quarry, groups find it necessary to muster their defenses quickly. When a coyote threatens mule deer, small bunches rejoin the others, and strays hurry back.[8] Wild cattle, such as musk oxen, respond to a threat by forming a circle with the adult males on the outside to fight off the enemy—like wagon trains attacked by Indians. Some birds and other animals emit warning signals picked up only within the species, causing those present to be ready for an impending attack.[9] Scattered birds can also respond to the alarm by flying at the invader, diverting its attention, harassing it, and driving it away. Some birds defecate or vomit on the enemy.[10] A wide range of species, including gulls, terns, and crows, engage in "mobbing"—the word for "bullying" in Swedish and some other languages, but in this case the word refers to defense.[11]

Potential victims of crime devise group defenses, sometimes assisted by technology. Alarm bells and buzzers, phone calls, shouts, screams—all of these can interfere with an offender after the target becomes aware of the risk. Some alarms are silent and others overt. A silent alarm helps organize the defenses without letting the attacker know. An overt alarm alerts more bystanders, perhaps convincing the attacker to quit now.

The ineffectiveness of the neighborhood watch can be explained by its lack of an alarm mechanism. Under normal circumstances, others in the neighborhood will not know an offense is in progress, hence not be able to intervene. Some years ago, British crime experts developed the *cocoon watch*.[12] If someone breaks into your home, officers then visit a handful of your nearest neighbors, asking their assistance for preventing a repeat victimization. Unlike the usual neighborhood watch, the cocoon watch focuses the alarm in space and time—asking local people to help prevent crime in nearby times and places. That's why it helps reduce repeat victimization. Vigilance works best if one can sound the alarm as soon as adversaries approach.

In general, an alarm works best if those alarmed already had some sort of relationship before the emergency.[13] Richard Ramirez killed and raped a number of women in the Los Angeles region before his capture in 1985. He became known as the "Night Stalker," and created a good deal of fear at the time. He finally left fingerprints, was identified, and the public was warned to watch for him. When he saw his own face in the newspaper, he took dramatic risks that led to his downfall. Ramirez attempted during daylight to hijack one car, then another, in a very tight Mexican-American neighborhood. His victims shouted for help, and the neighbors responded, with growing numbers chasing and catching him. He was lucky someone called the police, or they would have killed him.[14]

The Management of Snails and Slugs

A remarkable parallel can be found between crime prevention techniques and the methods used to keep snails and slugs out of the garden or away from the farm. The Cornell University Pesticide Management Education Program maintains a webpage on how to deal with the problem.[15] Although they do not use the words of criminal justice, they could just as well have. If you forgive my anthropomorphisms, police methods include searching and arresting pests about two hours after sunset, with help of a flashlight. Entrapment methods include baited coffee cans, inverted grapefruit rinds, or a yogurt cup with enough beer in it to drown the pests. Lethal injections by metaldehyde, methiocarb, or iron phosphate are also discussed. But these methods are not normally as effective as prevention. Cornell experts recommend a variety of preventive efforts, such as eliminating hiding places by removing boards, stones, and debris near the garden; clearing weeds; taking away daytime shelters; and tilling the garden. Effective physical barriers can include a layer of fine sawdust, a plastic bottle around seedlings, or a clean and dry buffer zone around the garden. Gardeners and farmers can create habitats for the pests' natural predators, such as ducks, geese, chickens, frogs, toads, hedgehogs, or opossums.[16] Like organic gardening, situational crime prevention reduces the natural habitat for one's adversaries.

Situational Crime Prevention

Crime control methods can be divided into three categories:

- *Intervention:* Arrest and control one offender at a time
- *Utopian:* Redesign society
- *Situational:* Reduce specific opportunities to carry out crime

Situational crime prevention is the intermediate approach between reforming individuals and redesigning society. Professor Ronald V. Clarke of Rutgers University has spent three decades originating and organizing that field. His research and applications have helped revolutionize how many people think about crime and its control.[17] Situational crime prevention emphasizes making crime (a) less rewarding, (b) more difficult, and (c) more risky to offenders. In ecological terms, (a) and (b) are primary defenses, while (c) coincides with secondary defenses.[18]

A community can develop many perimeters or circles of defense against crime. For example, parents and teachers monitor youths, and efforts are made to schedule their activities to keep them out of trouble. Malls provide security outside the mall, in the mall itself, and inside stores within the mall. Neighborhoods develop a local feel, and particular buildings are designed to make outsiders request permission to enter, or stand out if they do so without asking. The beauty of situational crime prevention is its ability to focus on immediate and direct methods to prevent particular crime problems, without waiting for the long term. It also has an ability to adapt, if offenders counter its earlier efforts.

Overview

This chapter and the last presented numerous types of defense against adversaries that apply to nature at large and to crime in particular. Exhibit 19.2 summarizes all 16 defenses. The nine primary defenses are applied prior to attack, usually before detection by one's adversary. The seven secondary defenses are used from the point of detection. Potential victims, actual victims, offenders, and even police use these methods to varying

Exhibit 19.2   Sixteen Defenses, in All

Type of Defense	Primary Defenses	Secondary Defenses
Response occurs	Before detection by adversary[1]	After being noticed by adversary

Subtypes	A. Hide
	  1. Avoidance
	  2. Camouflage
	
	B. Dissuade
	  3. Personal reputation
	  4. Batesian mimicry
	  5. Müllerian mimicry
	  6. Warnings
	
	C. Overwhelm
	  7. Physical defenses
	  8. Group defenses
	  9. Vigorous recovery
		D. Discourage
		  10. Move away from adversary
		  11. Communicate ability to escape
		  12. Distract, feign, or startle
		  13. Symbiotic protection
		
		E. Oppose
		  14. Chemical and weapon defenses
		  15. Sudden weaponry
		  16. Emergency social defenses

1. See notes for prior exhibit.

degrees. It is clear that offense relates to defense and hunting to security. It is also clear that natural variations apply, also, to the world of crime.

Central Points, Chapter 19

1. In some habitats, the defender can move away from adversaries more easily than they can pursue him.

2. Potential victims sometimes walk *toward* safe places or persons who will either protect them or appear to do so.

3. A speedy victim lets the offender know he is ready to run.

4. Where social ties are strong and others are nearby, endangered persons can shout for immediate help and count on some response.

5. Offenders and those seeking to control crime are locked into an "arms race." As one improves, the other answers.

6. Situational prevention is a noncoercive, nonutopian approach, seeking to prevent very specific types of crime by removing opportunities to carry them out.

Exercises

1. If confronted by an attacker, what should the victim do?

2. When walking down the street, what body language affects your security?

3. What are the most secure and least secure places to pick an apartment?

4. Compare and contrast the "neighborhood watch" versus the "cocoon watch."

Notes

1. American statesman, writer, and popular philosopher (1706–1790). Comment at the signing of the Declaration of Independence, July 4, 1776. Quoted in *Bartlett's Familiar Quotations*, 10th ed. (1919). Available from www.bartleby.com (accessed September 9, 2005).

2. British poet, dramatist, humorist (1572–1637). Quoted in *The Columbia World of Quotations* (New York: Columbia University Press, 1996).

3. Widely attributed. See Wikipedia, Wikiquote, http://en.wikiquote.org/wiki/Oscar_Wilde (accessed October 26, 2005).

4. Quoted in *Simpson's Contemporary Quotations* (New York: Houghton-Mifflin, 1988).

5. Witness intimidation is included, here.

6. This is a motion favored by Jeeves, P. G. Wodehouse's famous butler. See, e.g., P. G. Wodehouse, *Carry On, Jeeves!* (London: Barrie & Jenkins, 1976). For a biography of Wodehouse (1881–1975), see the Literary Heritage website, http://www3.shropshire-cc.gov.uk/wodehous.htm (accessed September 9, 2005). Also check http://www.todayinliterature.com/biography/p.g.wodehouse.asp (accessed September 9, 2005).

7. A wasp or yellow jacket can sting repeatedly. However, most bees sting once, then die. That's bad defense for the individual but a good one for the group.

8. S. Lingle, "Anti-predator Strategies and Grouping Patterns in White-Tailed Deer and Mule Deer," *Ethology* 107 (2001): 295–314.

9. An alarm call can backfire, alerting other predators to easy prey or causing counterproductive panic.

10. Mobbing does not work so well with the most dangerous species.

11. However, a British website on bullying states

> The word mobbing is preferred to bullying in continental Europe and in those situations where a target is selected and bullied (mobbed) by a group of people rather than by one individual. However, every group has a ringleader. If this ringleader is an extrovert it will be obvious who is coercing group members into mobbing the

selected target. If the ringleader is an introvert type, he or she is likely to be in the background coercing and manipulating group members into mobbing the selected target; introvert ringleaders are much more dangerous than extrovert ringleaders.

I cannot vouch for the psychological claim, but it is interesting. See Bully OnLine, http://www.bullyonline.org/workbully/mobbing.htm (accessed September 4, 2005).

12. See these papers and reports for a perspective:

    a. S. Chenery, J. Holt, and K. Pease, *Biting Back II: Reducing Repeat Victimization in Huddersfield* (London: British Home Office, 1997) (Police Research Group, Crime Detection and Prevention Series, Paper 82).

    b. G. Farrel and K. Pease, *Once Bitten, Twice Bitten: Repeat Victimization and Its Implications for Crime Prevention* (London: British Home Office, 1993) (Police Research Group, Crime Prevention Unit, Paper 46).

    c. G. Laycock, "Hypothesis-Based Research: The Repeat Victimization Story," *Criminal Justice* 1 (2001): 59–82.

    d K. Pease, "The Kirkholt Project: Preventing Burglary on a British Public Housing Estate," *Security Journal* 2 (1991): 73–77.

13. In various places, local residents have bonded together to mob and drive out local drug dealers. Even in countries with legalized prostitution, neighborhoods can act to force illegal salespersons to leave. But given the lack of an overt attack on these residents, this is not defense in the classic sense.

14. For an account, see Crime Library, the Court TV webpage, http://www.crimelibrary.com/serial_killers/notorious (accessed September 4, 2005).

15. Available from ibiblio, the Public's Library and Digital Archive, http://www.ibiblio.org/rge/s&s.htm (accessed September 4, 2005).

16. A similar set of strategies can be found for many other pests. A wasp control website offers details about control, with warnings not to swat at them one by one. "Natural Wasp Control" (2005), is available from Eartheasy, http://eartheasy.com/live_natwasp_control.htm (accessed September 4, 2005).

17. For summaries of the crime prevention work by Professor Clarke and others, see the Center for Problem-oriented Policing, http://www.popcenter.org (accessed September 4, 2005).

18. Situational crime prevention has expanded to include other categories. See "Situational Crime Prevention (SCP)—Techniques for Reducing the Opportunity for Crime" (2005), http://www.crimereduction.gov.uk/learningzone/scptechniques.htm (accessed September 4, 2005).

If men define situations as real, they are real in their consequences.

—W. I. Thomas and Dorothy S. Thomas[1]

What staggers me is not the persistence of illusion, but the persistence of the world in the face of illusion.

—A. G. Mojtabai[2]

Being fooled, by foolery thrive; There's place and means for every man alive.

—William Shakespeare[3]

I hope you have not been leading a double life, pretending to be wicked and being really good all the time. That would be hypocrisy.

—Oscar Wilde[4]

Lovers close their eyes when they kiss because, if they didn't, there would be too many visual distractions to notice and analyze.

—Diane Ackerman[5]

20

The Street Gang Strategy

In popular image, a juvenile street gang is a steady and stubborn group of young thugs. In 1980, Professor Walter B. Miller offered a more sophisticated definition of the gang. I disagree with his 51-word sentence:

[A gang is] a self-formed association of peers bound together by mutual interests, with identifiable leadership, well-developed lines of authority, and other organizational features, who act in concert to achieve a specific purpose or purposes which generally include the conduct of illegal activity and control over a particular territory, facility or type of enterprise.[6]

That makes a gang sound very organized, despite its young members. Often residents of gang areas, the police, and the general public see gangs that way, but that does not make it so.

To understand the gang, we should neither demonize nor sanitize it.[7] Gangs mix many features of real life, but we cannot consider them all, or we end up with confusion. Gang members might eat ice cream, but that's not why they join. Two living processes confuse the gang literature. First, groups of offenders diversify what they do and how they do it. Second, groups of professors diversify what they write and how they write it. Still it's possible to make sense of the gang.

Unfortunately, the public—even many police—subscribe to a well-known gang image: An exaggerated view of the gang, giving it too much credit for bad deeds, organization, leadership, unity, and enormity.

Scholarship repeatedly shows this image to be misleading, but it cannot be defeated without a clear alternative.

This chapter seeks the most essential feature of a juvenile street gang—the feature that *distinguishes* the gang from everything else. The goal is to understand the special service a gang offers its participants. Many youths confront a real problem—a dangerous local area.[8] *A gang promises them a specific solution to their security problem.* A gang's distinguishing feature is that it helps them intimidate others—not just one or two individuals, but more generally.[9] That does not mean a gang does this to the exclusion of everything else, but it does mean that intimidation is central for understanding it.[10] Combining to intimidate adversaries or repel intrusions is by no means new in natural history, as prior chapters indicate. But most combinations are for protection against other species. Dolphins are unique in forming gangs for security against other dolphins.[11] I suspect that dolphin gangs provide better service than juvenile street gangs.

Why Street Gangs Are Confusing

Several decades of juvenile street gang research yield a confusing reality. In particular,

- the word "gang" is overused,
- gangs have nongang features,

- gangs get too much credit,
- different gangs use the same name, and
- gangs are unstable.

Before deciding what to do about it, I explore the sources of confusion.

The Word Has Many Meanings

People use the word "gang" in too many ways, and I can't stop them.[12] The word has been applied to groups of motorcyclists, skinheads, and prisoners; organized crime; organized drug sellers, and more.[13] Gang experts help us by distinguishing types of gangs, such as "juvenile street gangs" and "drug gangs."[14]

Yet juvenile street gangs (this chapter's focus) still confuse people. Youths don't stand still for our academic convenience. Like the rest of nature, groups grow and diversify, combine strategies and make adaptations. Some try this and some try that. My challenge in this chapter is to sort some of this out.

Gangs Have Nongang Features

Gang youths have many nongang features. They eat and breathe. They go home to Mama. They can be friendly. They can be like other teenagers. Youths might join gangs like nongang youths join cliques. Gangs spend more time hanging out, doing nothing, than they spend committing crime. It's good to learn the total picture, but we still need to specify what's *unique* about a juvenile street gang.

Gangs Get Too Much Credit

We can never understand gangs by overcrediting their bad deeds. Contrary to popular belief, most youths in "gang areas" do not belong to gangs. Yet the gang makes its presence known because members commit a greater *share* of crimes than their share of the local youth population. On the other hand, nongang members commit more local crime than gang members *in absolute numbers.*[15] An area with 10 percent of youths belonging to gangs might have 25 percent of its crimes committed by gang youths and 75 percent by nongang youths. Of course, the gangs are falsely credited with most of it.

The gang problem is bad enough—we don't need to exaggerate it. Gangs tend to be more violent than other local offenders; but most gang youth crime is nonserious and nonviolent. Like other youths, gang youths are unfocused offenders: "Street gangs seem aimless. . . . Street gang members get into any and every kind of trouble. It's cafeteria-style crime—a little of this, a touch of that, two attempts at something else."[16]

In sum, the image of the gang exaggerates their bad reality, in a negative direction. That's not to deny the reality is bad. But our goal is to dissect the problem, not to pound the table.

Big Gang Theory

Sometimes gang observers draw a local map showing how a few huge gangs control large swaths of the city. If you keep questioning them, they admit that each "big gang" is really a bunch of little gangs. For example, about 200 different gangs in the Los Angeles region are classified as "crips."[17] These gangs cover a vast area, and range from the "Altadena Block Crip" to the "Most Valuable Pimp Gangster Crip." But what does that really mean?

Many people think of a huge gang with many little branches. *Big Gang Theory* makes a more dramatic story for the media, and most local people— even many police—believe that story. Perhaps government agencies provide more funding to fight a big gang than to oppose a bunch of little gangs. It is easier to blame your problems on something colossal, rather than a group of very local boys intimidating others. Unfortunately, rumor reinforces the dubious impression that many gangs are one.

Little Gang Theory makes much more sense.[18] The 200 gangs noted above do not usually see one another, so how can they be one gang? Gang experts tell us that many gangs are rivals and even fight one another, despite similar names. I believe that the colossal gang is largely an illusion—many independent gangs just using the same name over wider space and longer time. That implies that such terms as "crips," "bloods," and "latin kings," are really common nouns pretending to be proper nouns. If these are just synonyms for the word "gang," they should not even be capitalized. Yet small gangs portray themselves in big terms for good reasons, as you shall see.[19]

Gangs Disappear

Most turtle eggs fail to become turtles, and very few turtles reach old age. So it is with gangs. Media and police sources sometimes tell us about gangs that last for generations;[20] but researchers have noticed that most gangs disappear in a couple of years, or less.[21] Of course, we must distinguish between the survival of a name and the survival of a gang as a continuous group. The former *looks* like the latter.

Exhibit 20.1 speculates on the survival of juvenile gangs as continuous groups. I suspect that gang researchers miss a large number of start-up gangs

Exhibit 20.1   Which Gangs Draw Public Attention?

Duration of Gang Survival	Speculative Numbers	Attention Received
0 Number of gangs "born"	1,000	
1 Surviving less than a year*	788	
2 Surviving 1 to 3 years	200	✓
3 Surviving 4 to 6 years	10	✓✓
4 Surviving to the next generation**	2	✓✓✓

✓ Relative attention received.

*Speculation 1: These gangs are very numerous but escape notice.

**Speculation 2: These are long-lasting *names*, not long-lasting gangs.

that disappear (as a group) in a matter of months.[22] The exhibit speculates that only two of the 1,000 original gangs survive for generations. I also raise the issue that these might be illusory. In any case, gangs that make a good news story or draw police and academic attention are probably not representative.[23] Perhaps nobody notices gangs surviving less than a year.[24] In fairness, it is not easy to study gangs, and those who do so have to get what information they can.

Stillborn gangs point to an interesting issue.[25] Do they form in response to perceived incursions by other gangs, then evaporate when the threat dissipates? Does the new gang get absorbed by another one? Does counter-intimidation kill it off? Is the territory already staked out, preventing new gangs from forming? Does an incipient gang borrow the name of the existing gang that bothers it least, trying to thwart the one that bothers it most?

These speculations and gang research point toward this conclusion: Very few gangs survive long enough for fame; but famous and long-lasting gangs get more attention and affect community perceptions of all gangs.[26] Moreover, the road to gang fame is to use the same name over wider space and longer time.

The Gang Membership Problem

In 1959, Professor Lewis Yablonsky opened up a can of worms. He concluded that gangs are "near groups," with diffuse, limited, and shifting relationships.[27] In 1968, Professor Gerald Suttles found considerable turnover in gang membership.[28] Even while any given gang lasts, its instability is substantial. Other researchers have confirmed that gang "membership" is unstable and unstructured. Participants drift in and out—not day to day, but often enough to destabilize the group.[29] Moreover, gang "members" commit crimes as often with nonmembers as with one another. Scholars discovered that gangs are not very cohesive. On the other hand, gang cohesiveness can appear suddenly if an outside threat intervenes. Incursions by outside gangs, real or imagined, cause a gang to come together. Police interventions often backfire, causing the gang to become more cohesive and to survive longer. But juvenile gangs in general are not very coherent. Is there any glue at all holding them together?

Efforts to Find Gang Structure

Since the discovery of the amorphous gang, many scholars have tried to find other sources of gang structure. Some have depicted the juvenile street gang as a form of "social network," rather than a bounded organization. Unfortunately, even gang networks keep changing and lack clear boundaries.[30] At some point we have to wonder how a "changing network of gang youths" can really define a gang.

Professor Malcolm W. Klein has identified "core members" of gangs—those who participate longer and give more semblance of a group.[31] The gang "core" has helped make sense of some gang issues. But "core membership" is unstable, too, with individuals shifting away from the core or out of the gang entirely. Even "core members" often commit crimes with nongang participants. "Near group," "network," and "core members" are all useful ideas, but none pinpoints the juvenile gang. Thus gang scholars have killed off the traditional notion of a gang without developing a clear alternative. They have found many important pieces of the gang puzzle, but have not put the gang back together.[32] So what is going on with the juvenile street gang?

Signaling Strategy

In 1878, Fritz Müller (a German-Brazilian zoologist, 1821–1897, who studied the Amazon and southeast Brazil) realized that predators would learn from a bad experience with one species to avoid *several* other species that look like it.[33] Thus several individual species can gain maximum protection by standardizing the warning signals they send out. For example, different wasp species share a similar black-and-yellow striped body. A predator stung by one will then stay away from them all. This is referred to as *Müllerian mimicry*, meaning that several species have developed similar warning signals, in effect mimicking one another.[34] Together they scare off predators, who seem to *perceive* them as the same in response to their common signal.

Human beings also send out common signals.[35] Due to gossip and mass media, human nastiness is broadcast more widely than that of wasps. But that does not deny the benefits of *simple* signals that can be easily recognized. Plain colors can tell others to leave you alone.[36]

Rare is the boy so obnoxious on his own that his reputation reaches far and wide. But Müllerian mimicry can help an ordinary boy attain a higher level of obnoxiousness. People accomplish this with signals that other people recognize and link to a larger crowd of ruffians, real and imagined.

Gangs Rely on Signaling

The juvenile gang strategy is a specific case of Müllerian mimicry. I mean this literally, not as a metaphor. Moreover, I only arrived at this chapter's main points *after* discovering Müllerian mimicry.

Unlike organized crime—which prefers anonymity—street gangs seek visibility. The literature on juvenile street gangs makes it very clear that gang members use standardized signals. Street gangs communicate through their clothes, language, hand signs, and graffiti. Gang communication is often treated as a mere curiosity, or interpreted as fulfilling a psychological need that young people have for identity, recognition, love, and friendship. But you can join the stamp club for that. The "love and recognition" hypothesis misses the essential point of gang signals as a special feature distinguishing gangs from other groups.[37]

The Uses of Intimidation

At younger ages, it makes sense to go around in a pack, relying on immediate strength in numbers. But a pack is no longer sufficient for protection after youths are old enough to roam wider, and later into the day and night. A gang solves the problem, helping intimidate adversaries by drawing assistance from those not always present.

Nonviolent intimidation is everywhere. The library instructs you to return an overdue book immediately, threatening you with fines. But it does not send out a library strike force to beat students up. This chapter considers intimidation with potential violence behind it. We can distinguish three types of coercion:

1. Unvoiced intimidation (and general obnoxiousness)[38]

2. A verbal threat of violence[39]

3. Actual violent attacks

The second and especially the third forms of coercion tend to be illegal and to happen very quickly. They often force the victim to fight back, and the perpetrator can get hurt, too. Even the winner of a fight does not like getting hit in the process or getting arrested later. Moreover, an overt threat or attack might require the proximity of full forces to assure victory.

In contrast, unvoiced intimidation draws assistance from those not present. It avoids immediate counterattacks. Unvoiced intimidation is usually perfectly legal. Police cannot really do much to you for sending nonverbal signals, and might not even notice them. Most importantly, a nonverbal threat of violence is *enduring*. You can wear the gang colors for long periods, warning others on an ongoing basis. Nobody can prove you are trying to threaten others; the law might even view unvoiced signals as protected self-expression. You can carry your intimidation with you. Of course, you have to back it up sometimes, or nobody will believe you.

Of the three types of coercion listed above, *unvoiced intimidation* minimizes real combat, helping someone get what he wants at lower cost to himself. Smart intimidation is an effort to deliver the maximum amount of threat with the minimum risk to oneself. For those living in a tough area, a juvenile street gang offers a unique service, helping members intimidate others by signaling membership. Gang intimidation serves at least four purposes:

- To scare off your enemies
- To get your personal victims to comply with your wishes
- To discourage bystanders from interfering with your offenses
- To discourage witnesses from speaking against you later

Note how intimidation serves both offensive and defensive purposes. Many gangs form initially for defense. Even after a gang has become aggressive, many individuals join up for defensive reasons. In a crime-ridden area, there are very good reasons to intimidate others physically. Because intimidation is useful, many people would like to do a better job of it.

The Quest for a Nastier Image

The juvenile street gang provides each participant with an image nastier than his own. This nasty image shares and enhances the ability to intimidate others (see Exhibit 20.2, panel A).[40] Gang signals assist that process. A youth walking alone on the street, by wearing gang colors, hopes to gain an extra ability to intimidate. He hopes others will be convinced that he is tough. This will succeed if others believe that

Exhibit 20.2   The Quest for a Nastier Image

A By displaying a gang symbol:	You can acquire a *nastier image*, and *intimidate* your adversaries, but gang symbols can *provoke counterattacks* on you.
B If it gets too dangerous to display gang symbols all the time, you might:	Pick your times carefully; use social skills, trying to have it both ways; stop displaying entirely; or find a way out of the gang.

- since he is in the gang, he *must* be tough and dangerous;
- the gang might swarm to assist him now (if they hear him call); and
- the gang will retaliate on his behalf later.[41]

Each participant can draw upon the nastiness of the whole by using common signaling. That does not mean that every gang youth is obnoxious at all times, to all people. It merely means he hopes to draw on his nastier image when he needs to. Thus the individual who cannot intimidate others sufficiently on his own can find collective efficacy for that special purpose. Even nice boys discover, in the tough city, the uses of seeming nasty.

A Gang Blends the Real and the Fake

Gangs spend most of their time in a peaceful state. They rely on some illusion to enhance their power to intimidate others. But they are not totally fake; they really can harm adversaries, and sometimes must do so to keep their image.[42]

Their exaggerated image becomes reality, so long as enough people believe it to be true.[43] Maybe fellow gang participants will later exact revenge on your behalf, and maybe they will not. What's important is that enough people *think* they will. That means that the gang must *sometimes* act as a gang, and the word of it must spread. Thus gang signals can intimidate others, even when your compatriots are not around.

I cannot overstate the importance of signals for helping every individual appear more dangerous than his naked reality. Without a gang, you have to stand on your own two feet. With a gang, you can gain a free ride on the toughness of others, even when they are not present.

That same free ride helps make gang participants more active offenders than the average local boy. By helping boys intimidate more effectively, a gang affiliation gives them a sense of impunity, so they can harm the community more than other boys. All this depends on the gang's signaling power.

To understand the juvenile gang, don't believe completely its story about itself, or the story told by others in the vicinity. The myth and reality are woven together—that's the point of it. In the life cycle of a gang, its myth describes reality better at some stages than others. But the myth should never be dismissed, since it has real consequences. That is, the gang's exaggerated threat affects how current gang participants behave and draws reactions from those around them. Research on the gang needs to find out how much is true, how much is myth, how the myth is useful, how the reality and myth mix together, and how the myth leads to greater complexity.

Compound Nastiness

Gang intimidation actually serves to *compound* Müllerian mimicry.[44] A victim of a local gang can come to fear signals from *any* gang. Thus the boys in blue and the boys in red help each other intimidate nongang members. Even nongang youths might help gangs intimidate, in this sequence:

1. Nongang youths commit a majority of crime in gang areas;

2. others wrongly credit that crime to the gang;

3. that credit enhances the gang's nasty aura;

4. helping the gang intimidate even more.

Thus gang members even gain a free ride from nongang offenders, and have reason to accept credit for what they didn't do.

In addition, a famous gang name assists the intimidation process. In-migrants are more likely to recognize the famous name and fear it. An older gang name helps intimidate older local residents who remember gang members from the past. Any of these fears can spread through the community and beyond. Thus local gangs have a strong incentive to use a famous gang name, spanning space and time, regardless of whether intergang affiliation exists in reality.

A gang's image should transcend each individual and each specific point in space and time; otherwise the gang is not doing its job. Herein lies the gang's strength, as well as its weakness. Its strength is its ability to exaggerate its power and reach, providing an intimidation service to participants. But events can expose to others a gang's true weakness—that it cannot deliver sufficient protection. A gang must make its members, even if they are temporary occupants, seem more obnoxious to others than they would be alone.

A gang that ceases to communicate fear, or that delivers occupants into more danger than it repels, no longer can serve them well, and might soon evaporate. Most gangs do just that.

Risks and Flexibilities

If a gang brought only security, we could expect gang membership to expand until every youth belonged. But the instability of juvenile gangs and their inability to absorb most youths tells us that the benefits they confer are not dependable. Panel B of Exhibit 20.2 considers how a gang can fail to deliver as much as it promises. It might become too dangerous to display gang symbols all the time or at all. That forces gang participants to adjust, try to have it both ways, or even to leave the gang.

The basic gang participation dilemma is quite severe. On the one hand, the security of all contributes to the security of one. But the enmity against all contributes also to the enmity against one. Thus displaying gang membership is risky. Gang members are subject to harm by parents, schools, police, rival gangs, and maybe one another. Sometimes gang colors protect from adversaries and sometimes exactly the opposite. Youths have strong incentives to wear blue in the heart of the territory of the blue gang, but to hide those colors in other territories or at the edges. The risks and advantages can easily shift from hour to hour, depending on what groups are most in proximity—police, parents, rival gangs, or one's own.

I would like to know whether gang youths vary their gang signals by the hour, according to who's watching.

Do they wear a color under a coat that can be zipped up or down?

Do they roll their sleeves up or down, displaying gang tattoos as needed?

Do they shift signals from weekday to weekend, or one week to the next?

Do they keep calculating what display is safest?

Is gang affiliation fluid, according to what threat is most proximate?

Does a fixed membership impair the flexibility they need to survive?

Have youths found ways to feign loyalty, while preserving flexibility?

The empirical question is when and where youths make gang displays and what they consider when they do so. Periodic or sporadic, repeated or occasional, here or there, this month or that, gang displays are a means of survival in a hostile environment.

Mass Media Assist Signaling

I am not enamored of the mass media theories of crime. Criminal action long preceded movies and telecommunications. But the life of the gang is a life of the image. Mass media spreads images; hence it can play a central role in the growth and persistence of juvenile street gangs. There is no primordial reason for Los Angeles gangs to spread to the rest of the world or even the United States.[45] But when such gangs are portrayed in movies and on television, they begin to take on a greater life.

According to some commentators, gangs are disseminated because youths simply *imitate* what they see in the mass media. But group intimidation is a basic feature of life, starting at a very young age; one hardly needs to learn that through modern technology.

Yet the mass media provide two important services to the gang. First, the media inform the general public about gang signals and names. Second, the media link these signals to the nastiest possible image. Movies and television are largely silent about the minor crimes that gang members do and the vast amount of time they sit around doing nothing at all. The media portrayal of the gang is so obnoxious that it provides an extra power to intimidate, clearly linked to particular signals. Local boys simply need to borrow these signals; then others start complying with their wishes.

A Very Basic Gang Definition

To define the juvenile street gang, we must first be careful not to mix in too many issues. Gang leadership, organization, and cohesiveness are all important. It is also important to learn what psychological benefits a gang member gains from affiliation. But these are matters for *research,* not definition.

We can also gain clarity by making a distinction between a single gang and an alliance of many gangs. Accordingly, I define a juvenile street gang as

> *a very local group of youths who intimidate others with overt displays of affiliation.*

This is not the same as a juvenile street gang *alliance.* I define the latter as *a very weak affiliation of juvenile street gangs, sharing signals to enhance intimidation.*

I do not assert that intimidation is the only feature of juvenile gangs or their members. But intimidation is the gang's distinguishing feature, along with the use of specific signals to accomplish it. A group that did not intimidate would not be referred to as "a gang."

I have surveyed some of the problems scholars find when studying gangs, and proposed a basic way to think about gangs. I defined gangs separately from gang alliances. In the process, I made it clear that gang reality includes a good deal of fakery. The next two sections elaborate on that point.

Batesian Mimicry and the Gang

If the king snake can model the coral snake, the nongang-member can model the gang member. Gang researchers are well aware of "wannabes," those who feign membership even though they might be too young to be accepted by the gang. Is this is Batesian mimicry, described in Chapter 18? Do others their own age feel intimidated by wannabes? Do adults feel intimidated, leaving them alone more? Are they really gang members, not counterfeits? Do real gang members ignore them, attack them, or include them? Are they merely imitating in order to feel older? Are they trying to look older to increase their ability to intimidate? I have no answers yet for these questions, but the field of mimicry helps us ask them.

A New Zealand police officer informed me that some youths walking home from school put on a gang color only while traversing a given territory. Some even put on a different color as they pass through a new territory. This is probably an example of Batesian mimicry, since—for security—they are pretending to be something they are not. This is a risky procedure that could result in attack by rival gangs in the area or by the neighborhood gang itself if they recognize the fraud. Gang signaling for whatever reasons can lead gang and nongang youths to respond to someone as if he is a gang member, leaving him no alternative but to join.[46] Perhaps a king snake has an easier time than a youth living in a gang area.

So What's Real?

The problem about interpreting the juvenile gang is that the real and the fake are so well blended. Perhaps the word "fake" goes too far. What we have in fact are three types of "reality":

- *Tangible and persistent gang realities*, for example: local boys display gang colors;
- *Tangible but intermittent realities*, for example: intergang fights; and
- *Inaccurate perceptions with real consequences*, for example: the view that "most crime is committed by gangs."

Interestingly, widespread misconceptions are often more stable than many of the tangible realities. They are real in their consequences, despite gross exaggerations, simply because so many people believe them.

Exhibit 20.3 sorts these three gang realities for very local areas and beyond. Persistent and tangible local realities include gang signaling, gang hangouts, and high levels of ordinary crime in gang areas. However, the public perceives a few huge, organized, and persistent gangs, doing most of the crime. Intermittent local realities include particular gang membership and participation, leadership, intergang violence, and police incursions. Many of these occur at the edges of the local area, where local people and property are more likely to be attacked by outsiders. We always have to remember that gangs get extra credit for crimes that others do. We also need to keep in mind that much of the local perceptions of a gang seep in from the wider urban area.

Gang Policy and Crime Prevention

One prefers to despise a juvenile gang, not the individual youths within it. By telling yourself that the evil resides in the gang, you can convince yourself that youths are basically good. I dispute the second point. Youths are often rather nasty, creating a security problem for one another. The gang promises them a solution for that problem. Of course, it also creates new problems for them, and harms the community. But it takes some youths a while to learn that's so.

A gang policy should have four main features:

1. Reduce *general* local crime rates in gang areas, to reduce the incentive to form gangs and join them.

2. Suppress places, not people. Remove as best you can the hangouts a gang uses to keep going. That might mean reclaiming the park it takes over for itself. Without a hangout, a gang will tend to fizzle naturally. I deal with this issue elsewhere.[47]

3. Stop publicizing the gang's evils or what you have done against it. Take down the antigang posters. That just makes gangs appear strong, enhancing their ability to intimidate, survive, and multiply.[48]

Exhibit 20.3   What's Real About Gangs?

	Where Are You Looking?	
What's Real?	*The Wider Urban Area*	*Very Local Area and Its Edges*
A Tangible and persistent realities	Gang name Antigang publicity	Gang signaling Gang hangouts High ordinary crime rate
B Tangible, but intermittent realities	Gang alliances	Gang membership Gang leadership Gang attacks on rivals Intergang fights Police incursions
C Inaccurate perceptions with real consequences	"A few huge, organized, and persistent gangs, doing most of the regional crime."	"Organized, persistent gang doing most of the local crime."

4. Every six months or less, erase the term "gang member" from individuals' police files and policemen's minds, unless there's real evidence that a gang still exists, and that the "members" still "belong." Try not to exaggerate the gang's impact in your own mind.

Squads of social workers and SWAT teams fall into exactly the same error: enhancing the gang's nasty image, hence augmenting its service to members. Gang prevention does best to reduce overall local crime, reduce gang hangouts, and avoid publicity about gang nastiness. A more controlled gang accreditation system can assist this process.

Police will tell you, "We're the biggest gang in town," and that has some truth. Police signal their membership. They seek to intimidate. They want you to know they can call on the others if you catch one or two of them alone. However, their intimidation sometimes backfires, endangering themselves. But they are required to follow the law, and cannot be everywhere. The police-as-gang strategy does not work so well in everyday life. Police protect society better when they outsmart their opponents by focusing their efforts on removing gang hangouts and enabling situational crime prevention.

Overview

A juvenile street gang is a form of multiplied reality, combining reality with a degree of fakery. This serves to enhance threat. This is accomplished by sharing signals, conveying a nastier image than any member could convey alone. Thus the juvenile gang helps its members intimidate others, at least until the process begins to unravel. A gang's specific signals persist even as specific participants change. After particular gangs fade away, emergent gangs can adopt the same old signals for quick intimidation. A gang benefits from widespread media coverage, police attention, and neighborhood gossip, helping scare the public and reinforce the signaling process. A broader natural perspective helps us understand the juvenile street gang and to sort out its important elements.[49] The juvenile street gang is an imperfect adaptation to its surroundings. We can only understand it by paying close attention to its trials and errors.

Central Points, Chapter 20

1. Despite many years of effort, scholars have been unable to find what structures juvenile street gangs.

2. Following ecological principles, gangs standardize the warning signals they send out.

3. This helps gang participants scare off enemies, gain compliance from victims, and discourage bystanders from interfering or turning them in.

4. Gangs mix real intimidation with exaggeration; the latter serves a practical purpose.

Exercises

1. Compare the juvenile street gang to adult organized crime.

2. Do police, citizens, professors, and gang members themselves have incentives to exaggerate gang features?

3. How can you find out whether the author's view of the gang is correct?

Notes

1. This quotation is often misattributed to Robert K. Merton, or others. It was in fact stated by W. I. Thomas and Dorothy S. Thomas, associated with the "Chicago School of

sociology." Quoted from W. I. Thomas and D. S. Thomas, "The Methodology of Behavior Study," Chapter 13 in W. I. Thomas, *The Child in America: Behavior Problems and Programs* (New York: Knopf, 1928). The full quotation follows:

> He had killed several persons who had the unfortunate habit of talking to themselves on the street. From the movement of their lips he imagined that they were calling him vile names, and he behaved as if this were true. If men define situations as real, they are real in their consequences.

2. U.S. novelist (1937–). Quoted in *The Columbia World of Quotations* (New York: Columbia University Press, 1996).

3. *All's Well That Ends Well,* end of act IV, scene iii.

4. *The Importance of Being Earnest* (1895) act 2, ed. R. Berggren (New York: Vanguard, 1987). Original edition published 1895.

5. U.S. poet, nonfiction author (1909–1981). Quoted in *The Columbia World of Quotations* (New York: Columbia University Press, 1996).

6. W. B. Miller, "Gangs, Groups, and Serious Youth Crime," in D. Shichor and D. Kelly, eds., *Critical Issues in Juvenile Delinquency* (Lexington, MA: Lexington, 1980).

7. For more on gangs in a community context, see I. A. Spergel and I. Kantor, *The Youth Gang Problem: A Community Approach* (New York: Oxford University Press, 1995).

8. Crime victimization falls disproportionately on youths, so they might even have security concerns outside the worst neighborhoods. Indeed, adjacent areas face risks, encouraging gang activity to spread geographically.

9. Many gang scholars will disagree with this chapter. In personal communication (April 2005) Malcolm W. Klein, a leading gang expert, tells me that an earlier version of this chapter "vastly overstates the intimidation purpose. Generally you put too much emphasis on the crime component of gangs, too little on the social and personal motives." I am not sure the final version satisfies that criticism. However, social and personal motives cannot alone distinguish gangs from other forms of social participation. A juvenile street gang must offer something special to its members. I do not think demonizing gangs or their participants serves any useful purpose, but neither can we forget that people get something out of scaring others.

Much of my information about gangs came from what Professor Klein wrote or said while we were colleagues at the University of Southern California. See especially M. W. Klein, *The American Street Gang: Its Nature, Prevalence and Control* (New York and Oxford, UK: Oxford University Press, 1995). Also see his other writings cited below, and those of Professor Cheryl Maxson at the University of California, Irvine. You will notice that I offer my own view of juvenile street gangs, going beyond the published literature and sometimes in conflict with it. This just goes to show that much of science has to do not with the facts themselves but how they are arranged to tell a story. My emphasis is different from that of most gang scholars, even though I work with some of the same data. A subsequent note from Professor Klein indicated concern about my lack of direct familiarity with gangs. I cannot deny this. Perhaps time will tell whether my explanation of gangs serves a useful purpose. I'm optimistic.

10. The work of Scott Decker and colleagues at the University of Missouri–St. Louis is very important for understanding gangs. For example, see S. Decker and B. van Winkle, *Life in the Gang: Family, Friends, and Violence* (Cambridge, UK: Cambridge University Press, 1996). Also see M. Colvin, *Crime and Coercion: An Integrated Theory of Chronic Criminality* (New York: St. Martin's, 2000).

11. R. C. Connor, R. M. Heithaus, and L. M. Barre, "Superalliance of Bottlenose Dolphins," *Nature* 371 (1999): 571–572. Connor and colleagues studied dolphins at Shark Bay, Western Australia. Connor discovered that two or three dolphins form a gang. Dolphin gangs might be more stable than gangs devised by juvenile *Homo sapiens*. In addition, dolphins form bilevel gang alliances, so the smaller gangs band together for joint security. This

might help explain the gang alliances among humans, too. But we should not mistake an alliance for a gang. This chapter defines these separately.

12. I would rather drop the word entirely, if others would go along.

13. I think that research money feeds this confusion. Grants are available for studying "gangs," so researchers have an incentive to squeeze many offender groups into this category. But science cannot live by money alone.

14. One should distinguish a drug gang from a juvenile street gang that assists drug sellers *on the side*. See definitions offered in

    a. M. W. Klein, *Gang Cop: The Words and Ways of Officer Paco Domingo* (Walnut Creek, CA: Altamira Press, 2004).

    b. M. W. Klein and others, *Eurogang Paradox: Street Gangs and Youth Groups in the US and Europe* (Dordrecht, Holland: Kluwer Academic, 2001).

    c. M. W. Klein, "Street Gangs: A Cross-national Perspective," in C. R. Huff, ed., *Gangs in America III* (Thousand Oaks, CA: Sage, 2005).

15. For more about the gang share of crime, see C. L. Maxson and M. W. Klein, "Street Gang Violence: Twice as Great, or Half as Great?" in C. R. Huff, ed., *Gangs in America* (Newbury Park, CA: Sage, 1990).

16. M. W. Klein, "Attempting Gang Control by Suppression: The Misuse of Deterrence Principles," *Studies on Crime and Crime Prevention* 2 (1992): 88–111.

17. See StreetGangs.com, http://www.streetgangs.com/crips/ (accessed September 4, 2005). I admit that not all of these use the term "crip," and some are designated "crips" by police and gang observers. But I still maintain that gang unity over broad areas is grossly exaggerated.

18. We could divide Little Gang Theory into two versions: (1) Unlinked Little Gang Theory, and (2) Bilevel Little Gang Theory. The former suggests that little gangs sharing the same name in part are still totally independent. The latter involves a loose alliance, for occasional purposes, among little gangs that are independent on a day-to-day basis.

19. Occasionally someone might call the newspapers to announce a big gang meeting; but that does not prove the big gang exists on a daily basis.

20. Even these gangs are likely to be ignored in the media unless they do something very unusual.

21. This does not deny that they can do substantial harm before departure.

22. Gang experts made me aware that gangs tend to die more quickly than their image. But I have gone farther than available evidence in suggesting that more gangs last less than a year. This remains an empirical question.

23. M. W. Klein, *Street Gangs and Street Workers* (Englewood Cliffs, NJ: Prentice Hall, 1971); M. W. Klein, "Gangs," in R. J. Corsini and B. D. Ozaki., *Encyclopedia of Psychology* (New York: Wiley, 1987).

24. Some have suggested that short-lived gangs are not the ones that create the danger; hence attention for the more noticeable gangs is commensurate with their threat. There's some truth to this. But many gangs that survive only a year or two are indeed threatening to the community. Moreover, much of the threat created by longer-lived and wider-ranged gangs is a product of their image and multiplied reality.

25. I use the word "stillborn," since the gang forms, only to die before it does anything.

26. Some organized crime groups demand permanent membership, but have to work very hard to achieve it. Traditionally, Sicilian Cosa Nostra members could not easily drop out. Japanese organized criminals (*yakuza*) are easily recognized from their tattoos and missing finger joints. Tattoos are used by some American gangs, especially in prisons, and might contribute to longer-term affiliations. In Chicago and other cities, some gangs use tattoos, and these might freeze membership in time. But I wonder if tattoos are sometimes hidden under clothing. In places with very low migration rates and little chance to escape, these methods might work. However, most American street gangs are located in more fluid settings. Concerned that gangs would spread to new areas, American government agencies have funded

research on gang *in*-migration. But gang *out*-migration is also important. It helps disrupt gang membership. Perhaps new arrivals are also disruptive.

27. Y. Yablonski, "The Delinquent Gang as a Near Group," *Social Problems* 7 (1959): 108–109. Also see G. M. Knox, *An Introduction to Gangs* (Buchanan, MI: VandeVere, 1993).

28. See
   a. G. D. Suttles, *The Social Order of a Slum* (Chicago: University of Chicago Press, 1968).
   b. M. W. Klein and L. Crawford, "Groups, Gangs and Cohesiveness," *Journal of Research in Crime and Delinquency* 4 (1967): 63–75.
   c. P. G. Jackson, "Theories and Findings About Youth Gangs," *Criminal Justice Abstracts* 21 (1989): 313.
   d. S. H. Decker and J. L. Lauritsen, "Leaving the Gang," in C. R. Huff, ed., *Gangs in America III* (Thousand Oaks, CA: Sage, 2005).

29. See prior note.

30. Several scholars have worked on the gang network issue. See, e.g., M. S. Fleisher, "Doing Field Research on Diverse Gangs: Interpreting Youth Gangs as Social Networks," in C. R. Huff, ed., *Gangs in America III* (Thousand Oaks, CA: Sage, 2005). Also see J. Sarnecki, *Delinquent Networks: Youth Co-Offending in Stockholm* (Cambridge, UK: Cambridge University Press, 2001). This idea goes back at least to D. J. Bordua, "Delinquent Subcultures: Sociological Interpretations of Gang Delinquency," *Annals of the American Academy of Social Science* 338 (November 1961): 119–136.

31. See references to Professors Klein and Maxson.

32. I rely heavily on gang scholars in this chapter. But I also dismiss some of their claims. For example, it is easy to be distracted by the social normalcy of gang participants hanging out.

33. See D. A. West, *Fritz Müller: A Naturalist in Brazil* (Blacksburg, VA: Pocahontas Press, 2003). Also see James Mallet's 2004 review of this book in *Quarterly Review of Biology* 79 (2004): 196.

34. D. D. Kapan, "Three-butterfly System Provides a Field Test of Müllerian Mimicry," *Nature* 409 (2001): 338–340.

35. In this paper I use the word "signal" rather than "symbol." One reason is to link gangs to larger nature. The main reason is that the word "symbol" often implies diffuse communication, while "signal" has a more focused message, such as, "Don't mess with me, or you'll get the worst of it."

36. Müllerian mimicry is not an afterthought. I figured out the main point of this chapter *only* because I read about that form of mimicry and the wasp example.

37. In very local settings, faces are known and colors might not be necessary. It is also possible that symbols and identities serve additional sociopsychological purposes. But these are not the *central* reasons for the gang to exist.

38. I use the word "obnoxious" for a reason. Intimidation is usually directed at particular persons, organizations, and situations. Obnoxiousness is broader, and can be carried with you. We might think of poison ivy as obnoxious, even if it is not intimidating you personally. Of course, I intend to include intimidation, too, in explaining gangs.

39. This list could have added "explicit nonverbal threats," such as moving your finger across your throat to show somewhat what will happen to him.

40. Of course, a group of youths walking down the street or hanging out in a park can be intimidating, even without common colors. But gang signals imply an ability to draw upon a larger group.

41. B. A. Jacobs, "Typology of Street Criminal Retaliation," *Journal of Research in Crime and Delinquency* 41 (2004): 295–323.

42. Fascinating social psychological research indicates that many people respond more to their bad experiences than good ones. If so, a gang does not have to hurt you every time to stick in your mind. A review of the issue is found in R. F. Baumeiser and others, "Bad is Stronger Than Good," *Review of General Psychology* 5 (2001): 323–370.

43. Scholars are aware of gang images as an issue. See, for example, S. H. Decker and K. Kempf, "Constructing Gangs: The Social Construction of Youth Activities," *Criminal Justice Policy Review* 5 (1991): 271–291.

44. I made this term up, and I wonder if it has parallels among animals. Humans belong to nature, but they also add to it.

45. On gang migration, see C. L. Maxson, "Gang Members on the Move," *Juvenile Justice Bulletin,* October (Washington, DC: U.S. Department of Justice, Office of Justice Programs, Office of Juvenile Justice and Delinquency Prevention, 1998). Also see C. L. Maxson, K. Woods, and M. W. Klein, "Street Gang Migration: How Big a Threat?" *National Institute of Justice Journal* 230 (February 1996): 26–31.

46. For raising these issues, I thank Professors Malcolm W. Klein of the University of Southern California and Dr. Arlen Egley of the National Youth Gang Center.

47. See M. Felson, "The Process of Co-offending," in M. J. Smith and D. B. Cornish, eds., *Theory for Practice in Situational Crime Prevention* (Monsey, NY: Criminal Justice Press, 2003) (Volume 16 *in Crime Prevention Studies* series).

48. Although my theoretical approach differs from his, my policy prescription overlaps somewhat with that of Professor Malcolm W. Klein. See M. W. Klein, "Attempting Gang Control by Suppression: The Misuse of Deterrence Principles," *Studies on Crime and Crime Prevention* 2 (1992): 88–111.

49. As I stated earlier, Müllerian mimicry was essential for my thought processes in writing this chapter. This is not an analogy. I intend this as a literal example of signaling for purposes of scaring off one's enemies or gaining compliance to commit criminal acts. To be sure, human gangs compound what's found in nature, adding the impact of the media and historical reputation.

PART V

Synthesis

Science is the knowledge of many, orderly and methodically digested and arranged, so as to become attainable by one.

—J. F. W. Herschel[1]

In the theater of confusion, knowing the location of the exits is what counts.

—Mason Cooley[2]

The only way humans can do better than computers is to take a chance of doing worse.

—John W. Tukey[3]

The wonderful thing about science is that it's alive.

—Richard P. Feynman[4]

21

Classifying Crime

A classification is a "definition comprising a system of definitions.[5] Of course, acting outside the law is also acting beyond legal categories. To classify everyday crime, we need a more direct classification system, based on life—not law books. This chapter proposes a taxonomy for organizing what we know (and hope to know) about crime, in its many varieties. The goal is to list all forms of crime in a sensible order—that is, to find a crime taxonomy. But first, let's learn how naturalists learned to organize what they know about life.

Exemplar

In school, most of us learned about kingdom, phylum, class, order, family, genus, and species—a carefully *ordered* system. Carl Linnaeus (1707–1778), from southern Sweden, invented the taxonomy of living things. To this day, naturalists around the world use a variation of his taxonomy to classify organisms.[6]

A taxonomy not only organizes information, but also helps people communicate, fill in details, and expand when more is learned. To this day, Linnaean taxonomy helps naturalists to go from general to specific, and back again, without getting lost.

Linnaeus took his first trips to gather plant specimens in his early 20s.[7] His *System of Nature*[8] began with a small pamphlet, then grew into multiple volumes.[9] Linnaeus sent some 20 students on botanical adventures around the world, collecting specimens and taking voluminous notes.[10] Some of these students faced terrible tragedies at young ages. Anton Martin suffered Arctic frostbite and spent the rest of his life in misery. Peter Forsskål died of malaria at age 33, after a horrible expedition in 1762. His book about North African plants was brought back by the sole survivor and published posthumously. Fredrik Hasselquist died in Smyrna, but his collections were not lost. These student projects made their way back to Sweden, changing the history of science.

From these pioneers we learn

- that classification is very valuable for orderly progress in knowledge,
- that a strong substantive basis for classification is essential, and
- that a classification system must transcend time and space.

Legal classifications are not general enough to transcend time and space. This chapter formulates a crime taxonomy with a single intellectual framework, based on ecological theory, not tied to any particular time or place. Most importantly, the proposed taxonomy allows future scholars to make improvements as they learn more.

This chapter is a natural culmination of the theoretical work contained in this book. But I do not believe in using *every* feature of a crime to classify it, since that would make classification too cumbersome. It's more useful to organize crime's many types, taking into account how these acts occur within the daily ecosystem. *In particular, it makes sense to classify crime in terms of the trip toward the crime target and the main features of daily life that enable or impede that trip.* But first, let me explain why taxonomy is important at all.

What Taxonomy Can Do for You

Today's students don't have to risk their lives to study nature. For example, they might use the Texas Natural History Collections, which preserve about a million specimens in jars and on slides, plus 250,000 dried pinned insects, and many frogs, salamanders, caecilians, lizards, snakes, amphibians, tuataras, crocodilians, and turtles in a searchable online database that does not bite. Without a taxonomy, there would be nothing but messy piles. Naturalists show us how to clean piles up.[11] Even crime information can be put in order, if we set our minds to it.

Naturalists have made their taxonomy *universal*. Whether you live in Missouri, California, the Smoky Mountains, Kansas, Japan, Spain, or China—the same system applies. You can classify a single bug walking on the floor of your bathroom by kingdom, phylum, class, order, family, genus, and species. Even if you have never seen a platypus you can still find out where it fits and talk about it with people elsewhere.[12] Accordingly, a single taxonomy could help overcome the local inconsistencies among legal codes.

A taxonomy is a living system, growing new limbs, expanding and adapting over decades and centuries. Since Linnaeus, naturalists have named, coded, and classified some 1.5 million types of living things.[13] By the time this book gets to you, new specimens will be found and categories slightly altered. If Linnaeus returned to life today, he would recognize his taxonomy in broad terms; but naturalists could still give him a good briefing.

What a Crime Taxonomy Cannot Do

Classifying requires cooperating. It is not handed down from Heaven but, rather, represents a human effort to work together. A classification scheme does not use all of nature's details. Instead, it uses a *subset* of those details to help systematize the rest.

To organize what we know and want to know about crime, we must decide what unit to classify. We cannot get very far classifying people. As several chapters have shown, offenders are highly inconsistent. For more than 100 years, offenders have defied classification. To confuse the classifiers, "violent offenders" commit mostly property offenses. As I explained in earlier chapters, most offenders are generalists. "Property offenders" suddenly do something violent. Nonoffenders become offenders, and offenders become nonoffenders. Thus a burglar today might be a shoplifter tomorrow or stay on the right side of the law for months at a time. Differentiating offenders *as people* is not a dependable enterprise. That's why a crime taxonomy needs to classify types of criminal *acts*, not criminals.

What happens *afterward* should not bias how we see the crime incident (look back to Exhibit 2.2). In its aftermath, a crime could change from petty larceny into grand larceny or assault into murder. Moreover, varying local legal codes and their inconsistency in application cannot help us here (see Chapters 2 and 3). As stated earlier, a taxonomy must find an organizing principle that transcends local times and specific places.

Our best chance is to focus on *types of behavior,* going beyond any individual. The proposed taxonomy bypasses individual innocence or guilt, justice or injustice, or the final outcome of a criminal act. Indeed, such a taxonomy *will not even distinguish between assault and murder.* Murder depends on differences in medical treatment, and how a local justice reads intent. Many offenders do not really know how much they are going to harm the victim, and injuries might not run their course for months. Thus a universal classification of crime bypasses many important and difficult decisions made by local justice systems, and many issues important to society.

Now that I have shown what a crime taxonomy can and cannot do, the remainder of the chapter proposes one. The first step is to state its underlying organizing basis.

The Physical Story of a Crime

In Chapter 3, I offered a way to describe and diagram a crime, taking into account the offender's motives. That was useful for linking the world of individual offenders to the ecology of crime. But it stopped short, for it did not tell us how the offender arrived in that spot, or link the offender beyond the immediate setting.

This chapter proposes a crime taxonomy building on *crime's universal features*—as defined by the offender's motion toward the target (or object) of the crime. Every criminal act has a physical story.[14] An offender works his way toward a target, then acts upon it. He moves along various paths toward that target. He encounters barriers, sometimes overcoming them, often with the use of tools. At last he converges with his crime target. This very general physical story applies to a vast variety of specific crime types and makes possible a single crime taxonomy. I propose using five main levels, kept straight with symbols:

$\not\Rightarrow$ Paths

‖ Barriers

Θ Tools

⌐⌐ Convergences

⦿ Targets

Paths are legitimate systems the offender uses to move toward his target. A burglar might use highways, byways, walkways, and streets to get to the house he burgles. As the offender proceeds, he will often need to overcome *barriers* in order to carry out his crime. A fence or lock is a barrier, but even weak barriers (such as a sign) affect some offenders some of the time. *Tools* include a burglar's crowbar to force open a door or a hacker's software to steal his way into a computer system, as well as fake keys and drivers' licenses. Offenders then have a variety of *convergences* with the *targets of crime*.

The Electronic ⚡Path

Modern life provides rather new pathways to crime. Telecommunications systems open up tremendous additional crime opportunities. The ⚡ *electronic path* includes society's electronic hardware and software, by which people send and receive information. Offenders often divert these processes for criminal purposes.[15] The electronic path helps us classify a growing variety of criminal convergences using coaxial cable, conventional telephone, cell phone, microwave, radio, satellite, television, and the Internet. These media provide a means to reach crime targets beyond face-to-face contact, yet taking advantage of routine activities.[16]

The Organizational ⚡Path

Through most of human history, "white-collar crime" hardly existed because there were no official, impersonal, rules to violate. White-collar crimes are an artifact of modern society's reliance on formal organizations and role requirements. Over the past 200 years, formal organizations transformed the crime landscape. Social historian and theorist Max Weber defined formal organization by its clear-cut hierarchy of offices, specialized competencies and duties, obligations (without favoritism), and written rules, as well as hiring and promotion based on merit alone.

Under these rules, an individual only *occupies* the office, but does not *own* it. The rules subject each employee and manager to strict and systematic discipline and responsibilities.[17] Formal organization is supposed to separate official tasks from personal gains. However, in real life many people also use their official positions for personal purposes, even as a path toward crime. Thus formal organizations can put someone in just the right position to do the wrong thing.[18]

The *organizational ⁊path* enables crimes by providing those in official or business roles with access to people, data, or things. Someone can easily misuse that access, perhaps in violation of law. I have suggested calling these *crimes of specialized access,* since each offender abuses a specific role that offers access to a crime target.[19] Such infractions are often called "white-collar" crimes, forgetting that blue-collar workers can also abuse their positions, as might any employee inside a modern school, university, business, or government agency. The organizational path to crime is quite a large system linking companies, clients, patients, customers, professions, and government agencies for legitimate purposes. Hence it offers tremendous opportunities for abuse. The main point is that legitimate roles provide a path toward crime. The same point applies, whether a boss pressures his secretary for sex, or the boy behind the counter gives ice cream away to his friends. Of course, we know that real people often do favors for family, friends, and themselves.

How ‖ Barriers Block Crime Access

Oscar Newman, a famous architect-intellectual, explained that even informal boundaries can make a difference for crime. As I explained before, Newman distinguished private, semiprivate, semipublic, and public space, according to the degree of exclusion. Even a publicly *owned* housing project has private *access* if nonresidents need permission to go there. Of course, Newman's categories take into account many dimensions of human activity and architectural design. I focus mostly on tangible barriers.

Exhibit 21.1 presents five ways that barriers affect crime. (1) ‖ *Enclosures* are the most significant barriers to crime access. These include buildings as well as corrals for cattle and fences for schools. Doors, gates, and walls also block or impede physical paths to crime. However, not all barriers enclose fully. (2) ‖ *Impediments* are often placed in paths to slow down intrusions, not to prevent them entirely. Speed bumps slow traffic; streets narrow to discourage rapid entry. Many residential areas are constructed with curves in order to give a moderate sense of localism. Thus people or nature (or both) create impediments to crime.

Exhibit 21.1   A Proposed Taxonomy for Criminal Acts

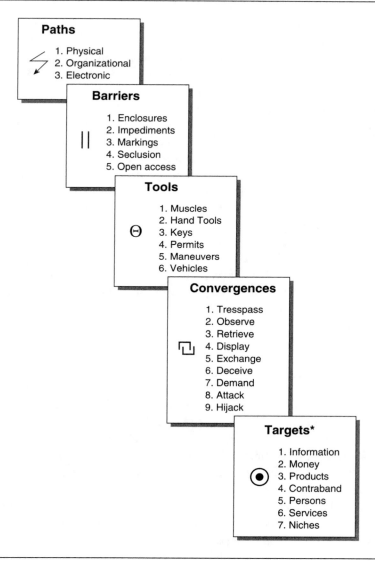

*Or Objects

The University of Southern California was the site of the Olympic village during the 1984 Olympics. Kicking me out of my office during August, the university cordoned off the sensitive area. They also constructed an attractive iron security fence around the entire campus. After the Olympics, the fence remained, but the gates were usually left open. The result was a major decline in thefts on campus, even though the public could still enter if they wished. Impeding free movement and entry is a matter of degree, affecting security accordingly.

(3) || *Markings* are often used to indicate private property or limited access. These include any cues or signs that tell people that access is not open. A marking does not physically prevent someone from entering, but it has some impact. Many people will comply voluntarily. Others comply because they fear standing out like a sore thumb. (4) || *Seclusion* is an important barrier against crime. Any location remote to or hidden from likely offenders impedes their ability to commit crime. Finally, some areas have (5) || *open access,* and hence throw up no barriers against crime.

Electronic and organizational paths toward crime also erect barriers. They are not always physical in the sense of a wall, but they work in similar fashion. It is no mistake that computer systems provide firewalls and passwords, or give instructions to keep out. It is no mistake that businesses have areas for customers and other areas for employees only. Businesses also divide their premises, and not every employee is supposed to be everywhere. These exclusions, too, are a matter of degree. Breaching barriers is an important task for criminal action. The proposed taxonomy classifies crime in part by how offenders do so.

How Θ Tools Assist Crime

Tools (broadly defined) help an offender overcome barriers to his crime target.[20] Tools include (1) Θ *muscles* alone, but these can be supplemented by (2) Θ *hand tools*, including any crowbars, hammers, screwdrivers, glass cutters—even rocks or junk sitting on the ground that can be used to break your way in and commit a crime. (3) Offenders also use Θ *keys*, whether authorized, stolen, or abused, assisting illicit entry without requiring smashing sounds. These include electronic cards used in hotels, as well as the passwords used in computers and combinations that open locks, or other relevant secrets. In addition, department stores have devices designed to remove security tags, and a "professional" shoplifter sometimes gets hold of one.

Offenders also gain entry by using (4) Θ *permits* or permissions of one form or another. A roommate or family member usually has a right to enter the home, making it easy to commit a crime there, including family violence. An employee has a right to enter the business establishment and vicinity of her own work. But people sometimes convert rightful permits to wrong uses, such as entering a part of the establishment they are not entitled to. Others obtain wrongful permits, such as fake identification or stolen passwords and combinations. Perhaps future versions of this taxonomy should distinguish permits that are rightful, wrongful, or converted to wrong uses, or distinguish written from unwritten rights of entry.

Many crimes are inconvenient for the average offender to carry out. To overcome this, offenders find ways to circumvent barriers. Thus some offenders' (5) Θ *maneuvers* help them get through or around barriers. This includes simply knowing where the fence has a hole, or how to get into the back of the dock without getting caught. (6) Θ *Vehicles* help offenders to circumnavigate a barrier or reach a remote target.

Nine Degrees of Crime 🖳 Convergence

Criminal acts vary greatly by how much the offender interplays with the target and engages with other people who might interfere with the crime. Nine steps are noted in Exhibit 21.1, and in the list below. As you go down the list, you will note growing interplay:

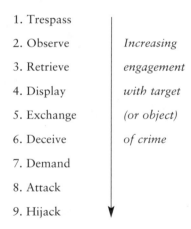

1. Trespass

2. Observe   *Increasing*

3. Retrieve   *engagement*

4. Display   *with target*

5. Exchange   *(or object)*

6. Deceive   *of crime*

7. Demand

8. Attack

9. Hijack

In some cases, offenders (1) 🖳 *trespass* quietly where they should not be—without taking, looking, doing, or retrieving anything tangible. For example, some people trespass across the property of another for sheer convenience. Other offenders illegally (2) 🖳 *observe* people or property, without retrieving anything or taking it elsewhere. Ordinary eavesdroppers and peeping toms fit this category, especially if unnoticed by the target. Perhaps some people enter the computer systems of others to take a look, no more. Other offenders (3) 🖳 *retrieve* something after encroaching, trying to take it away without a personal encounter and without being noticed. This includes shoplifting and most ordinary thefts and burglaries. Espionage normally involves retrieving documents or information for illicit use afterward. Of course, criminal retrieval often leaves footprints that are discovered later.

There's nothing more engaging than direct criminal interaction with other people. An offender might put on an illicit (4) 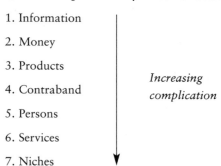 *display* for another person. That includes indecent exposure, obscene gestures, shouting at officers, disturbing public hearings, or showing illicit pornography. It also includes toughs showing guns, independent of any particular attack, to convince others of their own nastiness. A greater engagement occurs when offenders (5) *exchange* something with another person in consensual violation of law. This includes trade in hard drugs, selling on the street without a vendor's permit, or exchanging contraband via the Internet.

Some interplay between offenders and victims involve a degree of trickery.[21] For example, an offender might use eBay or other computer shopping methods to (6) *deceive* his victim into thinking she has bought something. In fact, the victim paid money but got nothing in return. Even more obtrusive crimes occur when offenders (7) *demand* something from a victim; but at least the victim can hand over what the offender wants and perhaps he will leave without further harm. But sometimes the offender subjects the victim to physical (8) *attack*, often including brief control (e.g., for less than a minute or two). In the most obtrusive crimes of all, offenders (9) *hijack* persons, property, or niches over longer periods. This includes rape, kidnapping, taking over aircraft, enslaving another person, hijacking a website, illegal broadcasting over the air, diverting company equipment to one's own use, and criminal seizure of land belonging to another.

Seven Types of Crime ⊙ Targets

Some crime targets are easily "attacked," with little notice, allowing the crime to blend into normal life afterward. Other targets create more complications. Seven nouns help us classify these variations in crime targets (or objects):

1. Information

2. Money

3. Products

4. Contraband   *Increasing*
                       complication

5. Persons

6. Services

7. Niches

The possibility of concealing a crime is paramount. (1) ⊙ *Information* can be stolen from files or traded illegally. But it often can be memorized or destroyed, limiting its complication for the offender. (2) ⊙ *Money* is easy to steal but then easily blends into the larger stock of money after the crime is over—especially when currency looks quite alike and is unlikely to be traced. Legal (3) ⊙ *products* provide tangible evidence and are often recognized, but also have a chance to regain their aura of legality. On the other hand, illicit drugs and other (4) ⊙ *contraband* never regain their innocence. A (5) ⊙ *person* can be the object of exchange, demand, or hijacking, involving even greater intrusion than the previous nonhuman targets. A personal target might fight back or otherwise produce complications for the attacker.

Illicit transactions also involve criminal gain of (6) ⊙ *services*. Sometimes an illicit exchange occurs by mutual consent (e.g., illegal prostitution, gambling, or loan sharking). Other times, the service itself is legal, but its seizure is not (e.g., theft of phone or cable services). Sexual assaults might be seen as illegal seizures of "services." Many sexual encounters would be legal if offered by consent. Other sexual activities are intrinsically illegal, such as consensual adult intercourse with children, but still produce special complications for the offender.

Perhaps the most interesting crime target is the (7) ⊙ *niche,* which an offender might seek to control for his own purposes. For example, some drug sellers use force or threat to commandeer a street corner from 5:00 to 10:00 p.m. for further illegal purposes. Organized violence is often directed at controlling a particular niche via multiple offenses against persons and properties.[22] This is the only item in the taxonomy that goes beyond single events. Experience will tell us whether this last category is practical to code, or will have to be removed later.

In light of the modern Internet, Professors Graeme R. Newman and Ronald V. Clarke have elaborated on the concept of a crime target.[23] For crime related to the Internet, they distinguish the following:

- *Prime targets,* such as intellectual property easily copied from electronic files
- *Convertible targets,* such as an employee access code stolen via the Internet, then converted for use in another crime
- *Transitional targets,* such as using an auction website as a means to defraud one of its customers
- *Incidental or undifferentiated targets,* such as a computer worm that threatens everybody connected to the Internet

Such elaborations will be necessary as a future crime taxonomy adapts itself, trying to keep up with a changing world.

Each Crime Is a Story

One bright and sunny day, a burglar traverses a physical ⚡ path, encounters an enclosed || barrier, uses a burglary Θ tool to break in, ⊡ retrieving legal ⊙ products, namely, jewelry. Next he exchanges ⊡ one piece of jewelry with a woman who deals in stolen goods. His own target is now money. He uses the electronic ⊙ path in ⊡ exchanging the rest of the loot via the Internet. The test of this taxonomy is its ability to tell this story many times over, working down the five levels, finding the right category on each, and knowing how to separate the various crimes that occur.

Future Expansions

Each level of the taxonomy can be supplemented and subdivided in the future. For example, a future taxonomy might distinguish offenses that

- use weapons, or use particular types of weapons;
- are committed within "outdoor enclosures," such as fenced college campuses;
- are carried out on foot, by bicycle, motorbike, motorcycle, cars, or trucks;
- elaborate primitive crime types, such as cheating the monarch; or
- elaborate modern crime types, such as Internet crime.[24]

Nevertheless, I have offered an orderly *start* for classifying crime, looking beyond a single nation, region, or period of history.

Overview

This chapter has shown what we learn from naturalists about the uses of a taxonomy and how to construct one. I have proposed a crime taxonomy with five levels, 30 categories within them, and many multiples.[25] The taxonomy helps us think about differences in how crime prevention is carried out. Police attend most to crime in the physical path, especially where access is open. Private security personnel often focus on enclosed parts of the physical path. Organizational crime draws attention of accountants, auditors, professional discipline boards, and governmental regulatory agencies (such as the Securities and Exchange Commission). Computer security personnel seek to block crimes in the electronic path—an area undergoing the most change in crime and crime prevention, due to the spread of the Internet and transformation of the telecommunications industries.

This taxonomy is a wine cellar with few bottles placed.[26] Its purpose is to classify a vast variety of crimes on a tiny number of dimensions. Experience and categories should grow in the future. Perhaps paleocriminologists will study extinct offenses. Perhaps changes in human society will force us to modify or even transform our crime taxonomy. But at least this can help us expand our knowledge without getting lost.

Central Points, Chapter 21

1. A taxonomy helps people discuss crime, using the same terms.

2. Order is essential for a taxonomy to help us study crime.

3. The proposed taxonomy organizes crimes by how the offender moves toward the target.

4. All criminal acts should fit into this taxonomy. If any crimes cannot be classified, the taxonomy must grow and change.

Exercises

1. Look up one of Linnaeus's students. Find out where he went, what he did, and what happened to him. Would you risk it?

2. Classify two different types of auto theft within this taxonomy.

3. Examine a newspaper story describing a crime. Try to fit the crime into this taxonomy.

4. Try to improve upon the author's list of tools that offenders might use.

Notes

1. British mathematician, astronomer, and philosopher of science (1792–1871). Quoted in *The Columbia World of Quotations* (New York: Columbia University Press, 1996).

2. Quoted in *The Columbia World of Quotations* (New York: Columbia University Press, 1996).

3. Remarkable statistical theorist and consultant, mathematician, and leader in research design (1915–2000). In "We Need Both Exploratory and Confirmatory," *The American Statistician* 34, no. 1 (February 1980): 23–25.

4. This quotation is widely attributed to Feynman. For example, see Wikipedia, Wikiquote, http://en.wikiquote.org/wiki/Richard_Feynman (accessed September 4, 2005).

5. Friedrich Von Schlegel, German philosopher (1772–1829). Quoted in *The Columbia World of Quotations* (New York: Columbia University Press, 1996).

6. Although the word "taxonomy" came to English via French, its original source is Greek. It combines two ancient words: "taxis" (arrangement) and "nomie" (method). The compound term "taxonomy" implies "method of arranging." Yet the word carries some extra connotation in life sciences, which uses the plural "taxes" to denote how a free-moving organism or cell responds to stimuli by moving toward or away from it. This connotation is especially appropriate in the current context, where an offender's approach toward the crime target is the organizing taxonomic principle. Grammarians differ in how they work the word, taxonomy, into a sentence.

7. Linnaeus became professor at the University of Uppsala, where his famous botanical garden receives visitors even today. Its website is http://www.linnaeus.uu.se/LTeng.html (accessed September 4, 2005).

8. *Systema Naturae*, written in Latin.

9. Much of his work is now housed in the Linnaean Society of London, which preserves 14,000 specimens of plants; 3,200 of insects; 1,700 of fish and shellfish—demonstrating the uses of organization. See the society's webpage at http://www.linnean.org/ (accessed September 4, 2005). For the letters of Linnaeus online, a pilot project is available at The Linnaean Correspondence, http://www.c18.org/pr/lc/index.html (accessed September 4, 2005). Many letters are in other languages, but English summaries are at the end of each. Future details of this project, as it progresses, should be available at the Linnaean Society website.

10. These pioneers included John Peter Falck (Russia and the Asian interior), Daniel Solander (Australia), Anders Sparrman (China and Africa), and Carl Peter Thunberg (Japan). Pehr Kalm traversed the Atlantic to study American plants, visited Benjamin Franklin, and gave the first scientific account of Niagara Falls.

11. Of course, they discover new things to mess piles up again.

12. From time to time, mistakes are found in taxonomy. Yet classified mistakes are more likely to be corrected than those that simply dangle. The presence of mistakes is a poor excuse for evading orderliness.

13. These include approximately 750,000 arthropod species, 280,000 miscellaneous, 250,000 plant species, and myriad fungi, protozoa, algae, bacteria, and virus species. I don't give a reference here, since each one has a different tally.

14. Really, this story is sociophysical, having both social and physical features. In this chapter I emphasize physical features because they are so useful for finding order.

15. See G. Newman and R. V. Clarke, *Superhighway Robbery: Preventing E-commerce Crime* (Cullompton, Devon, UK: Willan, 2003).

16. See M. Williams, "Understanding King Punisher and His Order: Vandalism in an Online Community: Motives, Meanings and Possible Solutions" (2004), *Internet Journal of Criminology,* http://www.internetjournalofcriminology.com (accessed September 4, 2005).

17. Weber's famous essay on bureaucracy and formal organization is part of *Wirtschaft und Gesellschaft,* and is outlined in almost any introductory textbook in organizations or in sociology. Or see *From Max Weber: Essays in Sociology,* H. Gerth and C. Mills, trans. and eds. (New York: Galaxy Books, 1991). I have combined Max Weber's concepts of "profession" and "office" to formulate the organizational path toward crime.

18. See Chapter 7 of M. Felson, *Crime and Everyday Life,* 3rd ed. (Thousand Oaks, CA: Sage, 2002). Organizational pathways do not include stealing a wallet at work, or selling drugs there, since the organizational role is incidental in these cases.

19. These crimes are part of a larger set of role infractions. The offender not only violates the written or implicit requirements of his work role, but also abuses that role's access to crime targets.

20. I do not include weapons here. They are considered under attack and defense methods in several chapters of this book.

21. The order of categories at this point is debatable. But an imperfect order is better than no order at all.

22. Laws often focus on single attacks rather than overall seizure of a niche. But the ecological perspective (developed in this book) tells us to think beyond the immediate action. Did violence occur because of something said, or because one party intruded on the territory of another? Answers to this and related questions will tell us whether a crime has occurred with a niche as its target.

23. See endnote 15.

24. For example, we might distinguish crimes that broadcast illegally to many receivers from those offenses transmitting just to one. Professor Johannes Knutsson of the Police Academy in Oslo, Norway, suggested this idea.

25. If every combination occurs, the taxonomy implies a total of $3 \times 5 \times 6 \times 9 \times 7 = 5,670$ possible crime types. Of course, some cells will prove to have no real crimes. And some crimes will not fit any cells, leading us to modify this first taxonomy with future experience. It will also be necessary to formulate protocols to make decisions and handle close calls.

26. Because they are centuries ahead of crime science, natural scientists have developed some nuanced terms for their classification process. Systematics is the branch of the life sciences dealing with classification. It includes neontology, which classifies organisms alive today, and paleontology, which considers prehistoric ones. The word "taxonomy" has evolved to mean describing and naming additional taxa, since the old ones are already widely disseminated. Classification arranges information into a formal hierarchy, hence this is the word commonly applied to the Linnaean system. Phylogeny studies the ancestral relationships of organisms, and increasingly coincides with classification.

All women become like their mothers. That is their tragedy. No man does. That's his.

—Oscar Wilde[1]

War will never cease until babies begin to come into the world with larger cerebrums and smaller adrenal glands.

—H. L. Mencken[2]

I have a brain and a uterus, and I use both.

—Patricia Schroeder[3]

I've never forgotten for long time that living is struggle. I know that every good and excellent thing in the world stands moment by moment on the razor-edge of danger and must be fought for—whether it's a field, or a home, or a country.

—Thornton Wilder[4]

It is even harder for the average ape to believe that he has descended from man.

—H. L. Mencken[5]

22

The Struggle for Existence

One organism alone on a nutritious earth would have a simple existence. But life with others defines a tougher task. It forces an organism to fight off enemies from other species, as well as adversaries of its own kind.

The struggle for existence goes far beyond the genes carried by any individual, or even by a population. Human genes allow tremendous adaptations as circumstances keep changing in daily life and over its longer course. The genes are like a backpack that each of us must wear through life without a chance to pack it. Hiking along, each of us must figure out some way to use whatever the backpack contains. We encounter various threats, organic and inorganic, from our own species and others. We look for easy ways to survive. We look for fun and excitement. We use illegal means for our own benefit, but try to keep others from using the same means against us. And so the struggle for existence unfolds, with crime as a part of it.

Crime, strictly defined, did not exist before humans appeared on earth. But crime in a broader sense was part of ancient natural history. Birds have long been accomplished thieves, eating the eggs and the young of others and sometimes their own. Squirrels and rats routinely steal from burrows and caches of others. Dormice raid the nests of birds, and birds raid the nests of dormice, too. Bears are effective burglars. Wild boars vandalize and leave a terrible mess of the natural habitat. Hyenas attack as a gang. Even forcible rape is part of the broader natural world—a common behavior of mallard ducks, geese,[6] and Drosophila flies.[7] The male rock scorpion (*Hadogenes*) even drugs the female to sedate her for nonconsensual mating.[8] Although plants lack brains, they still find ways to seize territory, strangle competitors, poison enemies, swallow prey, and drive away competitors. Make no mistake about it, theft, killing, predation and territoriality, attack and defense— these have long been central to nature. So why should anyone think of human crime as deviant or strange?[9]

Don't Study Aggression Isolated From Life

We should not focus upon aggression as an *individual* trait, but should study it within a larger perspective. To begin, an aggressive act is often defensive, too. If you approach a bear cub, her mother will attack you because you have become a threat to her offspring. While recovering in the hospital, try to look at her point of view.

It is a mistake to study "aggression" in isolation from the rest of life. Every pacifist lives behind the soldier's bayonet, every injured soldier is nurtured by a noncombatant, and every exhausted army hopes the diplomats will come up with a way out.

As the chapters on defense indicated, aggression and defense are very much intertwined. Although genetic programming provides abilities to attack, these are not fixed traits. They come out in the context of daily interaction.

Thus a well-fed lion is not much danger to the local cattle until he gets hungry again. Often we are surprised that human aggression bursts forth, even from those we think are passive.

Angelo Dundee was a legendary trainer of famous boxers, including the superstar, Mohammed Ali. As a teenager, Dundee kept teasing a passive youth who delivered groceries every day. One day that youth got fed up with him, put down the groceries, and beat him up, then went on to deliver the rest of the groceries.[10] Perhaps no beings exceed humans in the ability to shift from passive to aggressive, then back to passive, depending on environmental circumstances. In addition, the web of human interdependence links people who are more aggressive to those who are less so.

Human and Prehuman Origins of Offenses

Clearly crime is part of natural history. Yet the link between aggression and the struggles of nature is not always straightforward. The domestic cat tortures the mouse, removing its limbs one by one and playing with the dying remains. The cat does not need to be so violent in order to eat. Indeed, animals use violence for

- play and honing skills,
- taking over or holding territory,[11]
- winning a right to mate or denying it to others,[12]
- responding to any hint of interference by others,[13] or
- establishing their positions in the pecking order[14] (discussed later).

The hippopotamus, a vegetarian with massive teeth, kills far more humans than any other African animal. Annoyed when a person crosses its territory, the hippo leaves his dying body as it goes to eat more grass. This is part of a general category, "interference aggression," such as a plant driving its competitors away from its vicinity. Thus a mere threat of danger can evoke an organism's vigorous attack to keep others out of its way. It is obvious that, in nature, aggression occurs for many reasons.

The word "aggression" is often used carelessly. Some people classify all criminal action, even shoplifting and traffic violations, as "aggressive." Others use aggression as a synonym for violence. My brother—Professor Richard Felson of Penn State University—offers a way out of the woods by considering the offender's intent.[15] He minimizes the usual distinction between property and violent offenses, dividing crime another way. Harm to another is either *not intended,* or *intended.* In the second case, the offender is either *indifferent* to harming the victim, or *values that harm* for its own sake.[16] Here are some examples:

Exhibit 22.1   Natural Origins of Crime

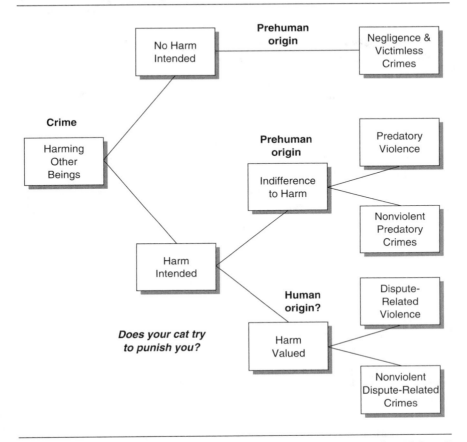

SOURCE: Modified from Figure 1 in R. B. Felson, "A Rational-choice Approach to Violence," in D. Zahn et al., eds., *Violence: From Theory to Research* (Cincinnati, OH: Anderson, 2004).

Harm not intended: crimes of pure negligence (reckless driving), or "victimless" crimes (possessing illicit drugs)[17]

Harm intended only as a means to an end, with indifference to the victim: predatory violence (robbery), or the usual nonviolent predatory crimes (stealing something you don't want to pay for)

Exhibit 22.1 borrows these distinctions to examine how crime might fit larger natural history. "Harming Other Beings" is a general category that includes human crime. Nature is permeated with unintended harms, such as the deer hosting ticks that transmit Lyme disease. There is also a long natural history of intended harm, as a means to another end. The same deer will rear up and use its horns if threatened, or to fight for a mate or grazing territory. These forms of harm apply to other species as well as to humans.

The third category is more interesting:

> *Harm intended, and valued for its own sake:* hitting somebody you are mad at (assault), or nonviolent predatory crimes (vandalism to get even with an enemy)

We know that people sometimes value harm as an end in itself. But do animals have the same tendency? Charles Darwin wrote an entire book titled *The Expression of the Emotions in Man and Animals.*[18] Many human emotions have their origins in natural history. It is less clear that animals value the harm they do to other beings, rather than using harm as a means to other ends. Yet a cat left alone too long is said to take revenge. This calls for further interrogation.

Security and the Struggle for Existence

To assure its survival, each creature must defend and preserve the product of its labor.[19] Professor Graham Farrell has catalogued many ways that human crime prevention mirrors how animals protect themselves, and how these relate to human security.[20] The armadillo has its plates, as did the dinosaur in its day. Animals know how to flee and to fight. Plants and animals color themselves, devise tough exteriors and spines, or sneak away. Living beings mimic others that are better killers or are not so tasty to eat. Trickery is also part of nature, with animals using camouflage and adaptive markings to thwart predators or lure prey—topics taken up in earlier chapters.

So it is with crime. People hide their car keys under the seat, and lock goods in the trunk or boot of the car, puff up their shoulders to look tough, and put securities in a safe deposit box. To quote Professor Nick Tilley,

> Surveillance has a very long history, going back to early developments in animal life where it triggered mechanisms enhancing the likelihood of survival from threats from predators; new forms of surveillance have been added over time with alterations in context and changes in the nature and sources of predatory threats and with the development of culture.[21]

Tilley links the development of sight in natural history to security needs. Crime is a part of a broad and natural struggle for existence. Thus it makes no sense to study human crime in isolation from the larger system of death and life.

The human species has its unique and nonunique features. In learning from larger nature, we need not confine ourselves to a narrow view. The goal is to broaden—not narrow—our horizons for studying crime. For example, humans have almost surely elaborated intentional harm, valued for its own sake, beyond anything found among most animal species. The human struggle for existence includes many indirect and elaborate features. Yet much crime is often crude, direct, and simple. It is quite a challenge to consider these variations. The rest of the chapter does so.

The Pecking Order Is Not Just a Metaphor

In a famous book, *The Territorial Imperative,* Robert Ardrey linked the animal pecking order to many forms of inequality and power in human society and among nations.[22] Modern research on this topic goes back to the barnyard—the ancestral home of the chicken. In a famous 1913 study, Norwegian zoologist Thorlief Schjelderup-Ebbe explained how chickens fight each other to establish their pecking order.[23] After that, chickens live in peaceful inequality until a new chicken enters to disturb the pecking order. That creates a new aggressive flurry. A new pecking order emerges, and it all settles down again.[24]

Unfortunately, the term "pecking order" has gotten out of hand. It is used now as a broad metaphor for money, status, power, popularity, beauty, and more. With all these implications, the metaphor confuses more than it helps. But when we take it literally and apply it to a specific situation, it helps us understand aggression.

Let's switch from barnyard to schoolyard. Boys establish *physical* dominance. They do this via fighting, shoving, shouting, and athletics, as well as feats of bravado and mischief. A good deal of crime is closely linked to *physical prowess, dominance, and daring.* To understand this, we must get rid of the metaphorical haze. It's an *empirical* question when physical dominance makes a person more popular or less so.[25]

The reputation as a good fighter or tough guy can be an asset among young men, or even at other ages. A nasty or daring reputation helps a youth gain compliance from others without fighting every time for his place. Boys establish a pecking order through verbal and physical contests and displays of prowess, including crime.[26] Sometimes George fights Gary to show him who's boss. Other times George fights Fred mainly to show off to John. Professor James Short, one of the world's leading gang researchers, emphasized group processes among boys leading them to commit criminal acts outside the group.[27] Even nonviolent actions can imply physical prowess, daring, and toughness. The boy who climbs the fence and steals the goods has put on quite a show for the others.

We should not be surprised if the arrival of a new boy at the playground upsets order and leads to a flurry of crime. A school disrupted by a high turnover rate will have trouble establishing a stable pecking order or peaceful routine.

Even a stable population of youths undergoes bodily changes, with disruptive consequences. The onset of puberty itself generates crime by producing muscle and sexual capacities. In addition, pubertal development is uneven from one boy to another, upsetting their pecking order. If boys grow unevenly in height, weight, and muscle, last year's whipping boy could become this year's bully. September's pecking order might dissolve in October.[28] Note that the timing of puberty is only partly a genetic trait. Better nutrition—especially protein—brings sexual maturation down to age 12 or younger.

Moreover, pecking orders are disrupted when youths begin to travel outside their own immediate neighborhoods, entering areas where they are not necessarily known. An individual or group that clashes with others might have to fight its way. Worse still, more fighting arrives with more traveling. Different trips upset different apple carts. The use of cars further expands the realm of youth contact and the potential for both violent encounters and nonviolent displays of prowess. With larger and larger settings for drinking and partying, more strangers come in contact as individuals and groups, needing to create pecking orders anew—at some cost to the community and to themselves.

Survival Is Not Always Direct

The most fundamental principle of ecology is a struggle for existence. That struggle is not always direct; indeed, many natural processes have hidden relationships to that struggle. Sex may give practical results, but that's not why we do it.[29] We have to understand both practical results and individual urges within a larger perspective. True, the sexual urge is essential for the survival of the species; yet most sexual acts do not *directly* assist human survival, and some are not helpful at all. Sexual acts and urges can help tie human couples together emotionally and economically, *indirectly* enabling children to survive until their own reproductive periods begin. But sexual impulses can also interfere with that survival by drawing fathers away to pursue sexual opportunities elsewhere, leaving their families to fend for themselves. Sexual acts can harm survival by spreading diseases, some of which lead to sexual dysfunction. Sexual urges can also entice a person to use dangerous force against others, or even to risk attacks by others (see Chapter 18). Nature's irony is that the sexual impulse provides for survival in general but not in every instance.

Mixed Consequences of Human Traits

A single human trait or tendency can feed both survival and crime. The tendency to acquire and hoard goods carries people through bad times. Yet human acquisition beyond real needs feeds aggression, entices thieves, and impairs the very ability to guard what's hoarded or notice pilfering. Surprisingly, thrift and theft derive from the same human tendency.

The traits that enable crime are far from unique in the repertoire of life. Hunting and foraging are standard behavior in the natural world, but people can search for illegal booty, too. Shopping and shoplifting have something in common. Play is a normal process that helps youths to gain physical skills, grow, and serve society, but also to harm others. Daring is useful for survival under threat, but sometimes gets out of hand.[30] Quoting Samuel Johnson, "Courage is a quality so necessary for maintaining virtue that it is always respected, even when it is associated with vice."[31]

Staking out territory and pushing limits are part of natural survival, but also can lead to fights and thefts. Selfishness is essential for each person to persist in adversity, but also creates conflicts of interest and fights. Crime ecology is born of imperfect and inconsistent processes of survival and adaptation to a larger environment.

Acquisition, domination, resistance, selfishness, retaliation—these are standard features of life, hence of crime. These features apply at all levels of class, status, and power, at varying ages, for all races, and for both sexes. Because these features assist adaptation and survival of the species, they can never be purged entirely from the human makeup. Thus crime motivation has no independent origins, but is merely the excessive application or misapplication of natural tendencies. Even if these tendencies can be channeled and contained, they always remain in the background. Crime is a harmful consequence of natural human motivations pushed too far or too wide. Crime motivation is deeply entangled with legitimate and necessary features of human life on earth; this impels society to search for controls that might reduce crime but can never extinguish it.[32]

Controls against crime are also part of the struggle of nature, as some seek to write and enforce laws to their own benefits and at cost to others, whether justifiable or not. Thus we see that nature, crime, and law are all enmeshed in an ongoing struggle that can only be understood as a human twist on ecological forces that were present long before man and woman came to earth. This is true even though human societies and individuals are not at the cusp of death or destruction. For the survival principle and the natural forces engendering it persist through eras of poverty or prosperity, and carry forth to all corners of the human population, however well they might be living at the time.

Human Struggle Easy to Ignore

Modern metropolitan life insulates most people from direct struggles with nature, at least in their own minds. Few of us in today's metropolitan world personally terminate living things to get our food. Few of us have jobs spraying swamps, crops, and warehouses to kill off insects and rodents competing with us for food. Yet somebody has to do it. Even an organic farmer serving vegetarian customers participates actively in the struggles for existence, decimating local swarms of insects as he shifts his crops or releases an army of predator insects to gobble up his agricultural enemies. The human vegetarian sits just a step away from mass killings.

The bulk of the population also insulates itself as best it can from direct involvement with the struggles of crime. We hire police as surrogates to use violence against offenders, and private security to do our risk management. We expect accountants and auditors to check on crime by and through organizations. We share the costs of shoplifting, without observing most of it ourselves. We concentrate criminal risk in specific locations and times, such as the vicinity of a heavy-drinking bar or the route home from a tough secondary school. Other crime is diluted by daily life, with offenders harvesting quietly and out of sight. Those living in areas of moderate crime are scarcely aware of it on a daily basis.

Mild arguments and disputes among people are numerous. A small subset of disputes leads to verbal threats. A small subset of threats is followed by violent acts. A small subset of such violence leads to serious physical harm. Thus serious acts of violence are nested within a much larger population of disputes. White-collar crime is nested within a multitude of legal economic transactions or conventional governmental activity.

Human struggle manifests itself in nonviolent forms of crime as well. Stealing the labor of another person or organization, evading taxes or administrative requirements, stealing property, trespassing, fighting in the schoolyard—all of these are means by which people pursue their selfish interests. We sometimes distinguish *predatory* crimes. In ecology, the word predatory means that one organism eats another. In crime ecology, the term "predatory crime" has a nonculinary meaning, referring to offenses in which one person takes or damages the person or property of another, who is not a coparticipant in this crime or repeat victim of this offender.

Predatory offenses can range from the tiniest theft to the most brutal murder. The continuing predatory offender steals from different persons and stores and punches different noses. (Chapter 13 discusses parasitic relationships, with one offender taking advantage of another person in ongoing fashion.) The point for the present is that crime is part of the larger struggles of nature, of survival and aggrandizement, as people abscond with the labor of others or seek to protect their own.

Ecological Proximity and Natural Struggles

Human beings have an ongoing struggle with some species, such as the mosquito. But people are not in direct struggle with most species on earth. Indeed, people struggle more with one another. This is consistent with a fundamental ecological principle explained by Darwin, that "the struggle will almost invariably be most severe between the individuals of the same species, for they frequent the same districts, require the same food, and are exposed to the same dangers."[33]

Active criminal offenders, too, are more likely to harm one another than to attack the population not actively involved in crime. We can well see that illegal actions fit within the natural struggle to secure person and property, draw resources from outside oneself, gain sexual gratification, and extend hegemony over others. Far from being an unnatural or strange set of phenomena, criminal actions fit within normal processes of natural history. Thus crime is not only a living activity within itself but is also intrinsic to the larger system of life. Given that predatory action fits within a long natural history, it will probably remain part of the human repertoire.[34] Paradoxically, crime rates can be reduced greatly through human action—but never washed away. Indeed, by accepting crime as a fact of life, we can do a better job of diminishing it.

Limits on Crime

Ecologists have long asked how much population a given environment could carry. Accordingly, does a given environment have a practical limit on how much crime it can support?[35] On the one hand, we are constantly surprised that crime rates that seem impossibly high can continue to increase. On the other hand, crime cannot grow infinitely if the number of targets is fixed. Thus one could infer theoretical limits for crime. Thefts cannot exceed what is available to steal. Robberies depend on persons and businesses storing cash or other items suitable to be robbed and carried. Stores cannot long sustain losses that destroy profitability. Dangerous drugs eventually sicken and even kill their abusers. Violent offenders themselves sustain injuries that impair their continued aggression. If they can find a way, residents might migrate away from places that are too dangerous to sustain their legitimate livelihoods. Even offenders might flee a high crime area, like smokers who crave fresh air.

Some crimes can persist without threatening the community itself. Violence against a few might leave the multitude untouched. Pilfering from stores need not cause them to close; costs can be passed on to customers, who pay a few percent more but still manage to live. Society has devised many means to adapt to crime rate increases without going out of business. Fearful people stay indoors or pick their times and places as best they can. Perhaps crime in most times and places is nowhere near its ceiling. Perhaps crime can survive as a set of activities nested within a larger system of human activities. Thus a high-crime neighborhood can drive out its legitimate activities, but survive nonetheless through relationships to its larger metropolis. Even if a whole society cannot live on drug dealing alone, a particular corner of that society might do just that. Many pipelines can carry resources into a crime-ridden area, keeping it from dying. Social benefits via government can arrive and assist it. Private charities can help sustain populations that are not themselves productive but continue to engage in criminal activities. Customers for illegal goods and services can enter from elsewhere. Local offenders can make field trips elsewhere to steal, sell, and bring back their illicit gains. Yet an extraordinary crime level sometimes destroys a local community in a literal sense, like a tapeworm that finally kills its host. Resources are closed off. Police interventions and other counterattacks push local crime below its peak. Neither occurs on an everyday basis, so empirical research cannot easily specify the carrying capacity of crime. We have to admit that not much is known about the absolute limits on crime.

To phrase the question somewhat differently, how and when does crime drive a community itself in a downward direction? Ecologists use the term serial *trap* to describe how the poor health of one species transfers to others until the whole community is destroyed. Sometimes, criminal activity causes its community to waste away, or even die. An example comes from Woodward Avenue, Detroit, which begins downtown and heads to the suburbs. This was the first paved road in America, touted on the webpage of America's Scenic Byways as follows:

Michigan's Woodward Avenue is to the American automobile industry what New York's Broadway is to the American theater—a lane packed with history and heritage. Woodward Avenue put the world on wheels, and the impact of America's automotive influence is represented along this corridor in famed industrial complexes, office buildings, residential mansions, world-renowned museums and cultural institutions. Cruise up this 27-mile (43 km) byway for a fun, educational and sporting experience that defines America's love for the automobile.[36]

At the University of Michigan, I was a graduate student in the Detroit Area Study, which required a week's stay at the Ansonia Hotel around the corner from Woodward Avenue. This saved the university money and also taught us more about a life most of us had not seen. At that time, this inner-city section of Woodward Avenue had become a headquarters for hookers, drug addicts, and psychotics, many of them staying at or near the Ansonia Hotel. The downtown section of Woodward Avenue and its environs had become the skid row of Detroit, sustained largely by the vice it provided for a somewhat broader community, but also allowing some legitimate activities to survive. Within a few years, Woodward Avenue deteriorated further until it sustained almost no life—criminal or legitimate. Vice had apparently destroyed its own habitat by driving almost everything out, even its customers.

In the extreme, a serial trap is an irreversible process. Yet given enough years, ecological wounds tend to heal. If trees and flowers return to the site of a volcanic eruption, can we expect a derelict part of the city to return to good health? Even after a devastating forest fire, reforestation occurs in time.

Woodward Avenue today offers a mixed picture. On the one hand, new immigrants and businesses include donut shops and gas stations. But consider the circumstances in which they work, with bulletproof glass on gas stations and minimarts, and people getting shot down on the street. I wonder what will happen to Woodward Avenue in the decade ahead.

Overview

Crime has elaborate and refined features, as well as those that are simple and crude. We must try to understand both. More generally, we must inquire about crime as it relates to the larger struggle for existence. Violent and nonviolent crime alike fit that struggle, although often indirectly. Crime is part of a long natural history of harm-doing. Although humans have some of their own versions and can do harm at a very substantial scale, they did not invent the concept. Security, too, is part of natural history long preceding the arrival of humans on earth. The field of ecology helps us understand how crime can be a minor problem, or can in other circumstances get completely out of control.

Central Points, Chapter 22

1. Crime and security from it fit within a long natural history, the struggle for existence.

2. Yet many people can insulate themselves from crime much of the time.

3. Active criminal offenders are more likely to harm one another than to attack the population not actively involved in crime.

4. Sometimes crime destroys its own best habitats.

Exercises

1. Compile your dog's criminal record.

2. Find and discuss a community almost destroyed by crime.

3. Find a high-crime neighborhood that regenerated.

4. How does the human sexual urge increase and decrease crime?

Notes

1. *The Importance of Being Earnest*, act 1, ed. R. Berggren (New York: Vanguard Press, 1987). Original edition published 1895.

2. Quoted in *The Columbia World of Quotations* (New York: Columbia University Press, 1996).

3. Former U.S. Congresswoman, on being an elected official and a mother. Quoted in *Simpson's Contemporary Quotations* (New York: Houghton-Mifflin, 1988).

4. *The Skin of our Teeth,* act III (New York: S. French, 1944).

5. From *A Mencken Chrestomathy* (New York: Knopf, 1949).

6. P. A. Gowaty and N. Buschhaus, "Ultimate Causation of Aggressive and Forced Copulation in Birds: Female Resistance, the CODE Hypothesis and Social Monogamy," *American Zoologist* 38 (1998): 207–225. Gowaty is professor of ecology and women's studies at Clemson University.

7. T. A. Markow, "Forced Matings in Natural Populations of *Drosophila*," *American Naturalist* 156 (2000): 1–4. Available from http://cis.arl.arizona.edu/markow_lab/articles/Forced%20matings%200f%20Drosophila.pdf (accessed September 4, 2005).

8. S. W. Bullington, "Natural History and Captive Care of the Flat Rock Scorpion, *Hadogenes Troglodytes*," *Vivarium.* 7, no. 5 (1996): 18–21.

9. Of course, this point is in no way new. Darwin compiles similar details in Chapters 17 and 18 of *The Descent of Man,* where he states, "All male animals which are furnished with special weapons for fighting, are well known to engage in fierce battles."

10. Personal communication via my television set.

11. R. S. Ostfield, "The Ecology of Territoriality in Small Mammals," *Trends in Ecology and Evolution* 5 (1990): 411–415.

12. G. Arnqvist "Pre-copulatory Fighting in a Water Strider: Inter-sexual Conflict or Mate Assessment," *Animal Behavior* 43 (1992): 559–567.

13. S. C. Walls, "Interference Competition in Post-metamorphic Salamanders: Inter-specific Differences in Aggression by Coexisting Species," *Ecology* 7 (1990): 307–314.

14. A rich tradition of research on dominance hierarchies is found in many fields. For a start, see T. Schjelderup-Ebbe, "Social Behavior in Birds," in C. Murchison, ed., *Handbook of Social Psychology* (Worcester, MA: Clark University Press, 1935).

15. See coverage of Tedeschi and Felson in Chapter 3 of this book.

16. See R. B. Felson, E. P. Baumer, and S. F. Messner, "Acquaintance Robbery," *Journal of Research in Crime and Delinquency* 37 (2000): 284–305.

17. Such offenses are victimless in a direct sense. But the offender might be victimizing himself, or harm others as time passes.

18. Charles Darwin, *The Expression of the Emotions in Man and Animals,* 3rd ed. (Oxford, UK: Oxford University Press, 2002). Original edition published 1898. Available from Human Nature.com, http://human-nature.com/darwin/emotion/contents.htm (accessed September 4, 2005).

19. Of course, the young are protected by parents. See prior chapters on defense.

20. G. Farrell, "Crime Prevention" in C. Bryant, ed., *Encyclopedia of Criminology and Deviant Behavior* (New York: Taylor and Francis, 2000).

21. N. Tilley, "Seeing Off the Danger: Threat, Surveillance, and Modes of Protection," *European Journal on Criminal Policy and Research* 3 (1995): 27–40.

22. R. Ardrey, *The Territorial Imperative: A Personal Inquiry Into the Animal Origins of Property and Nations* (New York: Atheneum, 1966).

23. See endnote 14.

24. Interestingly, the establishment of a paradigm and normal science follows a parallel process.

25. Professor Anthony Walsh of Boise State University argues that dominance hierarchies among male youths exist mainly to attract females. A. Walsh, "Companions in Crime: A Biosocial Perspective," *Human Nature Review* 2 (2002): 169–178. Available from http://human-nature.com/nibbs/02/ (accessed September 4, 2005).

26. This is not a new topic among students of crime. See E. Anderson, *Code of the Street: Decency, Violence, and the Moral Life of the Inner City* (New York: W. W. Norton, 1999).

27. See J. F. Short, "Social Structure and Group Processes in Explanations of Gang Delinquency," in M. Sherif and C. W. Sherif, eds., *Problems of Youth: Transitions to Adulthood in a Changing World* (Chicago: Aldine, 1969). Also see J. F. Short, and F. Strodtbeck, *Group Process and Gang Delinquency* (Chicago: University of Chicago Press, 1965).

28. The instability of adolescent physical dominance hierarchies is a topic of academic attention. For a review of adolescent status hierarchy, as it relates to crime, see Chapter 4 in M. Warr, *Companions in Crime: The Social Aspects of Criminal Conduct* (New York and Cambridge, UK: Cambridge University Press, 2002).

29. This is a slight modification of a phrase used by Richard P. Feynman.

30. Daly and Wilson pay special attention to biological adaptations linking crime to a larger set of human traits. But their emphasis is on male-female differences affecting violence rather than general human traits affecting general crime. See

    a. M. Daly and M. Wilson, *Homicide* (New York: Aldine de Gruyter, 1988).

    b. M. Daly and M. Wilson, "Evolutionary Psychology of Male Violence," in J. Archer, ed., *Male Violence* (London: Routledge, 1994).

    c. M. Daly and M. Wilson, "Competitiveness, Risk-taking and Violence: The Young Male Syndrome," *Ethology and Sociobiology* 6 (1985): 59–73.

    d. M. Daly, M. Wilson, and N. Pound, "An Evolutionary Psychological Perspective on the Modulation of Competitive Confrontation and Risk Taking," in D. Pfaff and others, *Hormones, Brain and Behavior* (San Diego, CA: Academic Press, 2002).

31. Quoted in James Boswell, *Life of Samuel Johnson*, G. B. Hill and L. F. Powell, eds. (Oxford, UK: Clarendon Press, 1934–1964).

32. Otherwise incompatible criminological theories have a common ecological thread, namely, a need to contain human acquisition, domination, selfishness, retaliation, or any other traits that lead to crime, even as they serve a positive purpose. Even though control theory and normative theory are incompatible in criminological terms, both consider ways to contain a crime tendency. Control theory is closer to ecology in considering that tendency to be part of nature rather than something that must be learned. Crime ecology does not reject normative controls, but merely regards them as impotent without assistance from the sociophysical world. Inequality theories are ecological insofar as they focus on acquisition. But crime ecology allows acquisition to impel crime at all levels of wealth, status, and power.

33. Chapter 3, p. iii, *The Origin of Species* (London: John Murray, 1859). Available from the Online Literature Library, http://www.literature.org/authors/darwin-charles/the-origin-of-species (accessed September 7, 2005) (Full title: *On the Origin of Species by Means of Natural Selection, or the Preservation of Favoured Races in the Struggle for Life*).

34. Professors Daly and Wilson have elaborated the survival of such tendencies in homicide and other aggression. See prior endnote.

35. Do offenders as individuals have satiable thirsts? I do not know the answer. On the one hand, substance abuse pushes upward. On the other hand, one goal of crime is to avoid working too hard.

36. The National Scenic Byways Program is part of the U.S. Department of Transportation, Federal Highway Administration, www.byways.org (accessed October 31, 2005).

Science is the belief in the ignorance of experts.

Richard P. Feynman[1]

A good writer is basically a story teller, not a scholar or a redeemer of mankind.

—Isaac Bashevis Singer[2]

Our remedies oft in ourselves do lie,
Which we ascribe to Heaven.

—William Shakespeare[3]

Why did the Lord give us agility,
If not to evade responsibility?

—Ogden Nash[4]

Epilogue

Crime is impelled by life itself. All people have a natural capacity to discover and enjoy what they are not supposed to do. Sometimes people stumble across illicit opportunities quite by accident. Other times they set out to find these opportunities, perhaps with care, perhaps without.

Life also impels people to seek security. The human capacity to counter crime draws upon the 15 natural defenses, and all their permutations. These defenses are imperfect because nature is imperfect. Yet such defenses can be effective precisely because they are diverse, flexible, and capable of adaptation and creativity.

We might use the term "natural crime reduction" to describe measures that shrink a crime's niche, or otherwise thwart its growth or luxuriance or help avoid it. Such reduction includes a family of ideas and techniques known as situational crime prevention,

crime prevention through environmental design,

secure by design, and

problem-oriented policing.

Such prevention draws upon nature's realities, not an idealized version of life. Natural crime reduction can be tailored to the fine points of particular offenses, narrowly specified but broadly conceived. Natural reduction is often imposed near the moment of the crime, or at least with that moment in mind. Thus natural crime prevention seeks to design products that are hard to steal and settings that are more suitable for human use and safety— taking into account the human capacity to break rules.

This book has discussed crime and security as part of nature, drawing from the scientific outlook of the life sciences. Such thinking helps us understand crime better, and to concoct better solutions to specific crime problems. Accordingly, natural crime reduction prevents crime with actions that are as direct and tangible as possible. It does not promise human perfectibility or rely on eventuality. Rather, it looks toward changes that are quickly evident and verifiable. Ironically, tougher thinking about crime leads to gentler policies, for natural crime reduction avoids heavy-handed interventions, such as genetic manipulation, wholesale repression, and social brainwashing.[5] Its pragmatism is possible because it accepts the facts of life, seeking better outcomes without trying to change people into something they are not.

Notes

1. See transcriptions from an interview made in 1981, in R. Feynman, *The Pleasure of Finding Things Out* (New York: Helix, 1999).

2. American Yiddish writer and Nobel Prize winner (1904–1991). *Day of Pleasure: Stories of a Boy Growing Up in Warsaw* (New York: Farrar, Straus and Giroux, 1969). Also note W. Somerset Maugham's remark,

> I have never pretended to be anything but a story teller. . . . It is a misfortune for me that the telling of a story just for the sake of the story is not an activity that is in favor with the intelligentsia.

—From the preface in W. S. Maugham, *Creatures of Circumstance* (New York: Arno, 1977). Original edition published 1947.

3. *All's Well That Ends Well*, act I, scene i.

4. Quoted in *Wikipedia* online encyclopedia, http://en.wikipedia.org/wiki/Ogden_Nash (accessed September 7, 2005).

5. Consider the eugenics movement that was popular among scientists, intellectuals, and reformers in the early 20th century. Its flavor is captured by the title of a 1910 book by the

eminent biologist, Charles B. Davenport: *Eugenics: The Science of Human Improvement by Better Breeding* (New York: Holt). Available online at www.eugenicsarchive.org (accessed September 5, 2005). Also see C. B. Davenport, *Heredity in Relation to Eugenics* (New York: Henry Holt, 1913). In addition, note F. Galton, *Inquiries Into Human Faculty and Its Development* (New York: Dutton, 1973). Original edition published 1883.

The original eugenics movement was humanitarian and idealistic, linked to the progressive movement. Its goal was to encourage larger families among better people. See D. Pickens, *Eugenics and the Progressives* (Nashville, TN: Vanderbilt University Press, 1968). Also see T. L. de Corte, Jr. "Menace of Undesirables: The Eugenics Movement During the Progressive Era" (1978). Available from Master Thinking, http://www.geocities.com/MadisonAvenue/Boardroom/4278/eugenics.htm (accessed September 6, 2005).

Eugenics was built on implied arrogance, but not implicit cruelty. The progressives did not wish to snatch people from their homes. Some European nations did just that. In the 18th and 19th centuries, the British shipped their undesirables to Australia. See C. Bateson, *The Convict Ships 1787–1868* (Glasgow: Brown, Son & Ferguson, 1985). Also see this webpage: Convicts to Australia: A Guide to Researching Your Convicted Ancestors, http://members.iinet.net.au/~perthdps/convicts/index.html (accessed September 6, 2005). Note also the French exiling of convicts to the colonies. See P. Redfield, *Space in the Tropics: From Convicts to Rockets in French Guiana* (Berkeley: University of California Press, 2000).

In greater Germany during the 1930s, the Nazis diverted eugenics into racism, eradicating those they considered inferior to themselves. France, Britain, and Germany apparently did not succeed in purging their gene pool of crime. Australia has a high crime rate, but bear in mind that it is almost entirely urban, and most of its modern population did not get there in convict ships.

Moral repugnance against eugenics misses the essential point that it is an impractical method for controlling crime. The crime potential resides in the genes of all, and cannot be purged through eugenics or isolated with imprisonment or social prevention.

Crime Ecology Glossary

[The prime chapter that considers each concept is bracketed.]

A crime: Any identifiable behavior that an appreciable number of governments has specifically prohibited and formally punished (comprehensive definition). [2]

Abandoned sites: Lots or buildings that are no longer used for legitimate activities, often taken over for crime purposes. [5]

Aegism: The first party draws protection from its counterpart, which is largely unaffected. See also *incidental protection*. [14]

Aggressive camouflage: A technique for blending into the surroundings as a prelude to committing a crime. [16]

Aggressive mimicry: A technique for getting closer to unsuspecting prey by mimicking something innocuous or even desirable. [16]

Aggressive parasites: A parasite that harms its host too much for its own ongoing benefit. [13]

Arms race: When offenders and crime adversaries keep adjusting to one another. [10]

Avoidance: A primary defense based on avoiding risky locations, times, and activities. [18]

Awareness space: The areas someone knows for relatively frequent trips; includes *personal nodes, paths,* and *edges.* [16]

Barriers: Impediments to the offender's movements toward the crime target. [21]

Batesian mimicry: Gaining protection from adversaries by imitating an obnoxious model. [18]

Behavior setting: A location for recurrent use, for a particular activity, at known times; the prime building block for everyday life, including crime. [6]

Behavioral ecology: The study of very local features and activities that stimulate crime. [4]

Big Gang Theory: The view that a gang is a large and powerful group covering much of the city. [20]

Browsing: Foraging for small gains, with a high chance of success each time. [15]

Colossalism: A huge activity or facility that creates local crime niches on a large scale. [8]

Commensalism: When one organism feeds off the unused food of another; when one offender grabs leftovers from another. [14]

Community crime ecology: The study of how the larger parts of a city or locality affect local crime. [4]

Camouflage: The ability to hide in plain site; includes *protective coloration* and *protective resemblance*. [18]

Competition: When crimes or offenders compete with one another or with legal activities. [9]

Complex symbioses: More than one symbiotic relationship occurring at roughly the same time among the same organisms. [11]

Complex web: The intricate web of relationships between criminal activities, shady activities, and legitimate activities. [11]

Comprehensive crime definition: A crime definition that transcends natural variations, while excluding oddball crimes. [2]

Conventional settings that invite crime: Settings that emit an excess of cues favorable to crime over cues unfavorable to crime. [6]

Covert criminal act: A criminal act that usually draws little immediate notice. [16]

CRAVED: An acronym that describes an item's suitability for theft, considering whether it is concealable, removable, available, valuable, enjoyable, and disposable. [8]

Crime ecology: The scientific study of the processes, interdependencies, transformations, distributions, and abundances of criminal activities. [4]

Crime event: A three-stage process, including a crime's prelude, the incident itself, and its aftermath. [3]

Crime food chains: Multiple interdependencies, with one offender feeding off another, who feeds off other people, still. [4]

Crime habitat: Provides crime's basic needs, including a favorable landscape and suitable locale; includes *specific* and *generic crime habitats*. [7]

Crime mutualism: When both parties relate with net benefit. [12]

Crime niche: The total requirements for a crime type to occur. See *fundamental niche, realized niche.* [8]

Crime sequence: When at least one criminal event flows into the next, without appreciable interruption. The aftermath of the earlier crime is the prelude to the later one. [3]

Crime symbiosis: A close and prolonged relationship between two parties, providing illicit benefit to at least one of them. [11]

Crime topography: The study of how fine features of landscape and cityscape affect crime. [4]

Crime triangle: Describes supervision that prevents crime. The inner triangle includes the offender, target, and place (or setting) where crime might occur. The outer triangle presents three actors preventing crime: the handler, guardian, and place manager. [5]

Crime web: A complex system of relationships among many legal and illegal roles and activities. [4]

Crimes of specialized access: A violation of the rules of formal organization, contrary to law. [21]

Criminal man: Traditional view of the offender, distinct from the rest of the population. [2]

Diet breadth: The diversity of booty an offender takes, or drugs he ingests. [15]

Diversification: How crime takes on diverse forms, giving offenders more options. [10]

Dupe: Somebody who falls for *mimicry.* [18]

Ecosystem: A dynamic, living, system of different activities, drawing upon one another and on nonhuman resources, environing crime and allowing it to survive and sometimes flourish. [4]

Edges (between communities): A generic crime habitat where offenders from two or more bordering communities avoid drawing attention. [7]

Exploitative competition: When competitors use the same scarce resources, to the disadvantage of one another. [9]

Facilitators: Diverse artifacts and accouterments of daily life that assist criminal acts. [4]

Fallacy of misplaced complexity: The tendency to imagine central coordination and fancy organization that does not really exist. [4]

Familiarity (opposite of anonymity): Often decreases crime since potential offenders can be recognized. [5]

Folds: Where abandoned sites create edge-like areas where offenders gain an extra ability to take over. [7]

Foraging: When offenders search for crime targets. [15]

Foraging ratio: The ratio of illicit gains to a combination of search time and handling time. [17]

Formal organization: A means for separating official tasks from personal gains; includes clear-cut hierarchy of offices, specialized competencies and duties, written rules, merit hiring, and merit promotion. "Crimes of specialized access" thwart these rules. [21]

Four misses: Crime increases when consumer products are misappropriated, mistreated, mishandled, or misused. [10]

Fragmentation of crime habitats: A process that serves to reduce crime in a *thick crime habitat* and interferes with its recolonization. See *habitat fragmentation*. [7]

Fundamental niche: Resources that offenders can use for a specific crime type under ideal conditions. [8]

Gang image: An exaggerated view of the gang, giving it too much credit for bad deeds, organization, leadership, unity, and enormity. [20]

Gang membership: See *gang participation*. [20]

Gang participation: An alternative to *gang membership*, taking into account unstable and unstructured features of juvenile gangs. [20]

Gang signaling: Colors, signs, or symbols that different youths use to scare off adversaries; a form of *Müllerian mimicry*.

Generic crime habitat: Fosters many different types of crime at a high rate, in a noticeable area or region; includes *edges* and *thick crime habitats*. [7]

Group protection: Traveling and lingering in groups, for security reasons. [18]

Guardian: Someone, usually an ordinary citizen, who looks after property or other persons, discouraging criminal attacks against them. [5]

Habitat fragmentation: When modern society fragments natural habitats, erodes interior habitat, threatens biodiversity, and interferes with recolonization. See *fragmentation of crime habitats*. [7]

Handler: A parent or other personal supervisor who discourages someone from committing crimes. [5]

Handling time: The length of time and the trouble an offender goes through to unload the booty, or otherwise bring the crime to fruition. [17]

Harmony: When crime lives in harmony with noncriminal activities, its harm is limited to particular victims, while the community itself remains healthy. See *healthy community, pathology*. [7]

Healthy community: A community that is able to manage human imperfections, preventing these from taking over the daily system of community life. See *harmony, pathology*. [7]

Host: The party upon which a parasite feeds. [13]

Hunting: Foraging with low probability of success, requiring rather large gains when success finally arrives. [15]

Hunting method: How the offender approaches, enters, and commits crimes on the ground. [15]

Illicit-trade setting: Where people transact illicit business. [6]

In-between areas: Between legitimate settings, helping offenders set up crimes. [6]

Insiders: Those who "belong" in an area, and can enter it without drawing undue notice. [16]

Interdependencies: A variety of relationships linking one crime to another, or to legal or marginal activities; includes symbiotic and nonsymbiotic relationships. [11]

Interference competition: When some offenders interfere with the foraging or life processes of others, perhaps by cornering some part of the habitat. [9]

Interior habitat: Hospitable to species that cannot survive at the edge of the habitat. *Thick crime habitat* derives from this idea. [7]

Intoxication setting: Where people can drink in excess, facilitating subsequent crimes. [6]

Irritability: A process by which people, including offenders, quickly respond to external stimuli. [1]

Juvenile street gang: A very local group of youths intimidating others with overt displays of affiliation.

Juvenile street gang alliance: A weak affiliation of juvenile street gangs that share signals to enhance intimidation.

Kleptoparasitism: Stealing loot from another offender, who has just obtained it. [13]

Law of local convergence: Crime stimuli vary greatly, based on the very local convergences of people and things. [23]

Law of universal response: Populations respond alike to the same crime stimuli. [23]

Little Gang Theory: Viewing most juvenile gangs as small and local. [20]

Local drug markets: Where friends, neighbors, or acquaintances make the drug deals, without a substantial search process. [17]

Marginal activities: Activities strongly disapproved by society or large segments of it, despite their legality. [11]

Maximum size rule: An offender does not usually forage for something he cannot carry. [17]

Metabolism: The rhythms of daily life, such as the hourly variations in crime and the activities upon which it feeds. [1]

Mimicry: When one organism (or crime participant) seeks to look like another. [16]

Motive: The offender's purpose for committing a particular crime, looking one step beyond the physical target. [3]

Müllerian mimicry: When several species use similar warning signals, together scaring off adversaries. Gang signaling serves this purpose.

Multiflow mutualism: When two parties illegally exchange several different resources, to mutual benefit. [12]

Neutralism: The absence of symbiosis between two parties; occurs because some offending makes few demands on other activities. [11]

Niche complementarity: When one crime fills illegal gaps left unfilled by another. [9]

Niche differentiation: When different crime niches coexist in the same area. [9]

Niche overlap: When two or more crime activities compete for the same resources, that is, have similar niche requirements. [9]

Niche requirements: The specific requirements of each illegal activity. [9]

Nodes: The places to which and from which someone travels often. [16]

Object: The person or thing that the offender attacks, or with whom the offender criminally interacts; includes *targets*. [3]

Oddball crime: Behavior that is criminalized in odd places and cases; it is excluded from the comprehensive crime definition. [2]

Offender convergence setting: Where offenders socialize, linger, find accomplices, and initiate illicit actions. [6]

Open-air drug market: An outside market for illicit drugs, in geographically well-defined areas at identifiable times; a market where buyers and sellers can locate one another with ease, and any plausible buyer is served. [6]

Outsiders: Those who do not "belong" in an area, drawing unwanted attention that interferes with their ability to commit a crime. [16]

Overt criminal act: A criminal act that draws human attention, perhaps with direct confrontation, noise, or violence. [16]

Parasitism: When one party benefits, harming the host little by little. [13]

Passive assistance: When crime draws resources from others not directly involved; includes *passive communication, passive feeding,* and *passive shielding.* [14]

Passive communication: Helping an offender transfer information to allure victims or reach co-offenders. [14]

Passive feeding: *Commensalism.* [14]

Passive shielding: When a nonoffender shields an offender, providing basic needs, such as transport, shelter, or refuge. [14]

Patches: Where an offender searches; often the *edges* of *nodes* and *paths.* [17]

Pathology: Crime only becomes pathological by taking over terrain and by driving out an appreciable number of legitimate activities. See *harmony, healthy community.* [7]

Paths: The routes someone takes among *nodes;* also the routes an offender takes toward his crime *target* or *object;* used in the proposed crime taxonomy. [16, 21]

Personal reputation: A tough reputation developed as a primary defense against adversaries. [18]

Physical dominance: A pecking order among boys, established through fighting, shoving, shouting, athletics, feats of bravado, mischief, and related crime. [22]

Place: A location clearly for human use that may or may not be recurrent. [6]

Place manager: Someone with formal or informal responsibility to look after a place or setting, often protecting it against crime. [5]

Primary defenses: Defenses usually applied before detecting the presence of an adversary. See *routine precautions.* [18]

Product life cycle: Changes in consumer products and their markets, during which their theft rates accelerate, then fall. [10]

Protective coloration: Blending in with surroundings by adapting colors or patterns similar to those of others, by reducing the contrast with the surroundings, or by hiding the eyes; a form of *camouflage.* [18]

Protective resemblance: Adapting the look, behavior, and motion of surrounding organisms; a form of *camouflage.* [18]

Prudent parasite: A parasite that minimizes its damage at any one time so it can take advantage of its host for a longer period. [13]

Racketeering: Complex relationships between organized crime and otherwise legitimate organizations; a *multiflow mutualism.* [12]

Range: The offender's normal search area when *foraging*. [15]

Rare crime: Widely criminalized behavior that nonetheless occurs rarely. [2]

Realized niche: Resources that offenders have actually used for a specific crime type. [8]

Recolonization: After criminal activity has been removed from a local area, through its connection to nearby areas, crime regains its foothold. [7]

Recovery: Crime's local ability to bounce back, after direct interference from police or others. [7]

Regional crime ecology: The study of how crime is affected by features beyond a single city or locality. [4]

Regional drug markets: Where strangers find each other by some sort of search process to complete a drug transaction. [17]

Relative generalist: An offender who commits a rather wide variety of crimes, but not all types. [15]

Repeat victimization: When the same type of crime victimization is experienced by the same victim or target within a limited period of time. [3]

Requirements of life: Organization, adaptation, metabolism, movement, growth, reproduction, and irritability. [1]

Routine precautions: A general term for a variety of primary defenses. [18]

Search time: Length of time an offender searches. [17]

Secondary defenses: Used to defend oneself from adversaries after detecting their proximity. [19]

Self-altering: How crime unfolds and transforms its own environment. [1]

Setting: See *behavior setting*.

Situational crime prevention: Preventing specific crime types by removing direct opportunities to carry them out. [19]

Social foraging: Foraging in groups to overcome a single offender's individual limitations. [15]

Space: A vague word referring to locations that may or may not be for human use. [6]

Specific crime habitat: Invites a particular type of crime to flourish in a noticeable area or region. [7]

Subject: The offender or offenders; used as part of a sentence to summarize a criminal act or acts. [3]

Susceptible host: Provides an environment meeting the parasite's needs. [13]

Target: A person or thing attacked or taken by an offender. [3]

Taxonomy: A classification system, with order among its categories. [21]

Territoriality: The tendency to defend an area larger than one's home nest but smaller than one's range of activity. [22]

Thick crime habitat: A generic crime habitat containing many *abandoned sites,* where offenders can escape controls, even near home. [7]

Tippelzone: A drive-in prostitution park found in the Netherlands. [4]

Tools: These help an offender overcome *barriers,* as he moves toward a crime *target.* [21]

Verb: The specific sociophysical act in committing a crime. Helps formulate a summary sentence about a crime or crime category. [3]

Virulent growth: When crime easily attaches, invades, colonizes, and poisons conventional activities. [7]

Web of crime: A complex living system that links legal and illegal activities within the larger ecosystem. [4]

White-collar crime: See *crimes of specialized access.* [21]

Appendix A

Main Points From
Crime and Everyday Life[1]

Chapter 1. Fallacies About Crime

a. The *dramatic fallacy:* Emphasizing crimes that are most publicized, while forgetting ordinary crimes.

b. The *cops-and-courts fallacy:* Overrating the criminal justice system's power over crime.

c. The *not-me fallacy:* Thinking that you are too good to commit a crime; believing that offenders are from a different population than you are.

d. The *ingenuity fallacy:* Overrating the skill required to commit a crime.

e. The *agenda fallacy:* Linking crime reduction to your favorite ideology, religion, or political agenda.[2]

Chapter 2. The Chemistry for Crime

a. An ordinary crime occurs when a *likely offender* converges with a *suitable target* in the absence of a *capable guardian* against crime.

b. Fights occur after a *sequence of events,* with someone perceiving an insult and *escalating* the insult process, leading to blows.

c. Criminal acts are highly responsive to *settings and the cues that they emit.*

d. *Place managers,* such as apartment doormen and office receptionists, are very important for preventing crime.

e. Certain car models are hundreds of times more likely to be stolen than other models. Crime risk is highly responsive to *situational factors* and *specific crime opportunities.*

Chapter 3. Crime Decisions

    a. Offenders act to gain *quick pleasure* and avoid *imminent pain.*

    b. Offenders make decisions, but plan very *little in advance* of their crimes.

    c. Offenders are *attuned to practical details* in choosing their crime targets and timing.

    d. *Each setting emits cues* that communicate temptations and controls, influencing the offender's action.

    e. Even strange offenders make decisions.

Chapter 4. Bringing Crime to You

    a. Crime shifts with *historical stages,* from village to town to convergent city to divergent metropolis.

    b. The *divergent metropolis* is especially criminogenic.

    c. *Stand-alone* homes are much easier for burglary.

    d. Cars parked in *public places* are much more likely to be stolen.

Chapter 5. Marketing Stolen Goods

    a. Thieves and burglars depend on *markets for stolen goods.*

    b. Such markets *depend on the public* to purchase used items.

    c. Reducing the chance to sell stolen goods also *reduces crime.*

    d. *Poverty areas facilitate* the sale of stolen goods.

Chapter 6. Crime, Growth, and Youth Activities

    a. Teenagers in the past had roles in agriculture and labor, impairing their participation in crime.

    b. Teenagers in the past reached sexual maturity at later ages.

    c. In recent decades, teenagers spend much more time away from parents.

    d. Crime involvement of teenagers is highest around 3:00 p.m. on school days, usually on the way home from school.

    e. Large high schools generate higher crime rates than small ones.

Chapter 7. White-Collar Crime

    a. Offenders can get to victims via (1) *overlapping activity space,* (2) *personal ties,* or (3) *specialized access* (via work roles).

    b. So-called white-collar crimes use the *third route,* above.

    c. Crimes of specialized access have *no special motives.*

    d. These offenders victimize (1) *employees,* (2) *customers, clients, or patients,* (3) *the public,* (4) *their own organizations,* or (5) *other organizations.*

Chapter 8. One Crime Feeds Another

    a. Committing one offense is a *slippery slope* leading to another.

    b. Many crime victims are *repeat victims.*

    c. Many criminal acts *generate other criminal acts.* Other criminal acts are largely *self-limiting.*

    d. Crime prevented here is generally *not displaced* there.

    e. Crime prevented here sometimes leads to declining crime in nearby times and places, a *diffusion of benefits.*

Chapter 9. Local Design Against Crime

    a. Environmental criminologists teach us how to *design buildings and settings* to reduce crime.

    b. It is possible thereby to control *natural access,* provide *natural surveillance,* and foster *territorial behavior.*

    c. *Natural strategies* are cheaper and more effective than providing guards or relying on equipment alone.

    d. New York's Port Authority Bus Terminal reduced its crime inside by 70 percent after *redesigning* its environment and *improving its management.*

Chapter 10. Situational Crime Prevention

    a. Situational prevention *does not seek to improve* human character.

    b. This method applies to *very specific slices* of crime, e.g., auto parts stripping.

    c. This method is *practical, natural, simple,* and *low in cost.*

    d. It seems to make each criminal act *difficult, risky,* and *unrewarding.*

Chapter 11. Crime Science and Everyday Life

The last chapter in *that book* introduced readers to the *current book*.

Notes

1. Marcus Felson, *Crime and Everyday Life*, 3rd ed. (Thousand Oaks, CA: Sage, 2002).
2. Only 6 of 10 fallacies are presented here.

Appendix B

Exhibits

Appendix Exhibit A   The Overlap Among Three Crime Definitions

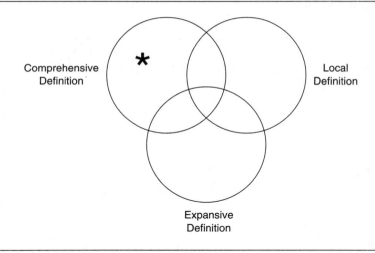

Comprehensive
Definition

Local
Definition

Expansive
Definition

Appendix Exhibit B   Crime's Verb, Direct Object, and Motive Phrase,
Various Offenses

Crime's Verb	Crime's Direct Object	Crime Motive Phrase
A. Nonviolent Offenses		
1. Steal	a car	for a thrill
2. Shoplift	a CD	to supplement collection
3. Trade for	illicit drugs	to get high
4. Paint graffiti on	a wall	to make yourself a big shot
5. Break into	a house	for quick money
6. Abscond with	a password	for Internet crimes, later
B. Violent Offenses		
7. Punch	the victim's nose	for revenge
8. Fight	another youth	to establish your position
9. Sexually abuse	a victim	to gain an orgasm
C. Illegal Services		
10. Provide	sexual services	in exchange for drugs
11. Assist	designer-drug production	to make money

Appendix Exhibit C   Crime Parasitism as an Overlap Between Exploitative
and Symbiotic Crime

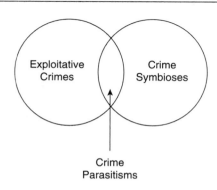

Appendix Exhibit D   Parasitic Versus Predatory Crime

Terms and Comments	What Repeats?	Examples From Larger Nature	Crime Examples
Parasitism	1. Same attacker, same target	A tapeworm in the tummy	Same bully attacks the same whipping boy
Included with parasitism	2. Same attacker, similar target	A flea bites this dog a few times, then moves on	Same burglar breaks into similar homes*
Borderline	3. Similar attackers, similar targets, localized	Similar fleas bite similar animals	Different local burglars choose similar homes*
Included with predation	4. Occasional repetition	Mosquitoes keep moving	After long delay, the robber might return
Predation	5. No repetition of target	Lion eats lamb once	The robber who never returns

* "Near repeats" include these two types of crime events, which are not identical. See Chapter 3.

Index

About the Author

Marcus Felson has been a leader not only in crime theory ("the routine activity approach") but also in applying that theory to reducing crime. His prior book, *Crime and Everyday Life*, is used in criminology classes throughout the world. His central argument is that everyday *legal* activities set the stage for illegal crime. Felson's work offers important examples of how crime has been reduced quickly by focusing prevention efforts directly onto local problems.

He is currently professor at the Rutgers University School of Criminal Justice; he has served as professor at the University of Southern California and the University of Illinois and as visiting scholar at the University of Stockholm, at Simon Fraser University in Vancouver (British Columbia, Canada), and at the Jill Dando Institute of Crime Science at University College London. He received his BA from the University of Chicago and his PhD from the University of Michigan.

Professor Felson has been a guest lecturer in many countries, including Argentina, Australia, Belgium, Canada, Chile, Denmark, England, Finland, France, Hungary, Italy, the Netherlands, New Zealand, Norway, Poland, Scotland, Spain, Sweden, Switzerland, and the United Arab Emirates. He is author of more than 90 professional papers, including *Redesigning Hell: Preventing Crime and Disorder at the Port Authority Bus Terminal*. He is coeditor (with Ronald V. Clarke) of *Business and Crime* and *Routine Activity and Rational Choice* and coauthor of *Opportunity Makes the Thief*.